# Expanding peace journalism: comparative and critical approaches

*Edited by Ibrahim Seaga Shaw, Jake Lynch, and Robert A Hackett*

D1417499

SYDNEY UNIVERSITY PRESS

Published 2011 by Sydney University Press
SYDNEY UNIVERSITY PRESS
University of Sydney Library
sydney.edu.au/sup

**National Library of Australia Cataloguing-in-Publication entry**
Title:     Expanding peace journalism : comparative and critical
           approaches / edited by Ibrahim Seaga Shaw, Jake Lynch,
           and Robert A. Hackett.
ISBN:     9781920899707 (pbk.)
Notes:    Includes bibliographical references and index.
Subjects: Peace--Press coverage.
           Mass media and peace.
           Social conflict--Press coverage.
Other Authors/Contributors:
           Shaw, Ibrahim Seaga.
           Lynch, Jake.
           Hackett, Robert A.
Dewey Number:
           070.44930366

Cover design by Miguel Yamin, the University Publishing Service
Printed in Australia

# Contents

# Preface

*Johan Galtung*

This book, so rich in content, is a testimony to the need for empirical, critical and constructive scrutiny of media. Each chapter opens a new window, a new angle; all of them important.

The problem some 50 years ago was what criteria an event had to meet to qualify as news, and we – my fine assistant Mari Holmboe Ruge and myself – came up with 12. When the news represents a distorted world image, the distortions are worth knowing. Recently I have added entertainment value as a news factor, in the form of 'infotainment'.

I then focused on four: high status of persons, countries, actor-orientation (as opposed to nature, culture, structure) and something negative. That high status – class, gender, race, whatever – attracts attention happens almost by definition, and actor-orientation is built into the Indo-European sentence structure: subject–predicate–object; not only a smoking gun, but 'who done it'. But negativism? Where does it come from? Media as we know them are Western efforts to mediate between the world and the reader/listener/viewer. But isn't the West based on an idea of progress? Maybe, but also on apocalypse. Negativism both highlights the abnormal and warns of clear and imminent danger. Then, Aristotle enters.

He did us a colossal disfavour by dividing the human drama in two: tragedy or comedy; Shakespeare being the showcase. Either it ends badly or it is laughable; the former for people high up, the latter for the rest. What is missing? Muddling through, regular life, the fact that we generally manage. And if literature is tailored to fit Aristotle, then why not also the lesser fry among authors – the journalists? Maybe mainstream journalists are as afraid of peace as authors are of the human condition of happiness, tearing at it the moment it rears its smiling face? Or, even worse, they do not even recognise it when it is there?

My basic concern was and is peace; and the four factors, with negativism up front, make peace journalism – as opposed to violence and war journalism – an uphill struggle. And yet it is possible: I have witnessed its increase in the last decades. But there are plenty of hurdles to overcome, like the strange idea that firing a bullet is somehow objective whereas saying or doing peace is not.

Happy reading – and please join the search for better media!

Versonnex, France, April 2011

# Introduction

## Expanding peace journalism: comparative and critical approaches

*Jake Lynch, Robert A Hackett and Ibrahim Seaga Shaw*

In a single month – January 2011 – a million Egyptians created their own accounts on Facebook. Weeks later, after a series of eye-catching demonstrations coordinated via social media, the hated regime of Hosni Mubarak was gone. State TV was still giving out the official line – that the actions were the work of foreign infiltrators and 'terrorists' – even as negotiations were underway for the military to take temporary charge, pending the adoption of a new constitution, leading to free elections.

The protests in Cairo drew inspiration from the ousting of Tunisia's President Ben Ali, weeks before. Here, another iconic new media phenomenon, Wikileaks, was implicated in social upheaval. According to 'Sam', a Tunisian blogger, 'Wikileaks revealed what everyone was whispering', thereby playing an important catalysing role as the first domino in the fall of repressive Arab governments began to wobble.

'President Ben Ali and his regime', the US Ambassador in Tunis had written, 'have lost touch with the Tunisian people ... They rely on the police for control and focus on preserving power'. Following its disclosure by Wikileaks, the cable was published in a Lebanese newspaper, launching Tunisia's web-savvy youth on a game of cat and mouse with the censors to devise ways to access the pages via internet proxies.

Most research on social movements supports the notion that internet usage – putting in the hands of activists more tools and opportunities for symbolic production – has had an effect on the capacity to bring about extra-movement outcomes, of 'simple accentuation' (Earl et al.

2010, p426). After all, other communications technologies had already played important enabling roles in social transformations: from newspaper journalism, then SMS messaging, in the two 'people power' uprisings in the Philippines which deposed presidents in 1986 and 2001 respectively; to the production and circulation of VHS cassettes of demonstrations against martial law in Thailand in 1992, drawing on the resources of Bangkok's large-scale pirate video industry (Williams & Rich 2000).

The events of the so-called Arab Spring may signal a further intensification of a syndrome identified by Manuel Castells as 'an evolution [now underway]: a historic shift of the public sphere from the institutional realm to [a] new communication space' – one in which 'insurgent politics and social movements can intervene more decisively' (Castells 2007, p238). Castells goes as far as to argue that 'the media have become the social space where power is decided' (2007, p238). One need not accept the media-centrism of this position to recognise that further scrutiny of the power relations at work within media domains, and of attempts to challenge them, is warranted.

It is in this context that interest in peace journalism has grown rapidly over recent years. Peace journalism (PJ) emerged in the mid-1990s as a new, transdisciplinary field of interest to professional journalists in both developed and developing countries and to civil society activists, university researchers and others interested in the conflict–media nexus. Significantly, it drew impetus by looking through Castells' telescope, as it were, from the other end: the insight sharpened in particular by experiences in the 1991 Gulf War, that militaries increasingly viewed the communication space as a crucial battleground, and that journalists were therefore 'caught up, whether they like[d] it or not, in the loops and coils of conflict and political process' (Lynch 2008, p193).

Perhaps the largest single category of published PJ research takes the form of operationalising the PJ model to derive sets of evaluative criteria to gauge the extent of peace journalism in the manifest content of mainstream media: usually newspapers for ease of access, television and radio. And in non-research environments, PJ supporters have sought to catalyse immanent critique, using the legitimating norms of journalistic

8

practice to call for reforms in professional standards, urging the case for peace journalism as 'good journalism' (Patindol 2010). Most PJ activity, then, has focused on the representation of conflict in corporate media, often called mainstream media – a category encompassing public broadcasting as well as journalism commercially produced and sold.

A growing number of PJ researchers advocate, instead, a root-and-branch critique of mainstream journalism as a privileged professional practice, indissociable from the predominant 'war journalism' style of reporting that PJ sets out, in scholarly research, to problematise; with adjacent exhortatory and pedagogical initiatives typically promoting feasible and preferable alternatives. Instead of examining or championing the case for marginal reforms in corporate media, these scholars argue that PJ should concentrate on 'the tradition of radical journalism [openly] committed to progressive social change' (Keeble 2010, p50); a tradition now enlivened and greatly expanded by new media technologies.

According to Hanitzsch (2007), on the other hand, journalism can be distinguished, as a form of public communication, precisely by its declared commitment to 'internal goals', in contrast to such endeavours as, say, political advertising, which are avowedly instrumentalist. This, Kempf argues (2007), accounts for the 'trust bonus' that journalism still enjoys, and PJ advocates would squander it at their peril.

Interest in PJ spans many fields, but its main 'home' has been in peace research, which is characterised by a value-explicit approach: 'with both a positive valuation of peace ... and a commitment to examine trade-offs between values' (Stephenson 1999, pp810–11). It shapes a key question: if the focus of PJ research, advocacy and training were to switch, from mainstream to alternative media, would it – in the classic PJ definition – 'create [more] opportunities for society at large to consider and value non-violent responses to conflict'? (Lynch & McGoldrick 2005, p5) Would it further the value-explicit remit of peace research, and the mission of peace activism to 'give peace [more of] a chance' by boosting the potential for extra-movement outcomes?

'Alternative media' represent a 'challenger paradigm', Robert A Hackett writes, in his contribution to this volume, to the objectivity regime, as its own structural underpinnings erode; one that opens up new 'vistas' for PJ by offering 'new venues and allies' for implementation. But Hackett chooses, as a spatial metaphor to convey the relationship between mainstream and alternative media, the word 'parallel', implying that they never meet. The much wider access to media per se now supplements, without necessarily challenging, what Molotch and Lester (1997) call the 'habitual access' to the privileged domain of mainstream media journalism enjoyed by official sources. Non-elite peace actors may therefore remain stuck in what the peace researcher John Paul Lederach termed the 'interdependence gap ... the lack of responsive and coordinated relationships up and down the levels of leadership in a society' (Lederach 1999, p30).

Gamson (1975) proposed 'acceptance in [a] polity' as the presumed aim of any social movement. It implies traction in what McKee calls the 'official public sphere' (McKee 2005, p41): a connection between Lederach's 'grassroots leadership' and 'top-level leadership' – being the level where institutional decision-making takes place. If such distinctions are under erosion by the evolution identified by Castells in the assessment quoted above, then he himself adds a reminder of the continuing salience of what Bennett (1990) described as 'indexing': factors limiting the range of reported political viewpoints and issues to those expressed within the mainstream political establishment, that still 'weigh heavily ... on the process of events-driven reporting' (Castells 2007, p241).

This is the very pattern – events-driven, and dominated by official sources – that is problematised as 'war journalism' in the PJ model. PJ, in Shinar's definition, is distinguished by:

1. Exploring backgrounds and contexts of conflict formation, and presenting causes and options on every side so as to portray conflict in realistic terms, transparent to the audience

2. Giving voice to the views of all rival parties

3. Offering creative ideas for conflict resolution, development, peacemaking and peacekeeping

4. Exposing lies, cover-up attempts and culprits on all sides, and

revealing excesses committed by, and suffering inflicted on, peoples of all parties

5.  Paying attention to peace stories and postwar developments (Shinar 2007, p200).

Bennett's indexing model is just one of a range of scholarly accounts of the relationship between structure and agency, as they bear upon the everyday working life of the journalist. Assessments of the unexploited scope for individual reporters, even editors, to shape their coverage in terms recognisable as belonging under Shinar's list of headings, vary accordingly. Lynch declares, simply, that in every case where the PJ model has been applied in exercises of content analysis, 'there is some peace journalism, even if not known, to its creators, by that name; so there could be more' (Lynch 2008, p234).

This statement highlights one of the significant ambiguities contained in such studies – necessitating, as an opening gambit, a threefold distinction. First, PJ may be a consciously applied editorial philosophy – still a relative rarity in conventional media (though it has occurred in particular circumstances of time and place, as with several Indonesian newspapers – see Lynch 2008, pp92–112). Second, some media may intentionally pursue practices that challenge war journalism, such as seeking common ground between contending parties, or reporting events from the viewpoint of all victims of war; but the practitioners are not necessarily informed by or trained in the PJ model as such. (A good example would be the Al Jazeera satellite television network, whose proponents have proclaimed that while Western-owned media like CNN report what happens when the missile is launched, Al Jazeera reports what happens when it lands.) Finally, there is 'accidental' peace journalism – news patterns that resemble those of peace journalism, but that are contingent byproducts of routine news imperatives in specific situations, such as the geopolitical locus of the news organisation in relation to a particular conflict.

This last factor may account for the apparently high PJ quotient in the editorials of Indian newspapers in the wake of the attack by masked gunmen on civilian targets in Mumbai in November 2008 – discussed in the chapter by Sudeshna Roy and Susan Dente Ross. Among the prevalent framings characteristic of the hegemonic 'war on terrorism' discourse, there remain, they record, 'infrequent yet rich "seams" in which resources of resistance can be mined' – linked, it is suggested, with key ambiguities over India's strategic orientation vis-à-vis the US.

Despite evidence of what Freedman (2009) calls 'plurality … and variegation' in the outputs of mainstream media, of the enduring 'trust bonus' that professional journalism may enjoy, and of the continuing salience of distinctions between the official and alternative public spheres, several of the contributors to this book make strong arguments for PJ to find what they see as more fertile ground in various branches of alternative media.

This emerging debate in peace journalism overlaps with another: whether PJ should, in keeping with the value-explicit approach of peace research, take an avowedly 'proactive' role. The community media, identified in the chapter by Lioba Suchenwirth and Richard Lance Keeble as the most promising milieu for PJ, 'actively promot[e] human rights and social change'. In chapter 3, Ibrahim Seaga Shaw's rallying cry for human rights journalism – as a complementary strand to the existing conceptual framework – urges journalism 'not only [to] illuminate the problems but also identify, recommend, advocate and mobilise actionable solutions to address them'.

There are, as Elissa Tivona shows in her account of women engaged in grassroots peacebuilding, plenty of actionable solutions being implemented around the world, all the time. They exemplify a different, more nurturing and more sustaining set of values and ideas than the male-dominated realist paradigms that exert hegemony over economic development and international relations; but mainstream media representations are complicit in keeping them in the background. It took a collaborative, non-commercial journalistic initiative – assembling the stories of 1000 peacewomen to be nominated for the Nobel Prize – to draw this narrative together, in what amounts to a notable paradigmatic exercise in peace journalism.

Matt Mogekwu calls on PJ to 'free itself from the mainstream journalism strait-jacket to be able to focus on bringing about change, preventing the escalation of crises, and doing its utmost to institute dialogue among people with conflicting ideas and values'. And even Rob McMahon and Peter Chow-White, although their data are drawn from examples of 'accidental' PJ in a mass-circulation newspaper, characterise PJ's theoretical stance as one that 'incorporates principles of conflict analysis to promote news production practices that *aim towards* conflict transformation' (emphasis added).

## Peace journalism and its critics

Rhetorical commitments such as these will potentially reactivate an important line of critique encountered by PJ in response to earlier iterations, which sees it as a threat to journalists' professional objectivity and integrity, imposing on them criteria external to their proper purpose. From a scholarly perspective, such a position begs the question of whether any form of journalism can be truly neutral vis-à-vis its broader political, economic and ideological contexts. One of the chief journalistic foes of PJ, the BBC correspondent David Loyn, accepts that 'objectivity' may be 'chimerical', but argues that it remains an appropriate aim in reporting and preferable to any attempt to 'load' the job with 'unhelpful ... prescriptions' for what it should and should not do (Loyn 2007).

Attempts to engage with this view, in order to mobilise journalistic agency around the distinctions in the PJ model, have led its advocates to confine their rhetoric instead to forms that mesh naturally with the branch of professional journalism most committed – notionally, at least – to openness and transparency, namely public service broadcasting. The editorial policies adopted by the doyen of the genre, the BBC, commit its journalists to '*enable* national and international debate' (emphasis added) – rather than, say, attempting to lead it. This is the significance, in the Lynch and McGoldrick definition of PJ, cited earlier, of the emphasis on 'creating opportunities' for audiences to consider and value non-violent responses. If society, furnished with such opportunities, decides it still prefers violent responses, then 'there is nothing more journalism can do about it, while remaining journalism' (Lynch 2008, p4).

13

Liberate PJ from the expectation that journalistic agency in mainstream media can be cultivated and cajoled to bring about a significant expansion of such opportunities, according to several contributors to this book, and such restraints can be thrown off. This more avowedly radical critique suggests that peace journalism has not sufficiently challenged professional norms, and has unwittingly mirrored war journalism by focusing on media roles in armed conflict at the expense of attention to structural violence and peacebuilding.

One critic who draws elements from both the professional/conservative and radical perspectives is Thomas Hanitzsch (2007), who throws nearly everything but the kitchen sink at peace journalism. Epistemologically, he accuses PJ of a näively positivist faith in untrammeled 'truth' (which in Galtung's model was counterposed to war journalism's 'propaganda' orientation). Theoretically, Hanitzsch sees in PJ an outdated conception of media effects as powerful and linear. Normatively, he says that PJ calls for 'bad news' to be suppressed when it jeopardises peaceful outcomes, and for journalism to take on inappropriate advocacy, peacekeeping or campaigning tasks that are better left to political, legal or military actors.

PJ advocates have effectively refuted these particular criticisms. PJ theory has been updated since Galtung's original model, to recognise epistemological pluralism and the de-centring of meaning-making: rather than reflect *the* truth as such, PJ aims to identify and deconstruct propaganda, and can be recognised as supplying 'cues to form negotiated and/or oppositional readings' of dominant iterations of meaning (Lynch 2008, p143). Media effects are not in fact conceived as linear; Lynch and McGoldrick (2005) hypothesise a 'feedback loop' whereby previous patterns of news reportage influence the expectations and strategies of political actors as sources, who shape reportable news events in conflict situations. As for how to handle news that is 'inconvenient', such as atrocities committed by one side that has already been demonised, peace journalists call not for censorship but for contextualisation.

But Hanitzsch offers several criticisms that are more telling. The peace journalism research tradition needs to attend more to the institutions and contexts of journalism itself. In Hanitzsch's view, PJ

14

is prone to equating journalism with media in general, collapsing it with public relations, advertising, entertainment, and more recently the hybrid forms of quasi-journalism emerging in social media and the blogosphere. It over-blames journalism for militarising popular consciousness and state policies, implicitly letting other social and political forces off the hook. News values, the criteria that govern news selection and framing, cannot take hold without a purchase in popular culture. In addressing the alleged shortcomings of journalism, structural factors must be given their due weight, including workaday news routines; media organisations' need for reliable and credible flows of news, technology, budgets, relationships with advertisers, and the legal framework (Shoemaker & Reese 1996).

Such insights can be synthesised into a conceptual schema flexible enough for PJ to be modelled as potentially influential on journalistic practice. We do not need to conclude that editors and reporters are mere cogs in a machine not of their own making, and that therefore efforts to reform journalism from within are pointless. Structural constraints govern the content of news, but they do not altogether determine it. Pressure from without and renewal from within are not mutually exclusive avenues, an issue explored by Jake Lynch's chapter in this volume; they may, indeed, be necessary counterparts.

To Majid Tehranian's aphorism – 'structural pluralism [in media] may be considered a *sine qua non* of content pluralism' (Tehranian 2002, p58) – one might add that PJ reform efforts have generally devoted themselves to attempts to invoke and implement the political and perspectival pluralism already notionally provided for, whether in public service agreements – the particular terrain identified in Lynch's chapter as a promising milieu – or the general transmitted assumption about the essential honesty of journalism, inscribed in Kempf's formula of a 'trust bonus'. Such a strategy is capable of extending the writ of PJ only so far, of course, and the differences of emphasis among its exponents, briefly rehearsed in this introduction, encompass, between them, a range of agendas, explicit or otherwise, for more thoroughgoing structural changes.

## Organisation of the book

*Part I. Conceptualising peace journalism: limitations and extensions*

The first part of this book is devoted to the conceptual and organisational frameworks that have produced the dominant patterns of war journalism, and to prospects for them to be transcended and transformed.[1] Titled 'Conceptualising peace journalism: limitations and extensions', contributions trace and traverse boundaries between peace journalism and other paradigms with potentially overlapping assumptions and orientations.

War journalism attained dominance within structures constitutive of the political economy of media. Such journalism should be seen, in other words, not merely as a successful product but as an epiphenomenon of a 'world information and communication order' – a formulation coined as part of a systematic attempt to promote reforms.

Robert A Hackett considers, in comparative analysis, the respective strengths and weaknesses of 'challenger paradigms' as candidates to overturn and supplant what he calls 'the arguably disintegrating but still dominant regime of objectivity'. He urges a creative synergy of reform efforts, with peace journalism seen as capable of breathing new life into the movement for a new world information and communication order, following the UNESCO initiative of a previous generation, and of reaching out to social movement activists responding to a broad range of concerns – from human rights abuses to environmental degradation – and seeking to exert political agency in symbolic domains.

Alternative media provide new venues, he suggests, for a struggle to democratise the communication field itself, to complement and strengthen existing calls for democracy *through* media. Examining the nature and extent of 'counter-hegemonic' impetus to be found in each of these challenger paradigms enables a systematic appraisal of the potential for a shared project or 'coalition' for social, political and communicative change to be formed between them.

---

1  Borrowing terms from Johan Galtung – see Galtung 2004.

Birgit Brock-Utne draws attention to the gendered character of cultural production, locating, as she does so, continuities between the representational conventions of news – with a dominant strain of war journalism – and those of school textbooks which inculcate, in the impressionable young, a flat, realist view of our shared human history. And the story is usually 'his-story', in both fields.

Not that peace research itself is always much better, she points out. 'The structure of foreign news', the 1965 essay that provides the starting-point for peace journalism, was itself co-authored by a woman, Mari Holmboe Ruge, who is often, Brock-Utne remarks, forgotten. In tracing the 'euphemistic language' devised by male 'defence intellectuals' to disguise the horror of war, in particular nuclear weapons, she reminds us of how familiar such phrases have become over the years through repetition in the news. News of effective nonviolent actions is, by contrast, generally ignored and suppressed, and it is not coincidental that such actions are often devised and carried out by women.

Ibrahim Seaga Shaw extends the dimensions of peace journalism to include human rights. It's an enticing step, given the common presentation in media reports of human rights as an unalloyed 'good thing'. It is also a risky one. The list of conflicts in which advocates of peace and human rights have found themselves on opposite sides, in particular debates – over 'humanitarian' military interventions against abusive governments in South East Europe and West Asia, for example – testifies to some cognitive dissonance in the formation and application of starting assumptions.

Human rights journalism can be seen as a counter-hegemonic paradigm and practice, Shaw argues, if it is conceived with attention to the 'unjust political economic structures, put and kept in place for the benefit of powerful interests in the rich world, [which] have the effect of keeping people in the majority world from realising the rights pre-scribed for them in the wellknown international instruments' of human rights. He deploys, and significantly elaborates, Lisa Schirch's (2002) enterprising attempt to devise a conceptual framework in which peace and human rights can be seen as mutually reinforcing, rather than as a set of forks in a road – over how to respond to individual culpability, for instance, for crimes against humanity committed in the context of deficient structures and cultures. Human rights journalism is presented as a complementary strand of peace journalism, and one that opens up new lines of attack, so to speak, on mainstream reporting.

Annabel McGoldrick situates peace journalism in a collocation of current challenges, with a multitude of disciplinary tributaries, not merely to the hegemonic 'objectivity' paradigm in reporting conflict but to the dominant assumptions of Western political discourses, and their conceptions of human motivation and behaviour. She draws on her own experience as a psychotherapist, helping patients to heal family relationships by a series of steps founded on acknowledging the validity of multiple perspectives on the same issue: an acknowledgement enabled, in turn, by harnessing innate capacities for empathy.

'Empathy' is named as an essential attribute of peace journalism in Galtung's original PJ table (Galtung 1998), one that can be activated by 'giving a voice to all parties', in multi-perspectival construction, not merely the two counterposed protagonists – 'goodie' and 'baddie' – familiar from war journalism. But it is a human quality that is routinely downgraded, McGoldrick argues, in the assumptions shared by both scholarly endeavour and public policymaking, in fields including economics and social policy as well as international relations. Friendship, emotional responses and fellow-feeling are seen as relatively weak and ephemeral compared with 'hard' calculations of optimality, in accounting for – and attempting to regulate – the social behaviour of individuals, communities and nation states alike.

However, a swelling stream of research has taken up findings from neuroscience to argue that humans are 'soft-wired for empathy', and that emotional responses are far more influential on behaviours than is allowed for in such doctrines as neoclassical economics, or realism in international relations, or the characteristic policy sets built upon them. The dominant representations of war journalism, being 'dehumanizing of "them"', as Galtung puts it, abrogate and suppress a key part of our meaning-making and relational capacity, thus exerting influence towards competitive, hostile and ultimately violent relationships. Peace journalism supplies opportunities for readers and audiences to activate their empathic capacities, and can therefore be seen as a form of representation that is preferable, because it appears more authentic to their needs and instincts.

### Part II: Peace journalism in wartime and peacebuilding

The chapters in this section focus on media framing of, and attention to, conflict situations. Each author offers some assessment of media representations in relation to criteria of war and peace journalism, while also pointing to new areas of (usually comparative) research and/or to conceptual revisions of the PJ model.

Stuart Allan's chapter calls for peace photography rather than war photography, and advocates expanding PJ into the analysis of photojournalism (both as a practice and as visual texts). It reinforces arguments advanced by other authors in this book (Shaw, Mogekwu & Hawkins) that PJ focuses too heavily on conflict at the manifest/visible level, and ignores peacebuilding processes or resolving conflict at the latent/invisible level. Allan argues that documenting the horrors of warfare is of vital importance, but so is the need to devise and offer visual representations of alternatives in the name of peace. In order to address the deficit identified in Susie Linfield's (2010) observation that 'seeing the images of war does not necessarily translate into believing, caring or acting', Allan proposes the need to 'reconsider anew photography's potential contribution to ongoing efforts to reinvigorate peace journalism'.

The chapter calls for the urgent need to document the lived realities of human suffering in all of their complexities while, at the same time, engendering opportunities to visualise alternatives. Peace photography constitutes more than anti-war photography, namely because disrupting the logics of familiar binaries ('good' and 'evil', 'victim' and 'oppressor', 'us' and 'them') is only the initial step. But, by way of expanding PJ and reinforcing the important human rights and peace nexus as discussed by other authors of this book, Allan proposes a second vital step in which peace photography calls for nothing less than a profound reimagining of photographic form, practice and epistemology in order to move beyond the imposition of binaries in the first place, and thereby contribute to the re-articulation of visions of the world in the service of human rights and social justice.

Lioba Suchenwirth and Richard Lance Keeble offer a critical appraisal of the mediascape of a country, Guatemala, now in a phase routinely described as 'post-conflict' but still, as they explain, replete with conflict issues and abundant cultural and structural violence, bequeathed by a history of colonialism and civil war (the latter triggered by the installation and maintenance of a repressive US client regime). The political economy of the Guatemalan media places the lion's share of resources for symbolic production in the hands of a local oligarchy and branches of the state (though they are linked at multiple levels).

Opportunities for PJ are therefore to be found in independent or 'alternative' media sectors – rich in ideas, creativity and grassroots connections, if not in physical or political capital. Indigenous media were provided for by the country's 'post-conflict' Constitution, they observe, but with a twist: radio stations can only gain legal status if they have successfully competed in a franchise auction for the entitlement to broadcast on allotted frequencies, thus institutionalising a bias in favour of those wealthy enough to clear this hurdle.

The chapter by Sudeshna Roy and Susan Dente Ross critically analyses and compares the editorial commentary about the 2008 terror attacks in Mumbai, India, in leading newspapers of India and the US: the *Hindustan Times* (*HT*), the largest-circulation English-language newspaper in Mumbai, and *The New York Times* (*NYT*). The authors examine Indian and US media coverage of the terror event in Mumbai to explore distinctions in the embedded ideology of terrorism and the (mis)alignment of the two nations' media commentaries with the tenets of war or peace discourse.

They suggest that media in both India and the US perpetuate global ideological discourses around terror that reify social identities, promote nationalistic support for government actions, and call up religious and political divisions between India and Pakistan as a primary cause for the terror attacks. The analysis also indicates alignment of the above three characteristics with the propaganda and elite orientation of war journalism, and the 'giving peace a chance' category with the truth and solution orientation of peace journalism (Lynch & McGoldrick 2005).

Still, the finding that a well-established newspaper like the *HT* can create space for at least some peace journalism, expanding and rendering, replete with contestation, the political context of the Mumbai terror attack, unlike the foreign *NYT*, suggests that peace journalism is 'doable', even in conditions of stress. This analysis can serve to answer criticisms that PJ is mere rhetoric. This chapter's major contribution to the expansion of PJ is not so much in theory as in the application of PJ as a critical method: it offers a useful contrast between a US and a major non-Western newspaper and their political context, and enables discussion of the local inflexion of globalising/US discourses on terrorism.

While recognising Galtung's PJ model as a useful tool or checklist both for journalists and peace researchers, Stig-Arne Nohrstedt and Rune Ottosen suggest conceptual limitations. They recommend extending the model in three ways: first, methodologically, to critical discourse analysis (CDA); second, in scope, to other stages of the conflict cycle (a theme in other chapters also); and third, conceptually, to Bourdieu's 'doxa' or blind spots in the news.

The CDA approach to media studies incorporates levels of meanings and the relations between different actors in the discourse analysis as part of the context. Public debates in society have influence on the intertextual meanings generated in response to media texts, as do a gamut of other discursive forms including, but not confined to, the speeches and writings of political and military leaders, rhetorical interventions by PR firms and spin-doctors, and popular conceptions of national and security identity. The authors draw on their empirical study of media silence around certain critical aspects of the plans for closer military cooperation between Finland, Norway and Sweden, and the hidden assumptions concerning the wider context of the US-led 'global war on terrorism', as some such important influences, the salience of which are in no way diminished by their remaining tacit in media texts.

By using CDA as a supplement, the authors suggest a more comprehensive analysis that reveals the systematic stifling of both ordinary people's voices, and certain crucial aspects of debate, with the objective of disclosing the complex discursive constructions and referential structures that contribute to conflict escalations and wars. Nohrstedt and Ottosen make the argument that this silence (or doxa) about potential conflict-risks and possible involvement in future wars is not reflected in Galtung's model for war and peace journalism.

If Nohrstedt and Ottosen's observations mandate PJ's increased attention to strategic silences that may prevent timely discussion of trajectories ultimately leading to violence, then Matt Mogekwu's chapter picks up the theme by calling on peace journalists to intervene in that key phase of conflict where violence is 'latent', rather than waiting for it to become manifest. Drawing on an exploration of the coverage of the Niger-Delta crisis by the local Nigerian media, Mogweku calls on journalists to promote dialogue among the parties in conflict before things get out of hand.

Mogweku argues that, if local journalists in the Niger-Delta region had taken up the responsibility of 'managing' the crisis at the level where listening would have been a crucial factor in resolving the issues raised by the region's indigenes, the eventual violence might have been avoided.

Virgil Hawkins' chapter finds that, relative to the coverage of the violent phase of the conflict, the proportion of coverage of the peace process was considerably less for the Democratic Republic of the Congo (DRC) than it was for Israel–Palestine, even when the death toll (threshold) was much higher in the former than the latter. He argues that the problem of war journalism is not only limited to the idea of 'stealth' conflicts but also 'stealth' peace processes.

The reasons for this marginalisation are complex, Hawkins notes, but they include the lack of involvement and interest of elite nations and persons; the perceived failure of a predominantly white and affluent audience to identify with the human stories within the intimidating statistics; the sheer complexity of the conflict; the fact that events in the DRC had been consistently marginalised in the past (continuity); commercial factors such as the lack of reporters permanently stationed in the vicinity; and the gravitational pull of powerful agenda-setters in the media. Hawkins calls for an expansion of the peace journalism movement to encourage 'improvements in the quantity, as well as quality, of journalism related to armed conflict and its resolution'.

## Part III. Agencies and openings for change

The chapters in this section overlap conceptually with those in Part II, but they place more emphasis on opportunities and avenues for change, politically as well as academically, in the practice of journalism, of research, and of peacebuilding.

Jake Lynch considers the potential for PJ to serve as a rallying cry for social movement activism, seeking to exert influence in the form of extra-movement outcomes in the particular case of representations in Australian media of the Israel–Palestine conflict. Is there, he wonders, sufficient 'commensurability' between the distinctions in the PJ model and what social movement activists would consider as motivating goals in response to 'hot poker' issues, for coalitions of interest to form around demands for reforms to media practices and structures?

Lynch describes an experiment in which two focus groups of activists from Sydney's Muslim community each saw a different version of a set of television news stories, including an episode of the Israel–Palestine conflict, in which Muslim people featured strongly as subjects ('or objects, in the sense of having things done to them'). One version was framed as war journalism, the other as peace journalism. There was, Lynch recounts, an 'incipient generation gap' in the responses, with younger activists prepared to notice and appreciate the differences, while their older colleagues saw them essentially as variants of the same thing: 'it's not different enough for the community here', one said; 'you'd have to hit us in the face with a wet fish, I think'.

Elissa Tivona's chapter builds on calls to expand PJ to incorporate coverage of largely invisible peacebuilding efforts such as those of social movements described in the chapters by Suchenwirth and Keeble, and by Lynch, by calling for similar attention to women's roles in peace-building processes. Tivona's point of departure is that intellectual elites, with the collusion of every form of recorded media from the beginning of history, have marginalised and obscured the identifiable agency of women and their particular capacity for compassion.

Drawing on the findings of her research based on the peace stories of nine women randomly selected from among the 1000 peacewom-en collectively nominated for the Nobel Peace Prize in 2005, Tivona calls for a shift in the gendered assumptions of news discourse, from 'if it bleeds, it leads' to 'it heals if it reveals'. However, she warns that to achieve this requires a reformulation of the performances that are highlighted on a day-to-day basis – performances modelled by women activists across the globe. She calls for a move away from the narrow spectrum of rhetorical performance currently featured in headlines, which freezes human activity in images of intractable and often violent conflict, while creative and salient models for conflict mitigation and resolution, such as those by the nine peacewomen in her study, are systematically overlooked.

Rob McMahon and Peter Chow-White develop the notion of 'empathy' for all in conflict resolution and peace building by proposing the 'cold conflict' model that they say would help peace researchers investigate the more subtle discursive terrain of 'cold' conflicts, which other authors in this volume call 'latent/indirect/invisible' conflicts. They propose the concept of 'legacy' racism as an alternative to 'old' racism, to recognise the continuing impacts of past racist policies and practices on groups and individuals. They critically analyse a case study of news coverage about 'reconciliation' activities between First Nations and non-aboriginal communities in Canada. Their analytical model reveals the strains of 'legacy racism' and 'new racism' that exist alongside already existing examples of PJ in news coverage of Canada's Truth and Reconciliation Commission.

The McMahon and Chow-White model exposes nascent tendencies towards peace journalism, enabling them to highlight examples of discourses that challenge stereotypes, expose the structural effects of violence, demonstrate the fluid and contingent nature of group-based identities and offer appropriate contextual explanations. Their case study underscores questions asked by PJ researchers and their critics as to whether mediated approaches to peacebuilding are effective in securing material change and transforming conflict.

## Future directions for peace journalism: research and strategy

Elissa Tivona builds up a qualitative document analysis through 'local focus dyads' – juxtaposing and contrasting the 'background [1000]

*Peacewomen across the globe* narrative ... with a foreground news story'. The latter was taken from mainstream media, in acknowledgement of their power *to* foreground, through such effects – wellknown to media research – as agenda-setting and framing, which make salient particular aspects of the reality in which we are daily immersed. Some 'knowns' – things we know, as a human community – are systematically rendered 'unknown' by this power, Birgit Brock-Utne notes, adding a category to the (in)famous typology of intelligence material proposed by Donald Rumsfeld. The 'unknown knowns' – knowledges and understandings we need, to build peace – have to be disinterred from where hegemonic forces have buried them under mounds of euphemism and strategic silence.

It is by claiming a share of this power – to bring aspects of background into the foreground, Tivona suggests – that extra-movement outcomes might be brought within reach for movements committed to progressive social change: what she names as a 'globalisation of compassion ... to move empathic sensitivity from a theoretical ideal to a practical reality', by 'regularly highlight[ing]' the acts performed daily by 'peacewomen' across every continent, thus bridging Lederach's interdependence gap.

Crucially, the binary of 'foreground' and 'background' ('highlight' and 'shadow') has to remain in place, at least to some extent, for this to work. The 'trust bonus' accorded to mainstream media is what enables them to do ideological work, in the Gramscian sense of camouflaging points of view as 'common sense', or appearing to place them in the realm of the 'factual'. 'The [journalistic] acceptance of representational conventions as facticity', Gaye Tuchman noted in a landmark study of newsroom procedures, is what 'leaves reality vulnerable to manipulation' (Tuchman 1978, p109). Success in penetrating and transforming the category of mainstream news – its values, practices and definitions – to give peace more of a chance, by claiming part of its lasting 'trust bonus', still presents a glittering prize for PJ in non-research contexts and an attractive prospect for researchers to devise ways to investigate further.

In the upheavals of the Arab Spring, and other examples of extra-movement outcomes, this may entail looking both before and beyond the 'new media moment' to disclose relations of cause and effect in longer perspective: how did the moment arrive, and what happened next? Egypt's Facebook phenomenon did not, by itself, bring about a revolution, any more than Wikileaks' crib to the real thoughts of the US Ambassador in Tunis 'caused' the fall of the Ben Ali regime. The 'risks to [its] long-term stability' were pinpointed, in his cable of 2009, as 'anger … at Tunisia's high unemployment and regional inequities'. New media placed organisational and ideological resources in the hands of activists at what proved a crucial moment, thereby lowering a barrier to mobilisation in response to grievances long in the gestation.

It still leaves open the question of how this momentum came to exert such powerful political agency, and this is where alternative and conventional media may converge after all. The inchoate cry of tweets from Tahrir Square appeared to acquire political heft only when they attained 'crossover' into the mainstream, notably through coverage on Al Jazeera, and thence into the 'official public sphere'. An email circular from one of the best-known online activist groups, Avaaz.org, thus described the fruits of its actions in 'Syria, Yemen, Libya … our support to activists has created global media cycles with footage and eyewitness accounts that our team helps to distribute to CNN, BBC, Al Jazeera and others'.

Wikileaks itself apparently made the calculation that, in order to attain due prominence and salience for the disclosures in its leaked diplomatic cables, formal arrangements with professional news organisations were required. The catalysing influence ascribed to them may be attributable, in part, to the phenomenology of their appearance, not on a campaigning website or in other 'alternative' media but in a context where traditional safeguards – trained observers, edited copy – had built up reputational resources to support them.

This pattern of 'crossover' from alternative to mainstream media, presaging extra-movement outcomes, is apparently being recapitulated in other, quite different mediascapes and political milieux at the same time. In a contemporaneous example, campaigners successfully halted the privatisation of forestry management by the UK's new Conservative-led Coalition government: an extension of neoliberal economic policy identified by activists as a threat to cherished rights of access. Ministers were responding, Attorney General Dominic Grieve declared, to 'a spontaneous combustion brought about by the internet [a half-million strong online petition organised via social media], which grew a momentum of its own. National newspapers jumped on the bandwagon once it started, but actually the bandwagon started without them'.

Matt Mogekwu, in his contribution to this volume, argues that PJ must 'free itself from the mainstream journalism strait-jacket' if it is to fulfil its representational potential, but also that it must reach out across the divide between the parallel fields of alternative and mainstream media to 'work hand-in-hand with existing journalism practice'. Robert A Hackett ends his chapter by making the case for 'challenger paradigms' to combine, in different permutations to suit different circumstances. Exponents of peace journalism, alternative media and communication rights could, he suggests, join forces, if their efforts are calibrated with due sensitivity to context.

It is possible, indeed, to extrapolate, from most if not all of the chapters in this volume, trajectories in which these approaches mesh to become greater than the sum of their parts. 'Movements for media democratisation are pursuing communication rights that are formally recognised in national and international law', Hackett observes; Jake Lynch, in his chapter, identifies the removal of bureaucratic filters to the ABC honouring its (notional) mandate to diversity; and Lioba Suchenwirth and Richard Lance Keeble point to reforms needed for indigenous Guatemalan media to fulfil their potential – these are all demands for structural changes whose focus is sharpened by the application of PJ analytical techniques.

There are roles for PJ research, then, in identifying, documenting and fostering the dynamics of 'crossover' between alternative and mainstream media, and thence into official public spheres, while those categories retain their applicability. PJ advocates must develop, between them, strategic approaches capable of motivating exponents in both fields – acknowledging that these will inevitably differ, and that they can draw strength from each other. 'Giving serious *attention* to nonofficial sources is discouraged as unnewsworthy', Shoemaker and Reese wrote

(Shoemaker & Reese 1996, p235), in journalism that thinks itself 'objective'; but this is a generalisation that dates from before the 'accentuation' of social movements' potential for political agency brought about by new media and its boost to multiple traditions of radical, openly committed journalistic practice.

In addition to the question of the potential for agency and change within the existing structures of media, future research could also explore the question that underlies the call by some of the authors in this volume for a more proactive role for PJ in preventing conflict escalation and violence. Could the practices of peace journalism, if embedded more widely in public communication processes and institutions, make a significant difference to conflict cycles? Could they change or break the hypothesised destructive 'feedback loop' noted above? Under what conditions could this occur? More empirical evidence on the potentially positive as well as negative impact of media practices and content would provide a stronger ethical case for a more consciously interventionist role for journalism in promoting and protecting peace and human rights.

Media, Schudson points out, 'are formally disconnected from other ruling agencies, in that they must attend as much to their own legitimation as to the legitimation of the capitalist system as a whole' (Schudson 1995, p270). They can ill afford, in other words, to appear less wellinformed or more credulous than their readers and audiences. Peace journalism, if it grows into a role connecting the alternative and mainstream media fields and speaks in ways intelligible to both, can come to be seen as offering means for journalists to 'wise up', for activists to bring their messages from background to foreground, and for democratisation agendas to acquire content to sharpen and promote their calls for structural reform.

## References

Bennett, W Lance (1990). Towards a theory of press-state relations. *Journal of Communication*, 40(2): 103–25.

Castells, Manuel (2007). Communication power and counter-power in the network society. *International Journal of Communication*, 1: 238–66.

Earl, Jennifer (2000). Methods, movements and outcomes. *Research in Social Movements, Conflicts and Change*, 22: 3–25.

Earl, Jennifer, Katrina Kimport, Greg Prieto, Carly Rush & Kimberly Reynoso (2010). Changing the world one webpage at a time: conceptualizing and explaining internet activism. *Mobilization*, 15(4): 425–46.

Freedman, Des (2009). 'Smooth operator'? The propaganda model and moments of crisis. *Westminster Papers in Communication and Culture*, 6(2): 59–72.

Galtung, Johan (2004). *Transcend and transform: an introduction to conflict work*. London: Pluto Press.

Galtung, Johan (1998). High road, low road: charting the course for peace journalism, *Track Two*, (7): 4, Centre for Conflict Resolution, South Africa. [Online]. Available: ccrweb.ccr.uct.ac.za/archive/two/7_4/p07_highroad_lowroad.html [Accessed 23 July 2011].

Gamson, William A (1975). *The strategy of social protest*. Homewood, Ill: Dorsey Press.

Hanitzsch, Thomas (2007). Situating peace journalism in journalism studies: a critical appraisal. *Conflict and Communication*, 6(2): 1–9. [Online]. Available: www.cco.regener-online.de/2007_2/pdf/hanitzsch.pdf [Accessed 23 January 2011].

Keeble, Richard Lance (2010). Peace journalism as political practice: a new, radical look at the theory. In Richard Lance Keeble, John Tulloch & Florian Zollmann (Eds). *Peace journalism, war and conflict resolution* (pp49–68). London & New York: Peter Lang.

Kempf, Wilhelm (2007). Peace journalism: a tightrope walk between advocacy journalism and constructive conflict coverage. *Conflict and Communication Online*, 6(2). [Online]. Available: www.cco.regener-online.de/2007_2/pdf/kempf.pdf [Accessed 20 July 2011].

Lederach, John Paul (1999). Justpeace: the challenge of the 21st century. In *People building peace: 35 inspiring stories from around the world* (pp27–36). Utrecht: European Centre for Conflict Prevention.

Linfield, Susie (2010). *The cruel radiance: photography and political violence*. Chicago: University of Chicago Press.

Loyn, David (2007). Good journalism or peace journalism? *Conflict and Communication Online*, 6(2). [Online]. Available: www.cco.regener-online.de/2007_2/pdf/loyn_reply.pdf [Accessed 20 July 2011].

Lynch, Jake (2008). *Debates in peace journalism*. Sydney: Sydney University Press.

Lynch, Jake & Johan Galtung (2010). *Reporting conflict: new directions in peace journalism*. St. Lucia: University of Queensland Press.

Lynch, Jake & Annabel McGoldrick (2005). *Peace journalism*. Stroud: Hawthorn Press.

McKee, Alan (2005). *The public sphere: an introduction*. Cambridge: Cambridge University Press.

Molotch, Harvey & Marilyn Lester (1997). News as purposive behaviour: on the strategic use of routine events, accidents and scandals. In Daniel Berkowitz (Ed.). *Social meanings of news: a text reader* (193–209). London: Sage.

Patindol, Jean Lee (2010). Building a peace journalists' network from the ground: the Philippine experience. In Richard Keeble, John Tulloch & Florian Zollmann (Eds). *Peace journalism, war and conflict resolution* (pp193–206). London & New York: Peter Lang.

Schirch, Lisa (2002). Human rights and peacebuilding: towards just peace. Paper presented to 43rd Annual International Studies Association Convention, New Orleans, Louisiana, March 2002.

Schudson, Michael (1995). *The power of news*. Cambridge, MA: Harvard University Press.

Shinar, Dov (2007). Peace journalism: the state of the art. In Dov Shinar & Wilhelm Kempf (Eds). *Peace journalism: the state of the art* (pp199–210). Berlin: Regener.

Shoemaker, Pamela J & Stephen D Reese (1996). *Mediating the message: theories of influences on mass media content.* 2nd edn. White Plains, NY: Longman.

Stephenson, Carolyn (1999). Peace studies, overview. In Lester Kurtz & Jennifer Turpin (Eds). *The encyclopaedia of violence, peace and conflict* (vol. 2) (pp809–20). San Diego, CA: Academic Press.

Tehranian, Majid (2002). Peace journalism: negotiating global media ethics. *Harvard International Journal of Press/Politics,* 7(2): 58–83.

Tuchman, Gaye (1978): *Making news: a study in the construction of reality.* New York: Free Press.

Williams, Louise & Roland Rich (Eds) (2000). *Losing control: freedom of the press in Asia.* Canberra: Asia Pacific Press.

# PART I

CONCEPTUALISING PEACE JOURNALISM:
LIMITATIONS AND EXTENSIONS

# Chapter 1

## New vistas for peace journalism: alternative media and communication rights[1]

*Robert A Hackett*

I once asked a California-based public health advocate, concerned with the media's impact on community violence, about her group's strategies for changing the media. 'Bob,' she replied, 'the point isn't to change the media. The point is to change the world'. It was a useful reminder. Like many other forms of citizen intervention in the media field, peace journalism (PJ) is not simply about journalism. PJ is part of much broader processes and movements to challenge cultural, structural and physical violence and to achieve a more peaceful world. Communication practices and institutions (particularly journalism as a culturally central form of storytelling) are interwoven with movements for and against social justice, with contemporary processes of peace and war,[2] and with other intersecting crises facing humankind – impending climate catastrophe, humanitarian emergencies, terror, war, poverty, forced migrations, and human rights abuses (Cottle 2009, p15). Addressing those crises requires, *inter alia*, addressing the structured communication paradigms that (however unwittingly) may contribute to them. The task is gargantuan, but the good news is that PJ has potential allies

---

1 I thank Jake Lynch, Rune Ottosen, Ibrahim Shaw and other members of the international peace journalism research group for comments and advice, and Angelika Hackett for editorial assistance. An earlier version of this paper was published in 2010 as 'Journalism for peace and justice: towards a comparative analysis of media paradigms', in *Studies in Social Justice,* 4(2): 145–64.

2 Indeed, it can be argued that increasingly 'the news media do not only communicate or "*mediate*" the events of war; they enter into its very constitution shaping its course and conduct' (Cottle 2009, p109; emphasis in original).

outside the media field, including a natural affinity with longstanding and emerging campaigns and movements to democratise media.

Drawing from secondary literature, this chapter makes a case for common ground between PJ and other 'challenger paradigms'. Each paradigm mobilises energy, generates incentives and institutional logics, organises ways of producing, legitimising and disseminating knowledge, and reinforces, challenges and/or creates power relations. While interested in the prospects for change, I start with the arguably disintegrating but still dominant 'regime of objectivity' (Hackett & Zhao 1998) characteristic of North American journalism's period of 'high modernism' (Hallin 2000). I then situate PJ in relation to that dominant paradigm, and turn to two other challengers, each of which can be considered a form of media democratisation. If PJ has so far been an effort to reform dominant media from within, alternative media bypass dominant media by creating a parallel field, and the communication rights movement seeks to reform dominant media from without by changing the legal and political-economic contexts within which media operate. Both of these latter paradigms can be considered forms of media democratisation, which has a double sense: democratisation *through* the media – using media to democratise other areas of society (a longstanding practice of progressive social movements), and democratisation *of* the media field itself (Hackett & Carroll 2006).

To make a case that PJ might find new venues and allies in movements for media democratisation, I explore the extent to which each of the three challenger paradigms can be considered counter-hegemonic (i.e. actively opposed to some form of domination or oppression), and identify their core principles, strategies, allies and opponents. To what extent, then, do they share a project of social, political or communicative change?

## The regime of objectivity

Given the centrality of the value of objectivity in discussions of journalism's public philosophy, including debates between critics and defenders of PJ, I begin with a discussion of this concept that has dominated Anglo-American journalism for much of the 20th century and that is acquiring global significance as journalists seek new roles and institutional supports within formerly authoritarian regimes elsewhere. So long as we take it as a heuristic framework and not an empirically existing object, objectivity could be described as a paradigm or a regime, a metaphor that calls attention to the interlinkage of practices, norms, epistemology and structures in journalism.

Objectivity has positive connotations, such as the pursuit of truth without fear or favour. What objectivity means in practice, however, and whether it is a desirable and achievable goal for reporting in a democratic society, are debatable questions. Objectivity is not a single, fixed 'thing'. Hackett and Zhao (1998) suggest that, in contemporary North American journalism, objectivity constitutes a multifaceted discursive 'regime', an interrelated complex of ideas and practices that provide a general model for conceiving, defining, arranging, and evaluating news texts, practices and institutions. They identify five general levels or dimensions in this regime.

First, objectivity comprises goals that journalists should strive for – values concerning journalism's ability to impart information about the world (accuracy, completeness, separation of fact from opinion), and values concerning the stance that reporters should take towards the value-laden meanings of news (detachment, neutrality, impartiality and independence, and avoiding partisanship, personal biases, ulterior motives, or outside interests) (McQuail 1992, chapters 16 and 17). Second, such values are assumed to be embodied in a set of news-gathering and presentational practices, discussed below. Third, this paradigm implies assumptions about knowledge and reality, such as a positivist faith in the possibility of accurate descriptions of the world as it is, through careful observation and disinterested reporting. Fourth, objectivity is embedded in an institutional framework. It presumes that journalism is conducted by skilled professionals, employed within specialised institutions – news organisations, usually corporate-owned, but in which editorial and marketing functions are separated. In their relations with the broader society, journalists and news media are assumed to enjoy legal guarantees of free speech, and independence from the state, political parties and other outside interests. And fifth, objectivity provides language for everyday assessments of journalistic performance. This language includes terms like 'fairness' and 'balance', which some see as more flexible and achievable substitutes for objectivity. Objectivity is often counterposed to propaganda, and personal or partisan 'bias'.

Who are the beneficiaries of the objectivity regime, and what functions does it serve? Notwithstanding the apparently high-minded altruism and universalism of its ethos – telling truth in the public interest without fear or favour – the historical and sociological roots of journalism objectivity reveal that it serves quite specific interests (Bennett 2009, pp189–92; Hackett & Zhao 1998). Nonpartisan reporting helped the commercial daily press, oriented towards emerging mass consumer markets, to displace the party-oriented papers of the 19th century, and to aggregate the broadest possible readership for advertisers. Similarly, the news agencies that emerged during the 1800s had a vested interest in providing politically neutral wire copy to newspaper clients with diverse partisan orientations. To the extent that objective reporting requires specialised skills, it enhances journalists' claim to professional status. The objectivity regime helps to manage the symbiotic relationship between news media and the state. Politicians gain access to media audiences and an opportunity to shape the public definition of political issues; conversely, so long as they follow the rules of objectivity, working journalists gain relatively stable access to senior officials and politicians, without sacrificing their public image of political independence and neutrality. Indeed, the objectivity doctrine 'obscured and therefore made more palatable [journalists'] unprofessional compromises with managerial imperatives and corporate politics' (Bagdikian 1997, p180). The claims of objectivity and professionalism also provided ideological cover for media monopolies against the threat of government antitrust legislation or regulation (McChesney 2004, pp63–64). Finally, the practices of objectivity, such as the 'balanced' reporting of political issues, opened the public forum to interest groups that had the resources and willingness to play the game (Hackett & Zhao 1998, chapter 3). A powerful coincidence of interests underpinned the longevity of the objectivity regime.

In addition to demystifying its social and political roots, academics have repeatedly demonstrated the shortcomings of existing journalism when measured against the stated ideal of objectivity, while others have advanced telling critiques of the epistemological foundations of journalism objectivity (see, for example, Hackett & Zhao 1998, chapter 5). It is more relevant here, however, to consider the regime's key narrative and reportorial practices and their systematic political consequences. These practices include 'documentary reporting' that allows journalists to transmit only facts that they can observe or that 'credible' and authoritative sources have confirmed (Bennett 2009, p193). Journalists also practise 'balance' when covering controversies that are regarded as legitimate, providing access to the most dramatic or authoritative leaders of 'both sides'. Other conventions include the separation of 'fact' from 'opinion', and the privileging of personalities over structures, political strategies over policy analysis, and discrete and timely events over long-term processes, conditions or contexts.

When measured against sensationalism or wilful propaganda, these objectivity practices have much to recommend them (Bagdikian 1997, p179). Yet they also have predictable consequences that are highly problematic for informing public opinion, or incentivising remedial action, in relation to global crises of conflict, ecology and poverty. Take the practices of 'balance'. In American environmental journalism, 'balance' gave undue weight to climate change deniers, resulting in inaccurate reporting at odds with the scientific consensus (Bennett 2009, pp108–12). Balance constructs and reduces complex issues to two sides, marginalising other perspectives, and giving excessive weight either to dramatic and polarising voices, or to the usual official sources (such as political party leaders). Balance also naturalises the construction of conflicts as two-sided zero-sum contests, in which one party can only gain at the expense of the other; alternative conflict resolution and win–win options are thus marginalised (Lynch & McGoldrick 2005a, pp203–12).

Other practices are equally problematic. The reliance on credentialed facts from elite sources, and the privileging of events over contexts, reinforce a global status quo of misery for millions of people, sidelining issues such as poverty, labour exploitation, or private sector corruption that are not on official agendas until they erupt in catastrophic upheavals. Such journalism can contribute to social turbulence as 'unestablished groups' adopt disruptive tactics to attract media attention (Bagdikian 1997, p213). Balance and official orientation can also make it difficult for 'objective' journalism to challenge governments' war-making policies, even when they are founded on dubious motives and evidence, in the absence of oppositional elite voices. The American media's virtually free pass to the Bush administration as it prepared to invade Iraq in 2003 is now widely recognised as a tragic case in point (DiMaggio 2009, see especially chapter 3). In a parallel fashion, the journalistic privileging of events and personalities over contexts and structures makes it easier for political leaders to foreground and demonise figures like Saddam Hussein, and to deflect attention from their own motives and contributions vis-à-vis conflict escalation, and from the 'collateral damage' of their own policies (such as the massive civilian cost of the pre-2003 sanctions imposed on Iraq).

A related line of critique asserts that the objectivity ethos directly contributes to the production of systematically one-sided or ideological news accounts, and legitimises media practices that undermine democratic public life, such as a stance of cynical negativism divorced from coherent analytical perspectives, and the framing of politics as a game of insiders motivated only by electoral success (see, for example, Bennett 2009, chapter 6).

Such critiques are contentious, but there is widespread agreement that the objectivity regime is in crisis. Anglo-American journalism is increasingly dissolving within profit-driven conglomerates, its economic basis threatened by audience fragmentation, and its occupational ethos shifting from public service (however conservatively defined) to consumerism and commercialism. No single paradigm has replaced objectivity, but several promising challengers have emerged that include PJ as an internal reform movement, operating in the corners of journalism education and news organisations to revise professional practices.

## Peace journalism

Like objectivity, PJ is a multifaceted paradigm. I do not repeat here the descriptions of PJ offered elsewhere in this book and in other publications (for example, Lynch & McGoldrick 2005a). Instead, I focus on several questions relevant to its philosophical and strategic prospects.

### Is peace journalism counter-hegemonic?

First, does PJ constitute a counter-hegemonic challenge to journalism, or to broader social structures? There is no unequivocal answer. While its advocates ask journalists to engage with concepts and ideas from the academic discipline of conflict analysis, they often prefer to speak in the language of journalistic professionalism. Indeed, when initiating PJ as a reform campaign within the journalism field, Lynch preferred to avoid the term 'peace journalism' which for some may imply an illegitimate prior commitment to extraneous values. He labelled the new initiative 'reporting the world' (Lynch 2002). Indeed, in justifying PJ's prescriptions, Lynch and McGoldrick (2005a, pp9, 185, 223, 242) are able to quote from formal editorial guidelines published by one of the world's bastions of the objectivity regime, the BBC, and to use its language – balance, fairness, responsibility (Lynch 2002, p3). One scholar characterises PJ as a prerequisite of good journalism, one 'which only forbids the unacceptable', such as the narrowing of news perspective to that of 'war-making elites', or acting as a conduit for propaganda (Kempf 2007a, p4; cited in Lynch 2008, pxvi). In this view, PJ embodies the best ideals of journalistic professionalism – including comprehensiveness, context, accuracy, and the representation of the full range of relevant opinions – and it critiques existing journalism from that standpoint while providing practical alternatives (Lynch 2008, pxviii).

Notwithstanding its toehold in the established media field however, PJ also has some of the characteristics of an oppositional social movement. Consider the contrasts between conventional journalism and the peace movement as paradigms for structuring thought and action. The peace movement values long-term peacebuilding processes, collective decision-making, political commitment, human solidarity, social change, and low-cost grassroots mobilisation. Dominant journalism favours timely events, official hierarchies, a detached stance, dyadic conflict, a consumerist worldview, and costly production values (Hackett 1991, pp274–75). While PJ should not be equated with the peace movement, it shares with it some of the above-noted incompatibilities vis-à-vis dominant news discourse.

PJ constitutes, first, an *epistemological challenge* to the objectivity regime. In this view, journalism inherently involves choices; it is a matter of representation, not of reality-reflection. Notwithstanding its professed disinterestedness, conventional 'objective' journalism enshrines practices that predictably favour some outcomes and values over others – including, too often, war over peaceful conflict transformation. For example, in conflict situations, far from being passive observers, journalists are often caught in a 'feedback loop' with political players. Frequently, based on their previous experience of the media, powerful sources create 'facts' that they anticipate will be reported and framed in particular ways. Thus, every time journalists re-create those frames, they influence future actions by sources. By focusing on physical violence divorced from context, and on win–lose scenarios, conventional 'objective' news unwittingly incentivises conflict escalation and 'crackdowns,' impeding a morally and professionally justifiable incentivisation of peaceful outcomes (Lynch & McGoldrick 2005a, pp216–18). Objective journalism can thus be 'irresponsible', in that it shuns Max Weber's 'ethic of responsibility' in public affairs – the idea that 'one should take into account the foreseeable consequences of one's actions … and adjust one's behaviour accordingly' (Lynch & McGoldrick 2005a, p218).

PJ thus challenges the very epistemological basis for a stance of detachment, calling instead for journalists to be self-reflexive vis-à-vis the institutionalised biases of their routine practices, the dangers posed by certain framing and sourcing choices, the non-passivity of sources, the interventionist nature of journalism, and the potential of its becoming an unwitting accomplice to war propaganda (Lynch 2008, pp10–14). That said, PJ is not renouncing the commitment to truthfulness, only questioning why some kinds of facts and sources are privileged, and how these feed into conflict cycles (p9). PJ rejects both the positivist stance that journalism simply reports self-evident facts, and the relativist position that 'it's all spin', that there is no independent basis to separate truth from propaganda. Instead, PJ offers interdisciplinary intellectual anchorage in peace and conflict studies, pursues the rigour of social science, and is reflexive, explicit about its normative commitments, open to justification, and aware of participant/observer interaction (ppxv, 21).[3]

Second, beyond epistemological differences, PJ challenges dominant *news values*, the taken-for-granted and usually implicit criteria that routinely guide journalists in selecting and constructing news narrative. In a recent update of a classic study by Galtung and Ruge (1965), Harcup and O'Neill (2001) identify ten dominant characteristics of newsworthy stories in the British press: power elite, celebrity, entertainment, surprise, bad news, good news (events), magnitude or scope, relevance (to the audience), follow-up (continuity), and the newspaper's own agenda. PJ's emphases on conflict formation and resolution, on win–win positive outcomes, on long-term processes and contexts, and on grassroots sources, challenge the news values of violence, negativity, unambiguity, timeliness, elite nations, and elite people.[4] Indeed, PJ's prescription to broaden the range of *sources* by consciously searching for the voices and options for peaceful resolution can be considered a third dimension of its challenge to conventional war reporting.

Some observers see PJ as offering an even more fundamental challenge – not just to the professional conservatism of journalists who cling to 'objectivity', and the routinised market share-building formats of profit-oriented news corporations – but also to the entire global war system and its 'deadly forms of propaganda', the 'lethal synergy of state,

---

3  A critical realist epistemology is evident in PJ's call to critically assess the claims of war propagandists; to distinguish between stated demands and underlying needs, goals and interests; to look beyond direct physical violence to explore its 'invisible' effects (such as cultural militarisation or psychological trauma), and the underlying patterns of cultural and structural violence (Lynch & McGoldrick 2005a, pp28–31; Hackett & Schroeder with NewsWatch Canada 2008, p44).

4  Although some PJ scholars suggest otherwise, pointing to specific failures in specific cases, such as the 'peace euphoria' framing of the Oslo 'peace process' in Israeli media (Mandelzis 2007).

corporations, think tanks, and the media' (Richard Falk in Lynch 2008, ppv, viii).

Other critics fear that PJ challenges a liberal value central to democratic journalism – that of freedom of expression. In the view of Hanitzsch (2004), PJ implies that 'bad news' and controversial topics, whose dissemination could contribute to the escalation of conflict, should be avoided. There is no evidence, however, that peace journalists actually make such a claim. They may well recognise legitimate limitations on free speech, such as prohibitions on hate speech, but this position is shared with many others, including some communication rights theorists, discussed below.

In one sense though, PJ does challenge the currently limited definition of free speech as the right of individuals to speak without fear of state punishment. PJ implies not just a right to speak freely, but also a right of access by all significant voices to the means of public communication. Free speech needs a chance to be heard in order to be effective – a normative imperative that underpins alternative media and media democratisation movements.

*What is an enabling environment for PJ?*

Given that PJ is, to some extent at least, counter-hegemonic, it will encounter obstacles and opponents. Thus, a second critical question arises. What are the prospects for actually putting it into practice? What strategies, and what political, cultural and institutional enabling environments, would help it to flourish?

One broad strategy is to reform the journalism field from within. A landmark review of scholarship on 'influences on media content' suggests that there is some degree of agency for newsworkers in traditional mass media (Shoemaker & Reese 1996). Excellent context-providing documentaries, or news reports on grassroots bridge-building across political divides, can be found within conventional news media – such as a Canadian national television news report that features an association of Israeli and Palestinian families who have lost loved ones in the ongoing conflicts. And there is experimental evidence that structural themes and de-escalation-oriented coverage can stimulate audience interest as much as escalation- and elite-oriented war journalism (Kempf 2007b).

Still, the barriers to PJ within conventional media are wideranging. They include the difficulties of constructing 'peace' as a compelling narrative (Fawcett 2002), the national basis of much of the world's news media and their audiences (notwithstanding the recently hypothesised emergence of 'global journalism'), and the embeddedness of dominant media and states in relations of inequality (as the New World Information and Communication Order [NWICO] movement had argued in the 1970s and 1980s) (Hackett 2007).

Unfortunately, it seems that in the Western corporate media, journalists have neither sufficient incentives nor autonomy vis-à-vis their employers to transform the way news is done, without support from powerful external allies. While systematic comparative research is lacking, it seems that PJ is likely to find more fertile ground in societies where the media is perceived to have contributed to socially destructive internal conflict or ethnic tensions, and in news organisations that have a stake in avoiding their audiences' dissolution into opposing camps. Moreover, in 'transition societies' emerging from authoritarian rule, the political roles and professional norms of journalism may be more open to self-reflexive change than they are in Washington, London, or other imperial citadels of the objectivity regime.[5] The uptake of PJ in Indonesia, the Philippines and some sub-Saharan African states offers preliminary support for these hypotheses.

PJ advocates focus on the dominant institutions of public communication, since these are presumably those with the greatest influence on conflict cycles. The current crisis in North American journalism presents opportunities for PJ as there are more footholds in the system for different and experimental forms of journalism. But in light of blockages to PJ in the dominant media, as well as the growing hybridity and complexity of the global media field,[6] it is worth exploring other spaces

5  I am indebted to Jake Lynch for some of these points; interview, University of Sydney, 25 June 2010.

6  Grassroots internet-based outlets are introducing new voices and expanding the definition of journalism, but, at the same time, dominant media corporations

for peacebuilding communication. If indeed PJ is to become 'more than an argument at the outer margins of political debate' (Richard Falk in Lynch 2008, pix), it must become part of a broader project. One approach is to build a new field parallel to currently existing journalism. This field would draw on alternative organisations and networks and would be supported by civil society, relatively autonomous vis-à-vis corporate or state power, and potentially capable of putting into practice the ethos of PJ.

## Alternative media

Compared to PJ, alternative media constitutes a less coherent field or paradigm. Debates in the burgeoning scholarly literature reveal its heterogeneity on core questions. How should the phenomenon be demarcated and labelled? Various adjectives have been deployed: alternative, alterative, radical, autonomous, independent, tactical, citizens', participatory, and community media (Kidd & Rodriguez 2010, p1). Each of these terms, which I use somewhat interchangeably below, has distinct connotations and limitations, reflecting disagreement over other questions, including:

- What are 'the descriptive features to which we give the greatest priority' for categorising media, and for empirical investigation? (Couldry 2010, p25)
- Should such media be defined on the basis of its own characteristics, and, if so, what – its content, or its egalitarian, participatory and/or noncommercial processes of production?
- Or, should it be defined by what it differs from – presumably the 'mainstream', corporate or state media?
- If so, how should such difference be understood – simply as divergence from a dominant model (perhaps meeting needs unmet by it) or as opposition and resistance to it?
- If alternative media is oppositional, what is the object of its

---

are extending their influence transnationally, through a multifaceted and uneven process of globalisation of media markets, firms, formats, governance and (ambiguously) effects (Zhao & Hackett 2005, pp6–8).

contestation – the institutionalised forms and concentrated nature of 'media power' (Couldry 2003), or broader forms of social and political domination?

- If the latter, and if alternative media is contesting political domination, are such political challenges necessarily 'progressive', in the broad sense of seeking a more equitable distribution of social, economic, cultural and political resources? (Hackett & Carroll 2006)

- Or can media of the radical right (for example, racist or religious fundamentalist websites) also be considered alternative? (Couldry 2010, p25; Downing et al. 2001)

No attempt is made here to resolve these questions, beyond noting that repressive and exclusionary alternative media are unlikely to constitute communicative spaces for nonviolent conflict resolution. For analytical purposes, an ideal type of alternative journalism might include these characteristics: participatory models of production; challenges to established media power (including the professionalisation and highly capitalised economy of commercial journalism, and the division between media producers and audiences); more 'bottom-up' ways of scanning and reporting the world, challenging conventional elite-oriented and ideologically conservative news values; and a positive orientation to social change, social movements and/or marginalised communities (Hackett & Zhao 1998, pp206–13; Atton 2009; Atton & Hamilton 2008, p1). In light of this description, one can see that alternative journalism is complementary to PJ in several ways.

First, like PJ, alternative journalism represents dissatisfaction not only with mainstream practices or coverage, but also with the epistemology of news (Atton & Hamilton 2008, p1). By contrast with the objectivity regime, citizens' journalism often valorises indigenous knowledge, personal testimonials and participant accounts over those of professional observers, constructing 'a reality that opposes the conventions and representations of mainstream media' (Atton 2008; Brooten 2008). Both participatory researchers and practitioners of alternative media embrace 'praxis as a method – learning by doing – and as an epistemological point of departure – knowledge starts from the experience (stories) of participants – that encourages critical thinking towards social change' (Riaño-Alcalá 2006, p273, cited in Rodriguez 2010, p137). While alternative journalists are likely to more stridently reject the very possibility or desirability of objectivity, they share with PJ a skepticism towards dominant journalism's claims to have achieved it.

Alternative journalism also shares with PJ a commitment to move beyond the reporting of daily events, to analyse contexts and to critically explore structures of power. Moreover, alternative journalism is opposed to poverty, the political exclusion of the poor, and top-down approaches to development (Bekken 2008; Wilkins 2008; Brooten 2008). It also resists domination along axes of gender, class, and ethnicity, and seeks to reverse the under- and mis-representation of subordinate groups. These commitments align well with PJ's call for the voices of victims and peacemakers to be heard, and for structural and cultural violence to be exposed and analysed.[7]

*The environment for alternative journalism*

What about the institutional framework for the practice of alternative journalism? PJ has relatively well-defined institutional locations – journalism education and established news organisations – albeit to date it generally operates in the margins of these. By contrast, alternative journalism is more variegated, hybrid and complex, spanning the continents and the centuries (see Downing et al. 2001). Moreover, in a

---

7 One example of such alternative journalism is the national magazine *Canadian Dimension*. Its masthead 'For people who want to change the world' is an unabashed rejection of the objectivity regime. By contrast with the corporate press, its decision-making is collective, its financing is readership- rather than advertiser-based, and its editorial content interweaves analysis and reports from a consistently progressive and bottom-up standpoint. Consider coverage of the Toronto G20 summit. While the corporate press focused on a handful of violent protesters and on security costs to taxpayers, *Canadian Dimension* (issue of September/October 2010) highlighted the mass arrests of protesters and human rights violations by Toronto police, explored the political issues the protesters were raising, and critically analysed (from a standpoint sympathetic with their goals) the tactics of various groups associated with the protests.

mediascape which is increasingly globalised, digitalised and networked, and where the producer/user distinction is blurring, it is more difficult to specify the institutional and technological scope of alternative media. Alternative media's contemporary constituencies include 'youths, immigrants, minorities, social movements, and cultural and political outsiders' (Bekken 2008). Its technological and organisational forms include community radio (arguably the most important form globally), internet 'radio', small print publications (like the Samizdat underground papers of the Soviet era), weekly urban newspapers, audiocassettes (during the 1979 Iranian revolution), public access television in the US, documentary and eyewitness video for social movements, political and citizens' journalism websites, blogs by unaffiliated individuals, and the anti-copyright open source movement. This list is illustrative only, and is far from being exhaustive or systematic. Of its various forms, those alternative media that most closely match PJ's ethos are probably those linked to communities seeking to protect themselves from direct violence, or to oppositional social movements seeking the 'four Rs' of democratisation – recognition, representation, rights, and redistribution (Sreberny 2005) – in the face of structural violence.

Under what conditions is alternative journalism likely to flourish? Alternative media faces a paradox: it tends to emerge in periods of upheaval, and in conditions of violence, repression or exclusion, to express needs ignored or actively suppressed by official or commercial media. Political or social repression obviously hinders the production and distribution of alternative media. Yet a supportive political communication regime that lowers the *costs* of mobilisation and enhances alternative media's sustainability (effective guarantees of free speech, recognition and even subsidisation by the state) would also reduce the *incentives* to mobilise. The decline of participatory underground media as post-communist regimes in eastern and central Europe consolidated offers one historical example (Sparks 2005).[8] Quite possibly, the perceived need for PJ arises similarly in situations of

---

8  But for a somewhat contrary view, see Bresnahan (2010), who argues that neoliberal media policies, more than changed political conditions, accounted for the decline of Chile's alternative media after Pinochet's downfall.

crisis, when societies are drifting towards avoidable violent conflict, or struggling to rebuild and engage in processes of reconciliation.

There are, to be sure, tensions between PJ and alternative media. First, PJ calls for responsibility and reform within the field of institutionalised journalism. It accepts the presence and desirability of professionalism, and thus the distinction between journalists and citizens/amateurs, with the former privileged in the construction of public discourse. Accordingly, PJ exhibits more concern with the framing of news *content* (in so far as it feeds into feedback loops and conflict cycles on a broader scale), than with news production *processes* as such, except for the reform of certain practices such as sourcing.

Alternative and citizens' media, by contrast, prioritise participatory processes, and people telling their own stories. Such media are (by definition) seeking to build a parallel and alternative set of practices and organisations that will often be consciously oppositional to dominant media, and competitive for some of the same resources (audiences, credibility, and occasionally revenues). Moreover, citizens' media is inherently more precarious than state-owned or market-oriented media. The seeds of PJ may find fertile soil in some corners of the alternative media field, but, organisationally, they would need frequent replanting. And, while alternative media may have profound long-term significance (Downing et al. 2001), its typically marginal status in the short-term means that it often cannot influence the immediate trajectories of conflict cycles.

Second, some alternative media advocate for one side of a conflict. These media may constitute organs of political contestation, linked to movements that advocate violence or that lack a commitment to universal human rights and/or other-oriented ethics. Within the broad spectrum of ethnic diaspora media, some amplify the most militant or uncompromising views, such as those of the Australian Muslim leader Sheik Hilaly, discussed in Jake Lynch's chapter in this volume. Such media may see themselves as representing particular communities, but the concept of 'community' is politically ambiguous: it can be employed to help construct essentialist and exclusionary identities (Downing et al.

2001, pp39–40). That kind of 'community' media may reject PJ's precept of productive dialogue between the different parties in a conflict.

There are, nevertheless, profound complementarities between PJ and alternative media. Both share a commitment to social justice, and to the critical analysis of social structure beyond the quotidian spectacles of conventional news. PJ's epistemological stance of critical realism, and its call for the exposure and removal of cultural and structural violence, offers two fundamental conceptual links between PJ and many alternative media. Both paradigms reject the epistemology of the regime of objectivity, insisting that journalists acknowledge they are embedded in social processes and communities, and act ethically on that basis. Both seek to challenge elite war propaganda, and to broaden the range of voices accessed to the public arena, especially those of peacebuilders and the victims of violence in conflict situations.[9]

---

9 One overlap between PJ and alternative media is provided by the 18 community radio stations in the Magdalena Medio region of Colombia, home to one of the worst internal armed conflicts in the world. The stations' participants may never have heard of PJ, but they have participated in local peacemaking processes – mediating between armed factions, cultivating nonviolent conflict resolution in a culture where violence is normalised, and buffering civilians from the negative impact of direct violence. They have done so in 'complex, multifaceted, and context-driven' ways (Rodriguez 2010, p143). The stations' mediating role included providing a public forum for discussing, negotiating and finding common ground between communal groups and between bitterly opposed political candidates. Despite her own theoretical preference for the term 'citizens' media, Rodriguez suggests that these community radio stations are 'almost' alternative media, in so far as they opened 'communication spaces in which communities can consider, experiment with, and witness' alternative, nonviolent ways of dealing with conflict, understanding difference, and developing collective imaginaries (2010, p151). The stations' active mediation role, however, distinguishes it from PJ: 'The stations are not sending messages to the community *about* how to solve conflict in nonviolent ways. Instead, the stations themselves are mediating conflicts; their communication competence is not being used to design messages about peaceful co-existence, but instead the stations are constructing peaceful co-existence through communication'. (Rodriguez 2010, p151; emphasis in original)

PJ, then, could profitably seek its expansion in alternative and community media. Sometimes community media can have a direct bearing on conflict resolution, as with the abovementioned Colombian radio stations. In especially repressive regimes like Iran's, citizens' underground media may be virtually the only internal communication option for promoting peace and democracy.

At the same time, given the limitations of alternative media discussed above, and the need to address the commanding heights of public communication in most conflict situations, another paradigm that challenges the concentration of 'objective' symbolic power in the media field should also be considered. By intervening in politics and other adjacent fields to change the environment of journalism and the gravitational pulls to which it is subject, movements for reforming media policy and structure may offer new spaces for public communication favourable to peaceful social relations.

## Media reform and communication rights

Throughout the twentieth century, social movements used communications to mobilise, to gain standing with publics and policymakers, and to pursue political and social change. Implicitly, most movements thereby accepted the media system as an obdurate part of the political environment (Hackett & Carroll 2006). Recent decades have added a new dimension, however. Citizens' movements have emerged in a number of countries, demanding democratic reform of media industries and state communication policies, in order to change the media field itself (see, for example, McChesney 2004; Hackett & Carroll 2006). Social movement organisations and less formal networks operate both locally (e.g. the Media Alliance in San Francisco) and nationally (e.g. the media reform groups Free Press in the US, Campaign for Press and Broadcasting Freedom in the UK, or the citizens' online campaign against restrictive copyright regimes in South Korea [Lee 2009]). In recent years, similar efforts have been directed towards democratising global media governance, such as CRIS – the Campaign for Communication Rights in the Information Society (Ó Siochrú 2005). Such groups are not necessarily directly engaged in producing or advocating new models of journalism. Rather, campaigning around a range of issues – intellectual property and the public sphere, broadcast content and regulation, foreign and concentrated media ownership, competition policy and the internet's accessibility and architecture – they seek to change the structures that currently constrain more diverse and democratic forms of public communication in general.

Thus, the threat against which such movements are mobilising is the democratic deficit of corporate and state media and telecommunications – a deficit often masked by claims of objectivity and responsiveness to consumers. That deficit has multiple dimensions, including the failure to constitute a democratic public sphere in the face of commercial pressures; the centralisation of political and symbolic power; the conversion of economic inequality into unequal media representation and access; the homogenisation of discourse and the displacement of civic engagement by consumerism, masked by the proliferation of channels and technologies; the loss of localism in many commercial media; the corporate enclosure of knowledge through restrictive user-pay and intellectual property regimes; secretive and elitist communications policymaking; and the erosion of privacy and free expression rights in the post-9/11 climate of surveillance and national security (Hackett & Carroll 2006, chapter 1).

Many of these democratic shortcomings are related to the commodification of communication and the global expansion of market relations. Other media deficits derive from state coercion, which, notwithstanding the claims of neoliberal ideologues, is not a phenomenon separate from and opposed to the 'freedom' of market relations. To the contrary: coercive state policies, from intellectual property regimes to growing military and prison expenditures, are integral to maintaining the inequalities generated by a market-oriented, neoliberal order (Hackett & Carroll 2006, p10).

*Is media reform counter-hegemonic?*

Against this democratic deficit of the corporate media and the social order in which they are embedded, what alternative principles do media reformers propose? And do emerging media reform movements challenge existing media and/or the social order? As with peace journalism and alternative media as challenger paradigms, the answer is complex. Normative principles may command widespread support in the abstract, but they are multifaceted and susceptible to different and perhaps contradictory emphases. Media diversity, for instance, could refer to types of programming or ownership, ideological frameworks, competitive markets, language of service provision, or the representation of various social groups in media content and employment. Moreover, the constituencies promoting media democratisation are themselves diverse, ranging from relatively privileged professionals in academic and media institutions, to minorities of colour in the global north, to communities and social movements struggling against authoritarian regimes and/or the impact of neoliberalism in Latin America and elsewhere.

It is not surprising then, that the media reform movement is heterogeneous. At one end of the scale, liberals advocate limited reforms to state policies and legislation, with no necessary linkage to broader transformations beyond improving the operation of liberal democracy. One example is the Free Press group's advocacy of restrictions on media ownership concentration, and for non-discriminatory traffic management policies on the internet – net neutrality. This strand of activism invokes mainstream liberal values – freedom of expression, consumer choice, innovation, journalistic professionalism, media independence from the state, and indeed the protection of news objectivity – but extends them to include struggles against corporate as well as state abuse of power.

At the other, more radical end of the scale, the Media Justice campaign, articulated in particular by American activists of colour, emphasises the struggle against broader forms of domination, and links with social justice movements outside the media field (see Arevalo & Benfield 2009). This tendency has much in common with the alternative media paradigm, rejecting dominant media's claims to a universalising stance of objectivity, and pointing to the imbrication of media power with an unjust social order. If liberal reformers emphasise procedural changes, Media Justice proposes substantive moral reform and the redistribution of resources and values. If free press advocates emphasise freeing individuals from external constraints, Media Justice may seek to forge or reinforce new collective identities, asserting the dignity and equality of subordinated communities (Hackett & Carroll 2006, p81). If liberal reformers begin with 'the set of legal circumstances' that may encourage progressive social outcomes, social justice advocates emphasise 'evident realities and verifiable injustices [–] ... the actual conditions that people live in' (Ó Siochrú 2010, p51).

One approach that in many ways straddles the liberal and media/social justice strands is the international civil society movement for *communication rights*. First articulated within UNESCO in 1969 as the 'right to communicate', it gained traction during the highly polarised NWICO debates of the 1980s, in the context of the East–West Cold War and demands from governments of the Non-Aligned Movement for a more 'balanced flow' of media content and technology between the global north and south (Padovani & Nordenstreng 2005). Hampered by its own contradictory stances (for example, grassroots participatory democracy versus national 'cultural sovereignty' exercised by authoritarian governments) and by the bitter opposition of media corporations and neoliberal governments in the West, NWICO was defeated as an intergovernmental movement in the 1980s. But in today's vastly different geopolitical and technological context, the torch for redressing unjust imbalances in communication structures and policies has been picked up by certain academics, NGOs and civil society advocacy networks (such as CRIS), and redefined as an effort to implement existing internationally recognised communication rights, in the plural.

On the one hand, this nascent movement shares liberalism's commitment (widely accepted in principle if not practice) to human rights. At first sight, a 'human rights' framework for media activism could have quite conservative implications. As a leading theorist and strategist for the CRIS campaign puts it, the current human rights regime 'was carefully circumscribed at the time of its drafting in the mid-twentieth century to exclude' radical changes to fundamental social structures (Ó Siochrú 2010, pp51–52). Allegations of human rights violations – including violations of press freedom – have been selectively and tendentiously used by the US and its allies (the 'international community') to justify military and other interventions against politically hostile states in the global south (Bricmont 2006). One example is the hue and cry against alleged violations of freedom of expression by Venezuela's leftist government of Hugo Chavez, even though most of the private mass media actively oppose the government and 'continue to have an unfettered right to disseminate unsubstantiated rumors ... and completely partisan anti-Chavez propaganda' (Golinger 2008, p120). Quite apart from such propagandistic uses, conventional legal protection of press and speech freedom may sometimes increase communicative inequalities; for instance, it has yielded judicial support for media corporations seeking to prevent public interest regulation of their power (Hackett & Zhao 1998, p80).

In principle, however, the defence of communication rights for all – even the important but relatively narrow principle of free expression and press freedom – can be pushed in progressive directions. First, successful resistance to authoritarian states' repression of free expression would be a radical step on the ground, potentially empowering subordinated groups and contributing to political pluralism. Think of the consequences for Burma, for instance, if opposition groups were allowed to publish and campaign on an equal footing with the military junta.

Moreover, like peace journalism, communication rights pushes conceptually beyond a narrow focus on the 'negative' right of free speech. Even within a legalistic (rather than social justice) framework, the meaningful exercise of free speech entails other 'flanking' rights, such as privacy and the right to one's reputation. Furthermore, the international legal instruments, which inspire the communication rights movement, entail a positive rather than merely negative view of rights. Article 19 of the Universal Declaration of Human Rights (UDHR) acknowledges not only freedom of expression, but also the right 'to seek, receive *and impart* information and ideas through any media', (emphasis added), implying not only *freedom from* state repression, but also *access to* the means of communication. Other provisions in the UDHR also arguably imply a positive conception of rights, such as Article 22 ('economic, social and cultural rights indispensable for ... dignity and the free development of ... personality'), Article 26 ('education ... directed to the full development of the human personality'), and Article 27 ('the right freely to participate in the cultural life of the community'). Hegemonic discourses on communications and cultural policy in the global north typically downplay such participatory dimensions, and also downplay real-world blockages to the effective and equitable use of people's right to free expression. These include the centralisation of means of symbolic production, illiteracy, language barriers, government and corporate secrecy, fear of surveillance, hierarchies of cultural capital (such as the privileging of written documents over oral traditions), and inability to afford schooling (CRIS Campaign 2005, pp19–24).

The communication rights movement highlights such social and economic blockages. It also challenges the epistemological underpinning of the established human rights standards as premised on a model of communication as 'a linear, one-way process' rather than one of 'sharing [and] making common or creating a community' (Hamelink 2003, p155). If democratic communication is a multi-staged cyclical social process of dialogue, 'free speech' addresses only part of that cycle: the ability to seek and receive ideas, to generate ideas and opinions, and to express or speak them. Free speech does not guarantee a right to be heard and understood (or the reciprocal obligation to listen and understand), nor does it address the learning/enhancing/creating and responding/sharing stages of the communication cycle (CRIS Campaign 2005, pp25–26).[10] This analysis extends beyond the legal framework to more broadly address the social, cultural, economic and

---

10 Conversely, some forms of speech (e.g. incitement to hatred or war) may not constitute a process of dialogue aiming towards consensus or mutual understanding, and may therefore not merit legal protection as communication (Dakroury 2009). The appropriate limits to free speech comprise an ongoing challenge within both PJ and communication rights paradigms; arguably, however, it can be addressed by working for dialogic cultural and communication environments in which hate speech can be readily countered, not least by its victims, and in which it is less likely to occur in the first place.

political environment needed to nurture democratic public dialogue – and thus points in the direction of social justice.

## Common ground?

Not all media reform groups adopt the rubric of communication rights, which currently has more resonance in activism oriented towards international than local or national venues. Some potential allies are sceptical for principled reasons; journalists' federations, for instance, worry that it might give governments or interest groups a tool to hamper independent journalism on grounds of accountability and responsibility. Others, including many within CRIS, worry about its strategic limitations: its complexity, the wide range of issues it encompasses, and the lack of intuitively obvious connections between communication deficits and their victims (Ó Siochrú 2010, p54).

Nevertheless, behind the diversity of declarations, frames and campaigns for media reform, it is possible to discern a reasonably coherent paradigm of democratic communication. An analysis of the People's Communication Charter, a landmark document extrapolating from international covenants and circulated by NGOs in the 1990s, suggests that democratic communication includes the following elements: independence from both government and commercial/corporate control; popular access and participation in communication and policymaking; equality, not just of rights, but of access to the means of communication; diversity and pluralism; human community, solidarity, and responsibility; and universal human rights (Hackett & Carroll 2006, chapter 4). A more recent discourse analysis of CRIS and other transnational civil society advocacy groups reveals a similar set of principles: freedom, inclusiveness, diversity, participation and knowledge as a common good (Padovani & Pavan 2009).

The overarching paradigm, arguably, is the institutional organisation of public communication so as to enable all segments of society to actively participate in constructing public cultural truth (White 1995) and to be in a position 'to introduce ideas, symbols, information and elements of culture into social circulation' so as to reach all other segments of society (Jakubowicz 1993, p41). This paradigm entails the intertwined projects of both democratisation *of* media, and the use of media for broader social change – democratisation *through* the media. Clifford Christians (1995) identified an ethics of listening to, and taking into account, the needs of the other, as a nucleus for both democratic communication and social justice. It is encouraging that at the World Summit on the Information Society, the World Social Forum and elsewhere, communication rights activists were able to achieve 'a degree of convergence of agendas and actions' with other civil society organisations working on human rights and social justice (Ó Siochrú 2010, p53).

Peace journalism and media reform/communication rights could similarly envisage strategic alignment and common principles. Strategically, they have common opponents, most notably in war propaganda and the institutions that support it, authoritarian governments that stifle press freedom, the post-9/11 political climate of fear and 'terror war' (Kellner 2003), and (in relatively democratic countries) the regime of objectivity that inhibits journalists from joining coalitions, or departing from established practices – like those of elite sourcing (Hackett & Carroll 2006, pp131–42). Opponents of the 'democratic ideal' in communication also include media conglomerates, and a 'conservative libertarian belief system that is broadcast widely across the globe', one centred on privatisation and the reduction of democratic citizenship to consumer choice within a hierarchical social order (Hamelink 1995, p33). Albeit more ambiguously, these forces are also blockages to PJ, in so far as they institutionally subordinate communication to the imperatives of profit and marketability, and ethically prioritise egotistic expression over the kind of dialogue intrinsic to PJ.

PJ and media reform campaigns may also have common allies. Media reformers have been able, unevenly and not without setbacks, to mobilise constituencies that can be roughly conceptualised as three concentric circles (Hackett & Carroll 2006, pp51–52). The first comprises groups working within and around media industries who may experience or perceive constraints on income, creativity and public information rights generated by state and corporate media – media workers, independent producers, librarians and communications researchers. In Britain, the work of the Campaign for Press and Broadcasting Freedom, and the National Union of Journalists, provides inspiring evidence that, even in a bastion of the objectivity regime, some journalists do actively support the intertwined agendas of democratic media reform, and defence of press freedom vis-à-vis government censorship (as in the Northern Ireland conflict) and state-promoted war propaganda, such as the Blair government's threat exaggeration prior to the 2003 invasion of Iraq (Gopsill & Neale 2007, pp270–74, 316–28).

A second constituency for media democratisation comprises subordinate or marginalised social groups, whose lack of social, cultural or economic capital is paralleled by lack of access or misrepresentation in traditional and networked media, and whose interests sometimes bring them into conflict with the social order – particularly social movements that need access to public communication in order to pursue their political project. The histories of two of the longest-standing media democracy groups in the US – the San Francisco-based Media Alliance, and the national media monitoring group Fairness and Accuracy in Reporting – indicates the potential for activists from other movements to turn 'media rage' into media activism (Hackett & Carroll 2006). Another example is provided in Jake Lynch's chapter in this volume: members of Sydney's Muslim community translated their discontent with their media representation into active participation in a protest coalition demanding that the Australian Broadcasting Corporation provide broader and more balanced coverage of the Middle East. One challenge is to convert particular grievances into support for universalising principles (such as those of PJ).

The outermost circle of potential constituencies for communication rights comprises more diffuse sectors for whom media issues are rarely paramount, but who may occasionally mobilise on the media front in order to promote other material or moral interests – for example, parents concerned with media impact on the young, citizens concerned with the disconnect between democratic and media agendas, or progressive religious or human rights groups advocating ethical conduct and governance. Some of these groups might find their primary interests compatible with the principles of both peace journalism and communication rights – and coalition-building would be aided by articulating the overlap between them. Peace journalism calls on media to heed the voices of victims and peacemakers, to exercise empathy and understanding, to promote agency and creativity in peaceful conflict resolution, and to render the conflict and the interests of all parties to it transparent. These ideas articulate well with the communications rights movement's conception of communication as a multi-staged cycle of society-wide dialogue. PJ's insistence on exposing the everyday, embedded patterns of structural and cultural violence that underlie and fuel physical violence, is a key link with the commitment of media justice activists to broader social transformation.

### A coalition of challenger paradigms?

This chapter has situated peace journalism, along with alternative media and communication rights, as paradigms that challenge aspects of established media structures and practices. I conclude with provisional thoughts on strategic directions for change.

First, we need to recognise, and turn to advantage, the ambivalent relationship of the challenger paradigms to conventional journalism, and to the broader social order of liberal capitalism. I have suggested that in certain respects they are counter-hegemonic, but they also draw upon such dominant ideals as freedom, democracy, diversity and human rights. In societies where such norms are well-established ideologically, if less so in practice, it is both principled and strategic to adopt the Habermasian approach of immanent critique, using the system's own legitimating norms to propose institutional reforms. PJ can legitimately present itself as a more complete and accurate form of journalism than the standardised and stunted practices of 'objectivity'. Movements for media democratisation are pursuing communication rights that are formally recognised in national and international law.

Indeed, from the viewpoint of democratic and antiviolent communication, the objectivity regime has normative dimensions that should be maintained: a commitment to substantive journalism and an ethic of truth-telling on matters of public interest; its capacity to cushion the intrusion of political and commercial interests on news, and its cultivation of ethical, skilled and independent professionalism. These ideals are understandably very attractive to pro-democratic forces in 'transition societies' emerging from authoritarian regimes. In North America, traditional journalism has been 'hollowed out' by the vectors of hyper-commercialism, media mergers, neoliberal deregulation, and corporate disinvestment in journalism, bringing to a new climax the longstanding tension between a free press and profit-oriented media industries (McChesney & Nichols 2010). In seeking to preserve and reinvigorate the best of the objectivity regime in a cluttered but still corporate-dominated new media ecology, new sources of innovation and renewal may be found in all three challenger paradigms.

As for those challenger paradigms themselves, while I have noted tensions between them, there is much common ground upon which to build. They generally share the objectives of expanding the range of media-accessed voices, building an egalitarian public sphere that can raise conflict from the level of violence to that of discussion, promoting the values and practices of sustainable democracy, and offsetting or even counteracting political and economic inequalities found elsewhere (Hackett & Carroll 2006, p88).[11] There are also potential strategic synergies between these paradigms. For instance, alternative media helps to foreground the democratic deficit of corporate media, and has been a key ally in media democratisation campaigns, the success of which in turn creates more space for PJ, given the ideological and economic entrenchment of war journalism within existing media structures. As

---

11  As an example of shared objectives, PJ has a 'democratic prospect' of promoting public deliberation on the question of war. Its critique of conventional war reporting identifies the 'missing pieces required to round out the generic war story that stifles democratic praxis'; when practised, it elevates public discourse to 'a level of complexity and awareness that confounds demonising images' (Ivie 2009, p6). Writing in the wake of the invasion of Iraq, two of the leading exponents of PJ similarly identify its relevance to the liberal-democratic ideal of free expression that can 'animate, and bring about a collision of, alternative views and propositions as to how progress can be made', a role particularly vital when political elites promote policies as drastic as war (Lynch & McGoldrick 2005b, p269).

Tehranian (2002, p80) notes, 'the structure is the message'. Particularly in the still-dominant 'legacy' news media – broadcasting and the press – structure largely governs journalism practices and content. Tehranian identifies the need for more 'structural pluralism in media ownership and control' as a precondition for more democratic checks and balances, and for more content pluralism, including the diversity of voices in conflict situations called for by PJ. Structural reforms applicable to all three challenger paradigms include public and community media that offset the biases of corporate and government media towards commercial and political propaganda; subsidies for media production and access in the global south; genuinely internationalist media; affordable and equitable access to networked digital media; and governance regimes that reinforce popular communication rights.[12] In the final analysis, all three challenger paradigms point beyond the objectivity regime, towards an ethos of dialogue and an epistemology of self-reflexivity, and to fundamental change in media and social structures.

## References

Arevalo, Joanna & Dalida Benfield (2009). You say media, we say justice! The Media Justice Delegation at the World Summit on the Information Society. In Laura Stein, Dorothy Kidd & Clemencia Rodriquez (Eds). *Making our media: global initiatives toward a democratic public sphere. Vol. 2: National and global movements for democratic communication* (pp123–37). Cresskill, NJ: Hampton Press.

Atton, Chris (2009). Alternative and citizen journalism. In Karin Wahl-Jorgensen & Thomas Hanitzsch (Eds). *The handbook of journalism studies* (pp265–78). New York: Routledge.

Atton, Chris (2008). Citizen journalism. In Wolfgang Donsbach (Ed). *The international encyclopedia of communication*. Malden, MA: Blackwell Publishing, Blackwell Reference Online. [Online]

12  Curran (2002, pp239–47) similarly proposes a working model of legal supports and state subsidies for diverse media to serve different democratic purposes – including social market/minority/civic/interest group and (as the central pillar) public service broadcasting sectors.

Available: www.communicationencyclopedia.com/subscriber/
tocnode?id=g9781405131995_chunk_g97814051319958_ss28-1 [Accessed
20 July 2011].

Atton, Chris & James F Hamilton (2008). *Alternative journalism: key texts.*
Los Angeles: Sage Publications.

Bagdikian, Ben H (1997). *The media monopoly.* 5th edn. Boston: Beacon
Press.

Bekken, Jon (2008). Alternative journalism. In Wolfgang Donsbach
(Ed.). *The international encyclopedia of communication.* Malden,
MA: Blackwell Publishing, Blackwell Reference Online. [Online]
Available: www.communicationencyclopedia.com/subscriber/
tocnode?id=g9781405131995_chunk_g97814051319956_ss39-1 [Accessed
20 July 2011].

Bennett, W Lance (2009). *News: the politics of illusion.* 8th edn. New York:
Pearson Longman.

Bresnahan, Rosalind (2010). Reclaiming the public sphere in Chile under
dictatorship and neoliberal democracy. In Laura Stein, Dorothy Kidd &
Clemencia Rodriguez (Eds). *Making our media: global initiatives toward
a democratic public sphere. Vol. 2: National and global movements for
democratic communication* (pp271–92). Cresskill, NJ: Hampton Press.

Bricmont, Jean (2006). *Humanitarian imperialism: using human rights to
sell war.* New York: Monthly Review Press.

Brooten, Lisa (2008). Grassroots media. In Wolfgang Donsbach
(Ed.). *The international encyclopedia of communication.* Malden,
MA: Blackwell Publishing, Blackwell Reference Online. [Online]
Available: www.communicationencyclopedia.com/subscriber/
tocnode?id=g9781405131995_chunk_g978140513199512_ss29-1
[Accessed 20 July 2011].

Christians, Clifford (1995). Communication ethics as the basis of genuine
democracy. In Philip Lee (Ed.). *The democratisation of communication*
(pp75–91). Cardiff: University of Wales Press.

Cottle, Simon (2009). *Global crisis reporting: journalism in the global age,*
Maidenhead, UK: Open University Press.

Couldry, Nick (2010). Introduction to Section I. In Dorothy Kidd, Clemencia Rodriguez & Laura Stein (Eds). *Making our media: global initiatives toward a democratic public sphere. Vol. 1: Creating new communication spaces* (pp39–54). Cresskill, NJ: Hampton Press.

Couldry, Nick (2003). Beyond the hall of mirrors? Some theoretical reflections on the global contestation of media power. In Nick Couldry & James Curran (Eds). *Contesting media power: alternative media in a networked world* (pp39–54). Lanham, MD: Rowman & Littlefield.

CRIS Campaign (2005). *Assessing communication rights: a handbook.* CRIS. [Online] Available: www.centreforcommunicationrights.org/ images/stories/database/tools/cris-manual-en.pdf [Accessed 20 July 2011].

Curran, James (2002). *Media and power.* London and New York: Routledge.

Dakroury, Aliaa (2009). *Communication and human rights.* Dubuque, IA: Kendall Hunt.

DiMaggio, Anthony (2009). *When media goes to war: hegemonic discourse, public opinion, and the limits of dissent.* New York: Monthly Review Press.

Downing, John DH with Tamara Villarreal Ford, Geneve Gil & Laura Stein (2001). *Radical media: rebellious communication and social movements.* Thousand Oaks: Sage.

Fawcett, Liz (2002). Why peace journalism isn't news. *Journalism Studies* 3(2): 213–23.

Galtung, Johan & Mari Holmboe Ruge (1965). The structure of foreign news: the presentation of the Congo, Cuba and Cyprus crises in four Norwegian newspapers. *Journal of International Peace Research,* 1: 64–91.

Golinger, Eva (2008). *Bush vs. Chavez: Washington's war on Venezuela.* New York: Monthly Review Press.

Gopsill, Tim & Greg Neale (2007). *Journalists: 100 years of the NUJ.* London: Profile Books.

Hackett, Robert A (2007). Is peace journalism possible? In Dov Shinar & Wilhelm Kempf (Eds). *Peace journalism: the state of the art* (pp75–94). Berlin: Verlag Irena Regener.

Hackett, Robert A (1991). *News and dissent: the press and the politics of peace in Canada.* Norwood, NJ: Ablex Publishing.

Hackett, Robert A & William K Carroll (2006). *Remaking media: the struggle to democratise public communication.* London: Routledge.

Hackett, Robert A & Birgit Schroeder with NewsWatch Canada (2008). Does anybody practice peace journalism? A cross-national comparison of press coverage of the Afghanistan and Israeli-Hezbollah Wars. *Peace and Policy,* 13: 8–25.

Hackett, Robert A & Yuezhi Zhao (1998). *Sustaining democracy? Journalism and the politics of objectivity.* Toronto: Garamond Press.

Hallin, Daniel C (2000). Commercialism and professionalism in the American news media. In James Curran and Michael Gurevitch (Eds). *Mass media and society,* 3rd edn (pp218–37). London: Arnold.

Hamelink, Cees (2003). Human rights for the information society. In Bruce Girard and Seán Ó Siochrú (Eds). *Communicating in the information society* (pp121–63). Geneva: United Nations Research Institute for Social Development.

Hamelink, Cees (1995). The democratic ideal and its enemies. In Philip Lee (Ed). *The democratisation of communication* (pp15–37). Cardiff: University of Wales Press.

Hanitzsch, Thomas (2004). The peace journalism problem: failure of news people – or failure on analysis? In Thomas Hanitzsch, Martin Loffelholz, Friedrich Ebert Stiftung & Ronny Mustamu (Eds). *Agents of peace: public communication and conflict resolution in an Asian setting* (pp185–209). Jakarta: Friedrich Ebert Stiftung.

Harcup, Tony & Deirdre O'Neill (2001). What is news? Galtung and Ruge revisited. *Journalism Studies* 2(2): 261–80.

Ivie, Robert L (2009). Breaking the spell of war: peace journalism's democratic prospect. *Javnost – The Public* 16(4): 5–22.

Jakubowicz, Karol (1993). Stuck in a groove: why the 1960s approach to communication democratisation will no longer do. In Slavko Splichal &

Janet Wasko (Eds). *Communication and democracy* (pp35–54). Norwood: Ablex Publishing.

Kellner, Douglas (2003). *From 9/11 to terror war: the dangers of the Bush legacy.* Lanham, MD: Rowman & Littlefield.

Kempf, Wilhelm (2007a). Peace journalism: a tightrope walk between advocacy journalism and constructive conflict coverage. *Conflict and Communication Online* 6(2). [Online]. Available: www.cco.regener-online.de/2007_2/pdf/kempf.pdf [Accessed 20 July 2011].

Kempf, Wilhelm (2007b). Two experiments focusing on de-escalation oriented coverage of post-war conflicts. In Dov Shinar & Wilhelm Kempf (Eds). *Peace journalism: the state of the art* (pp136–57). Berlin: Verlag Irena Regener.

Kidd, Dorothy & Clemencia Rodriguez (2010). Volume I, Introduction. In In Clemencia Rodriguez, Dorothy Kidd & Laura Stein (Eds). *Making our media: global initiatives toward a democratic public sphere. Vol. 1: Creating new communication spaces* (pp1–22). Cresskill, NJ: Hampton.

Lee, Kwang-Suk (2009). The electronic fabric of resistance: a constructive network of online users and activists challenging a rigid copyright regime. In Dorothy Kidd, Clemencia Rodriguez & Laura Stein (Eds). *Making our media: global initiatives toward a democratic public sphere. Vol. 2: National and global movements for democratic communication* (pp189–206). Cresskill, NJ: Hampton Press.

Lynch, Jake (2008). *Debates in peace journalism.* Sydney: Sydney University Press.

Lynch, Jake (2002). *Reporting the world.* Taplow Court, UK: Conflict & Peace Forums.

Lynch, Jake & Annabel McGoldrick (2005a). *Peace journalism.* Stroud, UK: Hawthorn.

Lynch, Jake & Annabel McGoldrick (2005b). Peace journalism: a global dialogue for democracy and democratic media. In Robert Hackett and Yuezhi Zhao (Eds). *Democratising global media: one world, many struggles* (pp269–88). Lanham, MD: Rowman and Littlefield.

Mandelzis, Lea (2007). Representations of peace in news discourse: viewpoint and opportunity for peace journalism. In Dov Shinar & Wilhelm Kempf (Eds). *Peace journalism: the state of the art* (pp97–110). Berlin: Verlag Irena Regener.

McChesney, Robert W (2004). *The problem of the media: US communication politics in the twenty-first century.* New York: Monthly Review Press.

McChesney, Robert W & John Nichols (2010). *The death and life of American journalism: the media revolution that will begin the world again.* Philadelphia: Nation Books/Perseus.

McQuail, Denis (1992). *Media performance: mass communication and the public interest.* London, Newbury Park, New Delhi: Sage.

Ó Siochrú, Sen (2010). Implementing communication rights. In Marc Raboy & Jeremy Shtern, with William J McIver. *Media divides: communication rights and the right to communicate in Canada* (pp41–59). Vancouver: UBC Press.

Ó Siochrú, Seán (2005). Finding a frame: towards a transnational advocacy campaign to democratise communication. In Robert Hackett & Yuezhi Zhao (Eds). *Democratising global media: one world, many struggles* (pp223–42). Lanham, MD: Rowman & Littlefield.

Padovani, Claudia & Kaarle Nordenstreng (2005). From NWICO to WSIS: another world information and communication order? Introduction. *Global Media and Communication,* 1: 264. [Online]. Available: http://gmc. sagepub.com/content/1/3/264 [Accessed 27 July 2011].

Padovani, Claudia & Elena Pavan (2009). The emerging global movement on communication rights: a new stakeholder in global communication governance? In Dorothy Kidd, Clemencia Rodriguez & Laura Stein (Eds). *Making our media: global initiatives toward a democratic public sphere. Vol. 2: national and global movements for democratic communication* (pp223–42). Cresskill, NJ: Hampton Press.

Riaño-Alcalá, Pilar (2006). *Dwellers of memory: youth and violence in Medellin, Colombia.* New Brunswick, NJ: Transaction.

Rodriguez, Clemencia (2010). Knowledges in dialogue: a participatory evaluation of citizens' radio stations in Magdalena Medio, Colombia. In Dorothy Kidd, Clemencia Rodriguez & Laura Stein (Eds). *Making our media: global initiatives toward a democratic public sphere. Vol. 1: creating new communication spaces* (pp131-54). Cresskill, NJ: Hampton Press.

Shoemaker, Pamela & Stephen Reese (1996). *Mediating the message: theories of influences on mass media context.* 2nd edn. White Plains, NY: Longman.

Sparks, Colin (2005). Civil society as contested concept: media and political transformation in Eastern and Central Europe. In Robert Hackett & Yuezhi Zhao (Eds). *Democratising global media: one world, many struggles* (pp37-56). Lanham, MD: Rowman & Littlefield.

Sreberny, Annabelle (2005). Globalisation, communication, democratisation: toward gender equality. In Robert Hackett & Yuezhi Zhao (Eds). *Democratising global media: one world, many struggles* (pp256-67). Lanham, MD: Rowman & Littlefield.

Tehranian, Majid (2002). Peace journalism: negotiating global media ethics. *Harvard Journal of Press/Politics,* 7(2): 58-83.

White, Robert (1995). Democratisation of communication as a social movement process. In Philip Lee (Ed). *The democratisation of communication* (pp92-113). Cardiff: University of Wales Press.

Wilkins, Karin Gwinn (2008). Development communication. In Wolfgang Donsbach (Ed). *The international encyclopedia of communication.* Malden, MA: Blackwell. [Online]. Available: www.communicationencyclopedia. com/subscriber/tocnode?id=g9781405131995_chunk_g97814051319959_ ss20-1 [Accessed 25 August 2011].

Zhao, Yuezhi & Robert Hackett (2005). Media globalisation, media democratisation: challenges, issues, and paradoxes. In Robert Hackett & Yuezhi Zhao (Eds). *Democratising global media: one world, many struggles* (pp1-33). Lanham, MD: Rowman & Littlefield.

# Chapter 2

# International security and language: expanding the peace journalism framework

*Birgit Brock-Utne*

In this chapter I first discuss the peace journalism framework, then look at the types of language being used in security discourses, and finally propose ideas for expanding the peace journalism framework in two important ways – in scope, from journalism to school textbooks to computer games; and conceptually, to address gender equality criteria. I point out that war journalism styles of writing about global events not only dominate the news media, but also school textbooks (especially history ones) all over the world. In this sense, those who control the present also control the past. Students from a young age are taught a special version of the past. One-sidedness and violence dominate the entertainment industry too, even as this industry claims to portray the truth (and I demonstrate this here by pointing to an analysis of the '*Black Hawk down* document complex'). I also make a point of the fact that not only are nonviolent solutions to conflict generally under-reported but so too are the peace actions and writings of women. Writing from a peace journalism perspective means giving a voice to the voiceless. Women, however, are often made invisible not only as victims but also as peace activists.

## Peace journalism

Peace journalism derives from insights first introduced in 1965 by peace researchers Johan Galtung and Mari Holmboe Ruge in an article featured in one of the first issues of *The Journal of Peace Research*. The article, 'Structure of foreign news', examined the presentation of the Congo, Cuba and Cyprus crises in four Norwegian newspapers (Galtung & Ruge 1965). In this article, the authors showed how dominant conflict reporting patterns emphasise official sources over 'people sources', events over process and violence over peace. In further writings on peace journalism, Johan Galtung (2002, 2006) makes a distinction between 'war journalism' and 'peace journalism' and proposes four main points of contrast between the two approaches:

| War journalism | Peace journalism |
| --- | --- |
| War/violence-oriented | Peace/nonviolence-oriented |
| Propaganda-oriented | Truth-oriented |
| Elite-oriented | People-oriented |
| Victory-oriented | Solution-oriented |

Adapted from: Galtung 2006, p1.

Rune Ottosen (2010, p259) notes that peace journalism is people-oriented in the sense that it focuses on the victims (often civilian casualties) and thus gives a voice to the voiceless. In their book on peace journalism, Jake Lynch and Annabel McGoldrick emphasise that journalists have a set of 'choices of what stories to report, and how to report them – that create opportunities for society at large to consider and to value nonviolent responses to conflict' (Lynch & McGoldrick 2005, p6).

*The language used in security discourse*

Language can be used both to generate and conceal meanings and to distort extra-linguistic realities. The same phenomenon can be given different names depending upon who does the naming. The same person may be called a freedom fighter by some and a terrorist by others for committing exactly the same acts. Carol Cohn (2009) notes that the way 'security' is employed by both academics and policy elites, in what is commonly referred to as 'security discourse' (for example, 'international security' or 'national security' discourse), has nothing to do with the everyday meaning of this word – that is, 'freedom from danger and fear'. It has implicit in it extraordinarily narrow assumptions about the nature of security. During the Cold War, the Norwegian Parliament changed the name of its 'Military committee' to 'Defence committee', which seemed to sound more reassuring (Brock-Utne & Garbo 2009). But the term 'defence' is also dubious, not least in a world where nuclear powers like the United States (US) and other North Atlantic Treaty Organization (NATO) member states insist on their right to use thermonuclear bombs, while seeking to prevent 'rogue states' from imitating them. Can anything be 'defended' through the use of atomic weapons?

In the dominating security discourse, this question is neglected through euphemistic language that defence intellectuals have developed for military hardware and its impact on human life. In 'rational' expert speak – the war journalism framework – human beings, human deaths and suffering, as well as dying humans, are made invisible. When the term *security* is used in what among defence intellectuals is called 'security discourse', it means something totally different from daily concerns. It also means something different from the way peace researchers talk about security. It does not refer to the social and economic conditions and relations within which people live. Among peace researchers this security discourse is often discussed in the context of Galtung's negative and positive peace concepts. While negative peace can be seen in terms of security from physical and direct violence, positive peace is seen also as security from structural and cultural violence (Brock-Utne 1989, 2008, 2009; Galtung & Vincent 1992; Ife 2007).

Abstract terms, which stand in for real weapons, conceal the reality of these weapons and how they would function under real-world conditions. This professional terminology serves to make questions from concerned citizens seem uninformed and naïve. Through her own work with defence intellectuals, Carol Cohn (1987a) has come to understand that 'security discourse' is not a discourse about the multiple dimensions and determinants of 'security' broadly writ; but rather, it is a discourse which has as its principal referents 'weapons' and 'war'. Cohn (2009) discusses what she describes as the American civilian nuclear defence intellectuals. These intellectuals are mostly men, who, from the time of the first nuclear bomb, have formulated the paradigms most commonly used to think about the use of nuclear weapons, strategies for 'nuclear war fighting', deterrence, and nuclear arms control, all within a war journalism framework. Elsewhere Cohn has argued that both the specific language that they use and the professional discourse within which it is embedded serve to radically disconnect defence intellectuals from the very realities they purport to be addressing (Cohn 1987a, 1987b).

Cohn's exploration of the language of security started in the mid-1980s (Cohn 1987a, 1987b). The community of nuclear defence intellectuals she studied was located at a prominent, elite university in the north-eastern US. She explains that the highly specialised professional language these men used was so riddled with acronyms and abstractions that it was practically opaque to her. She explains that when she began to be able to decode the language, she realised that the acronyms and abstractions often functioned as a kind of euphemism. She adds:

> One particularly stunning example is the term 'collateral damage' (which at the time only appeared in nuclear weapons discourse, although it has since become common in the discourse of 'conventional' wars, such as the current war in Iraq). The term 'collateral damage' sounds like it refers to something minor, something peripheral to the main event, a reference to some kind of objects that get in the way. So I was stunned when I first learned that 'collateral damage' is the phrase the defence intellectuals were using to refer to human beings, human deaths. Suffering, dying human beings are made invisible in the strategists' focus on destroying the other side's weapons, their 'targets'. As one defence intellectual commented ironically, 'The Air Force doesn't target *people*, it targets shoe factories'. The people killed are no more than 'collateral damage'. (Cohn 2009, p35)

The 'technostrategic discourse' that Cohn learned to understand did not only consist of acronyms, abstraction and euphemisms. It also consisted of sexual and domestic metaphors. Sexual metaphors were liberally sprinkled throughout the discussions the defence intellectuals carried out. Cohn tells how she listened to very serious men in suits and ties sitting around conference tables, talking about 'thrust to weight ratios', 'soft lay-downs', 'deep penetration', 'the comparative advantage of protracted versus spasm attacks', or what one military adviser to the US National Security Council called 'releasing seventy to eighty percent of our mega-tonnage in one, orgasmic, whump'.

> Additionally, there was an anxious preoccupation with 'hardening our missiles' and worry that the Russians were 'harder than we are'. Of course, what we needed, it was said, was better 'penetration aids'. As these conversations wore on, I would glance around and wonder if at some point someone would realise what it sounded like, and perhaps give me a glance that was a bit embarrassed or sheepish – but it never happened. (Cohn 2009, p36)

Cohn has also examined the language used by security experts and politicians to warn against 'nuclear proliferation'. This term does *not* mean a multiplication of nuclear weapons or 'new generations' of weapons in the nuclear arsenals of the US. It means nuclear weapons in *other people's* hands, people described as primitive, rogue and unpredictable. This racialised imagery serves to legitimise the responsible Self's access to weapons which should be denied to primitive Others. This kind of rhetoric is likely to make the possession of nuclear weapons even more attractive to the have-nots. It is a rhetoric that fits perfectly into the elite-oriented war journalism framework which makes human suffering invisible.

### Who controls the present controls the past

In his book *Nineteen eighty-four*, George Orwell (1949) described a superstate called Oceania. The language of war in this state was a language full of invented lies that passed into history and became truth. 'Who controls the past', ran the Party slogan, 'controls the future and who controls the present controls the past'. What appears in the news media today will be recorded in the civics and history books of tomorrow. It has taken me many years to realise that the history we study in school is a highly political subject. Some facts are deemed important enough for us to study, others are left out of the history books because they are disturbing and may give a negative picture of the 'mother' land. Some facts are distorted. Howard Zinn and Anthony Arnove's 2004 book, *Voices of a people's history of the United States*, and Howard Zinn's 2007 book, *A young people's history of the United States*, both give another version of US history than the one normally found in history books in the US. In the book *Lies my teacher told me: everything your American history textbook got wrong*, James W Loewen (2007) analysed 18 leading history textbooks in common use in high schools all over the US. He shows the embarrassing combination of blind patriotism, mindless optimism, sheer misinformation and outright lies found in these books. They omit the ambiguity, passion, conflict and drama of the past and make history a dull and uninteresting subject. Zinn and Arnove (2004) and Zinn and Stefoff (2007) deal with the truth about Columbus' historic voyages. They tell about the injustices done to 'Indians'.[1] These authors use a peace journalism framework looking at events from the perspective of the victims. Loewen does the same, but he also tells how these voyages and the resistance by the Indians have been portrayed in school history textbooks. Loewen deals with the immediate past as well as the more distant one and has an eye-opening chapter on the lies surrounding 9/11 and the Iraq War.

Textbooks play a dominant role in schools and ought to be of great interest as research topics for subject specialists. Yet normally they are not. One Norwegian political scientist claims that there exists within Norwegian cultural and political debate no other examples of literature published in such quantity, being read by so many unsettled minds and with such controversial content that is 'left in peace' or as unscrutinised as textbooks within social science (Koritzinsky 1972). Analysis of school textbooks for elementary and secondary schools does not carry high prestige among researchers. This is a pity, since in most countries textbooks largely determine the mode and scope of teaching and studying. Several studies show that teachers regard textbooks as national curricula in hard copy, dominating the work in the classroom with the same legitimacy (Kilborn 1982; Gustafson

---

1 The original inhabitants of the US were called Indians by Columbus and his sailors because Columbus thought he had come to India.

1982; Svingby 1986). There is a need for international and comparative textbook research, as there are many unanswered questions begging for answers. For example, are textbooks mirrors of a war journalism framework? How is peace defined in various textbooks around the world? How are human rights defined? What parts of the whole human rights construct are emphasised? How is development defined? How are the causes of underdevelopment explained? How are conflicts that have been resolved nonviolently treated? How are women's human rights addressed? (Brock-Utne 2007, 2010a). How are the accomplishments of women treated? Are they treated at all?

Ladislav Bognar (1996) has analysed books used in Croatian primary schools both before and after the Croatian war of independence. He found that, before the war, equal numbers of texts existed that spoke positively and negatively about other nations. There were three times more texts that spoke in favour of war and violence as a way of national conflict resolution than in favour of peace. After the war there were more texts that spoke negatively about other nations, especially about Croatia's neighbours, but fewer texts that spoke out in favour of war (however, these still numbered twice those that actively spoke *against* warfare). His analysis of primary school books before the war showed that 17 percent of the texts dealt with war. Of these texts, 73 percent spoke positively about war, 25 percent of the texts advocated peace, and two percent were neutral in that regard. An example of a poem from one book from the fourth grade of primary school follows:

> The war is, my brothers, the war for heroes.
> Take the gun, point the sabre.
>   Saddle the horse, let go the infantry.
> Let that be where our fame is!
>   The greatest happiness is to be killed in war:
>   Be happy, sad mother.
> Your worthy sons have fallen
>   Like heroes, like Croats.
> They have shed blood for their homeland.
> (cited in Bognar 1996)

Bognar concludes, through his analysis of Croatian primary school texts from before the war, that these texts provided children with a positive image of the war. What changed after the war? According to Bognar's analysis, there are now fewer texts on the theme of peace and war. They have been reduced from 17 percent to eight percent, but most of them still speak in favour of war. In the second grade, children are already learning that a homeland is something they have to defend at all times and in different ways, but, primarily, with a gun. In the third grade, children are asked to give their lives for Croatia.

Texts concerned with Croatia increased from six percent before the war to 19 percent after the war. Most of these texts focus on the Croatian language and on negative relations with other countries. The following nationalities are portrayed in a negative light: Turks, Hungarians, Venetians, Bulgarians, Austrians, Serbs and Montenegrins. The poem 'The pit' figures in a reading book for the seventh grade. Here the crimes of Croat fascists in the Second World War are described. Below the poem appears the question: 'Are you reminded of the present crimes against Croatians in this poem?' (cited in Bognar 1996)

In the new books there are valuable texts against war and for peace. In one text, the possibility of nonviolent conflict resolution is described. This is a text about the Croat King Kresimir, who tried in a peaceful way to resolve problems between Croats and Venetians. In a paper presented in Norway, Ladislav Bognar (1996, p7) noted: 'In our history the Republic of Dubrovnik maintained freedom for many centuries in a nonviolent way, but we have no texts about this in our reading books'.

Bognar (1996) sees the non-existence of a paradigm of nonviolent conflict resolution in Croatian education as a big problem. He quotes Marko Hren from Slovenia who thinks that a main reason for the war in the former Yugoslavia is that in the period after the Second World War there was a dearth of education and promotion of nonviolent change methods. He proposes that the best way to build peace would be for Croatians to gradually affirm nonviolent communication on a micro-social level – within families, peer-groups, schools and in everyday life.

Borgnar contends that a number of good people from many countries have been of assistance to Croatians in developing resources on nonviolent change, and there are now books about nonviolent communication, conflict resolution, cooperative games and human rights in Croatia. He argues that the next step must now be taken to develop nonviolent conflict resolution in the other states of the former Yugoslavia, especially in Bosnia and Hercegovina, and Serbia. It is important, he maintains, that Croatians connect with people in other parts of the former Yugoslavia who are ready to do the important work of peacebuilding. The project 'Peace Bridge', based in Mohács, Hungary, has done a great deal of this work in Serbia. So too has the Peace Centre based in Osijek, Croatia. Some peacebuilding activities have also started up in Bosnia and Hercegovina where a group of peace activists connected to the Bahai faith have been running a peace education program, supported economically first by Luxembourg and then by Switzerland.

### The invisibility of nonviolence in textbooks

The phenomenon examined by Bognar – the lack of a paradigm for nonviolent conflict resolution in textbooks – is not limited to Croatia. In fact it is a problem faced by peace educators all over the world: peace journalism approaches have not yet influenced textbooks. War and violence have much higher visibility both in the media and in history books than do accounts of conflicts that have been solved nonviolently. For instance, in 1905, Norway and Sweden were on the verge of war over the dissolution of their erstwhile union. There were armies lined up on both sides of the frontier. The war was avoided through diplomacy, yet this accomplishment is hardly mentioned in the history textbooks. If there had been a war, however, it would probably have filled several pages.

Christopher Krügler and Patricia Parkman (1985), from Harvard University's Program on Nonviolent Sanctions in Conflict and Defense, found in their research that history books give more attention to violent struggles that fail to achieve their objectives than to nonviolent struggles that succeed. There is a vast history of nonviolent sanctions but these do not reach the history books. Gene Sharp defines nonviolent sanctions as pressures that do not kill or threaten physical harm but which, nonetheless, thwart opponents' objectives and cause them to alter their behaviour (Sharp 1980, p289). Forty years ago, he described 85 major cases where nonviolent sanctions have been used (Sharp 1970). Yet conflicts that have been resolved through nonviolent means are both under-researched and are made invisible in history's record. Krügler and Parkman (1985) show through their analysis that when both violent and nonviolent actions have been used in a conflict, it is the violent ones that are described in history and that are celebrated, and they describe the case of the uprising against the dictatorship of Martinez in El Salvador in 1944. The violent actions of 2 April did not succeed in getting the dictator to resign. The nonviolent actions of 9 May *did* succeed. Yet 2 April is the date celebrated, not 9 May!

When violent sanctions fall short of achieving their objectives, the conclusion is rarely drawn that violence has been tried and found wanting. Instead, military analysts ask what conditions favoured the winner, and where did the loser go wrong? The assumption is not made that there is something wrong with the whole idea of using violence to solve a conflict. When nonviolent struggles are not successful, however, it is frequently concluded that nonviolent methods are not useful. Questions should be asked about ways of improving nonviolent means of conflict resolution. In most cases where nonviolent sanctions have been used, they have been improvised under harsh conditions, with little or no advance preparation on the part of those using them.

In an article in the *Bulletin of the Atomic Scientists*, peace researcher Elise Boulding (1982) holds that our whole educational system should be geared toward creating more confidence and competence in conflict resolutions by means other than violence. When the capabilities for nonviolent problem-solving are not developed at lower levels in the education system, it becomes more difficult to develop them later on. Formal education, it seems, does little to teach young people nonviolent conflict solutions or to train their capacity for visionary thinking. History books concentrate on violent solutions to conflicts between states such as wars, ignoring the fact that, statistically, the normal relationship between states is one of non-war, or peace, and that most conflicts in the world, both between people on the micro-level and between states, are solved through nonviolent means. School children could benefit from learning more about nonviolent solutions to conflicts, and less about violent ones. This would necessitate more research on nonviolent conflict resolution, and a rewriting of history.

It is extremely important that such a review be done in a scientific manner, whereby the nonviolent actions started and led by women are not to be left in the hidden history. Any such omissions would make this rewriting of history incomplete. It should be remembered that Mahatma Gandhi stressed time and again that he had learned most of his nonviolent tactics from the British suffragettes (Gandhi 1939; Gandhi in Hunt 1981). Indeed, insofar as Gandhian thought, comprising the principles of *swaraj* (self-rule), *ahimsa* (non-violence), *swadeshi* (use of local goods and products) and *sarvodaya* (universal welfare), is a critique of the masculine ideology of colonialism, it is defined as feminist (Poonacha 2008, p52).

There is also a whole African history of nonviolent conflict resolution and indigenous approaches to building peace which is under-researched and has frequently been overlooked by Western researchers. In a couple of interesting articles, the African peace researcher Tim Murithi (2006, 2009) shows how indigenous traditions with regard to governing and resolving disputes in African societies were corrupted by the centralising power of colonialism. He notes, however, that the Truth and Reconciliation Committee in South Africa is rooted in an African worldview, the worldview of *ubuntu* or social solidarity. A person who possesses *ubuntu* is a person who is considered to be generous, hospitable, friendly, caring and compassionate. The idea behind *ubuntu* is that a person is a person through other people. We are human because we live through others – we belong, we participate and we share (Murithi 2006, p17). According to Desmond Tutu (1999), a person with *ubuntu* is open and available to others and does not feel threatened when others achieve, because he or she recognises that they belong to a greater whole. The principles of forgiveness and reconciliation, which this tradition advocates, provide us with strategies for peacebuilding.

*The 'unknown knowns' – the role of the entertainment industry*

Young students not only learn of the one-sided glorification of violence in school textbooks, but also from the entertainment industry. Most young people, especially in the industrialised West, spend more time watching television or playing computer games than reading history textbooks. The German peace researcher Holger Pötzsch (2009) has analysed the 'Black Hawk down document complex' – a succession of Western mass-media representations dealing with the US intervention in Somalia in 1992–93.

In the middle of the 1990s, journalist and author Mark Bowden started to conduct research regarding the failed US intervention in Somalia. He succeeded in making contact with US soldiers involved in what had happened and began collecting their stories. The results of his work were published in the *Philadelphia Inquirer* between November and December 1997.[2] He later reworked and published them in the historical novel *Black Hawk down* (1999). Bowden's novel served as the factual basis for Ridley Scott's (2001) tremendously successful screen adaptation of the same title. The movie was followed by *The true story of Black Hawk down,* a documentary produced for the History Channel – and the release of the video game *Delta Force Black Hawk down* in 2002. In 2004, some of the involved soldiers' tales were published in a separate volume (Eversmann & Schilling 2004).

Taken together, these representations form what Pötzsch terms the 'Black Hawk down document complex', a clearly biased account where the American soldiers are depicted as humane helpers, while the Somalis are dehumanised and depicted as an invisible threat. The soldiers' tales, collected and reproduced by Bowden, are the source of the ideological and perspectival bias found in the narrative. The fact that interviews were largely carried out within military facilities and that interviewees had to obtain official permission from their superiors is not made apparent to audiences.[3] Bowden relied almost without exception upon material presented to him by military sources. These factors throw significant doubt over the neutrality of the dataset on which his account is based.

---

2  The newspaper series can be accessed on: inquirer.philly.com/packages/somalia/sitemap.asp [Accessed 28 October 2007].

3  On Bowden's methodology and sources, see Bowden 1999, p481.

Pötzsch argues that the documents forming the complex reproduce a biased narrative that implicitly privileges military approaches to the resolution of conflicts. He draws attention to a US Department of Defense press briefing from 2002[4] regarding developments of the war in Afghanistan and the ongoing debate at that time about alleged Iraqi weapons of mass destruction. In connection with this press release, the then Secretary of Defense Donald Rumsfeld made his notorious remarks regarding different categories of knowledge: the known-knowns (the facts we know that we know), the known-unknowns (the facts we know that we do not know), and the unknown-unknowns (the facts we do not know that we do not know). The latter category is the one claimed by Rumsfeld to be of most importance for war planners. Pötzsch points out that there is a fourth category that was evaded by Rumsfeld and that proves even more crucial for war preparation – the unknown-knowns, the knowledges we do not know we have, the attitudes and conceptualisations which subconsciously guide and influence individual and collective behaviours.

Today, the mass media play a major role in the formation of such unknown-knowns. Through the application of a particular set of cinematic techniques, representations reproduce unknown-knowns – myths concerning the Self, the Other, and the nature of conflict between the two. Pötzsch shows that, in spite of its explicit claim to realism, *Black Hawk down* employs the same representational strategies as do fully fledged, fictitious action and horror movies when representing the Self and the Other. He demonstrates that in order for the audience to distinguish between dichotomies such as self/other, good/evil, and order/chaos, the film places the US soldiers and their enemies in very specific surroundings. The enemy stronghold is characterised by filth and decay where chaos, danger and deadly threats lurk behind every corner. The American soldiers, however, are located in surroundings where order, sanity, technological confidence and control are paramount. The type of analysis that Pötzsch adopts in his article is one in which our teachers should be trained. Although we cannot prevent young people from

---

4  February 12, 2002. [Online]. Available: www.globalsecurity.org/military/library/news/2002/02/mil-020212-usia01.htm [Accessed: 7 March 2008].

watching films and playing games that focus on violence, we could nonetheless make what Kellner (1995) refers to as critical media literacy part of the school curriculum.

### The invisibility of peace actions and writings by women

As history is presently taught, important phenomena like the effective use of nonviolence and the important role of women are made invisible, hidden, or forgotten. For example, the achievements of Austrian heroine Bertha von Suttner (1843–1914) who devoted her life to nonviolent conflict solutions and to disarmament have been made virtually invisible, if not to her own generation, then to those that have followed. She was the founder of the International Peace Bureau and, without her, there would have been no Nobel Peace Prize. Yet Nobel, who took the money for the prize from his profits on weapons and dynamite, is the one who is remembered (Brock-Utne 1985, pp37–45; Heffermehl 2010). She is hardly mentioned in any history books, and there is no statue of her in the Nobel Institute in Oslo.

Some years ago I was asked by a Swedish research unit working on peace education to evaluate a set of eight publications in peace education which were in use in Swedish schools (Brock-Utne 1992, 2010b). The publications had been launched under the name *Fred, frihet, rättvisa* (*Peace, freedom, justice*) and sponsored by the Myrdal Foundation, the UN Association of Sweden, and the Red Cross. My main criticism of the teaching material had to do with the invisibility of women in the textbook and accompanying teacher guide meant for secondary education. The teaching guide gives advice to teachers to see to it that certain books are in the school library. Under the heading: 'Some classical books which ought to be found in the school library', they name ten books. All of the books were written by men! They also encourage students to search for books in the library under the heading; 'Books you can ask for in the school library'. Here they supply a short list of four books, none of them written by a woman!

They do not mention, for example, the beautiful novel *Die Waffen nieder* (*Lay down your arms*) by Bertha von Suttner (1889). Leo Tolstoy wrote to her that he thought her impressive novel would make an end to all war in the same way that Harriet Beecher Stowe's book *Uncle Tom's cabin* had contributed to the end of slavery (Brock-Utne 1985). Neither do the authors behind the guide for Swedish teachers in secondary schools mention many other topical books by women, including *Väckerklocka (Alarm clock)* by the Swedish author Elin Wägner (1941), one of the earliest books written on the human destruction of our environment; *Silent spring* written in 1962 by Rachel Carson on the same theme; Rosalie Bertell's (1985) tome on the destruction of the environment by nuclear testing, that combines data from stillbirths and births of deformed babies with data from nuclear fallout; and Susan George's writings (1989, 1994) on the debt crisis. In my analysis of the Swedish teaching material, I provide a list of more than ten wellknown works, from the many available, on peace issues written by women (Brock-Utne 1992). The experiences of women, especially when it comes to war and peace, have been silenced all over the world, in industrialised as well as in developing countries.

Turshen and Twagiramariya (1998) are aware of the fact that mainstream studies of wars in Africa generally suppress women's voices in recounting and interpreting their own experiences of wars or violent conflicts. That is why they edited the book *What women do in wartime: gender and conflict in Africa*, which gives voice to the silent victims of war in Africa (Turshen & Twagiramariya 1998). In this sense, the book is written from a peace journalism perspective. The concept of the 'unknown-knowns' employed by Pötzsch, in other words, the knowledge people do not know they have, can be put to use when analysing why men, even within peace studies, render invisible the contributions of women. I do not believe in any conspiracy theories among men aiming at the suppression of women, but, rather, in subconscious attitudes that achieve the same results.

Almost 40 years ago, I sat on the board of the Norwegian film making company, Norsk Film. It was once suggested that we have a day's workshop discussing ideas for new films. Each board member listed ten creative people in Norway whom they would like to invite for that day. The people did not have to be filmmakers, but people with creative ideas. Of the nine board members, I was the only woman. I had written down a list at home with ten names. Being gender conscious, my list consisted of five women and five men. Three men read out their lists before it was my turn. Each list featured ten men. Without frowning or saying a word, I silently changed my list and read out the names of ten women. And *then* they all reacted: 'You've just concentrated on women'. I answered: 'And what have you done?' The point of the story is that these men had not noticed their bias before they heard my list. When they were asked to think of creative people, their thoughts did not extend to women! Even though they seemed like nice men, they still held sexist attitudes and that subconsciously influenced their behaviour.

It is sad to see that even an edited volume created to celebrate peace on the occasion of Johan Galtung's 80th birthday features 30 male and only six female authors (Johansen & Jones 2010), none of which focuses on peace actions started and/or led by women. And this in a country where women like Ingrid Eide and Mari Holmboe Ruge, the co-founders, alongside Johan Galtung, of the Peace Research Institute of Oslo (PRIO), have been peace activists all their lives and active in the Norwegian chapter of the Women's International League of Peace and Freedom. The book *Bestemødrene på Stortings plass* (*Grandmothers in front of Parliament*) tells about an organisation of older women who, from 1983 to 2003, gathered in front of the Norwegian parliament once a week and distributed leaflets to make people aware of current conflicts and the importance of protest and action (Aas 2006). A new organisation, 'Bestemødre for Fred' (Grandmothers for Peace), has taken up the same work. Yet these women are not heard from in the abovementioned book celebrating peace research. In my book *Educating for peace: a feminist perspective* (Brock-Utne 1985, pp33–69), I write about peace activities started and led by women. I note the following three characteristics among the women:

They are concerned about human life, especially that of children.

They make use of a varied set of nonviolent techniques, actions and strategies.

They work trans-politically and often trans-nationally, aiming to reach people, especially other women, in the opposite camp.

I conclude in my book (Brock-Utne 1985, p63) that women's struggles for peace and human rights have for the most part been made invisible, and have sometimes been met with opposition. I mention, for example, the 1982 peace march by Nordic Women for Peace to the Soviet Union. The male-dominated peace organisation 'No to Nuclear Arms' did not want to have anything to do with this peace march as the women were visiting 'the enemy', and it actively discouraged its members from participating or giving money to the march (Brock-Utne 1985, p69).

## The role of the mass media

British academics David Edwards and David Cromwell have published *Media Lens*, a publication that since 2001 has observed the treatment of international affairs by mass media in Britain and also, to a degree, in the US.[5] When Edwards and Cromwell detect biased reporting, direct lies, or the neglect of relevant news, which they do continually, they try to engage the responsible journalists or editors in an exchange of views on the reports. Their book *Newspeak in the 21st century* contains a gold-mine of knowledge about the ways in which mainstream descriptions of world events are being produced (Edwards & Cromwell 2009).

One of the most striking examples presented in *Media Lens* was the political treatment of data presented in several articles in the *Lancet* medical journal (2004 and 2006) concerning the issue of mortality after the 2003 invasion of Iraq. There is no easy way of finding out the precise number of Iraqi fatalities, but a group of trained experts had carried out a cross-sectional cluster sample survey of the same kind that is used in opinion polls. Doctors collected data from 1849 households in 47 population clusters across Iraq. They estimated that after the invasion, 655,000 more Iraqis had died than would have been expected in a non-conflict situation. However, the British government refused to accept the results, claiming that the findings were based on too thin a sample. US President Bush asserted that the methodology

---

5 I must thank the author and journalist Gunnar Garbo for opening my eyes to this very valuable source in a lecture to my peace studies class at Wartburg College on 1 April 2010.

had been discredited, even though the survey used methods that were recognised by statisticians all over the world. All mainstream media then backed the position of the two governments. The same group of expert researchers also carried out a study to estimate mortality in the Democratic Republic of the Congo, using precisely the same methods. These findings received widespread media attention and were accepted without reservation by the US and British governments. Unlike Iraqis, the Congolese were not killed by Western powers.

Mass media sometimes refer to a decline in war deaths due to 'smart' bombs and different strategic priorities. This is not a reflection of reality, as is made obvious by news reports from Afghanistan. In a US opinion poll where people were asked to estimate the number of deaths during the Vietnam War, the average estimate was 100,000. According to a similar opinion poll in Vietnam, however, the war resulted in three million deaths, 300,000 missing persons, nearly four and a half million wounded persons, and two million people harmed by toxic chemicals. In 2008, the *British Medical Journal* published a study estimating that 3.8 million Vietnamese were killed during the war; close to the country's citizens' own calculation. The editors of *Media Lens* add that to turn a blind eye to our own crimes, while focusing on the crimes of others, is to guarantee more of both. Unfortunately, this is what mass media tend to do through their use of war journalism.

## A visit to the peace researchers

While Carol Cohn, whose work I mentioned in the beginning of this chapter, made a study of the defence intellectuals working in institutes for strategic studies, Lothar Brock (2009) is more concerned about discussions taking place among peace researchers. To what extent do peace researchers play on the same field as strategic analysts, using their vocabulary and their concepts? Are peace researchers afraid of being branded as näive if they use the concept of 'peace', or if they study peaceful and nonviolent solutions to conflicts? It could be argued that the name change of the *Bulletin of Peace Proposals*, edited by the Peace Research Institute of Oslo, to *Security Dialogue*, is more than just a name change.

There is no doubt that armament complexes use dangers previously met by civilian bodies as justification for increasing their own budgets. NATO refers to perceived threats such as climate change, globalisation, computer attacks, migration, or breaks in the flow of resources as reasons for strengthening its military forces. Challenges of this kind are best managed through the use of peaceful means and international cooperation. To what extent the *securitisation* discourse within peace circles has contributed to the opposite tendency is a question worthy of further investigation.

With reference to the first Gulf War, President Bush (Sr) proclaimed: 'What *we* say goes'. His son's administration followed in his footsteps. Gunnar Garbo (2009, pp58–59) describes an incident in which Ron Suskind, a veteran Washington columnist, happened to mention the intellectual principles of empiricism and the Enlightenment in a conversation with a presidential adviser, one year after 9/11. 'That's not the way in which the world really works anymore', was the response he received.

> We are an empire now, and when we act, we create our own reality. And while you are studying that reality, we'll act again creating other new realities, which you can study too. We are history's actors, and all of you will be left to just study what we do.

If we undertake to study the issues that the presidential adviser recommends, we discover how much the military powers lie about security matters. Former president Bush Jnr and UK prime minister Blair started their war against Iraq allegedly to liquidate the country's (non-existent) weapons of mass destruction, and to cut off Saddam Hussein's support to al-Qaeda, which had never existed either. When foes become friends or vice versa, terminology also changes. US representatives had once labelled the Kosovo-Albanian UCK (Kosovo Liberation Army) a terrorist organisation. When Washington saw fit to support these 'terrorists' in order to punish Milosevic and to remove Kosovo from the Federal Republic of Yugoslavia, the UCK suddenly became fighters for a just cause. Dominant media in the West readily adopt this sort of rhetoric, as exemplified when then US President Bush Jnr started his 'war on terror'.

The UN General Assembly has defined terrorism as the use of violence against a population in order to pressure its leaders to change policy. Hitler did that by bombing London and carrying out mass murders of Poles and Russians. The allied powers also consciously used state terrorism towards the end of the Second World War, killing several million civilians by firebombing German cities and dropping atomic bombs over Hiroshima and Nagasaki. The allied powers have never asked to be forgiven for this cruel use of state terror. Neither have they accepted their behaviour as such. From their perspective, terrorism is violence performed by resistance movements, the weapon of the poor, exemplified by suicide bombers, although these so-called terrorists will never possess the power to carry out atrocities comparable to the enormity of state-sanctioned terror. Neither have atrocities committed at Abu Ghraib, Guantanamo Bay, and in bombed Afghan civilian areas been defined as terror, but, rather, as pacification efforts by democratic states. The same language is used to describe Israel's bombing of Palestinians in Gaza. There is a need constantly to look at the language employed in journalism, as well as in the writing of history.

## Conclusion

The information disseminated by journalists is frequently hotly debated. As demonstrated in this chapter, news items and journalists' comments are often misleading and very often focus on violent drama, with detrimental humanitarian implications. Such journalism can inadvertently support violent rather than peaceful solutions. 'The gentlemen of the press' have a tendency to respond to the sort of criticism I have levelled here by insisting that their task is to act 'professionally', and they define professionalism in terms of producing stories that sell well, regardless of content or consequence. This definition has been and must continue to be opposed.

After many years of confrontational attacks from Western media institutions, the General Conference of UNESCO in 1978 adopted by acclamation a Mass Media Declaration regarding the contribution of the media to strengthening peace and international understanding. Article III, Point 2, of the declaration (UNESCO 1978) states:

> In countering aggressive war, racialism, apartheid and other violations of human rights which are inter alia spawned by prejudice and ignorance, the mass media, by disseminating information on the aims, aspirations, cultures and needs of all peoples, contribute to eliminate ignorance and misunderstanding between peoples, to make nationals of a country sensitive to the needs and desires of others, to ensure the respect of the rights and dignity of all nations, all peoples and all individuals without distinction of race, sex, language, religion or nationality and to draw attention to the great evils which afflict humanity, such as poverty, malnutrition and diseases, thereby promoting the formulation by States of the policies best able to promote the reduction of international tension and the peaceful and equitable settlement of international disputes.

Unfortunately, to date, this important declaration has seemingly made little impact.

In this chapter I have shown the importance of including nonviolent historical narratives in textbooks. What appears in the media today will be recorded in the textbooks of tomorrow. Textbook writers coming from a peace journalism perspective should rely on the broader, expanded vision of peace journalism I have outlined here, which I argue must give due recognition to the work of women peace activists and writers. This in turn may lead to a revision, or at least to an important expansion, of the field of peace journalism.

## References

Aas, Randi (2006). *Bestemødrene på Stortings plass* [The grandmothers in front of Parliament]. Oslo: Emilia Press.

Bertell, Rosalie (1985). *No immediate danger? Prognosis for a radioactive earth*. London: The Women's Press.

Bognar, Ladislav (1996). Orientation to peace and war in the reading books of Croatian primary schools. Paper presented to Second European

Education for Peace Congress: 'Educating for Human Rights: From Vision to Reality, Lillehammer, Norway, July, 1996.

Boulding, Elise (1982). Education for peace. *Bulletin of the Atomic Scientists,* 38(6): 60.

Bowden, Mark (1999). *Black Hawk down: a story of modern war.* New York: Atlantic Monthly Press.

Brock, Lothar (2009). The problematic securitisation debates. In Birgit Brock-Utne & Gunnar Garbo (Eds). *Language and power: the implications of language for peace and development* (pp48–57). Dar es Salaam: Mkuki na Nyota Publishers Ltd.

Brock-Utne, Birgit (2010a). Victims of sexual violence. In Nigel Young (Ed). *The Oxford international encyclopedia of peace: volume 4* (pp292–94). New York: Oxford University Press.

Brock-Utne, Birgit (2010b). Gender, socialization and militarism. In Nigel Young (Ed). *The Oxford International Encyclopedia of Peace: volume 2* (pp207–10). New York: Oxford University Press.

Brock-Utne, Birgit (2009). A gender perspective on peace education and the work for peace. *International Review of Education,* 55(2–3): 205–20.

Brock-Utne, Birgit (2008). Education for a culture of peace in a globalised world: strategies for curriculum development and implementation. Paper presented to the World Council for Curriculum and Instruction (WCCI) conference in Antalya, Turkey September 2008.

Brock-Utne, Birgit (2007). Education for and education about peace: a feminist analysis. *Bridges,* 14 (1/2): 1–18. [Online]. Available: ubcncm. wordpress.com/2007/05/02/letter-from-brock-utne/ [Accessed 25 August 2011].

Brock-Utne, Birgit (1992). *Evaluering av undervisningsmateriell til bruk i fredsundervisningen. (Evaluation of teaching material to be used in peace education).* Malmö: Institutionen för Pedagogik och Specialmetodik.

Brock-Utne, Birgit (1989). *Feminist perspectives on peace and peace education.* New York: Pergamon Press.

Brock-Utne, Birgit (1985). *Educating for peace: a feminist perspective.* New York: Pergamon Press.

Brock-Utne, Birgit & Gunnar Garbo (2009). Language is power. In Birgit Brock-Utne & Gunnar Garbo (Eds). *Language and power: the implications of language for peace and development* (pp1–32). Dar es Salaam: Mkuki na Nyota Publishers Ltd.

Carson, Rachel (1962). *The silent spring.* London: Penguin Books.

Cohn, Carol (2009). International security, language and gender. In Birgit Brock-Utne & Gunnar Garbo (Eds). *Language and power: the implications of language for peace and development* (pp33–47). Dar es Salaam: Mkuki na Nyota Publishers Ltd.

Cohn, Carol (1987a). Sex and death in the rational world of defense intellectuals. *Signs: Journal of Women in Culture and Society,* 12 (4): 687–718.

Cohn, Carol (1987b). Slick 'ems, glick 'ems, christmas trees, and cookie cutters: nuclear language and how we learned to pat the bomb. *Bulletin of the Atomic Scientists,* 43: 17–24.

Edwards, David & David Cromwell (2009). *Newspeak in the 21st century.* London & New York: Pluto Press.

Eversmann, Matt & Dan Schilling (2004). *The battle of Mogadishu: first hand accounts from the men of Task Force Ranger.* New York: Ballantine Books.

Galtung, Johan (2006). Peace journalism as an ethical challenge. *Global Media Journal Mediterranean Edition,* 1(2): 1–5.

Galtung, Johan (2002). Peace journalism: a challenge. In Wilhelm Kempf & Heikki Loustarinen (Eds). *Journalism and the new world order. Vol. 2: studying the war and the media* (pp260–80) Gothenburg: Nordicom.

Galtung, Johan & Richard C Vincent (1992). *Global glasnost: toward a new world information and communication order?* Cresskill, NJ: Hampton Press.

Galtung, Johan & Mari Holmboe Ruge (1965). The structure of foreign news: the presentation of the Congo, Cuba and Cyprus crises in four Norwegian newspapers. *Journal of Peace Research*, 2(1): 64–90.

Gandhi, Mahatma (1940). What is women's role? *Harijan*, 24 February 1940.

Gandhi, Mahatma (1939). Swaraj through women. *Harijan*, 2 December 1939.

Garbo, Gunnar (2009). Selling war. In Birgit Brock-Utne & Gunnar Garbo (Eds). *Language and power: the implications of language for peace and development* (pp58–65). Dar es Salaam: Mkuki na Nyota Publishers Ltd.

George, Susan (1994). *Faith and credit: the World Bank's secular empire.* Harmondsworth: Penguin Books.

George, Susan (1989). *A fate worse than debt: a radical new analysis of the third world debt crisis.* Harmondsworth: Penguin Books.

Gustafson, Christina (1982). Läromedlens Styrande Funktion i Undervisningen [The governing influence of textbooks and teaching aids on the teaching process]. In Ulf Lundgren, Gunilla Svingby & Erik Wallin. Läroplaner och läromedel. [Curriculum guidelines and teaching aids] *Rapport* no.13/ 1982 (pp75–107). Stockholm: Hogskolan for Lararutbildning. Institutionen for pedagogik.

Heffermehl, Fredrik (2010). *The Nobel Peace Prize: what Nobel really wanted.* Oxford: Praeger.

Hunt, James D (1981). Suffragettes and Satyagraha. *Indo-British Review*, 9 (1): 65–76.

Ife, Jim (2007). Human rights and peace. In Charles Webel & Johan Galtung (Eds). *Handbook of peace and conflict studies* (pp160–72). London: Routledge.

Johansen, Jørgen & John Jones (2010). *Experiments with peace: a book celebrating Johan Galtung's 80th birthday.* Cape Town: Pambazuka Press.

Kellner, Douglas (1995). *Media culture: cultural studies, identity and politics between the modern and the postmodern.* Routledge: London.

Kilborn, Wiggo (1982). Är läromedlet den verkliga läroplanen? [Do textbooks constitute the real curriculum?] In Ulf Lundgren, Gunilla

Svingby & Erik Wallin Läroplaner och läromedel (Eds). [Curriculum guidelines and teaching aids] *Rapport* no.13/ 1982 (pp107–153). Stockholm: Högskolan för Lärarutbildning. Institutionen för pedagogik.

Koritzinsky, Theo (1972). *Samfunnsfag og påvirkning* [Social studies and indoctrination]. Oslo: Universitetsforlaget.

Krügler, Christopher & Patricia Parkman (1985). Identifying alternatives to political violence: an educational imperative. *Harvard Educational Review,* 55(1): 109–117.

Lynch, Jake & Annabel McGoldrick (2005). *Peace journalism.* Stroud: Hawthorn Press.

Murithi, Tim (2009). An African perspective on peace education: *Ubuntu* lessons in reconciliation. *International Review of Education,* 55(2–3): 205–220.

Murithi, Tim (2006). African approaches to building peace and social solidarity. *African Journal on Conflict Resolution,* 6(2): 9–33.

Orwell, George (1949). *Nineteen eighty-four.* London: Secker and Warburg.

Ottosen, Rune (2010). Galtung's theory on peace journalism and Norwegian journalism on Afghanistan. In Jørgen Johansen & John Jones (Eds). *Experiments with peace: a book celebrating Johan Galtung's 80th birthday* (pp258–67). Cape Town: Pambazuka Press.

Poonacha, Veena (2008). Interpreting Gandhi differently: portraying the lives and work of two Gandhian women. *Indian Journal of Gender Studies,* 15(1): 51–80.

Pötzsch, Holger (2009). Black Hawk Down: film zwischen repräsentation und konstruktion gesellschaftlicher wirklichkeit. *International Review of Education,* 55 (2–3): 269–84.

Scott, Ridley (2001). *Black Hawk down.* DVD.

Sharp, Gene (1980). *Social power and political freedom.* Boston: Porter Sargent.

Sharp, Gene (1970). *Exploring nonviolent alternatives.* Boston: Porter Sargent.

Suttner, Bertha von (1889). *Die Waffen nieder* [Lay down your arms]. Dresden: E. Pierson.

Svingby, Gunilla (1986). *Sätt Kunskapen i Centrum* [Place knowledge in the centre of teaching]. Stockholm: Liber.

Turshen, Meredeth & Clotilde Twagiramariya (1998). *What women do in wartime: gender and conflict in Africa.* New Jersey: Zed Books.

Tutu, Desmond (2000). *No future without forgiveness.* London: Rider.

UNESCO (1978). Declaration on fundamental principles concerning the contribution of the mass media to strengthening peace and international understanding, to the promotion of uhuman rights and to countering racialism, apartheid and incitement to war. [Online]. Available: portal. unesco.org/en/ev.php-URL_ID=13176&URL_DO=DO_TOPIC&URL_SECTION=201.html [Accessed 18 August 2011].

Wägner, Elin (1941). *Väckerklocka* [Alarm clock]. Stockholm: Delfin. Reprinted in 1978.

Zinn, Howard & Anthony Arnove (2004). *Voices of a people's history of the United States.* New York: Seven Stories Press.

Zinn, Howard & Rebecca Stefoff (2007). *A young people's history of the United States: Columbus to the Spanish–American War.* London: Seven Stories Press.

# Chapter 3

## 'Human rights journalism': a critical conceptual framework of a complementary strand of peace journalism

*Ibrahim Seaga Shaw*

In recent years, the main conceptual focus of human rights journalism has essentially been twofold: the first has been on the role of the journalist in exposing human rights abuses, popularly called human rights reporting, and, second, on free speech which is in itself a human right. More rarely explored is the conceptualisation of human rights journalism (HRJ) that I am proposing in this chapter – that is, a rethinking of the form based on the insights of peace journalism (PJ). HRJ is a rights-based journalism – journalism based on the human rights principles enshrined in the 1948 Universal Declarations of Human Rights (UDHR) to be enjoyed and respected by all human beings, and subsequently elaborated upon in the twin International Conventions of Civil and Political Rights, and Economic, Social and Cultural Rights, respectively, as well as subsequent legislative and normative frameworks espoused by the UN system and by UN member states.

The heads of government meeting for the UN Millennium Summit in September 2000 issued a declaration which, looking back over this record of human rights frameworks, consisted 'largely of pieties' according to Noam Chomsky (2000). 'At the rhetorical level', rights and freedoms are supported by most governments, Chomsky noted, and by most journalists. However, Chomksy also drew attention to significant lacunae in the declaration's text by comparing and contrasting the showpiece event in New York with an earlier conclave in Havana, the South Summit of the G77, which brought together leaders of the developing countries that met in 1964 for the first UN Conference on Trade and Development (UNCTAD).

The South Summit communiqué made extensive reference to the need, if human rights are to be meaningfully attained by the majority of humanity, for positive measures to extend security and opportunity in the economic and social spheres: 'Our highest priority is to overcome underdevelopment, which implies the eradication of hunger, illiteracy, disease and poverty'. The G77 leaders went on to 'urge the international community to adopt urgent and resolute actions, with a comprehensive and multidimensional approach, to assist in overcoming these scourges, and to establish international economic relations based on justice and equity'. It deplored the 'asymmetries and imbalances that have intensified international economic relations' to the detriment of the South, and called for reform of 'international economic governance' and 'international financial architecture' to make them 'more democratic, more transparent and better attuned to solving the problems of development'. The difference lay, in other words, in the acknowledgement, built into the G77 declaration but omitted or glossed over in the equivalent document from the UN meeting, that unjust political economic structures, put and kept in place for the benefit of powerful interests in the rich world, have the effect of keeping people in the majority world from attaining the rights prescribed for them in the wellknown international instruments.

Mainstream minority-world journalism generally sides with the official rhetoric and policy stances of the governments in the countries in which it is produced. Where human rights violations make the news, they are usually reported as the actions of individual perpetrators, not as the product of a system and of structures that construct and sustain long-term relations in conflict. This is one of the key critiques put forward by PJ advocates, and it relates to majority-world mainstream journalism as well. 'The predominant war journalism of conflict reporting in the wealthy northern hemisphere also dominates global news flows', Lynch wrote (2008, p79).

> By excluding or downplaying backgrounds and contexts, it privileges
> dispositional – often essentialist – explanations for people's behaviour

in conflict over situationist ones. It therefore obscures longstanding structural inequities, in favour of discussions about self-professedly well-meaning interventions' (2008, p79).

Mainstream journalism has failed to communicate not only peace, but also human rights in ways that have the potential of illuminating the important nexus between them. Perhaps more importantly, mainstream journalism has failed to focus on the potential for positive peacebuilding and on positive human rights to match the dominant negative peace and negative rights emphasised within the cosmopolitan context of global justice. Moreover, apart from the growing body of peace studies and peace journalism research in recent times (see, for example, Galtung & Vincent 1992; Galtung 1994, 1996; Lynch & McGoldrick 2005; Lynch 2008), which has at least attempted to illuminate the failure of the media to contribute to or highlight positive peacebuilding initiatives, there is little scholarly work focusing, first, on the journalism–peace–human rights nexus and, second, on critical discussion of the failure of mainstream journalism to foreground positive peace and positive rights issues. This chapter aims to address this gap in scholarship and support the development of human rights journalism as a new, complementary strand of peace journalism that can contribute meaningfully to the promotion and protection of peace and human rights.

This chapter also draws and elaborates on, because of its salience for considering issues in media domains, Lisa Schirch's 'justpeace' framework, which 'provides a setting for seeing how human rights concerns for justice support other peacebuilding activities' (2002, p209). It is in keeping with the PJ model, in favouring, with Galtung, the concept of positive peace over negative peace (1992, 1996). And it provides a conceptual underpinning for the call by other chapters in this volume for an expansion of peace journalism to incorporate ideas of human rights in tackling problems of visible, direct violence as well as invisible, structural and cultural violence.

The rest of this chapter will explore, first, the concept of justpeace within the context of the human rights, peace and communication nexus, and, second, the links between justpeace, PJ and HRJ. Finally, it will critically discuss how HRJ, through the justpeace approach, complements the PJ model and makes it even more focused on 'justpeace-building' approaches.

## The concept of justpeace and the human rights, peace and communication nexus

This section explores the intersection of the theories of communication, human rights and peace. Communicating a message can be both a means and an end in the promotion and protection of human rights and peace. By taking part in an act of communication you can contribute to creating peace, which can also be indispensable for human rights promotion and protection. Cycles of violence (structural, cultural or physical), involving multiple potential human rights violations, are readily legible in the communication – or lack of – between conflicting parties. The enjoyment of human rights on the other hand may lead to peace while both combine to guarantee the freedom and security to communicate. There is therefore a clear nexus between peace and human rights, and between these two concepts and communication. However, the putative tensions that exist between the notions of human rights and peace on one level, and between these two notions and the conventions of 'professional' journalism on another, have threatened the mutually beneficial coexistence of these three arguably interrelated and interdependent notions. In this section I draw on insights from Lisa Schirch's justpeace framework (2002) and Galtung's positive peace framework (1996) to give a brief overview of these tensions and how the approach of justpeace-building addresses them.

Schirch (2002) traces the tensions between human rights and peace to a number of philosophical and practical differences. On the one hand, the work of human rights organisations is often interpreted as advocacy against human rights violations and calls for punishment of the violators. Human rights workers aim to carry out their work according to standards of behaviour enshrined in the UDHR, 'and use the legal system in the pursuit of a justice where offenders are punished for their crimes' (Schirch 2002, p210). In human rights discourse, clear victims and offenders are identified, and both cannot be equally held culpable for the acts of human rights violations.

On the other hand, conflict resolution approaches give equal attention to victims of all sides of a conflict, typically in a longer timeframe, and view all sides as mutually responsible for the task of addressing the problem. In other words, conflict resolution approaches to parties to a conflict emphasise impartiality between them (though not over issues of principle, such as human rights per se); while those of human rights advocates emphasise clear distinctions between perpetrators and victims.

> The goal of being a mediating "bridge" between groups in conflict, helping each to empathise with the other, to share perspectives on "truth", and work together to find ways of moving forward, is often seen as incompatible with the goal of raising awareness and naming injustice' (Schirch 2002, p210).

The apparent incompatibility between these two positions might lead a human rights advocate to ask a peace worker: 'How can you work for peace without including a sense of justice for victims?' The peace worker might ask back: 'How will we ever move forward if we insist on punishing offenders?' (Schirch 2002, p210).

The emphasis, in the discourse of Western-based human rights organisations, on the accountability of individual perpetrators is in keeping with negative peace: if a particular person can be shown to have fired a gun in an illegitimate way (or caused others to do so), then she or he should be punished. This emphasis also informs the familiar human rights agenda in Western journalism, perhaps epitomised by the Crimes of War project, in which two journalists, Roy Gutman and David Rieff, teamed up with the International Committee of the Red Cross to produce a handbook and website furnishing readers with expert advice as to what constitutes a war crime in a range of different circumstances, with the aim of getting journalists to report it as such (Gutman & Rieff 2000).

Galtung defines peace as the absence of violence, but while negative peace – like a ceasefire – requires only the abstention from direct violence, positive peace implies programmatic actions to provide for social justice, limiting structural and cultural violence to enable people to fulfil their potential. Putting these forms on the same ontological footing, by labelling them both 'violence', as Galtung has done, means that when an act or threat of force is made, individual culpability is automatically diluted. This insight, Galtung contends, is potentially important in peacebuilding, because the 'nature–structure–culture model' is inescapably 'exculpatory'. He explains:

> A structure-oriented perspective converts the relation from inter-personal, or inter-state/nation, to a relation between two positions in a deficient structure. If the parties can agree that the structure was/is deficient and that their behaviour was an enactment of structural positions rather than anything more personal, then turning together against the common problem, the structural violence, should be possible. A culture-oriented perspective also converts the relation from interpersonal, or inter-state/nation, to a relation spurred by a deficient culture. (Galtung 1996, p65)

Justice for individual perpetrators must, this implies, be conceived in a context where deficient structures and cultures are also transformed, because the behaviours of the individuals concerned must be seen as having been, in an important sense, 'produced' by the structures within which their relationship with their victims was formed.

The concept of justpeace, which is a hybrid of human rights and peace, helps to provide answers to the questions posed by both fields. Justpeace goes beyond efforts to reduce direct violence. Justpeace-building efforts prioritise the proper transformation of principles and values over a long timeframe through an organised system of distributive justice, where resources and decision-making are shared. There is a substantial overlap, at least rhetorically, between the concept of justpeace and the statement issued by the South Summit. 'Moreover, the concept of justpeace builds on a restorative vision of justice, aimed at meeting basic human needs of both victims and offenders while holding the latter accountable for their crimes' (Schirch 2002, p212). Justpeace is only possible where there are sustainable structures and processes that allow humanity to meet basic needs. Hence there are no contradictions between human rights and peacebuilding goals within a justpeace framework. 'The field of human rights fits into a long-term plan for building justpeace by contributing analytical tools, value frameworks, and by playing a variety of roles in peacebuilding practice' (Schirch 2002, p212).

While social oppression, which people experience as a result of structural violence, may have the effect of mobilising people who are normally nonviolent to commit acts of violence, 'it is [nevertheless] more difficult to notice than direct overt violence' (Larssen 2009, p21). Achieving peace without human rights generally renders such peace as sterile (Ife 2007). As Frank (2007) posits, any peace that is not grounded in human rights cannot be said to be justpeace. The concept of negative peace resonates with Walzer's just war theory (1992): injustice leads to structural violence such as poverty, famine and forced migration, which in turn may lead to direct physical violence and to further human rights violations. Thus the concept of justice for all is equally important in positive peace as in justpeace.

Thomas Frank (2007) conceptualises the ethic of justpeace as comprising the following seven forms of reasoning:

- All people have an ontological claim to 'Being' and 'Being Responsible' for their own social agency, although societal conditions such as war can affect this.

- The idea of 'Being' and 'Being Responsible' is a global phenomenon which emphasises the 'equality of all social agents'.

- The equality and co-existence of all social agents is valued.

- The value of 'Being' implies that the global social agents' needs are global values – that is, that values (rights) are universal and not relative.

- Wrongs committed by a social agent can be condemned and corrected but their life cannot be taken from them as punishment. The being of social agents is radically dependent on others.

- The issue of compulsory trust and the need for external assistance in matters outside of one's control implies the global norm to value the trust of others.

- The social agent is the subject of the concept of justpeace, not the sovereign state or the international community.

The ethics of justpeace as summarised by Frank (2007) above are already present and emerging in the framework of international human rights law. Frank (2007) explains that the needs of the social agent and the principles or norms designated to meet those needs are very much 'represented in the human rights discourse and regime and the asymmetric identities constructed therein' (p84). The logic of justpeace is framed in the notion that 'we must be just if we want justice to come' (Frank 2007, p86). As Gandhi famously said: 'Be the change you want to see in the world'.

The Western philosophical foundations of the peace and human rights nexus can be traced to the work of Immanuel Kant and his notion of the 'cosmopolitan community'. Kant believed in both peace and human rights and saw a clear connection between the two concepts. He linked the moral development of any particular political community to 'the development of international law and a pacific federation of states' (Kant 1963 [1784], p18), and argued that war or even preparation for it brings into play attitudes and behaviours hostile to the realisation of human rights. Kant advocated a lawful form of international association based on the cosmopolitan condition of interdependence. In an ideal cosmopolitan world, human rights are held equally by all persons; if that is the case, cosmopolitans argue that there will be common interest in their promotion and protection. 'A cosmopolitan community comes into being when a violation of human rights is felt to be of concern to the whole international community regardless of where it occurs' (Kant 1963 [1784], p21). This rhetoric is fine, but unfortunately the reality often does not follow suit. Why the international community acted to avert mass killings in Kosovo, for example, but not in the cases of Somalia, Rwanda and Sierra Leone, to name but a few African crises (to which one might now add the intervention in Libya, but not Palestine, Yemen or Bahrain), exemplifies what I call a form of 'rhetorical cosmopolitanism' (Shaw 2011, forthcoming): honoured by rhetoric, but not with follow-through actions.

Frank's ethic and logic of justpeace (2007) and Kant's philosophical framework of the peace and human rights nexus resonate more closely with Schirch's (2002) human rights paradigm of justpeace than with a realist paradigm, especially as each values the important cosmopolitan justice-based values of equality and interdependence. I include below two tables reflecting a realist paradigm, and Schirch's justpeace human rights paradigm.

Table 1

| Realist paradigm: focused on meeting human needs and rights of self at expense of other |
| --- |
| • Human relationships are structured hierarchically where some people dominate others in an effort to meet their own needs and obtain their own rights. |
| • Humans are independent of each other so that one person's gain can be another's loss. |
| • Violence is often seen as the only way of pursuing one's human needs and rights. |

Table 2

| Justpeace human rights paradigm: focused on meeting human needs and rights of both self and other |
| --- |
| • Many human relationships are structured in an egalitarian, partnership model where people cooperate to meet each other's needs. |
| • Humans are interdependent with each other so that unmet human needs or rights of any individual or group ripple outward toward the whole of humanity. |
| • Nonviolent methods of ensuring human needs and rights are essential so that the very struggle to obtain rights does not violate the rights of an opposing group, thus reinforcing the cycle of violence. |

## Justpeace, human rights journalism and peace journalism

In this section I explore the links between justpeace and PJ on the one hand and between justpeace and HRJ on the other. Justpeace is seen as a holistic and practical framework informed by the idea that war is not simply an isolated event but very much rooted within the fabric of our societies, and by 'the hope that wars can be prevented from within by creating modes of negotiation and reconciliation practices to reduce and eventually end the necessity for violence' (Malone 2004, p8). Ury (2001, p38) conceptualises justpeace as having a 'third side' that is 'a kind of a social immune system that prevents the spread of the virus of violence'. Ury is critical of the Hobbesian notion that human nature's inclination to war can only be restrained by a strong government. He ponders how our ancestors were able to resolve conflict so successfully for so long (Ury 2001).

While carrying out research among the Kalahari Bushmen, in which he observed the ways in which family, friends and the extended community intervened to resolve issues between conflicting parties, Ury discovered that conflicts never take place just between two adversaries, but that there is always a 'third side'. This third side:

> is made up of people from the community using a certain kind of power, the power of peers, from a certain perspective, which is a perspective of common ground; supporting a certain process, which is the process of dialogue and nonviolence; and aiming for a certain product, which is a triple win – a solution that's good for the community and good for both of the parties. (Ury 2001, p73)

Ury perceives conflict as a natural phenomenon and calls for a positive interactive dialogue rather than mere opposition from external forces. He comes up with ten roles that 'third siders' can play in achieving justpeace:

Table 3

| | |
|---|---|
| 1. Provider | Helping people meet their frustrated needs |
| 2. Teacher | Instilling skills or attitudes to defuse tensions |
| 3. Bridge builder | Fostering good relationships across potential lines of conflict |
| 4. Mediator | Helping people reconcile their opposite interests |
| 5. Arbiter | Delineating the disputed rights |
| 6. Equaliser | Balancing the power between clashing parties |
| 7. Healer | Repairing injured relationships and defusing wounded emotions |
| 8. Witness | Taking heed and note of early warning signs of dispute |
| 9. Referee | Establishing objective rules for conflict |
| 10. Peace keeper | Stepping in to separate the fighting parties, even physically |

*Defining peace journalism*

Lynch and McGoldrick (2005, p5) define PJ as 'a set of tools, both conceptual and practical, intended to equip journalists to offer a better public service'. It is a journalism that helps reporters and editors alike to make informed choices about what stories deserve reporting and how the reporting itself is done, and that provides society at large with opportunities to consider and value nonviolent responses to conflict. Lynch and McGoldrick (2005, p5) present PJ as playing the following three key roles:

- It uses the insights of conflict analysis and transformation to update the concepts of balance, fairness and accuracy in reporting.

- It provides a new route map tracing the connections between journalists, their sources, the stories they cover and the consequences of their journalism – the ethics of journalistic intervention.

- It builds an awareness of nonviolence and creativity into the practical job of everyday editing and reporting.

Like all alternative journalism models, PJ has both supporters and critics. By recognising the debates in favour of and against peace journalism, Lynch (2008) challenges practitioners of war journalism to try an alternative paradigm – that of providing a more comprehensive diagnosis of conflict dynamics to aid news consumers' understanding of the issues, and encouraging a 'win–win' logic of finding solutions instead of just reporting the facts of violence in a 'win–lose' framing that often leads to more violence. PJ creates an enabling environment that helps people consider nonviolent approaches to ending violence and in this sense it resonates with the justpeace approach that favours dialogue and nonviolence. Both have elements of critical conflict analysis and creativity that help provide solutions to conflict. However, where justpeace goes further in the solution-orientated approach is where its own targeted end product is a triple win, a solution that meets the needs of the two parties in the conflict and the community as the 'third side'. Moreover, where justpeace goes further in the people-orientated and justice-orientated approach is where it is attached, rather than detached, to all vulnerable victims of human rights violations. Justpeace implies the provision for social justice, necessary for allowing the fulfilment of human potential that has been curtailed by structural and cultural violence. Lederach captures something of this sense by defining justice as 'the pursuit of restoration, of rectifying wrongs, of creating right relationships based on equity and fairness' (1995, p20).

*Defining human rights journalism*

Human rights journalism can be defined as a diagnostic style of reporting which offers a critical reflection of the experiences and needs of the victims and perpetrators of (physical, cultural and structural) human rights violations. It attempts to understand the reasons for these violations in order to prevent further violations and to solve current ones in ways that would not produce more violence. Moreover, it is a journalism that challenges, rather than reinforces, the status quo of the dominant voices of global and national societies. It is, in other words, journalism without borders, based on human rights and global justice, challenging political, economic, social and cultural imbalances of society at both local and global levels.

The HRJ strand of PJ is premised on the argument that if journalism is to play any agency role in society, it should focus on deconstructing the underlying structural causes of political violence such as poverty, famine, exclusion of minorities, youth marginalisation, human trafficking, forced labour and forced migration (to name but a few), rather than focusing merely on the attitudes and behaviours of the elite that benefit from direct and uncensored violence. In short, it calls for a robust, proactive (preventive), rather than dramatic, reactive (prescriptive) role for media in conflict. In an analogous dyadic diagnosis to that of 'war journalism/peace journalism', it identifies, as mainstream practice, a dominant strand of 'human wrongs journalism' (HWJ) – a journalism that reinforces, instead of challenges, the problematic representational imbalances in society and the concentration of power in the hands of the few people and political communities within global society (Shaw 2011, forthcoming).

Like PJ, HRJ resonates with the justpeace approach by valuing the critical conflict analysis and creativity that is needed to help people actively participate in the resolution of violent situations. HRJ, similarly to justpeace, adopts a global, long-term, proactive and sustainable approach to news coverage as it provides a critical reflection of the experiences and needs of not only the victims, but also of perpetrators or offenders. In this way, it ensures the prevention or resolution of all forms of future or present violence. Hence, HRJ has the potential to complement PJ's contribution to global, long-term, proactive and sustainable justpeace-building.

The orientation variables of peace journalism, as outlined by Galtung (1992) and reproduced in the first chapter of this book, are similar to those I have identified with human rights journalism, as can be seen in Table 4.

On the other hand, the orientation variables or principles of war journalism, as outlined by Galtung (1992), also share similarities with what I have identified as human wrongs journalism, as can be seen in the Table 5.

Table 4

| Peace journalism | Human rights journalism |
|---|---|
| 1. Peace/conflict orientated: prevention/win–win | 1. Nonviolence/structural/cultural violence orientated: proactive/ preventing direct violence/triple win |
| 2. Truth orientated: exposes all untruths | 2. Human wrongs orientated: exposes all human wrongs |
| 3. People orientated: names all victims | 3. People/human-face orientated: cares for and empowers all but is biased in favour of vulnerable people |
| 4. Solution orientated | 4. Holistic problem-solving: for present problems now/tomorrow; and surface/hidden problems |

Table 5

| War journalism | Human wrongs journalism |
|---|---|
| 1. War/violence orientated: reactive/first zero-sum/win–lose orientation | 1. Competition orientated: violence/drama/provocative: solution after damage/business profit or loss |
| 2. Propaganda/deceit orientated: exposes 'their' untruths/lies and covers up 'ours' | 2. Their propaganda/deceit/ conspiracy orientated: talks about 'their' conspiracies to commit human rights violations, and ignores 'ours' |
| 3. Elite orientated: focuses on 'those' evil doers and 'our' victims/friend (good), enemy (bad) | 3. Demonisation orientated: focuses on the human rights violations by 'them', 'others' or 'our enemies' against 'us' or 'our friends', the victims |
| 4. Victory orientated: peace=victory +ceasefire | 4. Partially solution orientated: focuses only on immediate physical needs at the expense of long-term structural solutions |

*How human rights journalism complements peace journalism*

Galtung's PJ model was conceived as a peace–conflict paradigm to counterbalance the war–violence model with a view towards moving from the current dominant culture of violence to a culture of peace. This called for a paradigm shift, coming as it did on the heels of the end of the Cold War which climaxed with the fall of the Berlin Wall in 1989, and which was characterised by the outbreak of wars in the Balkans, the Middle East Gulf, Africa, and Southeast Asia. Galtung's model was informed by the popular saying 'violence breeds violence' (Galtung & Vincent 1992).

According to Galtung (1992), PJ denounces mainstream journalism as war journalism mainly because of its focus on problems rather than solutions, on propaganda rather than truth, on its elite rather than people, and its win–lose rather than win–win orientated paradigms (Lovasen 2008). Lovasen, who agrees with Galtung, uses PJ's orientations to claim that it holds dear the values of humanitarianism, truth, holism and empowerment. But there is a problem with this claim. I argue that, despite ticking almost all the boxes of the abovementioned orientations and values, PJ, as it stands, is lacking in the four other orientations typically reflective of HRJ listed in Table 4 (working for a global, triple-win, rather than a selective win–win or win–lose solution, biased in favour of vulnerable voices, proactive rather than reactive, and justice orientated, siding with the victims of violence). To show how HRJ complements PJ's orientations outlined in Table 4 above, I argue that HRJ also problematises mainstream journalism, labelling it 'human wrongs journalism', because of its orientation to selective justice rather than global justice; its bias against, rather than for, vulnerable voices; its tendency to report reactively rather than proactively; and its detachment from victims of human rights violations. All of these orientations are the polar opposites of the four HRJ orientations in Table 4. The four values – humanitarianism, truth, holism, and empowerment – advanced by Lovasen (2008) resonate in certain ways with the five principles of the HRJ approach to journalism: linkages to human rights standards, participation, accountability, non-discrimination and empowerment. These principles are informed by both negative and positive rights, and by both negative and positive peace (Berman & Calderbank 2008; Galtung 1992, 1996; Nowak 2005). The four values and five principles of the HRJ also largely inform the justpeace-building approach advocated by Schirch (2002).

### Global, long-term, proactive and sustainable approaches of justpeace

In the remainder of this section I critically explore how HRJ can, through the global, long-term, proactive and sustainable approaches of justpeace, complement and strengthen PJ as a counter-hegemonic journalism practice. Drawing on these justpeace approaches, HRJ proposes a critical reflection of the experiences and needs of both victims and perpetrators of human rights violations. I look now at these justpeace approaches in the context of PJ's use of both realist and human rights paradigms, the debate about the place of objectivity and of advocacy in journalism.

In the context of realist and human rights paradigms, HRJ makes transparent, and problematises, power relations (at both national and supranational levels) that increase the powerlessness, helplessness, impotence, and apathy of those whose mobilisation would best serve the peace efforts (Carrol 1972; Dente Ross 2006). In 1972, Carrol argued the case that research failed to 'consider seriously the possibility that war is inherent not in human nature but in the power system of dominance in human relations', articulated through the nation-state. Political realists such as Hans Morgenthau believe that states are rational egoists seeking to promote their material interests in foreign policy (1967). Wheeler sees realism as predicated on a particular conception of the relationship between citizens and strangers that privileges what Robert H Jackson calls an ethic of 'national responsibility' (Wheeler 1999, p175; Jackson 1995). Realists believe that where there are competing interests, a country's vital strategic interests must be prioritised over actions to save human lives; this runs contrary to what cosmopolitans stand for. Mainstream journalism is overly manipulated by political, economic and cultural structures of hegemony and, hence, often leans towards political realism in its promotion of 'selective justice' than cosmopolitan 'distributive' justice. Realists argue that since journalists do not operate outside their immediate political, social, economic, and cultural communities, it would be naïve to think that their reporting could remain uninfluenced by these.

In his synthesis of the arguments and counter-arguments in the PJ debate, Kempf (2007) defends Galtung's (2002) criticism of the mainstream media for reducing conflict to a zero-sum game and Lynch's (2007) call to journalism to analyse and address its own role in creating realities. PJ is critical of the media for systematically concealing certain facts, especially those that favour the peace discourse, in favour of others such as those that favour the war discourse. Kempf (2007) sees conflict as an interactive process involving three kinds of reality: first, the subjective reality of one party; second, the subjective reality of an opponent (and both this and the first kind of reality can interact internally); and third, the kind of reality that can only be assessed from an external perspective. Kempf (2007) sees PJ playing the role of an external perspective that shows how the two internal subjective realities interact with each other.

In the context of the objectivity–advocacy journalism binary, PJ continues to face the daunting challenge of relying on its critical conflict analysis approach based on values (truth/honesty/humanitarianism) that are at odds with those of mainstream 'professional' journalism, notably 'objective journalism'. Peace journalists must strike a balance between reporting and informing (objectivity) on one hand, and caring for humanity (advocacy) on the other hand. Are they getting the balance right? Or are they leaning more towards objectivity than advocacy? Or vice versa? Both PJ and HRJ are putatively extra-linear; that is, not based on neutral/objective journalism but on honest/subjective journalism. However, this is not always the case with PJ, which oscillates between the two divides and tends to lean more towards the objectivity standpoint. Perhaps the most illustrative case of this tendency of PJ is that offered by Lee and Maslog (2005) and Lee et al. (2006) in their studies of the *Philippine Daily Inquirer* (*PDI*)'s coverage of political violence in the Philippines:

The peace journalism framing is highly dependent on criteria of a less interventionist nature, for example, an avoidance of good/bad labels, a non partisan approach, a multi party orientation and avoidance of emotive language. These four indicators, although important in the overall scheme of peace journalism ... are mere extensions of the objectivity credo: reporting the facts as they are. These indicators do not truly exemplify a strong contributory, proactive role by journalists to seek and offer creative solutions and to pave a way for peace and conflict resolution. (Lee et al. 2006, p512)

In portraying PJ in the Philippines as taking a somewhat neutral, or passive stance, Lee and Maslog (2005) argue that the PJ practised by the *PDI* is more closely related to the 'classic' tenets of 'good journalism', rather than the more radical interventionist approach called for by 'advocacy journalism' (Hanitzsch 2007, p3; Becker 2002, p14). Lynch (2008, p149) argues that while the Lee and Maslog (2005) and Lee et al. (2006) studies concentrate on 'passive' peace journalism indicators – coded as the *absence* of, for instance, demonising or partisan language – they ignore the more ideational, 'active' indicators of PJ, which, according to Shinar (2007, p200), work to 'explore context', 'challenge propaganda' and 'make peace visible'. In Lynch's study, the *PDI* exhibited the highest 'quotient' of active PJ, of any of the media examined, in their coverage of the communist insurgency in the Philippines, at 41.2 percent: significantly higher than international media covering the same story in the same period.

The percentages of the three 'passive' indicators – avoiding emotive or demonising language (40 percent), non-partisanship (49.4 percent), and avoiding labels such as 'good' or 'bad' (64 percent), present in the *PDI* coverage of the same story – were even higher than those of the active peace journalism indicators. The crucial distinction is whether indicators or issues are framed in ways that will not only illuminate the problems but also identify, recommend, advocate and mobilise actionable solutions to address them. The passive (neutral) peace journalism illustrated in the Lee and Maslog (2005) and Lee et al. (2006) case studies resonates with the 'impartial' conflict resolution approach, and the 'negative', retributive-justice-based human rights approach, as opposed to the 'positive' human rights, or justpeace approach outlined by Schirch and discussed above.

Not all writers in the broadly defined PJ 'camp' are inclined to this more radical approach. Kempf (2002) rejects advocacy explanations of PJ in favour of what he calls 'good' journalism, which he says has one aim: to represent reality accurately. Kempf (2002) presents objectivity, neutrality and detachment as means of reaching accuracy. While recognising the need to problematise the conventional journalistic appreciation of objectivity by way of liberating it from its shortcomings, Kempf cautions against turning away from it, as Lynch and McGoldrick (2005) or Hackett and Carroll (2006) have advocated, warning that this may undermine the 'trust bonus' that PJ currently enjoys (Kempf 2007, p7).

Kempf, like David Loyn (2007), prefers to reserve the name 'good journalism' for describing the opposite of what the former BBC correspondent Martin Bell called a 'journalism of attachment' (1996). Journalism, in Kempf and Loyn's view, must attempt to remain 'detached' – albeit with some caveats. Objectivity may, Loyn allows, be 'chimerical' – but it is still an essential goal of news. Nevertheless, Nordenstreng points out that the privileged place of journalism within the international human rights framework – explicitly provided for twice over in the twin 'Articles 19' of the Universal Declaration of Human Rights and the International Covenant on Civil and Political Rights – is not intended to enshrine the free flow of information as a goal in itself, but as a means to an external goal – that of peace (2001).

This is in keeping with the advocacy journalism which German political scientist Jorg Becker (2002, p14) sees as the political obligation of the media. That is, it should 'participate and stand for peace of its accord', and, I add, human rights. Becker looks to journalism not only to report reality 'as it is' but, rather, to create reality, set examples and call for change (Hanitzsch 2007, p3). This is what Siebert et al. (1963, 1956) call the 'social responsibility of journalism model': with their enjoyment of communications rights, journalists have a social responsibility to criticise those in power on behalf of peoples and societies, more or less serving as their watchdogs (Siebert et al. 1963, 1956; Hohenberg 1974;

Cater 1957; Cohen-Almagor 2001). Article 3 of the 1978 UNESCO Declaration, for instance, states that, 'the mass media have an important contribution to make to the strengthening of peace and international understanding and in countering racialism, apartheid and incitement to war' (UNESCO 1978, p1). The social responsibility role of journalism, grounded in communication rights, underpins Nordenstreng's call for initiatives 'to systematically monitor what the media tell about the world with a view to improving media performance and contributing to media ethics' (2001, p1).

It is this social responsibility role that Lynch and McGoldrick (2005, cited in McGoldrick 2006, p4 and cited in Kempf 2007, p3) allude to when they assert that journalists are responsible for the way they report, and even for the creation of 'opportunities for society at large to consider and to value nonviolent responses to conflict'. But Lynch and McGoldrick (2005) see this 'responsibility' not so much as an external goal imposed on journalism from outside, but, as they argue, an 'obligation to create these opportunities [that] results directly from the role assigned to journalism in democratic societies' (cited in Kempf 2007, p3). Lynch and Galtung (2010, p91) note that 'the external goal of peace is added instrumentally, to deliver more successfully on internal goals of accuracy and fairness'. HRJ, which, as an external goal, consistently draws on the principles of the human rights-based approach to journalism mentioned above, can therefore potentially strengthen PJ's call to journalists to be more socially responsible in creating opportunities for the nonviolent prevention or resolution of conflicts within a justpeace-building framework, without necessarily undermining the professional tenets of professional 'good' journalism such as accuracy and fairness. In fact, I have argued that the external goals of the HRJ principles assigned to journalism in democratic societies instrumentally reinforce professional journalism's internal goals of fairness and accuracy.

## Conclusion

In conclusion, the problems of war or mainstream journalism identified here are largely to blame for the under-reporting and/or misrepresenting of political and structural forms of violence – and, by extension, human rights violations – that permeate today's news media. Given these problems in mainstream journalism, it makes sense to incorporate HRJ as a complementary strand of PJ, to tackle these problems.

HRJ complements the four orientations of the PJ model advanced by Galtung (1992, 1996) and supported by Lynch and McGoldrick (2005) – namely: solution rather than victory oriented, truth rather than propaganda oriented, people rather than elite oriented, and win–win rather than win–lose orientated by introducing four others. These are: global rather than selective reporting, a bias in favour of vulnerable voices, a proactive (preventive) rather than reactive (prescriptive) approach to reporting, and an attachment to, rather than a detachment from, victims of violence. It is also human rights orientated. With these complementary attributes of HRJ, PJ, this chapter argues, will be able to lay justifiable claim to the observation of the values of 'humanitarianism, truth, holism and empowerment', as identified by Lovasen (2008) in support of the Galtung model. These four values resonate with the principles of the rights-based approach to journalism: participation, accountability, non-discrimination, empowerment, and linkages to human rights standards informed by both negative and positive rights on one hand, and negative and positive peace on the other (Berman & Calderbank 2008; Galtung 1992, 1996; Nowak 2005). (See also Shaw, 2011 for a detailed discussion of this connection.)

Below is a table showing my human wrongs and human rights journalism model.

Table 6 HWJ vs HRJ

| HWJ | HRJ |
| --- | --- |
| • Empathy/distance frame | • Empathy/critical frame |
| • Evocative reporting | • Diagnostic reporting |
| • Reactive | • Proactive |
| • Non-interventionist | • Interventionist |
| • War journalism | • Peace journalism |

The above model underscores the importance of the role of the media in the promotion of peace and human rights. The existence of any solution presupposes the existence of a problem that that solution is aiming to solve – hence my reasoning behind juxtaposing HWJ with HRJ in the table. Communication manipulated in favour of the dominant classes of society is bound to be produced when journalists employ HWJ (evocative empathy distance frames) that discourage advocacy or intervention. This is in contrast to HRJ (diagnostic empathy critical frames) that encourages advocacy and intervention to promote and protect peace and human rights (Preston 1996). I conclude with the argument that HRJ upholds the internal principles of human rights–based journalism which encompass the tenets of professional journalism to address the structural imbalances of global society at large, and in this way prevent or resolve direct physical violence within a justpeace framework. In this way, human rights journalists can complement peace journalists as 'third siders', taking on the roles of providers, teachers, bridge builders, or mediators to help parties in conflict reach their needs and achieve justpeace.

## References

Becker, Jorg (2002). Medien im Krieg. In Ulrich Albrecht & Jorg Becker (Eds). *Medien zwisschen Krieg und Frieden* (pp13–26). Baden-Baden: Nomos.

Bell, Martin (1996). *In harm's way: reflections of a war-zone thug.* London: Penguin Books.

Berman, Gabrielle & Daniel Calderbank (2008). *The human rights–based approach to journalism: training manual Vietnam.* Bangkok: UNESCO.

Carroll, Berenice (1972). Peace research: the cult of power. *The Journal of Conflict Resolution,* 16(4): 585–616.

Carruthers, Susan (2000). *The media at war: communication and conflict in the twentieth century.* New York: St. Martin's Press.

Cater, Douglass (1957). *The fourth branch of government.* Boston: Houghton Mifflin.

Chomsky, Noam (2000). World summits yield remarkable contrast. *Z Magazine*. [Online]. Available: www.progress.org/chomsky05.htm [Accessed 22 July 2011].

Cohen-Almagor, Raphael (2001). *Speech, media and ethics: the limits of free expression*. New York: Palgrave.

Dente-Ross, Susan (2006). (De)constructing conflict: a focused review of war and peace journalism. *Conflict and Communication Online*, 5(2). [Online]. Available: www.cco.regener-online.de/ [Accessed 22 July 2011].

Frank, T (2007). Idealist and realist aspirations for just peace: an analysis of ethics of military force and the discursive construction of an ethic of international policing within the framework of just peace and the contemporary hegemony of international law. Unpublished PhD Dissertation Submitted to the Theological Faculty, University of Aarhus.

Galtung, Johan (1996). *Peace by peaceful means: peace and conflict, development and civilisation*. PRIO–International Peace Research Institute, Oslo. London: SAGE Publications.

Galtung, Johan & Richard C Vincent (1992). *Global glasnost: toward a new world information and communication order?* Cresskill, NJ: Hampton Press.

Gutman, Roy & David Rieff (2000). *Crimes of war*. Geneva: International Committee of the Red Cross.

Hackett, Robert & William Carroll (2006). *Remaking media: the struggle to democratize public communication*. New York: Routledge.

Hanitzsch, Thomas (2007). Situating peace journalism in journalism studies: a critical appraisal. *Conflict and Communication Online*, 6(2). [Online]. Available: www.cco.regener-online.de [Accessed 27 July 2011].

Hohenberg, John (1978). *The professional journalist*. New York: Holt Rinehart Wilson.

Ife, Jim (2007). Human rights and peace. In Charles Webel & Johan Galtung (Eds). *Handbook of peace and conflict studies* (pp160–72). New York: Routledge.

Kant, Immanuel (1963 [1784]). *Idea for a universal history from a cosmopolitan point of view*. Translated by Lewis White Beck. [Online]. Available: www.marxists.org/reference/subject/ethics/kant/universal-history.htm [Accessed 18 August 2011].

Kempf, Wilhelm (2007). Peace journalism: a tightrope walk between advocacy journalism and constructive conflict coverage. *Conflict & Communication Online, 6(2)*. [Online]. Available: www.cco.regener-online.de [Accessed 27 July 2011].

Kempf, Wilhelm (2002). Conflict coverage and conflict escalation. In Wilhelm Kempf & Heikki Luostarinen (Eds). *Journalism and the new world order: studying war and the media*, 2nd volume pp59–72. Goteborg: Nordicom.

Larssen, Ingvild (2009). Peace and human rights: a comparative analysis on the role of human rights in Norwegian peace processes in Sudan. Unpublished Master's Thesis. Faculty of Social Sciences University of Tromsø, Norway.

Lederach, John Paul (1995). *Preparing for peace: conflict transformation across cultures*. New York: Syracuse University Press.

Lee, Seow Ting, Crispin Maslog & Hun Shik Kim (2006). Asian conflicts and the Iraq war: a compassionate framing analysis. *International Communication Gazette*, 68(5–6): 499–518.

Lee, Seow Ting & Crispin Maslog (2005). War or peace journalism in Asian newspapers. *Journal of Communication*, 55(2): 311–329.

Loyn, David (2007). Good journalism or peace journalism? *Conflict and Communication Online*, 6(2). [Online]. Available: www.cco.regener-online.de/2007_2/pdf/loyn.pdf [Accessed 27 July 2011].

Lovasen, Line (2008). Journalism and power: the role of media in building human rights and culture of peace. *Human Rights Defence.org*. [Online]. Available: www.humanrightsdefence.org/journalism-and-power-the-role-of-media-in-building-human-rights-and-a-culture-of-peace.html [Accessed 27 July 2011].

Lynch, Jake (2008). *Debates in peace journalism*. Sydney: Sydney University Press.

Lynch, Jake (2007). Peace journalism and its discontents. *Conflict & Communication Online, 6*(2). [Online]. Available: cco.regener-online.de. [Accessed 27 July 2011].

Lynch, Jake & Galtung, Johan (2010). *Reporting conflict: new directions in peace journalism.* St Lucia: University of Queensland Press.

Lynch, Jake & Annabel McGoldrick (2005). *Peace journalism.* Stroud: Hawthorn Press.

Malone, Naomi (2004). From just war to just peace: re-visioning just war theory from a feminist perspective. Unpublished Master's Thesis, Department of Political Science College of Arts and Sciences, University of South Florida, US.

Marshall, Rachelle (1991). Nothing without US pressure on Israel. *The Washington Report on Middle East Affairs,* X(4): 14.

McGoldrick, Annabel (2006). War journalism and 'objectivity'. *Conflict & Communication Online, 5*(2). [Online]. Available: cco.regener-online.de. [Accessed 10 February 2010].

Morgenthau, Hans (1967). To intervene or not to intervene. *Foreign Affairs,* 45: 425–36.

Nordenstreng, Kaarle (2001). Something to be done: transnational media monitoring. *Transnational Broadcasting Studies Journal,* Spring edition. [Online]. Available: www.tbsjournal.com/Archives/Spring01/nordenstreng.html. [Accessed 8 February 2011].

Nowak, Manfred (2005). The International Covenants on Civil and Political Rights and on Economic, Social and Cultural Rights. In Rhona Smith & Christien van den Anker (Eds). *The essentials of human rights* (pp193–200). London: Hodder Arnold.

Preston, Alison (1996). Television news and the Bosnian conflict: distance, proximity, impact. In James Gow, Richard Paterson & Alison Preston (Eds). *Bosnia by Television* (112–16). London, British Film Institute.

Schirch, Lisa (2002). Human rights and peacebuilding: towards justpeace. Paper presented to 43rd Annual International Studies Association Convention, New Orleans, Louisiana, March, 2002.

Shaw, Ibrahim Seaga (2011). *Human rights journalism: advances in the reporting of distant humanitarian interventions.* London: Palgrave Macmillan.

Shinar, Dov (2003). Peace process in cultural conflict: the role of the media. *Conflict and Communication Online,* 2(1). [Online]. Available: www.cco.regener-online.de. [Accessed 25 July 2011].

Siebert, Fredrick S, Theodor Petersen & Walter Schramm (1963 [1956]). *Four theories of the press.* Urbana: University of Illinois Press.

UNESCO (1978). Declaration on fundamental principles concerning the contribution of the mass media to strengthening peace and international understanding, to the promotion of human rights and to countering racialism, apartheid and incitement to war. [Online]. Available: portal. unesco.org/en/ev.php-URL_ID=13176&URL_DO=DO_TOPIC&URL_ SECTION=201.html [Accessed 19 September 2011].

Ury, William (2001). *Must we fight? From the battlefield to the schoolyard-a new perspective on violent conflict and its prevention.* New York: John Wiley & Sons.

Walzer, Michael (1992). *Just and unjust wars: a moral argument with historical illustrations.* 2nd edn. New York: Basic Books.

Wheeler, Nicholas (1999). Enforcing human rights. In Timothy Dunne & Nicholas Wheeler (Eds). *Human rights and global politics* (pp169–99). Cambridge: Cambridge University Press.

# Chapter 4

## Empathy and ethics: journalistic representation and its consequences

*Annabel McGoldrick*

Peace journalism was first proposed by Johan Galtung, as a development from his landmark essay published with Mari Holmboe Ruge in 1965, 'The structure of foreign news'. It takes the form of a set of recommendations for reporters and editors – 'the policy implications of the [1965] study', (Lynch & Galtung 2010, p10) – that have, over the last decade or more, been taken up by journalism advocates and professional trainers, and have also latterly been critically examined by scholarly researchers. Peace journalism claims to be a fairer and more accurate way of representing conflicts than the predominant strain of reporting, in most media, most of the time, which it identifies as 'war journalism'. PJ is normative and value-explicit: if implemented more widely in professional practice, its advocates say, it would lessen the influence of media in favour of violence and create social capital for peace, which is to be preferred.

To these claims, this chapter will examine whether it is possible to add another: that peace journalism produces more authentic and more healthy representations of human behaviour in conflict, enabling its audiences to respond, and make meanings, with parts of their relational instincts and meaning-making capacities that are habitually suppressed. Emerging evidence is considered, from neuroscience and several other fields, that we are 'soft-wired for empathy' (Rifkin 2009), a facet of human nature that scholarship in general – and science in particular – generally underplays, by focusing wholly on the functioning of the left hemisphere of the brain (McGilchrist 2010). These scientific propositions about our humanness provide further validation for peace journalism. In this chapter, I consider this evidence and what it adds to the peace journalism critique of mainstream news.

As a psychotherapist working in addiction recovery for the past ten years, I have witnessed at first hand, violent, aggressive, drunk and drugged people transform into caring, compassionate individuals. Change in such cases is predicated on challenging addictive behaviour by putting down drugs and alcohol, but that change is only maintained when they begin to see themselves and the world differently: to put on, in a metaphor favoured in the field, 'a new pair of glasses' ('C' 2003 [1955]). These people learn how to alter their perception of reality and become conscious of their own meaning-making process. Part of that transition is for them to acquire – or the therapist to impart – the concept of reality as multiperspectival: they can have a 'different reality' from someone else, and still stay in relationship with them.

The second, complementary step is to 'switch on' their instinct to empathise with the other. The self-help group Alcoholics Anonymous, whose formation was listed by *Time Magazine* as one of the 80 most important moments in human history (Poniewozick 2003), also heals through empathy, which is a remarkable quality to witness, especially where previously only violence and aggression were evident. It's a vivid illustration of a proposition I shall draw on in this study, that human beings are naturally fitted for, and inclined to, empathy in our relationships with others – a quality that can therefore be quite readily reached and activated even in highly disturbed, apparently maladjusted individuals.

Peace journalism embodies, and equips readers and audiences to apply, that same multiperspectival approach, prompting and enabling us to connect empathically with events we are not personally participating in, and with actors apparently at far remove. We can, if supplied with the right cues and clues, imagine ourselves 'in the shoes' of people in the news, even when we cannot, by definition, be there in person. To 'focus on suffering all over [and] on people peacemakers, giving voice to the voiceless' is, according to Galtung, one of the four main distinguishing features of peace journalism. Another is its 'truth orientation', which

Lynch (2008) has updated to denote forms and tactics of reporting that draw attention to dominant iterations of meaning, and enable us to inspect them from the outside, negotiating our own reading in the process.

Research in the growing field of peace journalism has adopted and elaborated a normative preference for 'nonviolent responses to conflict' (Lynch & McGoldrick 2005, p6). In Johan Galtung's original table setting out the peace journalism schema, the characteristics of peace journalism appear on the right-hand side; those of 'war/violence journalism' (Galtung 1998) on the left. Lynch and Galtung comment:

> The position taken here is not that good reporting on conflict is some kind of compromise with a little from the left hand column and a little from the right. The position taken is in favour of the second column, peace journalism, and against war journalism (Lynch & Galtung 2010, p15).

Elsewhere, Lynch defends this value-explicit stance as 'instrumental'; enabling journalism to deliver on 'internal goals [of] fairness and accuracy' (Lynch 2008, p4). Fairness because, peace journalism scholars argue, media conventions generally predispose the news, in most places, most of the time, to a predominance of war journalism, thus depriving peace of its chance. Accuracy because, while peace initiatives broadly defined, are present in all conflicts, they are usually excluded from the representations of those conflicts furnished by the news. Adopting a deliberate creative strategy, to seek them out and remit them into the public sphere, restores an important missing element.

As well as through scholarly research, the peace journalism field has developed through training and social movement activism, usually with a sense of swimming upstream against the current of established assumptions about the role of journalism, and the capacities and preferences of readers and audiences. Journalists' assumptions about audience preferences, and traditional news factors like 'simplification vs complexity', Kempf writes, 'are more compatible with escalation oriented than with de-escalation oriented coverage' (Kempf 2007, p138). The feeling is often that peace journalism advocacy amounts to a call for something to be imposed on 'normal' journalism; to offer an 'artificial prescription', in David Loyn's words; one that is 'uniquely unhelpful' (Loyn 2007, p2).

The contribution of this chapter is to add another layer to the claims of peace journalism to be preferred as a set of precepts and methods for representing conflict; and to be regarded as more conducive, not only to the social goal of peace (and as fair and accurate in respect of its subject matter), but also to the needs and instincts of its publics – publics that are human beings, not simply rational beings, but emotional too.

It is inaccurate to represent human responses and motivations, in situations of conflict, without allowing for this. Furthermore, the dominant representations of war journalism, being 'dehumanizing of "them"', abrogate and suppress a key part of our meaning-making and relational capacity.

The influence of war journalism therefore shrinks and distorts the social reality we shape and inhabit. Our reality is constructed through relationships, not separate from relationships. How we behave in relationships, as a result, is determined by the meanings we make. Responses in relationships can be cooperative and empathic, or competitive, suspicious and ultimately violent. With events and people we have not experienced personally, that relationship is necessarily formed and developed through media. This chapter draws together evidence to argue that peace journalism offers a more authentic and beneficial representation of human relations in conflict.

## A challenge to realism(s)

'They are our representatives, and where we can't be, they can be'. Stuart Hall is speaking about politicians, in a lecture for the Media Education Foundation. The ability to speak and act on behalf of other people is one of the meanings encapsulated in the word 'representation', he suggests. The other is 'the notion that something was there already and, through the media, has been *re*presented' (Hall 1997).

The stress on the first syllable is from Hall's original. A critical consideration of journalism, especially journalism about conflict, foregrounds yet a third meaning to go with the two proposed (only to be 'subverted') in the lecture, and it argues for the emphasis of the syllables to be reversed. Reports from battle-zones have concentrated increasingly on re-*present*-ing, dramatising a sense of excitement that we can be 'virtually there', albeit with a characteristically restricted view, down a gun barrel or missile sight. In Operation Desert Storm, the campaign to eject the forces of Saddam Hussein from Kuwait in 1991, pictures from the nose-cones of guided missiles, carrying out 'surgical strikes', played to a video game generation. In the invasion of 2003, embedded camera crews brought point-of-view shots of actual firefights to a 'first-person shooter' computer game generation.

Ottosen shows how 'the political and economic roots of computer games on war are entrenched in the military-industrial complex and the defence industry' (Ottosen 2008, p73), arguing that these play an increasingly important role as a recruiting tool and a means of disseminating war propaganda. Der Derian goes so far as to postulate 'a paradox … that the closer the war game [is] able to technically reproduce the reality of war, the greater the dangers that might arise from confusing one with the other' (Der Derian 2009, p14).

Audiences in the rich countries that engage in what Der Derian says is presented as 'virtuous war', are immersed in images that offer to reproduce the experience of waging it; especially as it is increasingly carried out from within a virtual realm, with remote-controlled drones bombing faraway places at the click of a mouse. War is being made 'present', in 'real' time, thanks to computer games, 24-hour news and the internet: a signifier lifted to a new position of prominence in the culture because it is attended by a feeling of accessible authenticity.

To adapt Der Derian's paradox still further, the virtual representation of war draws on, and reinforces, a realist view of conflict. Lord Palmerston, the 19th-century British Foreign Secretary and exponent of gunboat diplomacy, encapsulated this doctrine in a formula that is usually paraphrased as 'nations have no permanent friends, only permanent interests'. The realist paradigm of international relations constructs interests in conflict as phenomena confined and defined by state borders. Wars start when states declare them, in pursuit of their interests, and peace is what prevails when they cease firing.

Inscribed in this paradigm is the extension, to the imagined community of a nation, of a set of propositions about human nature, formulated by philosophers such as Hobbes and Descartes. The Cartesian dichotomy of mind and body exalted 'reason' above 'passion', which threatened to distort 'logical' thought. In the empiricist school, 'hard evidence', available through sensory contact with the material world, was valued above 'mere sentiment'. In *Leviathan*, Hobbes (1982 [1651]) developed his famous argument that the deterrent effect of a social contract is necessary to forestall a 'war of all, against all' as individuals pursue their narrowly defined, selfish interests. This can be – and, in the realist school, often is – conceived in analogous terms in the context of international relations. The United Nations, Galtung observes, has 'a Security Council (not Peace, or Peace and Security, Council)', based, as it is, on 'a security approach [that] sees some party as a threat to be deterred or eliminated' (Galtung 2007, p14).

One notable omission from this picture is any notion of empathy. Between them, the rationalist and materialist philosophies of 17th-century Europe instilled a cultural bias in favour of assumptions that human beings are essentially self-interested, and that appeals to friendship, emotional responses and fellow-feeling can be relegated (as means of explaining and regulating our behaviour) below what can be seen, measured and 'optimised' in a competitive world. The latter qualities are constructed as more realistic, more authentic to our true nature. This bias remains pervasive, in the mainstream of academic disciplines such as economics and political science, as well as international relations: all, coincidentally or not, fields of scholarship influential on journalism.

Objections to the realist paradigm often originate in the critical discourses that have successfully challenged it in other sections of academia, namely structuralism and post-structuralism. Within the field of journalism, these have supplied conceptual underpinnings for the movement, of ideas, social movement campaigns, professional training and, latterly, academic research interests, known as peace journalism. It has been articulated in calls for a critical self-awareness to be built into the job of reporting. 'Of course reporters should report, as truthfully as they can', Lynch says, 'the facts they encounter; only ask, as well, how they have come to meet these particular facts, and how the facts have come to meet them' (Lynch 2008, p4). Peace journalism is explicit in its commitment to get beyond 'the way it is' – the evidence immediately at hand to the reporter in the field – to enable readers and audiences to negotiate readings of 'how and why it came to be that way' (Lynch & McGoldrick 2005, p214) – and how it could be different.

However, efforts to promote such insights often call to mind Barbie Zelizer's observation about 'interpretive communities' (Zelizer 2004) that tend to talk past each other, inhabiting, perhaps, what CP Snow identified as the 'two cultures' of intellectual life – the sciences and humanities. David Loyn, the BBC reporter and leading critic of peace journalism, appealed to scientistic concepts of knowledge and evidence in his attempt to disprove its claims (Loyn 2007). Thus it is significant to find a challenge to realism, and validation for empathy, emerging from its own 'home ground' of the natural sciences.

## Empathy

In *The empathic civilisation*, Jeremy Rifkin subjects the inherited assumptions from rationalist and empiricist philosophies to critical examination, drawing on evidence from multiple sources, including a discovery by scientists at an Italian laboratory of connections in the brain they called 'mirror neurons'. Purely by accident, researchers found that when a monkey ate a peanut, the same parts of the monkey's brain lit up as when it watched a researcher eat a peanut. Giacomo Rizzolatti says what is most striking is that '[m]irror neurons allow us to grasp the minds of others not through conceptual reasoning but through direct simulation. By feeling not by thinking' (in Rifkin 2009, p83). We learn through mimicry – 'monkey see, monkey do' – and we feel what others are feeling in the same way. These have been dubbed empathy neurons, or 'Gandhi neurons', because their existence appears to validate claims that we humans – as individuals and, by extension, collectively – are capable of setting aside our own narrow self-interest, in order to put ourselves in others' shoes, utilising our emotions.

McGilchrist produces a reading of 'Western civilisation' as having been based on misplaced assumptions about the sovereignty of conscious reasoning, situated in the left hemisphere of the brain, in shaping human responses:

> [I]n the context of intellectual discourse we are always obliged to 'look at' the relationship of cognition to affect from the cognitive point of view ... Asking cognition, however, to give a perspective on the relationship between cognition and affect is like asking an astronomer in the pre-Galilean geocentric world whether, in his opinion, the sun moved round the earth or the earth round the sun. To ask the question alone would be enough to label one as mad. (McGilchrist 2010, p186)

Affect and emotions are experienced by the right hemisphere of the brain, which sees the whole and the context. Our awareness is about the interaction of both hemispheres – the left hemisphere sees the detail, is rigid, and is concerned with possession and manipulation. However, right hemisphere representations of reality have, McGilchrist argues, been subjugated by a dominant left hemisphere.

The counterpart of the evermore sophisticated 'simulation' of warfare, Der Derian writes, is 'media dissimulation' (Der Derian 2009, p264) over what Lynch, in reviewing his book, calls 'the grim reality of thousands killed' (Lynch 2009) when the weapons actually land. 'Dehumanization of "them"' is a standard propaganda tactic, and a staple of war journalism (Galtung 1998), used to inure target populations to campaigns of organised violence, implying that our empathic capacities have to be nullified, in order to enable us to go along with it. In a different setting – the US prison system – Ari Cowan, who devised a prevention and restoration model for intervention to lessen incidents of violence, finds that: 'Central to human ability to commit acts of violence is an "objectification/action" process in which the recipient of violence must be converted conceptually from a human being to an object' (Cowan 2011).

Reverse this conceptual conversion, Cowan has found, by reactivating our empathic connection with one another, and the incidence of violence falls steeply. Realism – in both senses, of the dominant international relations paradigm and the apparent re-*present*-ing brought about by innovations in war reporting – may not be as 'realistic' as is commonly supposed, since both depend on suppressing a substantial segment of reality in the way we relate to one another as human beings.

Then, we have been taught to mistrust our feeling selves, Rifkin writes, by psychoanalysis, where Freud's postulation of our aggressive 'drive', *thanatos*, required *catharsis* to render it manageable in everyday life. (Perhaps those violent computer games are good for us after all!) However, Freud may have simply missed a vitally important part of being human – the empathy. He mistook the bond between mother and child as satisfying the child's libido, discussing the infant feeding with its mother: 'I cannot discover this oceanic feeling in myself' (in Rifkin 2009, p52). (Perhaps it is purely coincidental that Descartes' mother died when he was a baby, and that Hobbes was born prematurely to a mother terror-stricken by news of the Spanish Armada on the way to invade England, and abandoned by his father at a tender age.)

My work as a psychotherapist has brought me into contact with research on child development, which has emphasised the primary importance of the attachment between child and mother, the formation of which then shapes the way we form relationships for the rest of our lives. When that attachment is not formed, the child can feel a deep sense of abandonment and act that out in later life. Results can include pathologies leading to obsession, addiction and antisocial behaviour. One study in the 1960s assessed babies into adulthood, and found that the more securely attached infants grew up to be more sociable adults, a general rule observed in countless individual cases by care workers such as Camila Batmanghelidjh, who set up Kids Company in London, in 1995.

[If] you actually look at what neuroscience is telling us about the way children's brains develop', she said in a recent interview, 'it is absolutely evident that the frontal lobe, which is the area responsible for pro-social behaviour and assessing consequences of your action doesn't develop robustly in males until they're 27 and in females until they're 25. (Batmanghelidjh 2010)

She continues:

> Neuroscience is saying the quality of attachment relationship that is
> provided for you sculpts your ability to control your behaviour, plan
> and be pro-social. It's saying if children are frightened and terrorised
> and impoverished nutritionally then there is an impact on the way
> their brain develops. It doesn't mean that we can't correct their
> behaviour, but we can't hold them criminally responsible at age ten.
> No child is born a criminal or a killer, any child who commits a crime,
> there is a legacy of crimes committed against that child, prior to the
> time they got to be the perpetrator. (Batmanghelidjh 2010)

Rifkin argues that many fields of research are simultaneously
supplying evidence that humans are 'soft-wired for empathy'. For
whatever reason, Freud's propositions about what 'really' determines
our responses – that human nature is aggressive and sexually driven
– are based on observations of pathologies, or at least a 'secondary
movement' after our primary movement towards nurture, relationship,
empathy and connection was not fulfilled in infancy.

The successful treatment of patients with addictions, referred
to above, has been based on treating the addiction as an attachment
disorder; in other words, the secondary movement of the person with
an addiction is towards a self-destructive behaviour. They are only
able to make that primary movement towards relationship, empathy
and connection in adulthood, by first attaching to a self-help group or
therapist – effectively being 're-parented' – before going on, in many
cases, to lead normal healthy lives, based on a reactivated capacity for
empathy and care for others. 'AA bridged the gap', Rifkin says:

> between the object relationship theorists and behaviouralists, by
> acknowledging the critical relational and emotional aspects of social
> well-being and the important role that empathic engagement plays in
> recovery, while at the same time creating a twelve-step program that
> contained elements of behavioural conditioning. (Rifkin 2009, p400)

'Some of the claims of peace journalism', Lynch and McGoldrick
write (2010, p95), 'are realist ... in the sense of fidelity' to a pre-existing

reality. Through its mission to 'highlight peace initiatives' (Galtung 1998), peace journalism 'connect[s] with visions and creative ideas for peace' (Lynch & McGoldrick 2010, p95) that are invariably present, in any conflict, but usually suppressed in media representations – the mainstream of 'war journalism' – which can therefore be seen as less accurate.

Among the other distinguishing features of peace journalism, in Galtung's original table, is its emphasis on the 'humanization of all sides' through 'empathy and understanding' (Galtung 1998). This, too, is therefore more realistic, both in the sense of depicting human relations and in the sense of prompting and enabling a response to the events and processes being depicted that is more authentic and more conducive to the needs and instincts of readers and audiences. Rifkin's narrative, re-examining dominant conceptual frames transmitted from various disciplines and discursive practices in light of multiple-sourced findings in support of an empathic human nature, may therefore be seen as lending a further authenticity-claim to peace journalism as a representation of conflicts and responses to them.

Lynch and McGoldrick draw attention to 'heroes of nonviolence': some wellknown, but others generally under-appreciated in their influence on our lives, because of 'cultural phenomena' such as the preponderance of depictions of violent heroes on American-made children's television programs (Lynch & McGoldrick 2005, p78). More coverage, not only of the Nelson Mandelas and Mother Teresas of this world, but also less heralded nonviolent change agents – such as those featured in chapter 12 of the present volume by Elissa Tivona – would contribute towards rebalancing a presently distorted picture.

For adult audiences, of course, our allegiances are manipulated in more sophisticated and often more ambivalent ways. In *Silence of the lambs*, serial killer Hannibal Lecter is consulted by FBI agent Clarice Starling because only he 'really' knows what is 'really' going on: his depravity having stripped away the 'illusions' the rest of us find necessary to carry on living. Anthony Hopkins' mesmeric portrayal seeps into us deviously; his is hardly a view of human nature that we would accept as 'the whole story', and yet – by squeezing out empathy

– the conventions of war reporting effectively conceptualise the human beings on the 'other' side – the 'Taliban', to take a current example – in the manner of a serial killer sizing up potential victims.

British psychologist Simon Baron-Cohen has suggested that we may substitute the words 'zero empathy' for 'evil' (Baron-Cohen 2011) and that people who perpetrate acts of violence without conscience – whether they be US soldiers, the Taliban, or Nazis exterminating Jews in the Holocaust – be regarded as having 'zero degrees of empathy'. The point is, we should be assessing anything that causes empathy-erosion – like war journalism – and seeking to reduce it.

Peace journalism, by humanising 'them', fires the mirror neurons and creates the scope for more mimicry and repetition. Among the research data adduced by Rifkin are findings that television viewers' facial expressions even match those of people they are viewing. These, in turn, echo findings from experiments on the psychological phenomenon of merging: asking people to put themselves in someone else's shoes, then write a 'day in the life' of, respectively, a senior, a cheerleader and a university professor (Galinsky et al. 2005). Participants unconsciously mirrored the behaviour and perceptions of their model: the first was observed to walk noticeably more slowly, the second saw herself as more physically attractive, and the third performed better in intelligence tests.

The relation between what we watch and the way we think, feel and behave may not be linear, or direct. But the explosion of evidence, appearing simultaneously in many fields, for believing that we are, in Rifkin's terms, soft-wired for empathy, may further explain the findings of my own earlier study (McGoldrick 2008) based on interviews with subjects about their experience of watching news in general, and about the distinctions in the peace journalism model in particular. In it, I quote Rollo May's study of our modern quest for meaning (May 1991, p134). May characterises Heidegger's theories as having 'made care (*sorge*) the basis of being: without care, our selves shrink up, we lose our capacity to will as well as our selfhood'.

In McGilchrist's account, the capacity for caring is situated in the right hemisphere of the brain, which gives the context, sees the whole, the big picture, while the left supplies language and sequence, being concerned with manipulation, possession, rivalry and power. Too much news 'gives us a long list of problems with no opportunities for us to *apply* our care', I argued, thus addressing only the left hemisphere. As a result, subjects in my study reported strong, overwhelmingly negative responses: the experience of watching news triggered 'lingering feelings of depression, helplessness, hopelessness and alienation' (McGoldrick 2008, p94). News about conflict, particularly war reporting, which is presented as such a realistic portrayal of such an authentic human experience, may actually be harmful to consumers precisely because it subjugates and misleadingly 'frames out' a substantial portion of human nature.

Indeed, journalism, as a report of 'just the facts' – which could therefore be construed as a Hobbesian practice – comes with the same, familiar in-built bias against empathy. The unrealistic human relations it constructs – and to which it contributes – can be glimpsed in the infamous picture of a starving Sudanese girl, watched over by a waiting vulture, that appeared in *The New York Times* (Carter 1993). The photographer Kevin Carter won a Pulitzer Prize, but unlike his fellow journalists, readers were less interested in the technical quality of the picture and more interested in what happened to the child.

In an editors' note four days after the photo first appeared, *The Times* said: 'The photographer reports that she recovered enough to resume her trek after the vulture was chased away. It is not known whether she reached the [relief] center' (in Moeller 1999, p148). Two months after receiving his Pulitzer, Carter would be dead of carbon-monoxide poisoning in Johannesburg, a suicide at 33. Did he lack the empathy to put down his camera and help her? His role as a journalist mandated a 'detachment' from his own feelings. Did the guilt of that contribute to his death? He told a friend: 'I'm really, really sorry I didn't pick up the child' (in Moeller 1999, p40). The science of trauma tells us that post-traumatic stress disorder (PTSD) is much more likely if people are unable to make sense, and a meaningful outcome, from a horrific incident. If you witness an atrocity and feel empathy for someone, then if you can somehow involve yourself in helping them – saving their lives, as in the case of the Sudanese girl, or joining in, however vicariously, efforts to prevent a repetition of such incidents – you are much less likely to develop PTSD, because the event thereby acquires more meaning.

## Group responses

If particular patterns of news reporting – encapsulated in Galtung's description of war journalism – can be regarded, on this basis, as potentially harmful on an individual basis, separate research has highlighted the importance of our empathic capacity, conveyed through mirror neurons, in governing group responses. If someone watches a report of an atrocity against another group – a white European, say, watches coverage of the bombing of Gaza, *with a Palestinian* – they are likely to feel the same feelings as the Palestinians (Argo et al. 2009, p30).

And this works the other way too: in experiments at MIT and Harvard – funded by Queen Noor of Jordan and Richard Branson – subjects have been shown to respond to an attack on a member of a group with which they identify by wanting 'revenge', more than if the attack is made upon them personally. Many researchers have made the link between group status, sense of self and personal self-esteem. Examples include the 1992 Los Angeles race riots where TV news showed repeated images of Rodney King being beaten by police officers – officers who were later acquitted in court. More recently, studies on the radicalisation of militants in Iraq have linked it to the humiliating images of prisoners in Abu Ghraib being mistreated by US soldiers.

Similar findings were repeated in laboratory conditions when 240 people in Boston watched violent vignettes:

> First, subjects were more likely to report a desire to retaliate at the perpetrator when their friend was the injured party than when they themselves were slighted or harmed. This finding was strongest for men, and strongest for subjects under age 30. Second, females were more likely to report that the perpetrator deserved to have retribution meted upon him when a group member was the injured party than when they themselves were. (Argo et al. 2009, p28)

Is it possible that these responses might now be more widespread and more rapid because of intensified media coverage? Here's the view of a young Palestinian in the occupied territories:

The difference between the first intifada and the second is television. Before, I knew when we were attacked here, or in a nearby camp, but the reality of the attacks everywhere else was not so clear. Now, I cannot get away from Israel – the TV brings them into my living room … And you can't turn the TV off. How could you live with yourself? At the same time, you can't ignore the problem – what are you doing to protect your people? We live with an internal struggle. Whether you choose to fight or not, every day is this internal struggle. (in Argo et al. 2009, p9)

Significant in this context is evidence that group information is processed in emotional centres of the brain. 'That is, group-related reasoning and perception may well be implicit, emotional, and untouchable via traditional cognitive and rational approaches' (Argo et al. 2009, p33). This holds profound implications for considerations of media influence on the actions and motivations of parties to conflict, whether direct or indirect, linear or extra-linear. It suggests we are more likely to find differential group responses to media representations of conflict through adjusting the more emotional, less explicit content, than the more cognitive, fact-based elements: revealing elements of context and background through telling a story based on human interest, perhaps.

A study of reader responses to crime stories in a US university showed greater receptiveness to 'peaceful' policy prescriptions – in the sense of attending to structural causes – among students whose empathic responses had been evoked by the news being framed in ways very similar to the peace journalism method for reporting conflicts. The Berkeley Media Studies Group, a lobby group for public health and social issues, carried out training with journalists in the newsrooms of five metropolitan newspapers. As with the experience of peace journalism training, participants were sometimes 'defensive and bristly', but many still said it had an effect on how they would cover crime in the future (Thorson et al. 2001, p414).

Precepts for the training were derived from the public health model of violence, adopted officially in the US by Surgeon General C Everett Koop in the 1980s, since the time when violence prevention became the domain of public health departments (Thorson et al. 2003, p53). In this model, death from violent crime is seen as preventable if the underlying causes are investigated, such as availability of alcohol, guns, unemployment, racial discrimination, violence in the media, lack of education, abuse as a child, witnessing violence, and male dominance over females. Researchers found that readers of crime stories framed with this public health model are more likely to be less blaming of the perpetrators and look to societal causes and want holistic social/political initiatives to address those causes (Thorson et al. 2003, p53).

'A good reporter does not stop a story of two cars shocking, known as a collision', Lynch and Galtung write, 'with an account of those killed or wounded, and material damage' (2010, p3). In an analogy intended to validate the peace journalism approach to reporting conflict, they go on to recommend consideration of the human cost of the rush-hour effect, with everyone attempting to drive to work at the same time and even – if alcohol is involved – the underlying reasons why people, in the society under discussion, use alcohol inappropriately or excessively. This, they say, is essential if journalism is 'to make the world transparent, unveiling causal chains' (Lynch & Galtung 2010, p4).

This is, in fact, an example of how expanding and spreading understanding of what Lynch and Galtung call the 'condition–consequence' relationship – the process leading up to an event – actually helped to bring about a change in outcomes. Until the 1960s, traffic accidents in the US were simply blamed on 'the nut behind the wheel' (Coleman & Thorson 2002, p403). Then 'the media began to include the type of cars involved, road and weather conditions, and whether people were driving drunk or wearing seatbelts'. It helped to create demand for safety features to be added to cars, for the wearing of seatbelts, and raised the social pressure against drink-driving – and the number of accidents fell.

## Ethics and consequences

Shinar (2007, p200) put forward a set of five headings for exercises in content analysis to identify and recognise peace journalism

1. Exploring backgrounds and contexts of conflict formation, and presenting causes and options on every side so as to portray conflict in realistic terms transparent to the audience

2. Giving voice to the views of all rival parties

3. Offering creative ideas for conflict resolution, peacemaking and peacekeeping

4. Exposing lies, cover-up attempts and culprits on all sides, and revealing excesses committed by, and suffering inflicted on, peoples of all parties

5. Paying attention to peace stories and postwar developments.

These all require and activate empathy in regarding and analysing conflicts, just like the reporting of road accidents, in allowing for a cataclysm, or an act of direct violence, to emerge from a background and provide a context resulting in an effort to understand how the perpetrators could have been brought to commit it. If the perpetrator is simply a 'nut', behaving with no discernible reason, then it apparently makes no sense to reason with them: for there to be scope for creative ideas of conflict resolution, there has to be an intelligible cause–consequence chain, and, for that to emerge, all parties – 'them' as well as 'us' – have to have a voice.

War journalism, on the other hand, in the original schema by Johan Galtung (in Lynch & McGoldrick 2005, p6), is journalism orientated:

- towards violence

- towards propaganda

- towards elites

- towards victory.

Why should the former be adopted, over the latter? When I was chairing the Reporting the World meetings in London in 2001 – a series of reflective discussions for professional journalists about their coverage of particular conflicts – a senior editor at the BBC World Service said:

> I do think there's a danger of seeing a coincidence of interest between people engaged in conflict resolution, and the media. Conflict resolution is something on which I report, not something in which I engage. A side-effect of my reporting may be that it makes conflict resolution harder or easier, but that's a judgment that is made after our reporting. (Bob Jobbins in Lynch 2002, p24)

This is the journalistic ethics of duty, or conviction – to report 'without fear or favour', in the classic phrase. It is the reporter's duty *not* to empathise, not to consider how he or she may be involved in the story or consider how the reporting may be adjusted, in advance, in light of any such involvement. This deontological ethic of journalism can, Lynch and McGoldrick suggest, be conceptualised with reference to the universalising principle of Immanuel Kant: 'I ought never to act, except in such a way that I would will that my maxim [in so acting] could become a universal law'.

However, journalism is 'always already' involved, Lynch and McGoldrick say – explicitly adopting a characteristic formula of the critical discourse of post-structuralism – in a 'feedback loop of cause and effect'. They quote Max Weber's concept of an 'ethic of responsibility', a teleological ethic, as the appropriate governing principle.

> One should take into account the *foreseeable* consequences of one's actions, [Weber] argued, and adjust one's behaviour accordingly – it is foreseeability that confers responsibility. A deontological journalistic ethic is, in this sense, merely a teleological one 'in waiting' – waiting for a convincing explanation of the relations of cause and effect. (Lynch & McGoldrick 2005, p218)

That explanation becomes more convincing when considering the rapidly growing body of evidence that war journalism, the dominant mode of news reporting, influenced, through different means of transmission, by Hobbesian empiricism and Cartesian rationality – both of which relegate empathic, emotional responses – has identifiable consequences, for both individual psychological wellbeing and group receptiveness to particular policy prescriptions.

If peace journalism can offer us more empathic responses to conflict, more examples of those working cooperatively for bridge-building or human rights, we have more behaviours to mirror. Whereas the exponents of war journalism can no longer hide behind claims that we cannot foresee the consequences of reporting in that way, this same evidence supports the claim that both war and peace journalism deserve their name: in general, the one makes more violence more likely, whereas the other makes it less likely. Journalism cannot be regarded as 'detached' – it is implicated in cycles of cause and effect.

It is in this context, among other senses, that Hall's less 'literal' concept of representation, set out in his lecture, acquires particular resonance. Representation is not separate from the event, he says, but 'constitutive' of it: 'one of its conditions of existence'. And it's interesting for our discussion that Mikhail Bakhtin, whose work is often seen as a forerunner of structuralism and post-structuralism, articulated his own philosophy of human nature in explicitly empathetic terms:

> To *be* means to *communicate* ... To be means to be for another, and through the other, for oneself. A person has no internal sovereign territory, he is wholly and always on the boundary; looking inside himself, he looks *into the eyes of another* or *with the eyes of another*. (in Rifkin 2009, p147)

The rhetorical connection with state sovereignty, which is the basis for the realist paradigm in international relations, is a clue as to the resonance of Bakhtin's insight for the entire philosophical tradition that Rifkin, McGilchrist and others are now reworking in light of these recent findings.

Clifford Christians argues from a standpoint of 'philosophical anthropology' (2010, p16) that peace journalism calls on the journalist's 'liberal self', based on 'social contract theory', transmitted from Hobbes through the work of such thinkers as Locke, Rousseau and Rawls. But the nature of journalism, and its inescapable involvement with causes and consequences, demands revision of the concept of self at the heart

140

of this theory: the 'Robinson Crusoe' figure alone on an island (Christians 2010, p17). Instead, Christians posits a 'relational self', which fits much better with the new paradigm of empathy. He writes:

> In addition to this demanding agenda – one could argue, our first order of business – peace journalism must transform its philosophy of the human. Rather than presuming the liberal/contractual self, the foundation of the new thinking is holistic humanness where community is ontologically and axiologically prior to persons. When we start intellectually with humans-in-relation, the golden rule becomes a credible normative standard for both the general morality and professional journalism ethics in this contentious age. (Christians 2010, p28)

## Conclusion

Peace journalism sets up a binary opposition, directing our attention to what is wrong with journalism as it has been practised, and enabling calls for its improvement. It creates a need and an incentive to find reasons why it should be preferred. The emergence of new evidence of our capacity for empathy, as part of holistic humanness, strengthens its claims. And the marshalling of that evidence into coherent challenges to the philosophical underpinnings of our inherited 'war system' – as per the work of Rifkin and McGilchrist – strengthens them still further, by tracing connections with the struggles underway around binary oppositions in other academic disciplines and in social movements.

For the journalist, rather than being asked to follow a prescribed set of ethical rules, mandating an unattainable aspiration to 'detachment', professionals can connect with, and trust, their most basic empathic human instinct to behave relationally, morally and ethically to inform and enlighten their audiences. In other words, peace journalism produces a more authentic and realistic representation of human relations in conflict, thereby offering humanity the best chance of being able to resolve differences nonviolently, and ultimately transform relationships into a more nurturing reality.

*References*

Argo, Nichole, Shamil Idriss & Mahnaz Fancy (2009). *Media and intergroup relations: research on media and social change.* Dubai: Alliance of Civilisations Media Fund.

Baron-Cohen, Simon (2011). The science of empathy. *The Observer*, 27 March.

Batmanghelidjh, Camila (2010). No child is born a criminal. In Natalie Hanman & Elliot Smith (Eds). *Hay Festival Video, The Guardian.* [Online]. Available: www.guardian.co.uk/commentisfree/video/2010/jun/05/child-criminal-camila-batmanghelidjh [Accessed 25 August 2011].

'C', Chuck 2003 [1955]. *A new pair of glasses.* Newport Beach, CA: New Look Publishing.

Carter, Kevin (1993). Vulture waits for starving girl. *The New York Times.* [Online]. Available: www.nytimes.com/imagepages/2009/04/15/arts/15jaar_CA0.ready.html [Accessed 25 August 2011].

Christians, Clifford (2010). Non-violence in philosophical and media ethics. In John Tulloch, Richard Keeble & Florian Zollmann (Eds). *Peace journalism, war and conflict resolution* (pp15–30). New York: Peter Lang Inc.

Coleman, Renita & Esther Thorson (2002). The effects of news stories that put crime and violence into context: testing the public health model of reporting. *Journal of Health Communication, 7*: 401–25.

Cowan, Ari (2011). *The violence integrative prevention and restoration (PAR) model.* [Online]. Spiritridge Institute. [Online]. Available: www.aricowan.net/pgs/par/01par.html [Accessed 25 July 2011].

Der Derian, James (2009). *Virtuous war: mapping the military-industrial media-entertainment network.* 2nd edn. New York: London: Routledge.

Galinsky, Adam, Gillian Ku & Cynthia Wang (2005). Perspective-taking and self–other overlap: fostering social bonds and facilitating social coordination. *Group Processes & Intergroup Relations, 8*(2): 109–24.

Galtung, Johan (2007). Introduction. Peace by peaceful conflict transformation: the transcend approach. In Johan Galtung & Charles

Webel (Eds). *Handbook of peace and conflict studies* (pp14–34). London: Routledge.

Galtung, Johan (1998). High road, low road – charting the course for peace journalism. *Track Two*, 7(4). [Online]. Available: www.ccr.uct.ac.za/archive/two/7_4/p07_highroad_lowroad.html [Accessed 25 August 2011].

Hall, Stuart (1997). *Representation and the media*. Media Education Foundation film, 55 minutes.

Hobbes, Thomas (1982) [1651]. *Leviathan*. Harmondsworth: Penguin.

Kempf, Wilhelm (2007). Two experiments focusing on de-escalation orientated coverage of post-war conflicts. In Dov Shinar & Wilhelm Kempf (Eds). *Peace journalism: the state of the art* (pp136–57). Berlin: Verlag Irena Regener.

Loyn, David (2007). Good journalism or peace journalism? *Conflict & Communication Online*, 6(2). [Online]. Available: www.cco.regener-online.de/2007_2/pdf/loyn.pdf [Accessed 25 July 2011].

Lynch, Jake (2009) *Review of Virtuous war, by James Der Derian*. [Online]. Available: www.warandmedia.org/reviews/book/derian.htm [Accessed 9 September 2011].

Lynch, Jake (2008). *Debates in peace journalism*. Sydney: Sydney University Press.

Lynch, Jake (2002). *Reporting the world a practical checklist for the ethical reporting of conflicts in the 21st century, produced by journalists, for journalists*. Taplow UK: Conflict and Peace Forums.

Lynch, Jake & Johan Galtung (2010). *Reporting conflict new directions in peace journalism*. St Lucia, Qld: University of Queensland Press.

Lynch, Jake & Annabel McGoldrick (2010). A global standard for reporting conflict and peace. In Richard Keeble, John Tulloch & Florian (Eds). *Peace journalism, war and conflict resolution* (pp87–104). New York: Peter Lang Inc.

Lynch, Jake & Annabel McGoldrick (2005). *Peace journalism*. Stroud: Hawthorn Press.

May, Rollo (1991). *The cry for myth*. New York: Delta.

McGilchrist, Iain (2010). *The master and his emissary: the divided brain and the making of the Western world*. New Haven: Yale University Press.

McGoldrick, Annabel (2008). Psychological effects of war journalism and peace journalism. *Peace and Policy*, 13: 86–98.

Moeller, Susan D (1999). *Compassion fatigue: how the media sell disease, famine, war and death*. New York: Routledge.

Ottosen, Rune (2008). Video games as war propaganda: can peace journalism offer an alternative approach? *Peace and Policy*, 13(1): 73–86.

Poniewozick, James (2003). 80 days that changed the world. *Time* Online edition. New York: Time Warner. Available at: www.time.com/time/magazine/article/0,9171,1004561,00.html [Accessed 10 January 2012].

Rifkin, Jeremy (2009). *The empathetic civilisation: the race to global consciousness in a world in crisis*. New York: Tarcher/Penguin.

Shinar, Dov (2007). Peace journalism: the state of the art. In Dov Shinar & Wilhelm Kempf (Eds). *Peace journalism: the state of the art* (pp199–210). Berlin: Verlag Irena Regener.

Thorson, Esther, Lori Dorfman & Jane Ellen Stevens (2003). Reporting crime and violence from a public health perspective. *Journal of the Institute of Justice and International Studies* 2: 53–66.

Thorson, Esther, Lori Dorfman & Jane Ellen Stevens (2001). Reporting on violence: bringing a public health perspective into the newsroom. *Health, Education & Behaviour*, 28: 402–19.

Zelizer, Barbie (2004). *Taking journalism seriously: news and the academy*. London: SAGE Publications.

# PART II

## CASE STUDIES: PEACE JOURNALISM IN WARTIME AND PEACEBUILDING

# Chapter 5

# Documenting war, visualising peace: towards peace photography

*Stuart Allan*

Engaging with peace journalism encourages one to pose awkward questions about familiar assumptions, to look afresh at reportorial conventions with enhanced self-reflexivity. This is as important for photojournalism as it is for other types of journalism, especially where its capacity to record distressing truths is concerned. For the photojournalist confronted with the challenge of bearing witness to violent conflict on our behalf, the effort to document its human consequences raises issues of perspective, judgment and interpretation. 'Photographers are many things – historians, dramatists, artists – and humanitarians', the photojournalist James Nachtwey recently observed. 'As journalists, one of their tasks is to reveal the unjust and the unacceptable, so that their images become an element in the process of change'. In this way, he added, photography 'gives a voice to the voiceless. It's a call to action' (2009, pp4–5).

Such a view renders problematic the longstanding principle that photojournalists must strive to be scrupulously impartial, an obligation to dispassionate relay recurrently expressed in the language of professionalism. At a time when the proliferation of digital technologies is helping to rewrite the relationship between professionals and their 'amateur' or 'citizen' counterparts, this priority acquires even greater salience. Still, one need not subscribe to a romanticised conception of the origins of photojournalism to appreciate that a pronounced reportorial ethic informed the ethos shared by many of its founding practitioners. To the extent that it is possible to discern the guiding tenets giving shape to photojournalism as a reportorial craft, it is striking to note how often a language of social – and moral – responsibility resonates within accounts from the outset (see Allan 2011). 'The earliest photojournalists [from the late 19th century] expected images of injustice to push viewers into action', Susie Linfield observes; 'photographs were regarded not as expressions of alienation but as interventions in the world' (2010, p59). From the vantage point of today, however, such ideals risk appearing naïve, even dangerous. As Linfield elaborates:

> To turn from the image and put right the world: this is the photographic ideal that still lives today. But like so many ideals, it has been chastened by experience. Now we know that pictures of affliction can be easily ignored – or, even worse, enjoyed. Now we know that photographs of suffering can be the start of human connection – and the endpoint to deadly fantasies of revenge. Now we know the fatal gaps that exist between seeing, caring, understanding, and acting. (2010, p60)

Important questions thus arise regarding 'our camera-mediated knowledge of war', to use Susan Sontag's phrase, which bring the exercise of communicative power to the fore. 'Look, the photographs say, *this* is what it's like. This is what war *does*. And *that*, that is what it does, too', she writes. 'War tears, rends. War rips open, eviscerates. War scorches. War dismembers. War *ruins*' (2003, p7). Such imagery, it follows, invites a shared stance or point of view with the photographer, regardless of its implicit claim of being a 'record of the real' faithful to journalistic impartiality. The ways in which a photograph of an atrocity privileges a moment, effectively making 'real' events which 'we' might otherwise choose to ignore, is as much a question of framing (including but also, by definition, excluding) as it is of objectification. Such photographs 'give rise to opposing responses,' Sontag points out; 'A call for peace. A cry for revenge. Or simply the bemused awareness, continually restocked by photographic information, that terrible things happen' (2003, pp11–12). In each instance, photography makes possible the means to apprehend – at a distance – other people's pain, with all of the moral implications such a form of spectatorship engenders.

Accordingly, this chapter signals its intention to contribute to this book's strategic agenda by exploring the significance of photographic images in reportorial terms. Realising this objective is not as straightforward as it may sound. When considering journalistic narratives of violence, it is worth noting the extent to which corresponding forms of news imagery have recurrently eluded sustained scrutiny. Here we recall Rune Ottosen's suggestion that 'in promoting a peace journalism strategy, more emphasis should be placed on visual elements' (2007, p2). He points to the ways in which internet-based digital technology 'offers new methods for mobilising sympathy for human suffering through visual documentation', thereby better enabling peace journalism to 'focus on the "true face" of war when the media fail to do so' (2007, p14). Similarly Frank Möller (2008) contends that peace studies 'have as yet been quite unaware of visual culture', not least with regard to how 'pictorial memory' – by which he means 'the huge reservoir of images that every person carries with them' – shapes our interpretation of incoming visual information. Previous exposure to images influences perceptions of new occurrences, yet he observes that the importance of photography in this regard has been largely ignored by peace researchers. Barbie Zelizer makes the further point that scholars have failed to fully grasp the ways in which photographs articulate a 'subjunctive voice' in the visual representation of death. 'Viewing death has long been associated with voyeuristic spectacles of suffering', she points out, 'where looking at those dead or about to die constitutes a public duty, often of an involuntary nature [...] and with an invitation to either empathise or dissociate' (2010, p25). Delving more deeply into this process of meaning-making, she suggests, promises to help reveal the extent to which opportunities for emotional engagement find expression in representational terms (see also Guerin & Hallas 2007).

At stake, then, is the need to reconsider war photography anew. This chapter, in seeking to disrupt the ideological purchase of its accustomed norms, values and priorities, aims to secure the conceptual space necessary to explore its capacity to visualise peace. Several examples will be scrutinised over the course of this discussion with a view to distinguishing the reportorial tensions negotiated by the photographer striving to bear witness. On this basis, it shall be argued that a photojournalism committed to peace raises pressing concerns about the re-mediation of discursive power, a process that will be shown to be uneven, contingent and frequently the site of resistance from those whose interests are called into question.

## 'Your photos pose a threat to us'

Typically working under intense pressure, photojournalists in today's conflict zones are recurrently forced to negotiate a range of formidable challenges. Longstanding professional ideals are certain to prove conditional upon the ad hoc negotiation of conflicting demands, not least where the perceived benefits of rolling deadlines, processing speed and heightened immediacy effectively streamline decision-making processes (see also Matheson & Allan 2009). Photojournalists 'embedded' with US or British troops in Iraq, for example, have evidently welcomed the mobility afforded by portable digital technologies (the capacity to relay images while travelling, for example, being a critical consideration when personal safety is threatened), yet recognise that the sheer range and volume of such images risks denying them sufficient explanatory context. Moreover, what the 'embed' gains by way of access to the war zone is countered, in turn, by a corresponding loss of journalistic independence, not least when photographs are perceived to have contravened the tacit rules of sanitisation enforced by military minders. Even the 'unilateral' photographer working without the benefits of military access or protection is likely to test the limits of what are relative freedoms at risk of censure on the basis of their images' possible impact on public support for the war.

A case in point is the experience of freelance photographer Zoriah Miller, who found himself barred from covering the US Marines in Iraq after he posted photos on the internet of three soldiers killed by a suicide bomber (having first waited for their families to be notified). 'It is absolutely censorship', he stated at the time. 'I took pictures of something they didn't like, and they removed me. Deciding what I can and cannot document, I don't see a clearer definition of censorship' (cited in

Kamber & Arango 2008). In a recent interview, Miller (2010) explained what he seeks to achieve as a photojournalist:

> I hope that my photographs make people think a bit about what it is like for others around the world. It is so easy to get caught up in our own lives, we forget that there are so many people struggling in some really terrible situations. I want to make photographs that hit people on an emotional level, punch them in their gut and make them feel something. If people can connect to those I photograph then they can empathise with them. This kind of understanding is the first step in changing the situations that affect these people.

> In the long term I would hope to leave behind historical documents, photographs documenting lives, situations and struggles that may otherwise have vanished and been forgotten. I hope that at some point there will be fewer conflicts in this world, and if this happens I want my photos to remind people of the horrible things people go through in war.

> Finally, I want my work to be art. I want to leave something behind that will inspire people to not only be creative but to also be kind to their fellow human beings, even the ones who live thousands of miles away that they may never meet.

Crucial here, his comments suggest, is the necessity for photojournalists to be compassionate, to see in their work the potential to forge connections between distant publics that encourages empathy and understanding in the face of indifference. Photography may be a modest 'first step' in this direction, but the value of its documentary evidence is such that the individual photojournalist must recognise the moral responsibility at the heart of their craft. 'It is just about being human', Miller adds; 'it is not hard, just something that some people forget to do at times'.

For photojournalists striving to extend this commitment to moral responsibility, tensions may arise with their sense of professionalism; that is, their personal adherence to the ideals of dispassionate, impartial reportage. Such tensions, under certain circumstances, may invite insidious forms of self-censorship in accordance with wider discourses of 'the national interest', 'patriotism', or 'support for our troops'. Compounding matters is the extent to which major news organisations are withdrawing their photojournalists from the field altogether, typically citing safety as the principal concern. There is little doubt that documenting events is often extraordinarily dangerous, which is why local Iraqis are being increasingly relied upon at the frontlines, many of whom are routinely risking their lives to document the human devastation left in the wake of military attacks. Several have been killed, while others have endured arbitrary arrest and imprisonment by US and Iraqi military authorities. The experience of Bilal Hussein is telling. Born in the Al-Anbar Province, he worked in several jobs over the years before he became involved with the Associated Press (AP), initially as a guide for its journalists and helper with interviews in Fallujah. A keen amateur photographer, he received training and equipment from AP's Baghdad bureau – initially being paid $50 a photograph on a trial basis as a local stringer – before being sent to Ramadi to work as a contract photographer (see also Arango 2007; Lang 2007b; Layton 2007). Carrying out a range of assignments, he sharpened his new craft, taking a number of impressive photographs, not least one of insurgent fighters in Fallujah in November 2004 included in an AP collection awarded a Pulitzer Prize the following year.

On 12 April 2006, Hussein's life was dramatically altered when he was held – without formal charge – for 'imperative reasons of security', with no opportunity to hear the evidence against him. He was subjected to intense interrogation, which included spells of solitary confinement and being blindfolded for nine days, in a facility in Ramadi, before being transferred to Abu Ghraib and then on to a detention facility at Camp Cropper. A 46-page report later prepared by Hussein's attorney alleges that US military interrogators initially sought to recruit the photographer as an informant working within AP, which he refused because of his ethical and professional commitments. The report went on to state:

> USM interrogators have focused, in particular, on several photographs taken shortly before his arrest showing Iraqi children playing with

[a] torn-off leg of an injured US or Iraqi soldier. One interrogator said to Hussein: 'Do you know what would happen if these photos were show[n] in the US? There would be huge demonstrations and we would have to leave Iraq. This is why you won't be released. Your photos pose a threat to us'. (cited in Lang 2007a)

AP worked quietly behind the scenes to secure his release, but, after more than five months without success, went public. 'We want the rule of law to prevail', Tom Curley, AP's president and chief executive officer stated in September of that year. 'He either needs to be charged or released. Indefinite detention is not acceptable. We've come to the conclusion that this is unacceptable under Iraqi law, or Geneva Conventions, or any military procedure' (cited in AP 2006). In a letter to *The New York Times*, Curley (2006) pointed out that no evidence had been provided by the military to support their claim – no formal charges having been filed – that Bilal had improper ties to insurgents, which left him incapable of mounting a defence. 'All we are asking is that Bilal have appropriate access to justice: charge him or let him go', Curley wrote. 'Likewise, due process should apply to the thousands of others [estimated by AP to be as many as 14 000 people] being held in the United States military vacuum'.

Pentagon insistence that Bilal Hussein was a 'terrorist media operative' who infiltrated AP was based on 'convincing and irrefutable evidence' that officials refused to disclose. Calls for his release, including from organisations such as the Committee to Protect Journalists, were ignored. As time wore on, several AP editors became increasingly convinced that Bilal's arrest was in retaliation for photographs he had taken. The company's Chief Executive Officer, Tom Curley (2007) stated in an interview with Salon.com:

Bilal Hussein was operating in Anbar Province. Anbar was a black hole in the coverage of Iraq. For most of the war, there have been virtually no journalists there or very few journalists, so getting any information from Anbar was difficult. These pictures came at a time when the U.S. was trying to say that things were OK, and we know now that they were deteriorating.

He continued, explaining that every single photograph taken by Hussein, including outtakes, had been examined by AP with a view to determining whether he may have somehow known about events before they took place.

> His images are very much what you'd expect from other parts of the country. It's all the aftermath of violence – not just US on Iraq violence, but Iraq on Iraq violence, foreign fighters on Iraq violence, shattered buildings, grieving families, burned out car shells. When there's damage to vehicles, it's obvious [from Hussein's photo] that has long since occurred. If there was an attack on a military convoy, they would lock it down, and by the time Bilal was able to take pictures, there would be children playing in the background.

Besides Hussein's own fate, he pointed out, the integrity of news reporting was at stake:

> Of course it's not just about one man. It's about our ability to operate as journalists in a war zone. It is the most important conflict on the planet today. This is about any journalist's ability to do their jobs without fear of open-ended imprisonment without charges. This is not treatment that would happen in the United States. (Carroll 2007)

This latter point was further underscored by one of the lawyers working on the case for AP. 'I am absolutely convinced', Scott Horton stated:

> that the ton of bricks fell on these two guys – Bilal Hussein and Abdul Ameer Hussein [CBS cameraman arrested and imprisoned in Abu Ghraib for one year before being acquitted by an Iraqi court] – because they were working as professional journalists. They were the eyes of the world, covering things that the Pentagon doesn't want people in America to see. (cited in Herbert 2006)

Intense pressure to avoid using this type of imagery has also been brought to bear on news organisations by a number of staunchly conservative, pro-war bloggers in the US. Several condemned Bilal Hussein and other photographers for producing propaganda for the insurgency, engaging in what Eric Boehlert (2008) aptly described as 'mob rule-style pseudo-journalism' to advance their accusations. Blogger Michelle Malkin was arguably Hussein's fiercest critic, but other warbloggers weighing in included 'The Belmont Club', 'Captain's Quarters', 'Federal Way Conservative', 'Flopping Aces', 'Infidels are Cool', 'Jawa Report', 'Little Green Footballs', 'PowerLine', and 'Wizbang', amongst others. Charles Layton (2007), writing about the controversy in the *American Journalism Review*, pointed out that the 'first word of Bilal Hussein's arrest seems to have come from the blog of Michelle Malkin, Hussein's long-time critic', which cited an anonymous military source maintaining that he had been 'captured' by US forces in a building in Ramadi 'with a cache of weapons'. The perception lingered that the military had fed the story to Malkin because of her past histrionic criticism of Hussein's imagery, which appeared consistent with a broader strategy articulated by the Pentagon and the Bush administration. Layton points to a radio address made by Bush in October of 2006, when the then president stated:

> [...] the terrorists are trying to influence public opinion here in the United States. They have a sophisticated propaganda strategy. They know they cannot defeat us in the battle, so they conduct high-profile attacks, hoping that the images of violence will demoralize our country and force us to retreat. They carry video cameras and film their atrocities, and broadcast them on the Internet. They e-mail images and video clips to Middle Eastern cable networks like Al-Jazeera, and instruct their followers to send the same material to American journalists, authors, and opinion leaders. They operate websites, where they post messages for their followers and readers across the world. (Bush 2006)

In this way, 'images of violence' documenting the atrocities 'they' commit become a strategic priority because of their perceived propaganda value to broader media campaigns to undermine popular support for the war. Photojournalism risks being regarded as serving the enemy's interests, by this logic, effectively complicit in extending the aims of those – in Bush's words – 'trying to divide America and break

155

our will'. For Hussein, this meant two years of imprisonment before the accusations (formal charges were never filed) against him were finally dismissed in April 2008. 'I think the case is more than Bilal Hussein', his lawyer said at the time of his release. 'He was part of a much larger issue, which is who is going to control the flow of information from the battlefield. ... I think he was someone who got caught up in the debate, and it will be a continuing debate and struggle between the media and the military' (cited in Lang 2008).

Further instances where Iraqi photojournalists endeavouring to provide firsthand reportage in a war zone have found themselves detained by US forces continue to be revealed by major news organisations. This form of intimidation is one strand of a broader effort to control disturbing imagery which has met with considerable success from a military vantage point. As Michael Kamber and Tim Arango (2008) of *The New York Times* observe, while 'the conflict in Vietnam was notable for open access given to journalists – too much, many critics said, as the war played out nightly in bloody newscasts – the Iraq war may mark an opposite extreme'. Five years into the war, and after more than 4000 US combat deaths, the searches and interviews they conducted 'turned up fewer than a half-dozen graphic photographs of dead American soldiers'. The newspaper's public editor, Clark Hoyt, referred to Kamber and Arango's findings in a column addressing the 'longstanding tension between journalists who feel a duty to report war in all its aspects and a military determined to protect its own'. Hoyt pointed out that commanders in the field will employ a range of tactics to try to prevent photographs of the dead and injured from being published, a problem compounded by the dwindling number of Western photographers deployed in the first place – evidently, the newspaper had only two in Iraq at the time. Bill Keller, the executive editor, is quoted in the column to underscore Hoyt's contention that a newspaper has an obligation to report all aspects of war, including death, even though it may be painful. 'Death and carnage are not the whole story of war – there is also heroism and frustration, success and setback, camaraderie and, on occasion, atrocity – but death and carnage are part of the story', Keller maintains, 'and to launder them out of our account of the war would be a disservice' (cited in Hoyt 2008).

This insight into journalistic reasoning usefully highlights aspects of decision-making processes concerning the handling of such imagery that seldom come to the fore for discussion. One exception to this general rule occurred in September the following year, however, when a news photograph depicting a US Marine mortally wounded in combat in Dahaneh, southern Afghanistan, sparked a controversy that proved sufficiently newsworthy to garner coverage in its own right. The image in question was taken by AP photographer Julie Jacobson, who later described the moment in her personal journal. 'For the second time in my life, I watched a Marine lose his. He was hit with the RPG [rocket-propelled grenade] which blew off one of his legs and badly mangled other', she wrote. 'I hadn't seen it happen, just heard the explosion. I hit the ground and lay as flat as I could and shot what I could of the scene' (cited in de Montesquiou & Jacobson 2009). Lance Corporal Joshua 'Bernie' Bernard, 21 years old, is shown lying on the ground, his fellow Marines tending to him before he was transported to a helicopter that would take him to a field hospital where he died on the operating table. When informed that he had passed away, Jacobson reflected: 'To ignore a moment like that simply … would have been wrong. I was recording his impending death, just as I had recorded his life moments before walking the point in the bazaar', she said. 'Death is a part of life and most certainly a part of war. Isn't that why we're here? To document for now and for history the events of this war?' (cited in AP 2009). In her journal, she mentions that Bernard's comrades asked to see the photos on her laptop computer she had taken of the 'Taliban ambush' that day. 'They did stop when they came to that moment. But none of them complained or grew angry about it', she recalled. 'They understood that it was what it was. They understand, despite that he was their friend, it was the reality of things' (cited in de Montesquiou & Jacobson 2009).

The 'reality of things' looked very different from Defense Secretary Robert Gates' perspective. Alerted about AP's intention to distribute the photograph as part of a larger package of related material, he made a personal plea to AP President and CEO Tom Curley to withhold pub-

157

lication.[1] Insisting it was a matter of 'judgment and common decency', he contended that its release would mark an 'unconscionable departure' from the restraint most journalists had exercised since September 11, 2001. Bernard's parents, who had been shown the photographs beforehand by an AP reporter as a courtesy (permission for their use was not requested), also demanded that the news agency reconsider a decision they believed would be disrespectful to their son's memory. Whilst mindful of these views, AP remained steadfast. 'We thought that the image told a story of sacrifice; it told a story of bravery', John Daniszewski, senior managing editor, explained. 'We felt that the picture told a story that people needed to see and be aware of' (cited in Bauder 2009). His colleague, director of photography Santiago Lyon, pointed out that AP had followed the military regulations set down for journalists 'embedded' with US forces. Moreover, they had allowed for

---

1 In addition to several related photographs (including of Bernard's memorial service), AP distributed a detailed account of what had transpired, excerpts from Jacobson's journal and a video she narrated, as well as an article outlining its rationale for publication. Gates' intervention took place after AP had wired the package to its outlets, but prior to the expiry of its embargo on its use (intended to give news organisations sufficient time to decide whether or not to proceed with it). 'Why your organization would purposely defy the family's wishes knowing full well that it will lead to yet more anguish is beyond me', Gates (2009) wrote. 'Your lack of compassion and common sense in choosing to put this image of their maimed and stricken child on the front page of multiple newspapers is appalling.' In actuality, the image at the centre of the controversy was more likely to feature on news websites than in newspapers, and when it did appear in the latter, it was on an inside page. Several newspapers refused publication outright on the grounds of 'poor taste', while others objected on patriotic grounds, amongst other reasons. Amongst those that did run the photograph was the *Intelligencer* (Wheeling, West Virginia), which sought to justify its decision – taken 'after hours of debate' – in an accompanying editorial: 'Too often, we fear, some Americans see only the statistics, the casualty counts released by the Department of Defense. We believe it is important for all of us to understand that behind the numbers are real men and women, sometimes making the ultimate sacrifice, for us' (cited in Bauder 2009). Such decisions were taken in the face of an onslaught of criticism from politicians, including Sarah Palin who condemned the release of the photograph as 'a despicable and heartless act by the AP' on her Facebook page. 'The family said they didn't want the photo published. AP, you did it anyway, and you know it was an evil thing to do' (cited in CNN 2009).

a 'period of reflection' and waited until after Bernard's burial, which took place ten days after he died, before releasing the images. 'We feel it is our journalistic duty to show the reality of the war' in Afghanistan, he maintained, 'however unpleasant and brutal that sometimes is' (cited in AP 2009).

Reactions from members of the public, appearing in 'letters to the editor' as well as on various online forums, tended to express strongly held opinions. While it is impossible to generalise, there is little doubt that a key factor prompting such intense discussion was the relative scarcity of such imagery in the first place. This point was underscored by Lyon, who felt that there was a journalistic imperative to show the 'real effects' of war otherwise being lost in a 'very incomplete picture' that amounts to sanitisation. 'What it does is show – in a very unequivocal and direct fashion – the real consequences of war', he argued. 'So I think it really becomes a very immediate visual record of warfare that, in and of itself, is compelling, and that becomes more compelling because of its rarity' (cited in Dunlap 2009). For Jacobson, the photographs she took that day were consistent with her conviction that journalists have a 'social responsibility to record *and* publish' images of what happens in war, even when they risk upsetting people. In her words:

> An image personalises that death and makes people see what it really means to have young men die in combat. It may be shocking to see, and while I'm not trying to force anything down anyone's throat, I think it is necessary for people to see the good, the bad and the ugly in order to reflect upon ourselves as human beings.

> It is necessary to be bothered from time to time. It is too easy to sit at Starbucks far away across the sea and read about the casualty and then move on without much of another thought about it. It's not as easy to see an image of that casualty and *not* think about it. I never expect to change the world or stop war with one picture, but only hope that I make some people *think* beyond their comfort zones and hope that a few of them will be moved into some kind of action, be it joining a protest, or sending that care package they've put off for weeks, or writing that letter they keep meaning to write, or donating money to

some worthy NGO, or just remembering to say I love you to someone at home. Something. (cited in Dunlap 2009)

And here she proceeds to underline a basic contradiction at work where editorial decisions about the use of such imagery come to bear. Pointing out that war photographers 'have no restrictions to shoot or publish casualties from opposition forces, or even civilian casualties', she asks: 'Are those people less human than American or other NATO soldiers'?

## Towards peace photography

Jacobson's question, together with her call for action (which resonates with Nachtwey's words quoted at the outset of this chapter), encourage new ways of thinking about what I propose be called 'peace photography'.[2] Documenting the horrors of warfare is of vital importance, but so is the need for visual alternatives in the name of peace. Every photographic image of suffering, as Susie Linfield observes, is also one of protest: ' "This goes on", but also, by implication: "This must stop" '. Such is the dialectic – and the hope – at the core of such photographs, and yet therein lies a paradox. 'There is no doubt', she writes, 'that photography has, more than any other twentieth-century medium, exposed violence – made violence *visible* – to millions of people all over the globe'. At the same time, however, 'the history of photography also shows just how limited and inadequate such exposure is: seeing does not necessarily translate into believing, caring, or acting' (2010, p33). To redress this failure, I would suggest, is to reconsider anew photography's potential contribution to ongoing efforts to reinvigorate peace journalism.

While photography has long been recognised as a tool to raise awareness, efforts to create spaces for public engagement struggle to claim a purchase in an image-saturated culture. One modest yet effective example is the 'Frames of war' exhibition currently touring different

---

2 For a more detailed elaboration of 'peace photography' as a concept, please see my book, Conflicting images: photojournalism and war, (Routledge, in preparation).

countries. Intended by its coordinator, *Nepali Times* editor Kunda Dixit, as a contribution to the reconciliation process underway in Nepal, it has garnered critical acclaim and widespread public interest. The collection of 179 photographs, selected by Dixit and photojournalists Shahidul Alam and Shyam Tekwani from an archive of over 3000 shot by both amateurs and professionals, documents the impact of the war on the Nepali people during and after the ten-year 'People's war' (which ended in 2006 with a death toll close to 15 000 people, the vast majority of whom were civilians). 'Pictures remind us to remember the brutality', Dixit explained in an interview about the exhibition. 'And also what the violence does to those who want no part in it'. Given the 'great care' taken by the news media 'to filter the images of war', he felt the exhibition's inclusion of 'raw' images was necessary to show the 'human cost' of the conflict – and, moreover, the fact that 'peace does not come at the end of war'.

In calling for a paradigm shift in journalism training from war correspondent to peace correspondent, Dixit proceeded to underscore the importance of reconceptualising journalistic priorities. 'Reporters who go to war are almost celebrities. They cover the war as a series of battles, they count the body bags and chronicle the carnage', he observed. 'War correspondents focus on the battle plans, the strategy of the warring sides, and the hardwares of killing'. A peace correspondent, in marked contrast, 'tries to look at the human cost so that the politicians who lead people to war understand the pain they have unleashed, or cover[s] stories that help in the reconciliation process rather than polarising society' (see also Keeble et al. 2010; Lynch 2008, 2010). Photography, it follows, can play a crucial role in this process. The exhibition attracted more than 350 000 visitors during its initial tour in Nepal, many of whom found it an intensely emotional experience as evidenced by comments inscribed in visitor books. 'Because of Nepal's low literacy rate, the picture is the only way to communicate', Dixit added. 'At many exhibition venues we saw young school girls reading aloud the captions of the photographs to their illiterate grandparents'. A follow-up film and book have further extended this initiative, enabling wider audiences to gain critical insights into the conflict and its aftermath.[3] In this way, then, 'Frames of war' exemplifies an alternative conception of photography, one that strives to create shared communities of interpretation in the hope of furthering mutual understanding.

Building on these insights, a further elaboration of what I am calling 'peace photography' extends this conception to consider the polysemic nature of war imagery. That is to say, the 'meaning' of any one image is subject to a multiplicity of possible readings, with much depending upon the subjective positionalites brought to bear by the viewer in what is a complex process of negotiation. Here we remind ourselves how precariously contingent this process always proves to be, with any invocation of significance at risk of being undermined by alternative interpretations. The oft-rendered assertion that the grisly representation of violence necessarily threatens public support for military intervention, for example, glosses over a range of prospective reactions, such as where revulsion solicits renewed determination in the face of adversity. Similarly, there is no necessary correlation between images of human suffering and compassion, let alone concerted action, in response. In other words, there can be no easy extrapolation of a singular, preferred meaning from visual evidence, and yet this is not to suggest that any potential reading is equally viable either. Rather, I would suggest, it is the subtly inchoate way in which images ostensibly invite certain readings over and above alternative ones that we need to foreground for exploration. Research into peace photography may then attend to the subjunctive, seemingly 'common-sensical' criteria shaping these tacit, unspoken rules of inclusion and exclusion so as to discern the extent to which they reaffirm militarist perspectives.

Of pressing importance, this chapter has suggested, is the need to document the lived realities of human suffering in all of their complexities while, at the same time, engendering opportunities to visualise alternatives. Peace photography constitutes more than anti-

3  Information about the exhibition, together with the quotations attributed to Kunda Dixit, have been drawn from the following sources: Buddha's Breakfast, 2009; Pacific Media Centre, 2010; Wilson, 2010a, 2010b. See also the video 'Frames of war'. [Online]. Available: www.youtube.com/watch?v=dMZnFwa6Xys [Accessed 12 August 2011].

war photography, because disrupting the logics of familiar binaries ('good' and 'evil', 'victim' and 'oppressor', 'us' and 'them') is only the initial step. As important as such efforts consistently prove to be, a second step is vital in this regard. It is my contention that peace photography calls for nothing less than a profound re-imagining of photographic form, practice and epistemology in order to move beyond the imposition of binaries in the first place. To succeed in challenging the codified strictures of war photography, I believe, it is necessary to recast anew the otherwise implicit assumptions, values and normative proscriptions shaping its priorities and protocols. It is in the creation of a new visual grammar resistant to the pull of binaries that the diverse array of ethical choices at the heart of photojournalism will be thrown into sharp relief. Searching questions then may be raised regarding how best photography may contribute to the re-articulation of visions of the world in the service of human rights and social justice.

*References*[4]

Allan, Stuart (2011). Amateur photography in wartime: early histories. In Kari Andén-Papadopoulos & Mervi Pantti (Eds). *Amateur images and global news* (pp41-59). Bristol: Intellect.

Arango, Tim (2007). Case lays bare the media's reliance on Iraqi journalists, *The New York Times*, 17 December. [Online]. Available: www. nytimes.com/2007/12/17/business/media/17apee.html [Accessed 25 July 2011].

Associated Press (2009). Associated Press says photo of Lance Cpl. Joshua Bernard shows realities of war, Associated Press, 4 September. [Online]. Available: www.liveleak.com/view?i=145_1252129188 [Accessed 25 July 2011].

Associated Press (2006). US holds photographer in Iraq. *The New York Times*, 18 September. [Online]. Available: www.nytimes.com/2006/09/18/world/middleeast/18photographer.html [Accessed 25 July 2011].

---

4 The access dates below refer to to the occasion when the url was checked to ensure it was active.

Bauder, David (2009). AP picture of wounded marine sparks debate. Associated Press, 4 September. [Online]. Available: www.huffingtonpost. com/huff-wires/20090904/afghan-death-ap-photo/ [Accessed 25 July 2011].

Boehlert, Eric (2008). Michelle Malkin and the warbloggers get everything wrong – again, *MediaMatters.org*, 23 April. [Online]. Available: mediamatters.org/columns/200804230002 [Accessed 25 July 2011].

Buddha's Breakfast (2009). *'People war' – photographs of war to promote peace in Nepal*. [Online]. Available: therightsexposureproject. com/2009/04/23/%E2%80%98people-war%E2%80%99-%E2%80%93-photographs-of-war-to-promote-peace-in-nepal/ [Accessed 25 August 2011].

Bush, George (2006). President's radio address, Transcript, The White House, 21 October. [Online]. Available: www.standardnewswire.com/ news/50761168.html [Accessed 25 July 2011].

Carroll, Kathleen (2007). Q&A: the case of Bilal Hussein. David Walker interview with Kathleen Carroll. [Online]. Available: PDNonline.com [Accessed 27 September 2011].

CNN (2009). Palin calls News Org 'heartless and selfish'. *Politicalticker. blogs.cnn.com*, 7 September. [Online]. Available: politicalticker.blogs.cnn. com/2009/09/07/palin-calls-news-org-heartless-and-selfish/ [Accessed 25 August 2011].

Curley, Tom (2007). Interviews with AP Executives on the Bilal Hussein Travesty. *Salon.com*. [Online]. Available: www.salon.com/news/opinion/ glenn_greenwald/2007/11/20/hussein [Accessed 25 August 2011].

Curley, Tom (2006). Charge our man, or let him go, *The New York Times*, 22 September. [Online]. Available: www.nytimes.com/2006/09/22/ opinion/l22ap.html [Accessed 25 July 2011].

de Montesquiou, Alfred & Julie Jacobson (2009). Calm – then sudden death in Afghan War, *Associated Press*, 4 September. [Online]. Available: www.msnbc.msn.com/id/32676734/ns/world_news-south_and_central_ asia/t/calm-then-sudden-death-afghan-war/ [Accessed 25 July 2011].

Dunlap, David W (2009). Behind the scenes: to publish or not?, *Lens Blog, The New York Times*, 4 September. [Online]. Available: lens.blogs.nytimes. com/2009/09/04/behind-13/ [Accessed 25 July 2011].

Gates, Robert (2009). *Letter to Thomas Curley, Office of the Secretary of Defense*, 3 September. [Online]. Available: graphics8.nytimes.com/ packages/flash/Lens/2009/09/20090903-Behind-Jacobson/20090903- Behind-Curley.pdf [Accessed 25 July 2011].

Guerin, Frances & Roger Hallas (2007). *The image and the witness: trauma, memory and visual culture*. London: Wallflower.

Herbert, Bob (2006). Due process, bulldozed, *The New York Times*, 25 September. [Online]. Available: select.nytimes.com/2006/09/25/ opinion/25herbert.html?_r=1 [Accessed 25 July 2011].

Hoyt, Clark (2008). The painful images of war, *The New York Times*, 3 August. [Online]. Available: www.nytimes.com/2008/08/03/ opinion/03pub-ed.html [Accessed 25 July 2011].

Kamber, Michael & Tim Arango (2008). 4,000 US deaths, and a handful of images, *The New York Times*, 26 July. [Online]. Available: www.nytimes. com/2008/07/26/world/middleeast/26censor.html [Accessed 25 July 2011].

Keeble, Richard Lance, John Tulloch & Florian Zollmann (Eds) (2010). *Peace journalism, war and conflict resolution*. New York: Peter Lang.

Lang, Daryl (2008). An Iraqi photographer's long wait for justice. *PDNonline.com*, 3 January. [Online]. Available: www.pdnonline.com/pdn/ Search-420.shtml?kw=An+Iraqi+photographer%E2%80%99s+long+wait+ for+justice&exposeNavigation=true&action=Submit&searchInterface=Ke yword&matchType=mode%2Bmatchallpartial&an=superPdn&x=46&y=8 [Accessed 27 July 2011].

Lang, Daryl (2007a). Interrogators told Bilal Hussein his photos were a threat, report says. *PDNonline.com*, 26 November. [Online]. Available: www.modelmayhem.com/po.php?thread_id=216867 [Accessed 25 August 2011].

Lang, Daryl (2007b). The man from Fallujah. *PDNonline.com*, 28 November. [Online]. Available: www.pdnonline.com/pdn/Search-420.sht

ml?kw=The+man+from+Fallujah&exposeNavigation=true&action=Subm
it&searchInterface=K [Accessed 25 July 2011].

Layton, Charles (2007). Behind bars. *American Journalism Review*
December 2006/January 2007. [Online]. Available: www.ajr.org/article.
asp?id=4225 [Accessed 25 July 2011].

Linfield, Susie (2010). *The cruel radiance: photography and political
violence.* Chicago: University of Chicago Press.

Lynch, Jake (2010) Peace journalism. In Stuart Allan (Ed). *The Routledge
companion to news and journalism* (pp542–53). New York: Routledge.

Lynch, Jake (2008). *Debates in peace journalism.* Sydney: Sydney
University Press.

Matheson, Donald & Stuart Allan (2009). *Digital war reporting.*
Cambridge: Polity.

Miller, Zoriah (2010). Interview with Zoriah Miller, by Michael Zhang,
*PetaPixel*, 3 June. [Online]. Available: www.petapixel.com/2010/06/03/
interview-with-zoriah-miller/ [Accessed 25 July 2011].

Möller, Frank (2008). Imaging and remembering peace and war. *Peace
Review: A Journal of Social Justice*, 20(1): 100–106.

Nachtwey, James (2009). Introduction. In Caroline Moorehead & James
Nachtwey (Eds). *Humanity in war* (pp3–5). London: New Internationalist.

Ottosen, Rune (2007). Emphasising images in peace journalism: theory
and practice in the case of Norway's biggest newspaper. *Conflict &
Communication Online*, 6(1): 1–16.

Pacific Media Centre (2010). Dixit photo exhibition handed over to
Amnesty International. Cited December 23, 2010. [Online]. Available:
www.pmc.aut.ac.nz/pmc-blog/2010-12-23/mijt-dixit-photo-exhibition-
handed-over-amnesty-international [Accessed 25 July 2011].

Sontag, Susan (2003). *Regarding the pain of others.* London: Hamish
Hamilton.

Wilson, Courtney (2010a). The power of a war-and-peace picture – all 179
of them, *Pacific.Scoop*, Pacific Media Centre. Cited November 27, 2010,

[Online]. Available: www.pmc.aut.ac.nz/articles/power-war-and-peace-picture-%E2%80%93-all-179-them [Accessed 25 July 2011].

Wilson, Courtney (2010b). Dixit challenges benefits and pitfalls of virtual world for investigative journalism, *Pacific Media Centre.* Cited December 6, 2010, [Online]. Available: www.pmc.aut.ac.nz/articles/mijt-dixit-challenges-benefits-and-pitfalls-virtual-world-investigative-journalism [Accessed 25 July 2011].

Zelizer, Barbie (2010). *About to die: how news images move the public.* Oxford and New York: Oxford University Press.

# Chapter 6

## Oligarchy reloaded and pirate media: the state of peace journalism in Guatemala[1]

*Lioba Suchenwirth and Richard Lance Keeble*

This chapter presents a case study of the state of peace journalism (PJ) in Guatemala, based on the critical assumption that analysts need to broaden the definition of PJ to encompass current local level and alternative media initiatives. It investigates current PJ in Guatemala through interviews with those who analyse the media (media experts), produce the media (journalists and volunteers), and those whose representation in the media is essential for the Guatemalan peace process (indigenous groups). While profound racism and a violent environment hamper peace journalistic work for both mainstream and alternative outlets, the chapter argues that the opening for media for the people and by the people in Guatemala is to be found within alternative channels rather than commercial outlets.

### What is PJ?

Peace journalism is a normative journalistic school critiquing mainstreaming 'war journalism' as introduced by Johan Galtung in 1965 (see Lynch & McGoldrick 2005, p6). By using conflict analysis techniques in reporting, its main purpose lies in both mapping out and actively supporting peaceful solutions to conflict. Rather than modelling its reports on sports journalism with its zero-sum games and focus on who is winning or losing, Galtung suggests that the PJ approach should be modelled on health journalism, which does not focus merely on

---

1 An earlier version of this chapter was published in *Ethical Space: The International Journal of Communication Ethics*, 8(1): 44–52.

disease, but also on possible ways to overcome it (Galtung 2002, p259). The core of the theory is formed by an awareness of conflict dynamics and an understanding that no information can be neutral.

According to PJ theory, every time a report goes public, it has an impact on the particular conflict. By reporting in a manner that gives undue attention to violence, journalists' reports may actually spawn a new chain of violent behaviour in a perpetuating feedback loop (Lynch & McGoldrick 2005). Consequently, PJ will be 'intended outcome programming' used as a tool for transforming attitudes, promoting reconciliation, putting the conflict sides together for resolution, maintaining 'a duty for journalists to use their potential for mediation between conflict parties' (see also Spurk 2002, p16), thus emphasising the responsibilities of journalistic actors to respond in ways that are supposed to maximise the chances for peace (Lynch & McGoldrick 2005).

While the definition of PJ provided by Lynch and McGoldrick (Lynch & McGoldrick 2005, p5) remains vague, making it very hard to measure PJ outcomes, they provide a clear list of practical/professional activities for peace journalists, comprising four major elements (based on Galtung 2002, p6). Reporting is:

- *peace/conflict-orientated*, making conflicts transparent, and, as such, is exploring conflict formation, proactive in the prevention of violence and empathetically humanising of all sides

- *truth-orientated*, exposing cover-ups on all sides

- *people-orientated*, focusing on giving voice to the voiceless and people peacemakers

- *solution-orientated*, highlighting peace initiatives, focusing on structure, culture, the peaceful society as well as resolution, reconstruction and reconciliation.

In contrast, core elements of war journalism are seen to be:

- *war/violence-orientated*, focusing on the conflict arena and a zero-sum orientation, 'us–them' journalism, dehumanisation, making wars opaque and reactively waiting for violent incidents before reporting

- *propaganda-orientated*, exposing 'their untruths' and helping 'our' cover-ups
- *elite-orientated*, focusing on able-bodied elite males, and on elite peacemakers
- *victory-orientated*, with coverage focusing on treaties, institutions and the controlled society (Galtung 2002).

### Critiquing the elite tradition in PJ theory

Despite critiquing elite-orientated journalism, a dominant characteristic of peace journalism theory focuses on the possibilities for transforming *professional* routines. Dov Shinar and Wilhelm Kempf, in their seminal work *Peace journalism: the state of the art* (2007) draw together some of the leading theorists in the field – virtually all of whom concentrate on professional issues, only occasionally acknowledging any 'alternative' outlet. Susan Dente Ross, for instance (in Shinar & Kempf 2007, pp53–74) ends an extraordinarily detailed and exhaustive review of the PJ literature with a passing reference to 'independent, self-critical media' (such as www.IndyMedia.org) and an emphasis on the 'norms of professional ethics and objectivity'. She calls for a 'journalism of symbolic rapprochement' involving a transformation of 'the images of the self and the others' to end intractable, essentialist, cultural conflicts. But no 'revolutionary' changes are needed. She concludes that 'peace journalism does not involve any radical departure from contemporary journalism practice. Rather peace journalism requires numerous subtle and cumulative shifts in seeing, thinking, sourcing, narrating and financing the news'.

In the final chapter, Dov Shinar (2007, pp199–210) outlines the conclusions of a two-year project by the peace journalism group of the Toda Institute for Global Peace and Policy Research. His priorities, too, are largely in the professional journalistic realm. Listing 'four promises of peace journalism', his first is 'professional improvement'. Peace journalism, he says, 'might change the seemingly inherent contradiction between the nature of peace stories and the professional demands of journalists' (Shinar 2007, p201). His fourth promise is to widen 'scholarly and professional media horizons' away from 'functionalism, hard core Marxism and technological determinism'.

We argue that this dominant strand of PJ theory focuses too closely on the notion of journalism as a privileged, professional activity and fails to take into account the critical intellectual tradition which locates professions historically and politically, seeing them as essentially occupational groupings with a legal monopoly of social and economic opportunities in the marketplace, underwritten by the state. Parkin (1979) and Collins (1990) explore the notion of social closure, according to which occupations seek to regulate market conditions in their favour by restricting access to a limited group of eligible professionals. Such a notion of closure can also help to explain the ideologies of professionalism and 'objectivity', which largely exclude alternative, campaigning, social media from the definition of 'journalism' (Illich 1973).

*Need for a radical redefinition of PJ theory*

Contrary to Dente Ross (see above), we argue that PJ theory does, in fact, need to embrace a radical political analysis of the media and society. This will incorporate an awareness of the possibilities of journalistic activities both within and outside the corporate media and as part of a broader political project to democratise the media and society in general (Hackett & Carroll 2006). The strategy will also ultimately involve a radical broadening of the definition of journalism to include intellectuals, campaigners and citizens – each articulating their ideas within the dominant, and alternative, global public spheres.

While alternative media can consist of very diverse groups and organisations, they can be explicitly partisan, characterised by efforts to disclose issues of exclusion, elite-bias and gaps in information left by the mainstream by providing room for alternative views and a voice to those who are not otherwise heard (Atton & Hamilton 2008, pp79, 86; Harcup 2007, p85). They are seen to 'challenge accepted news values and ethical frameworks of mainstream media' (Harcup 2007, p127), thus creating important counter-public spheres (Fraser 1993 cited in Keeble 2009, p197). Alternative media are often linked to identity and community building, according to Atton and Hamilton (2008, p122):

171

the strength of alternative media lie not only in their counter-information role but also in the provision of opportunities for ordinary people to tell their own stories, and to reconstruct their culture and identity using their own symbols, signs and language. In this way, they challenge social codes, validate identities and empower themselves and their communities.

Thus PJ can learn from development journalism, which has long argued for a transformation from imposition to collaboration. In her theory of citizens' media, Clemencia Rodriguez writes: 'Only when citizens take their destiny in their own hands and shape it using their own cultures and strengths will peace and social change be viable. In both cases power has diffused from being concentrated in a few experts into the everyday lives and cultures of civil society' (Rodriguez 2000, p150). It is the citizens' media, not the news media, which, in her opinion, can 'give voice to the voiceless', foster empowerment, connect isolated communities, foster conscientisation and serve as alternative sources of information (Rodriguez 2000, p151). She is convinced that peace media can learn from citizens' media – and address a gap which peace journalism has so far not addressed appropriately.

## Historic role of alternative peace media

When talking about peacebuilding within a society, it is, then, the local media which are of special importance, because they are concerned most directly with the communication between the different military antagonists and civil groups (see, for example, Blondel 2004). Historically, alternative peace media have played crucial roles in progressive struggles across the globe.

Following are several examples of the role of media in such struggles. Informal underground communication networks and the role of newspapers such as the *Sowetan* were crucial in the anti-apartheid struggle in South Africa in the 1970s and 1980s (Downing 2005, pp150–53). Jonathan Neale (2001, pp122–30), in his seminal study of the Vietnam War, identified around 300 anti-war newspapers in the armed services during the course of the conflict. From 1963 to 1983, the Bolivian miners' radio stations highlighted the rights of workers. In Poland during the 1980s, alternative publications of the Polish Roman Catholic Church and the *samizdat* publications of the solidarity movement played crucial roles in the movement against the Soviet-backed government of the day (Atton 2009, p269). In Nicaragua during the 1980s and 1990s, the Movement of Popular Correspondents produced reports by non-professional, voluntary reporters from poor rural areas that were published in regional and national newspapers – and they helped inspire revolutionary education and political activities. In the 1990s, the Revolutionary Association of Women of Afghanistan bravely reported on the abuse and execution of women under the Taliban by producing audio cassettes, videos, a website and a magazine (Atton 2009, p269). This century we have seen much use made of websites by reformist movements in Burma and more recently (with Twitter, Flickr, Facebook and YouTube) in Iran (Kirkpatrick 2009; Garton Ash 2009). Similarly, in Peru in 2009, indigenous activists used Twitter and YouTube to highlight human rights abuses as more than 50 000 Amazonians demonstrated and went on strike in protest over US–Peru trade laws that threatened to open up ancestral territories to exploitation by multinational companies (Schnieter 2009).

*Crucial political impact of peace media*

A sustainable peace can only be built when implicated local groups are willing to contribute. It is in the local settings that the soft power[2] of the media can completely fulfil its potential. This is because peacebuilding efforts must have as an overarching goal 'to enhance the indigenous capacity of a society to manage conflict without violence' (Schnieter 2009). This necessitates that 'external support for peace building is an adjunct to local peace building efforts and not a substitute for them' (Howard et al. 2003, p24). Wolfsfeld (2004, pp11–14) proposes four major types of political impact by local media on peace processes. Media:

define the political atmosphere;
influence the nature of debates;

---

2 Soft power is a phrase coined by Joseph Nye to describe a power that is not physical, but works on the basis of persuasion (2004).

influence the strategies and behaviour of the antagonists; and
raise or lower the public standing of antagonists.

## PJ initiatives in Guatemala: historical context

Fifteen years after the end of Guatemala's infamously brutal civil war,
armed groups and clandestine security networks have merged with
criminal organisations deeply entrenched in state institutions. Murders
and death threats to civil society activists undermine democracy, and
homicide rates have almost doubled since 2000. The UN development report comments: 'To put it bluntly: Central America is the most
violent region of the World, with the exception of those regions where
some countries are at war or are experiencing severe political violence'
(United Nations Development Programme 2010, p14).

Meanwhile, international actors such as the World Bank,
Organization of American States, the International Monetary Fund,
the United Nations Development Programme, religious organisations
as well as numerous NGOs and state development agencies have been
heavily involved in the country's affairs, though the effects of their
efforts remain dubious. Poverty rates remain at 51 percent, with 34
percent living in extreme poverty. Twenty-three percent of children are
malnourished. At least 26 percent of the population is illiterate (World
Bank 2010). Indigenous people, mainly Mayan groups, are affected
the most, because although they make up the demographic majority,
they are excluded politically, socially, economically and culturally.[3] In
short, the civil war is over, but violence and the underlying causes of the
conflict continue to exist.

The signing of the Guatemalan Peace Accords in December 1996
marked the official end of a 36-year conflict between army and guerrilla
groups. A CIA-sponsored coup had overthrown the democratically

---

3  Statistics concerning Guatemala are considered to be extremely unreliable
for a variety of reasons, yet Mayans are believed to number about six million
people, meaning that by all accounts they comprise one half or more of the total
population (Handy 2002). In addition, there are around 2000 Xinca (a different
indigenous group) and 4000 Garifuna, whose ancestors were African slaves
settling on the Caribbean coast at the end of the 19th century.

elected government in 1954, justifying the intervention in the light of a US Cold War interventionist strategy to contain the 'communist menace'. Land reforms seeking to redistribute unused land from large holdings to landless peasants were immediately reversed. Reformist dissidents were gradually eliminated as civil society was destroyed through targeted repression by the subsequent military dictatorship. Receiving extensive military and economic assistance from the US, Guatemala became a security state *par excellence*.

The consequent civil war took a tremendously heavy toll: a minimum of 200 000 deaths, in addition to 40 000 people who 'disappeared' after being arrested. More than 400 villages were destroyed; 200 000 people were forced to flee to neighbouring Mexico, and, of Guatemala's 10 million inhabitants, about one million were displaced internally (Handy 2002; Carey 2004, p70). Around 93 percent of the killings were inflicted by the army, according to the Guatemalan truth commission. As over 83 percent of the dead were Mayans, the army had committed 'acts of genocide' since they 'contemplated the total or partial extermination of the group' (Handy 2003, p279). Although the conflict had its origins in Cold War ideological differences, it soon took on distinct ethnic dimensions.

Clearly, the rift between the population of European descent (and those who could adopt a European identity), so-called Ladinos, and the majority indigenous population did not appear overnight. Shortly after the arrival of the Spanish conquistadors in 1524, Spanish distinctiveness was sharply separated from 'Indian' identity through the provision of different rights. During centuries to come, racism was rife, while political indigenous identification was discouraged at best and brutally suppressed at worst (Colop 1996; Watanabe 2000). 'To be indigenous was to be treated as the dangerous "Other" who had to be kept under control – if necessary by all means' (Warren 2003, p108).

*Elite-focus in the Guatemala mainstream media scene: it's a family thing*

Media ownership in Guatemala is marked (and marred) by monopoly, which both perpetuates the oligarchic system and prevents democratic change (Monzon 2010; Rockwell & Janus 2001). Monzon speaks of an 'ideological embrace' between media and company interests (2010, p60) and concludes: "They are [primarily] companies, not communication media" (Monzon 2010, p59).

All of Guatemala's national newspapers[4] are owned by two competing news groups, both of which are affiliated with the famous 20: elite Guatemalan families who control the country's major sources of income and wield considerable political influence (Casaus Arzu 2002). In addition, there is a 'monopoly of gate-keeping' within the media (Silvio Gramajo, personal interview, 2010). One example is the family Marroquin, who own the smaller publishing group. In addition, both the editor of *Prensa Libre*, the biggest broadsheet in the country, and the editor of another broadsheet, *El Periodico*, are Marroquin relatives. 'They are not [a] very powerful family as such, but it looks as if they might soon have the entire print output under control' (Silvio Gramajo, personal interview, 2010). While the Guatemalan readership is low, due to the country's high illiteracy rates, newspaper influence among the elites is deemed to be considerable (Silvio Gramajo, personal interview, 2010). This underlines a clear *elite-focus* as described in Lynch and McGoldrick's critique of war journalism (2005, p6) – that news is written by elites for elites, and reflects elite standpoints.

Infamously, the Mexican Angel Gonzalez (nicknamed 'the Angel of Democracy'), brother-in-law of the former minister of communication, owns all four commercial TV licences, as well as the main radio news channel, Radio Sonora, and a large portion of the commercial radio stations. When journalist and social scientist Gustavo Berganza wrote of favours exchanged between Gonzalez and certain politicians, he was made 'the target of a relentless attack of the news programs of the "national" TV channels owned by this Mexican' (*Guatemala Times* 2008). In a personal interview, Berganza (2010) said: '[Angel

---

4 Cooperacion de Noticias owns the broadsheet *Siglo Veintiuno* as well as the tabloid *Al Dia*. They are in fierce competition with the other, larger group, a news conglomerate controlling the biggest-selling broadsheet *Prensa Libre* and which also holds the most successful tabloid *Nuestro Diario*, as well as *El Periodico*, another broadsheet. In addition, the Prensa Libre group owns *El Quetzalteco*, Quetzaltenango's bi-weekly regional paper – the biggest regional in the country.

Gonzalez] doesn't distort reality as such, making up news that [is] pure government propaganda, but he omits information that could harm [the government]', clearly indicating that the Gonzalez's news coverage is both *elite-orientated* and *propanganda-orientated* (see Lynch & McGoldrick 2005, p6).

Radio ownership is similarly concentrated among a few major groups which mainly repeat the news broadcast by Radio Sonora, or printed in newspapers with allegiance to the Catholic and evangelical churches and the state. Due to the high illiteracy rate, radio is of particular importance, and more than 90 percent of the population of Central America is exposed to radio on a daily basis (Rockwell & Janus, cited in Salzman & Salzman 2010, p8).

Regional journalists often work parttime in public relations for local authorities, and parttime as correspondents for media in the capital, since the media organisations do not pay them sufficiently (Gramajo, personal interview, 2010). Hence journalists do not appear to stay in the profession for very long, as they receive low wages and have few career opportunities (Berganza, personal interview, 2010). A recent government drive saw the recruitment of large number of former mainstream journalists to government media outlets to increase the quality of their output (Berganza, personal interview, 2010). Consequently, the newspaper *Diario de Centro América* and various radio stations have had a strong rise in popularity. Silvio Gramajo elaborates:

> [At present] the government is putting [in place structures] for the formation of government media: they are calling them public media, but I doubt that. I think they are government media, yet with a different vision. In this country government media were imminently pro-government; propaganda. But now they also report from a different view. To put [it] simply, there is journalistic work now, when before it was propaganda work. Is it not the best [journalism possible]? Probably. But it exists. That is a step forward. (Personal interview, 2010)

A positive side-effect of the media's increased popularity and wider reach is that the government is less dependent on placing advertisements with commercial media to distribute official information, thus making them less vulnerable to corruption and favouritism (Berganza, personal interview, 2010). In PJ terminology, Guatemala's mainstream media consequently focus on elite orientation and propaganda orientation. Their coverage is both war/violence-orientated and victory-orientated in the sense that they focus on treaties, institutions and the elite of society.

*Proactive peace reporting in the alternative media: pirates, priests and communists*

One distinguishing feature of peace/conflict-orientated reporting is its proactive approach, and its giving of a voice to all parties. Although the right to indigenous and participatory media is actually part of the Guatemala Peace Accords signed in 1996, community radio stations are illegal, if they have not competed for their frequency in regular commercial auctions, which they can hardly ever afford. Yet there are more than 800 self-declared community radio stations in the country. Some promote mainly missionary content rather than news, such as the evangelical stations in association with Radio Cultural (Sywulka, personal interview, 2010). Others are essentially commercial pirate radio stations with local reach. Yet according to Martina Richards, country director of the German national development agency DED, community radio is at present the best media outlet for Guatemala, because 'it's where its audience is' (personal interview, 2010).

During the conflict, community radio was used both by guerrilla groups to keep in touch with their fighters and supporters as well as a nonviolent means of opposition (Viscidi 2004; Randall 1993, p633). Former broadcaster with legendary guerrilla radio station La Voz Popular, Tino Recinos is now coordinating Mujb'ab'l yol, a network of 205 community radio stations. Programs focus on human, indigenous and children's rights, freedom of speech, and other social and political themes and are conducted in indigenous languages as well as Spanish (personal interview, 2010). Mujb'ab'l yol sees its role clearly as proactive community-building. Its website states:

From our point of view a means of communication shouldn't just be about distributing and sharing information but rather it should be orientated around getting close to the community it serves. In this way it can supply the conditions needed to benefit society as a whole in terms of increased community awareness and cohesion. Establishing members of radio stations and other people as pillars of the community, who can promote progressive change, means leaving behind the image of just being distributors of information to being progressive activists who promote development within the community. (2010)

The network is peace/conflict-orientated in that it aims to open spaces for all, especially marginalised groups, exploring conflict formation, the prevention of violence, and the humanisation of stories. It is solution-orientated since much of its coverage highlights peace initiatives, focusing on culture, and in particular on peaceful society initiatives such as resolution, reconstruction and reconciliation (these fit with the elements suggested by Lynch & McGoldrick 2005, p6).

One of the biggest problems community radio is facing in Guatemala is that there exists no clear definition of what a community radio station is. The stations are too divided among themselves, which will make it hard for them to get legislation passed. This is why most community stations remain illegal to this day, according to Gramajo (personal interview, 2010). In terms of alternative television, the former military channel was given to the Academy of Mayan languages as part of the Peace Accords, and is now known as TV Maya. Expectations and demand were high, yet TV Maya is currently being kept in an economic limbo, as – being a public channel – it is not allowed to sell advertising space, yet it receives little public funding and cannot broadcast beyond its neighbourhood.

A rather more successful venture is the independent periodical *EntreMundo*s, a free magazine aiming to publish 'news and commentary on human rights and development in Guatemala'. Originating as a society magazine in Quetzaltenango, its current focus vastly increased its popularity and readers can now be found all over Guatemala. Theme-specific issue subjects include mining (May and June 2010), education (July and August 2010), and gender (March and April 2010), and its

2000 copies are distributed in cafes, universities and libraries, as well as through the internet. Valeria Ayerdi, editor of *EntreMundos*, elaborates on the magazine's agenda:

> [I want] to give a voice to news you normally wouldn't see or wouldn't notice ... You see I read the newspapers every day, and I take important news that I know the normal media won't cover and we publish it ... and sometimes small news become big articles for us ... In the mainstream, you see indigenous people just being used, or see them as patronising postcards, but they don't really tell about the story of those [people]. And we are focused; whenever we talk about a project or something from indigenous people or rural areas, we try to show the human side of them. (personal interview, 2010)

According to Ayerdi, *EntreMundos* is actively encouraging its readership to contribute articles. Yet talking about terms such as freedom or civil liberties is difficult, as they are often associated with communism. 'I want to be critical about both sides, both left and right, so that they can see that the fact that you are criticising and that you are talking about human rights doesn't mean that you are a communist' (Valeria Ayerdi, personal interview, 2010).

Again, clear links to PJ elements are apparent. *EntreMundos*' proactive approach, focuses on giving voice to all parties, and humanising of all sides shows a peace/conflict-oriented reporting, while the wish to expose untruths on all sides shows a truth-orientation. The magazine's focus is people-oriented in that it is giving voice to those 'rarely seen in the news', and it has a clear solution-orientation in its choice of topics.

Unsurprisingly, funding is a major point of concern for alternative media outlets. The axiom that 'community media lack power, because they lack economic power' (Evelyn Blanck, personal interview, 2010) was expressed commonly in interviews conducted for this chapter, especially by those who work in and with alternative media. Lucia Escobar, for example, laments that while her project, Radio Ati, is trying to change Guatemalan society as a whole, she often does not even have the fare to send a journalist to report from the next village (personal interview, 2010). A lack of funding for alternative media means that their employees need to have second and third jobs. These might affect their journalistic output, or vice versa. Valeria Ayerdi tells of the repercussions of her journalistic work for her second job, teaching English. After publishing an *EntreMundos* edition on mining, a particularly sensitive subject in Guatemala, she was called into the principal's office. Parents were apparently concerned about what she was teaching their children. She was given an official warning and told to stick 'only to teaching English' (personal interview, 2010).

However, besides these findings, interviewees also recounted some positive side-effects of economic pressure. Indeed, the tight financial situation appears to increase collaboration between activists. Julia Cajas, coordinator for AMOIXQUIC, an NGO for indigenous women's rights, explained how she turned to a community radio station to broadcast AMOIXQUIC's women's rights program, since AMOIXQUIC had no money to pay for space in a commercial station. Community radio makers taught the women how to produce a program and distributed the results using their wide network of community stations. Since the organisation had no funds to produce professional material, the women had to produce the shows themselves. 'It was problematic because I too didn't know how to do many of these things, but still we managed and that has more value than anything else because we learned it by doing it and between the women there were a lot of skills and originality'. Women did not only acquire more skills, but also gained self-esteem, Cajas said (personal interview, 2010). This precarious economic situation also has the potential to foster an increased sense of ownership and community for those involved, according to volunteer coordinator Ruben Dominguez. When the community radio station Doble Via had to raise 4000 Quetzales for equipment, the bill was footed by its 37 volunteers. This increased the sense, within the community, that the station belonged to them (Ruben Dominguez, personal interview, 2010).

*'Us' versus 'them' journalism: racism and indigenous inclusion in the Guatemalan media*

Racism in the media was rampant during and before the civil war. While certain expressions are no longer used after the Peace Accords of 1996, there was little inclusion of indigenous identity in the written mainstream press ten years later (Suchenwirth 2006). This is even more evident in the case of indigenous women (Tubin Sotz 2007). Even in political advertisements aimed at Mayans, indigenous people play subordinate roles (Conolly-Ahern & Castells i Talens 2010). Amilcar Davila, the director of a comprehensive study of the Guatemalan media over the last three years, conducted by Rafael Landivar University, has concluded:

> The racism has transformed a lot. But it does not disappear, it adapts, it camouflages. Very few people would now say strong insults in public... but is this progress? ... You can see it very well when there is a crisis of sort[s], let's say a demonstration. Nobody is a racist until there is a crisis ... and [then] everything comes out: [They say that the indigenous people] are behind the times, they don't want progress, they don't think about the future etc ... For me the biggest topic, more than the insults and stereotypes, which do still happen, is the exclusion of indigenous people. They are not covered. Not [even] important topics, not their points of view. They don't even think about them. The discourse goes in a different way ... The news is not aimed at them. (Amilcar Davila, personal interview, 2010)

According to a content analysis of Guatemalan media conducted by the university, an average of only six percent of all newspaper articles mention indigenous people or issues, and those mentions mostly have negative connotations such as that indigenous people are implicated in local conflicts, human rights issues and racism problems (Tubin et al. 2010). It was difficult for professional journalists to accept the outcome of the university's study.

> One reason mainstream journalists give is that the country is racist, so therefore the media will be racist, and that if sources are racist,

that translates to the article. But this, they claim, is not the journalists' fault. (Amilcar Davila, personal interview, 2010)

Davila's statement describes the classic perpetuating feedback loop examined by Lynch and McGoldrick (2005). However, interviewees for this chapter agreed that there had been improvements in employment policy, with more journalistic openings for indigenous people, even though they may not always campaign on indigenous causes. As Mayan professor of anthropology, Lina Barrios, comments:

> We have had some success in the promotion of indigenous identity [in the last five years]; for example, now there are TV programs which talk about the meaning of the Mayan calendar. This is some progress, but there is no significant progress. (Lina Barrios, personal interview, 2010)

## Constraints to freedom of speech: security

PJ critique is firmly based within a human rights approach to news coverage, making freedom of speech an integral part of the theory. Closed spaces and opaque wars are core elements of war/violence-orientated reporting. Legally, freedom of speech is part of the Guatemalan constitution, though Salzman and Salzman conclude, 'Media freedom is protected only in law. Even the application of that legal protection is not guaranteed' (2010, p10). Guatemala is regularly featured among the most dangerous countries to work as a journalist. In particular, threats related to drug trafficking and organised crime are having a serious impact on freedom of speech, as self-censorship is pervasive. Three journalists were killed in 2009 (CERIGUA 2010). Media outlets in the interior are particularly targeted. One common explanation is the increased visibility of the journalist. Cesar Perez Mendez, chief editor of *El Quetzalteco* (the largest regional newspaper in Guatemala) recounts:

> Here in the region, they have killed journalists. There is one well-known case of Jorge Merida whom they killed when he was at home writing a news article [in 2008]. We have had complicated issues regarding the topic of safety here at the *Quetzalteco*. We have received death threats. Last month one of our editors quit her job, because she

felt threatened, and it was true, they were threatening her, and also the director of the newspaper, with death threats. So she said: 'I'd rather go home and be alive and [not] expose myself'. These are things which one can't see, but the journalism in the regions suffers. (Cesar Perez Mendez, personal interview, 2010)

There is a consensus among those interviewed for this chapter that solely politically motivated threats seem to have given way to those stemming from a general sense of insecurity in the country (such as organised crime). Valeria Ayerdi states that for publishing *EntreMundos*, 'ten years ago, I would have been killed'. She described relations with the police now as passive aggressive (Valeria Ayerdi, personal interview, 2010). Yet, it is this same violent climate and the associated widespread impunity that makes threats based on political differences even easier to extend. For example, feminist journalist Lucia Escobar reveals she has received a public death threat from a member of the Catholic Church after writing a column about women's reproductive rights (personal interview, 2010). Evelyn Blanck, director of NGO Centro Civitas, tells of an office burglary, despite the office being in a compound guarded constantly by security guards, as well as having its own security guard. The only things stolen were the NGO's computer hard drives and a USB-stick, with everything else left behind (personal interview, 2010).

Conversely, Gramajo warns that many of the journalists working in the media now were around during or directly after the war, in which politically motivated violence against journalists was common. He speaks of the myth of the 'hero journalist', and is not sure of how many threats are bona fide. In addition, he thinks journalists may actively seek danger. 'Some might even say: "I want to die in service" and they go for whatever there is ... There can be a lack of consciousness' (personal interview, 2010).

Violence is not only directed *at* journalists, but can also stem *from* the media. Tino Recinos recounts how a visitor from a commercial radio station threatened to shut down the community station Doble Via, since they were a pirate station. Doble Via broadcast this threat – and asked for support from the population. When the visitor from the commercial station returned, there were about three hundred people waiting for him, armed with machetes and stones, ready to kill him. Recinos called the police and warned that the situation could get out of hand, while trying to calm the irate listeners. 'He realised what was going on and tried to escape, but they caught him. He was scared. In the end, he signed a paper that the commercial station would leave us in peace, and we have not heard from them since' (Tino Recinos, personal interview, 2010).

### PJ in Guatemala: it ain't what it says on the box

Peace journalism in Guatemala has been examined in this chapter as seen through the eyes of those who analyse the media (media experts), produce the media (journalists and volunteers), and those whose representation in the media is essential for the peace process (indigenous groups). We have attempted to test our assumption that analysts need to broaden the definition of PJ to encompass current local-level media initiatives, and two main points of critique have been highlighted.

In conducting a case study of the state of PJ in present day Guatemala, we looked at the political economy of the mainstream media in Guatemala and different alternative media outlets, and then explored two features that are distinctive of the Guatemalan situation: racism and security. Mainstream media appear far too involved with the Guatemalan oligarchy and too absorbed by economic goals to reflect alternative viewpoints, thus failing to give a voice to disenfranchised groups such as Guatemala's indigenous people. While there are examples of good journalism and voices of dissent, mainstream media output can hardly count as PJ, and is, in fact, mostly counterproductive to peace building in post-conflict Guatemala.

Alternative media are aiming to fill this gap. Community radio stations such as the Mujb'ab'l yol network are actively promoting human rights and social change while giving voice to those least heard. Situated within small communities, the stations have ideal access to local knowledge and cultural codes. However, community radio efforts are threatened by their legal situation and lack of definition. Since every station can be a self-declared 'community radio', news value for peace has to be scrutinised carefully in each individual case.

Indeed, as described by Recinos and others, on occasion, community stations may even incite violence. TV Maya has so far failed to reach out to its audience. *EntreMundos* appears the most successful project so far, as it is constantly growing, focusing more and more on peace journalistic issues such as proactive reporting, inclusion of minorities, and exposing untruths on all sides. The country's high illiteracy rate, however, means that the magazine is not for all. Profound racism and a violent environment hamper peace journalistic work even further for both mainstream and alternative outlets.

Yet despite these difficulties, the opening for media for the people and by the people in Guatemala is to be found within alternative channels rather than commercial outlets. The success of *EntreMundos* and the ever-increasing number of community radio stations tells of the population's interest. Peace journalism emphasises the moral responsibility of media involved in conflict. It is the people who should be able to recognise themselves in their media – expressing their own voice to determine their fate.

## References

Atton, Chris & James Hamilton (2008). *Alternative journalism*. London: SAGE Publications.

Blondel, Yvla Isabelle (2004). International media get the most attention, but don't ignore local media in defusing conflict. In Barry James & UNESCO. *Media Conflict Prevention and Reconstruction* (pp27–31). Paris: UNESCO.

Carey, David (2004). Maya perspectives on the 1999 referendum in Guatemala: ethnic equality rejected? *Latin American Perspectives*, 139(3/6): 69–95.

Casaus Arzu, Marta (2002). *La metamorfosis del racismo en Guatemala*. 3rd edn. Guatemala: Cholsamaj.

CERIGUA. (2010). *Estado de situacion de la libertated de expresion 2009*. CERIGUA: Guatemala. [Online]. Available: cerigua.info/nuke/especiales/

informe_primer_semestre_2009_estado_situacion_de_la_libertad_de_
expresion_en_guatemala.pdf [Accessed 10 November 2010].

Colop, Sam Enrique (1996). The discourse of concealment and 1992. In
Edward Fisher & R McKenna Brown (Eds). *Maya cultural activism in
Guatemala* (pp146–56). Austin: University of Texas.

Connolly-Ahern, Colleen & Antoni Castells i Talens (2010). The role
of indigenous peoples in Guatemalan political advertisements: an
ethnographic content analysis. *Communication, Culture & Critique*, 3(3):
310–33.

Downing, John (2005). Activist media, civil society and social movements.
In Wilma de Jong, Martin Shaw & Neil Stammers (Eds).*Global activism,
global media* (pp149–64). London: Pluto Press.

Fraser, Nancy (1993). Rethinking the public sphere: a contribution to
the critique of actually existing democracy. In Bruce Robbins (Ed). *The
phantom public sphere* (pp1–32). Minneapolis: University of Minnesota
Press.

Garton Ash, Timothy (2009). Twitter counts more than armouries in this
new politics of people power, *Guardian*, 18 June 2009. [Online]. Available:
www.guardian.co.uk/commentisfree/2009/jun/17/iran-election-protests-
twitter-students [Accessed 26 July 2011].

*Guatemala Times* (2008). In solidarity to Guatemalan journalist Gustavo
Berganza, *Guatemala Times,* December 16, 2008. [Online]. Available:
www.guatemala-times.com/news/guatemala/644-in-solidarity-to-
guatemalan-journalist-gustavo-berganza.html [Accessed 26 July 2011].

Hackett, Robert & William Carroll (2006). *Re-making media: the struggle
to democratise public opinion*. London: Routledge.

Handy, Jim (2003). Reimagining Guatemala: reconciliation and the
indigenous accords. In Carol Prager & Trudy Govier (Eds). *Dilemmas
of reconciliation: cases and concepts* (pp279–306). Waterloo, Ontario:
Wilfried Laurier University Press.

Handy, Jim (2002). Democratizing what? Some reflections on nation, state, ethnicity, modernity, community, and democracy in Guatemala. *anadian Journal of Latin American and Caribbean Studies*, 27(53) 35–71.

Harcup, Tony (2007). *The ethical journalist*. London: SAGE Publications.

Howard, Ross, Francis Rolt, Hans van den Veen & Juliette Verhoeven (2003). *The power of the media: a handbook for peacebuilders*. Utrecht: European Centre for Conflict Prevention.

Illich, Ivan (1973). The professions as a form of imperialism. *New Society,* September 13: 633–35

Keeble, Richard (2009). *Ethics for journalists*. 2nd edn. Oxon: Routledge.

Kirkpatrick, Marshall (2009). Dear CNN: 'please check Twitter for news about Iran', *ReadWriteWeb*, 13 June 13 2009. [Online]. Available: www. readwriteweb.com/archives/dear_cnn_please_check_twitter_for_news_ about_iran.php [Accessed 26 August 2009].

Lynch, Jake & Annabel McGoldrick (2005). *Peace journalism*. Stroud: Hawthorn Press.

Monzon, Marielos (2010). Guatemala: con los mismos anteojos. In Omar Rincon (Ed). *Porque nos odian tanto. Estado y medios de comunicación en América Latina* (pp55-70). Bogota: Centro de Competencia en Comunicación para América Latina, Friedrich Ebert Stiftung. [Online]. Available: www.c3fes.net/docs/porquenosodian.pdf [Accessed 25 August 2011].

Neale, Jonathan (2001). *The American war: Vietnam 1960–75*. London: Bookmarks.

Nye, Joseph S. Junior (2004). *Soft power*. New York: Public Affairs.

Parkin, Frank (1979). *Marxism and class theory: a bourgeois critique*. London: Tavistock Publications.

Rockwell, Rick & Noreene Janus (2001). Stifling dissent: the fallout from a Mexican media invasion of Central America. *Journalism Studies,* 2(4): 497–512.

Rodriguez, Clemencia (2000). Civil society and citizens' media: peace architects for the new millennium. In Karin Wilkins (Ed). *Redeveloping communication for social change: theory, practice, power* (pp147– 60). Boulder: Rowman and Littlefield.

Ross, Susan Dente (2007). (De-)constructing conflict: a focused review of war and peace journalism. In Dov Shinar & Wilhelm Kempf (Eds). *Peace journalism: the state of the art* (pp53–74). Berlin: Verlag Irena Regener.

Salzman, Ryan & Catherine Salzman (2010). Central American media: testing the effects of social context. *Journal of Spanish Language Media*, 3: 5–23.

Shinar, Dov & Wilhelm Kempf (Eds) (2007). *Peace journalism: the state of the art*. Berlin: Verlag Irena Regener.

Spurk, Christoph (2002). *KOFF – media and peacebuilding: concepts, actors and challenges*. Schweizerische Friedensstiftung. [Online]. Available: www.swisspeace.ch/typo3/fileadmin/user_upload/pdf/KOFF/Reports/medienstudie.pdf [Accessed 1 December 2010].

Suchenwirth, Lioba (2006). Mayans in the news: a study of the formation of post-conflict identities in Guatemala. Master's Thesis, University of Oslo, Norway. [Online]. Available: www.duo.uio.no/publ/statsvitenskap/2006/42403/42403.pdf [Accessed 22 November 2010].

Tubin, Victoria (2007). *Mujeres Mayas, racsimo y medios de comunicación*. Guatemala: Fundacion para Estudios y Profesionalzalion Maya (FEPMAYA). [Online]. Available: www.racismoenlosmedios.com/img/articulo_2.pdf [Accessed 10 October 2010].

Tubin, Victoria, Lucia Verdugo de Lima & Amilcar Davila Estrada (2010). *Racismo en los medios: hacia un espacio incluyente: informe final*. Guatemala: Universidad Rafael Landivar.

United Nations Development Programme (2010). *Opening spaces to citizen security and human development: human development report for Central America, HDRCA, 2009–2010*. [Online]. Available: www.scribd.com/doc/53638310/Human-Development-Report-for-Central-America-PNUD [Accessed 26 July 2010].

Viscidi, Lisa (2004). The people's voice: community radio in Guatemala.

*Americas Program of the Interhemispheric Resource Center.* [Online]. Available: www.cipamericas.org/archives/1402 [Accessed 27 July 2010].

Warren, Kay (2003). Culture, violence and ethnic nationalism. In R Brian Ferguson (Ed). *The state, identity and violence: political disintegration in the post-cold war era* (pp102–14). London: Routledge.

Watanabe, John (2000). Culturing identities, the state, and national consciousness in late nineteenth century western Guatemala. *Bulletin of Latin American Research*, 19: 321–40.

Wolfsfeld, Gadi (2004). *Media and the path to peace.* Cambridge: Cambridge University Press.

World Bank (2010). *Guatemala data.* [Online]. Available: data.worldbank. org/country/guatemala [Accessed 27 July 2010].

# Chapter 7

## The gaze of US and Indian media on terror in Mumbai: a comparative analysis[1]

*Sudeshna Roy and Susan Dente Ross*

To contribute to growing knowledge of how journalists fail to contribute to global reconciliation and peace and move outside the dominant scholarly focus on Western media, this chapter critically analyses and compares editorial commentary about the 2008 terror attacks in Mumbai, India, in leading newspapers in India and the United States. Examining how media of a dominant Western and a dominant non-Western nation represent terror events, this chapter explores distinctions in the embedded ideology of terrorism and the (mis)alignment of the two nations' media commentary with the tenets of war or peace journalism. Since the terror event occurs outside the geographic and ideological West, a concept utilising a binary of the 'West and the Rest' to emphasise European uniqueness and non-Western inferiority, this chapter illuminates the representation of terror events from two opposing ends of this constructed binary.

Our findings suggest that media in both India and the US perpetuate global ideological discourses around terror that reify social identities, promote nationalistic support for government actions, and call up religious and political divisions between India and Pakistan as a primary cause for the terror attacks. The newspapers differ, however, in their proposed solutions to terrorism and their proximity to the

---

1 A different version of two short sections from the Background and Method section in this chapter appear in the Sudeshna Roy and Susan Ross co-authored article titled 'The circle of terror: strategic localizations of global media terror meta-discourses in the US, India and Scotland' in *Media, War & Conflict*, 4(3).

practices endorsed by peace journalism. Commentaries in India are heavily critical of the role of the Indian state, indicating how internal corruption and politics are contributing factors for the attacks and arguing for a self-reflexive response to terrorism. Only rarely does the US newspaper challenge its dominant post-9/11 construction of terrorism as the product of the evil 'other'. Critiques of the power elite in the US are too few and far between to create real discursive seams in its overarching schema of war journalism.

## Background

On 26 November 2008, ten armed men coordinated attacks across Mumbai, India, damaging the iconic Taj Mahal Hotel and killing more than 250 people. This chapter compares and scrutinises media editorial commentary about the attacks in Mumbai in the *Hindustan Times*, an English-language newspaper with the largest Mumbai readership and the second-highest readership (6.3 million people) in India (National Readership Studies India 2006), with that of *The New York Times*.

The Mumbai attacks have been deemed a terror event by the media in India and around the world. Terror events have long been considered a global phenomenon with news of the events accessible worldwide through media coverage. In the past decade, diverse scholars have focused on the nexus of terrorism and the media. Post-9/11, media discourse on terrorism around the world changed dramatically (Ross & Bantimaroudis 2006). Around the globe, the meaning-making powers of media engaged the 'affective potential' of audiences in the construction of a polarised view of terrorism as absolutely evil and generally ignoring the systemic forces that drive terrorist acts (Chouliaraki 2004; Simmons & Lowry 1990). Hatfield (2008) examined the media construction and deployment of iconic images to create a culture of terror. Lazar and Lazar (2004) identified the recurrent pattern of Western media to toe the line of their respective governments with regard to constructed 'enemies' within the context of the 'war on terror'. Graham et al. (2004) found that the US media's 'war on terror' discourse consistently constructed terrorism victims as inherently good; terrorists as the evil Other; public support of national government as necessary, and government actions and policies as both legitimate and benevolent. Studies of media text and talk about 9/11, both in the United States and around the world, found that media relentlessly demonise terrorists in ways that distort and inhibit the free and fair flow of information (see, for example, Hackett 2007).

Yet seams in media's hegemonic discourse of terrorism provide instances of relief from this oppressive system of representation of terrorists through opportunities for effective social action (Ross 2009). Viewing discourse as fluid and shifting, Aly (2010) identified a 'series of critical points' through which terrorism discourse evolves in a meaning-making interplay between the audience and media outlets. Similarly, Ross and Bantimaroudis (2006) defined events as the locus of 'critical discourse moments' that permit shifts in media discourse.

While post-9/11 studies of the media have provided significant insights in the area of critical media studies, very few studies have focused on how media of different countries represent terror events that have occurred outside the geographic and ideological West. In examining the media commentary about the 26 November Mumbai attacks both in India and in the US, we address this gap in literature. By examining the Indian and the US media coverage of the non-Western terror event in Mumbai, we intend to explore any distinctions in the underlying ideological messages they convey about terrorism.

Studies have shown that terrorism/conflict coverage by Western media has predominantly grazed Galtung's (1998) four identified fields of war journalism practices. The coverage has often embraced a we-they orientation (Leudar et al. 2004); contains systematic 'blind spots' (Hackett & Gruneau 2000) about 'our' ideologies and mistakes; produces monologic discourses and non-reflective echoing of elite rhetoric (Bennett 2003; Billeaudeaux et al. 2003; Carruthers 2000; Hackett 2007; Lazar & Lazar 2004; Steuter 1990) and fails to provide solutions to problems like terrorism (Lynch & McGoldrick 2005). Western media consistently cast the beliefs and visions of identified 'enemies' as radical, oppressive, fanatical, irrational and antithetical to Western values as they normalise Western values and beliefs, making Western ideas appear devoid of politics and ideology. The discursive strategies of normalising the West and fanaticising the rest, taken together, construct binaries that naturalise divisions and undermine informed deliberation of the causes of and solutions to terrorism.

Terror events/conflicts in India have been an unfortunate but consistent part of society for a long time. India and Pakistan have fought three wars since 1947, the year of their independence from the British. Two of the wars were fought over the contentious Kashmir territory, which both countries claim to be theirs. Lee and Maslog (2005) found that Indian and Pakistani media coverage of the India–Pakistan conflicts had strong war journalism framing, with little attention to long-term solutions to religious and nationalistic frictions between the countries. Siraj's (2008) examination of US media coverage of the India–Pakistan conflicts revealed that the majority of media sources also adopted the war journalism frame. The overdependence on the war journalism frame is not unusual, as noted by Ross and Bantimaroudis (2006), mainly because journalists fail to break away from trained and deeply entrenched professional patterns; constantly face structural and financial constraints; seek drama to engage the audience; adopt 'logical' storylines to resonate with the human need for narrative; and are deeply invested in the socio-psychological drive to react to events in ways that reinforce their 'rightful' place in a nation.

Some studies found that Indian media's coverage of the terror attacks in Mumbai unsettled the public and increased negative images of the nation and the effectiveness of its government (Shekhar 2009). Kattarwala (2010) found that media coverage of terrorism in India exposed the nation's deep, societal schism between Islam and Hinduism, increasing tensions among people but making visible the hegemonic force of global media discourse linking Islam with terrorism. Indian media deployed the phrase 'India's 9/11' within their coverage of the attacks, thereby diminishing and deflecting harm to national identity raised by domestic threats to national security. This deployment served to align India discursively with the US and to build public demand for Indian policies and actions similar to those of the US government following September 11, 2001: striking hard and fast against 'the terrorists' (Rajagopal 2009; Chakravartty 2002).

Few studies have examined the media coverage of these terror attacks from a war or peace journalism perspective. Advocates of peace assert that more reflective, less polarised news texts can open public discussion to the root causes and sustainable solutions to global terrorism (Howard 2003; Lee & Maslog 2005). But scholars have found that media discourses often fail to provide solutions to problems like terrorism (Lynch & McGoldrick 2005). Using the case study of the attacks in Mumbai, this chapter attempts to address this gap in scholarly studies in the field by exploring the extent to which the contemporary media discourses of terrorism complement or challenge the tenets of peace discourse.

## Method

In this chapter, we employ a critical discourse analysis (CDA) of media commentary on the Mumbai attacks in the *Hindustan Times* in India and *The New York Times* in the US. Analysis of similarities and differences among the media's discursive treatment of the attacks adds to the literature on media's global construction and utilisation of terrorism discourse, its ideological functions, as well as its alignment with war or peace journalism. Editorials and op-eds in the leading newspapers of the two countries are juxtaposed to expose terrorism discourses that are constituted by and constitutive of a global media response to a terror event that occurs in a non-Western country.

Media commentary in the US was chosen for the purpose of comparison because the US is the locus of one of the world's most-publicised terror events, the 9/11 attacks, and the US media have long been understood to sculpt and lead global media discourses on international issues, including terrorism. Moreover, the mediated, discursive position of the US as a global superpower aligned with the ideological West will highlight any discursive tug-of-war between culturally embedded handling of terrorism-related events in one Western and one non-Western nation.

Critical analysis of media commentaries requires attention to the social, cultural and historical contexts from which these texts arise and in which they perform their meaning-making work. In this study, we employ CDA to identify the structure of mediated terror discourses employed by domestic and international media, acknowledging fully that this discourse structure is neither closed nor stagnant. Rather, the particular deployment of this discourse is deeply acculturated within specific national settings and shifts in response to dominant ideological forces. CDA uncovers the processes within media discourse that systematically link distinct types of talk and text into 'intertextual chains' of meaning (Fairclough 1998). The explicit and subtextual interplay of language, image and symbol across temporal and geographic space that constitutes the fluid intertextuality of media discourse both obfuscates and normalises the implicit ideological messages of the powerful. As the site of co-existence and struggle among various local and global social actors within and between nation-states, media discourse articulates, structures and delimits the nature of these interactions in harmony with hegemonic processes of power and politics (Fairclough 1998).

Van Dijk (1995, 2006) has documented the particular usefulness of CDA in studying ideological polarisation between 'us' and 'them'. Using van Dijk's approach to ideological discourse analysis, we therefore examine media text at the levels of structure, syntax, word choice, local and global semantics, schematics, and rhetoric. The analysis also includes critical examination of linguistic binaries and floating and sliding signifiers that consolidate the representation of the world in terms of dichotomised absolutes, and create and reinforce unequal relations of power in Western discourse (Altman & Nakayama 1991; Derrida 1978). Burke (1945) defined antithetical constructions in discourse as 'the placement of one thought or thing in terms of its opposite' (p403), that has the power to represent Others without explicit mention. Barthes (1957, 1977) and Derrida (1978) have both shown how the construction of discursive imprecision, instability and incessant deferral and sliding of meaning can undermine the relationship between the signifier, signified and referent. These strategies work together to obscure the hegemonic work of discursively separating the dominant and the dominated, the powerful and the powerless.

We also analyse the editorials relying on the observations of Hackett and Gruneau (2000) who identified how systematic media 'blind spots' can be recognised through careful attention to the content, sourcing and depth of coverage; dominance of influential players; impartiality in including and representing various viewpoints, and significant omissions about the other. Finally, borrowing from Galtung's (1998) categorisation of war and peace journalism, the authors utilise CDA to identify we–they orientation; (a) historicity and self-reflexivity, reactive and proactive rhetoric, and non-zero-sum solutions in the texts.

Editorials long have been the site of discourse analysis because they express both institutional and elite group opinions, perspectives, ideologies, positions and interests (Bolivar 1994). Moreover, editorials are widely circulated in society and play a significant role in shaping public opinion in alignment with government policy, especially during periods of crisis (Billeaudeaux et al. 2003; Zaller 1992, 1994). While created by contributors rather than newspaper staff, op-eds (commentary generally placed on the page opposite the newspaper's editorial) are selected by the newspaper (generally without review of specific column content) and placed in the influential locus of the newspaper's own opinions. Op-eds thus contribute to the ideological work for and of the newspaper, albeit with the nuances of an 'external voice'. Moreover, op-eds provide opportunities for intertextual dialogue within the newspaper through counterpoint to as well as amplification of the newspaper's own voice.

One month of editorials and op-eds from the *Hindustan Times* and *The New York Times* form the basis of this study. We have examined all editorials and op-ed commentaries related to the terror events for the month following the Mumbai attacks,[2] which yielded seven editorials and seven op-eds from the *Hindustan Times (HT)* and three editorials and five op-eds from *The New York Times (NYT)*.

## Findings

The editorials and op-eds of the two countries show considerable similarities as well as differences in their approach to the Mumbai attacks.

---

2 To capture immediate editorial and op-ed response to the events in the *Hindustan Times* and *The New York Times* between 27 November and 26 December 2008, we used the LexisNexis database and keywords such as "terror***," "India***," "Mumbai w/3 attack," etc.

The interplay of the local and global is captured by four identified categories: us vs them identity construction; nationalism is what the doctor orders; playing the India–Pakistan religious difference card; and giving peace a chance. The discussion illuminates distinctive local and global discourses that serve to complicate, contradict, strengthen and substantiate terror as well as peace discourses.

## Us versus them identity construction

The examined newspaper editorials and commentaries demonstrate that terror discourses function to construct identities for 'Us', the citizens of India and, through alignment, those of the US, and for 'Them', the terrorists. The editorials and op-eds of both countries identify Us as civilised, open, democratic, superior, peaceful, and so on, while the terrorists are repeatedly labelled as dangerous, shape-shifting, noxious, barbaric, backward, volatile and tangled.

In the *HT* editorials, the discursive identity construction of 'Our' moral, ideological, cultural superiority supersedes that of the terrorists. One *HT* editorial claimed that 'Mumbai is held hostage by *marauding terrorists*, with its *citizens forced to cower in fear* under a *fog of utter helplessness* ...' (*Hindustan Times* 2008a, emphasis added). The juxtaposition of 'marauding terrorists' and cowering citizens distinguishes Us from Them. The terrorists are identified with vigorous specificity, pinning 'their' identities to a few, debilitating terms and affording Them no discursive latitude in the process. 'They' are the 'marauding terrorists', akin to pillaging and raiding pirates with no conscience, wielding 'fear' as 'their' weapon of choice on unsuspecting, 'helpless', good citizens. The Others, the marauders, are socially constructed through alienation and association with violent, raw power over the helpless, nonviolent citizens of Mumbai. The commentary works to simultaneously bestow and remove power from the Others, giving them illegitimate power to terrify and chaining them to the narrow identity of a terrorist.

The 'fog' metaphor projects an amorphous and pervasive power onto terrorism, shrouding its operation in fear-inducing mystery and enhancing the association of terrorists with the dislocation, confusion and figurative obliteration of (civilised) society. The commentary evokes scenes from Hollywood and Bollywood movies where the 'enemy's' moves are dramatically shielded and rendered impenetrable through 'fog' that accentuates the terror and blinds good citizens to the source of their trauma.

The reference to the savage raider metaphor continues to appear in subsequent *HT* editorials describing the '*senseless terror* and *barbarity* unleashed on *innocent lives* of late' (*Hindustan Times* 2008b, emphasis added). The use of the term 'barbarity' contributes to the consistent discursive identification of 'terrorists' as less than human, less than thinking, sensible beings; closer or equal to uncivilised beings or even inhuman beasts. At the same time, citizens of India are bestowed the identity of the 'innocent' and their characters imbued with a sense of purity and clarity, childlike and free of blame. Indian citizens are innocent of provocation, innocent of all wrongdoing, and innocent of any and all of the actions the terrorists are blamed for as well as all similar acts of violence.

Ideologically, the terrorists' actions are rendered as stand-alone instances of rage by uncivilised savages upon the civilised, guilt-free people of Indian society. Terrorism is not presented as one of many forms of violent action against policies of injustice, inequality, and ideological, political, and religious alienation from mainstream society. It is presented as an aberration in society, which robs acts of terror of any ability to deliver an ideological message. The blatant discursive omission in this case is the ready and blameless employ of power and dominance by many of the citizens and the government of India through domestic and international policies embodying an ideology of force. Any correlation or cause and effect relationship between military and police violence by the legitimised powers and the acts of mass violence by illegitimate terrorists is strategically omitted from these texts.

The *NYT* commentaries employ similar discursive construction of Us vs Them. However, these constructions are given a global hue, with the people of the US alongside the people of India as inherently 'good' and terrorists worldwide as unequivocally 'evil'. Kristol (2008) observes that in Mumbai 'jihadists kill innocents'. The nature of this assertion is telling in its power to assign identities. The Mumbai attackers are 'jihadists,' only, unquestionably, unproblematically, undeniably and singularly that. The connotation of 'jihadists,' or Islamic militants, is far reaching, calling up age-old images of Oriental extremism and vengeful violence, people ready to destroy themselves for irrational religious causes that border on fanaticism. The evocation of the Islamic religion, as a given, is a taken-for-granted characteristic of all terrorists, expands and reinforces global discourses of the Islamic terrorist Other rampaging across the face of the earth. The construction of the attackers as 'jihadists' is made indisputable through the well-established, global authority of the *NYT*.

The Indian editorials use generous reference to the 9/11 attacks to align the Mumbai attacks with the attacks on the Twin Towers. The recurrent use of this strategy firmly establishes a deep connection between the US and India, providing an implicit justification for the appropriateness of a US-style response to the terrorist Others and constructing an idealised global citizen network united oppositionally to the 'terrorists'. One representative *HT* column said, 'the American nation stood united at that most critical moment of history … After the Wednesday attack, the Indian nation is united in condemning the dastardly attack on our soil' (*Hindustan Times* 2008c). The identification between the two nations is explicit.

Editorials in both nations adopt discursive strategies to close the membership of Us and Them. We are the people who stand united against a common enemy, the people who support their government against Others threatening the security of the country, the citizens aligned with their global friends, partners and allies from powerful nations through unified collective action against the 'terrorists'. They, those Others, are the people who help Us define 'our' shared identity.

This sentiment of solidarity is echoed in *NYT* editorials where the citizens of the US are constructed as standing steadfast with Indians during this time of crisis. Claiming that 'We share the horror, the pain and the disbelief that Indians are feeling as they absorb the appalling details of the terrorist attacks in Mumbai that left nearly 200 dead' (*New York Times* 2008a), the *NYT* explicitly constructs US identity as connected to, and 'shar[ing]' in the suffering of the people of India. Here 'we' also connotes the global, law-abiding Us of virtuous victimisation, the people stricken by sorrow, standing together in 'horror', 'pain' and 'disbelief' at the 'appalling', senseless attacks upon Us. Yet it is 'they', in this case the citizens of India, who must absorb the reality and the dead. Thus, while 'our' horror is shared, our loss – and the resulting necessary action – is not. Second, through the implicit evocation of 'our' 9/11 sufferings, 'we' are rendered both valiant and empathetic; 'we' understand and feel their pain; our compassion makes Indians, who are suffering now, a part of Us. Finally, this identification of/with Us makes clear through oppositional omission that the terrorists are *not* Us; they are distinct from the US, the Indian, and the collective 'we'. This distinction reifies the divide the *NYT* and the *HT* articulate between the terrorist Other and Us.

The collective construction of both countries' editorials and op-eds of terrorists as uncivilised, cruel and fanatical conveys a number of hegemonic and ideological messages. First, by presenting all terrorists as pillaging, heartless jihadists, any legitimacy of 'their' political and ideological argument is erased discursively. As extreme outliers, the perspectives of these Others are voided of credibility, respectability or rationality in modern society. Through opposition, then, 'our' ideologies become legitimate and appropriate as the taken-for-granted guide to a normal and secure world. Second, the *NYT* construction of Us welded together in the moment of suffering inflicted by 'terrorists' facilitates the conceptualisation of terrorism as a unitary global problem. The implied mutuality of/between the US and India initiates a subtle move toward public persuasion of the Indian Government to ally itself with the US-directed global response to terror, to conceive of the Indian national response to the Mumbai attacks *as part of* India's support of the US in the global 'war on terror'. However, India has, in the past, been critical of the US invasion of Iraq and has refused to send soldiers to participate in that war.

The identification of solidarity between the two nations constructed through the commentaries works strategically to forge a bond between the US and India to facilitate global collaboration motivated from the Western ideological standpoint. In these ways, media discourses work to promote a deep underlying sense of who 'we' are and who 'they' are, producing, amplifying and maintaining social identities through strategic Othering processes deeply infused with the ultimate goal of promoting Western ideological and political solutions to curb terrorism.

*Nationalism is what the doctor orders*

The terror attacks in Mumbai also brought to the forefront the ways in which media discourse works to call up nationalistic and patriotic fervour amongst the people in order to hegemonically unify disparate factions of society. Other political goals, such as the formation of international alliances and chalking specific regional objectives to curb terrorism, are also crafted and sustained through the nationalistic rhetoric. Media intertextuality, particularly the strategy of comparison (Fairclough 1992), helps build an argument for the proper understanding of these terror events in India and abroad.

For example, the *HT* uses discursive strategies to bolster the patriotic argument by comparing the Mumbai attacks intertextually to the 9/11 attacks. The recency of the terrorist attacks in the US renders 9/11 highly salient in the Indian public memory, but reference to 9/11 also symbolically links India to this other great nation through subtle identification. One editorial states:

> After September 11, 2001, *America came together* to fight a *common, shape-shifting enemy*. Can *we as a nation* that has known terrorism for far longer – and with far more wounds to show – *come together* to face this nation-crippling assault? (*Hindustan Times* 2008a, emphasis added)

The unified, collective support of Americans for their government following the 9/11 crisis is represented as an ideal response to terrorism. The notion that the 'American nation stood united' is repeated almost as a choral refrain to discursively highlight and recommend a unified national Indian response as *the* proper response to their own terror events. Unification and 'coming together', in the case of India, is represented as collective condemnation of the terrorists, mourning the victims and praising the work of the government forces that defeated the Mumbai terrorists in the end. Oppositionally, we are made unlike the 'shape-shifting', intangible, deliberately diffused and formless images of the 'terrorists'; 'we' have shape and character and symbolic unity in the form of our actions. The Indian editorials' reliance on the US response to terrorism as a core of its argument illustrates and enacts an elite Indian desire for political and cultural alignment with the US, even while rejecting some of its policies (like the invasion of Iraq, for instance). The discursive reference to the 'common' enemy prompts both international and local alignment and unification – alignment with the terror-fighting tactics of the US and unification through the 'coming together' of the Indian people in support of both US action and the home government's plans in response to domestic terror attacks.

In the *NYT*, there is explicit reference to the need for activating the nationalistic fervour in the people of India and in other terror-stricken nations in order to reduce terrorism in the world. For example, one op-ed states:

> But if terror groups are to be defeated, it is *national governments* that will have to do so. In *nations like India (and the United States)*, governments will have to *call on the patriotism of citizens* to fight the terrorists ... *Patriotism is an indispensable weapon* in the *defence of civilisation against barbarism.* (Kristol 2008, emphasis added)

This statement, at once, makes the response against the Mumbai attacks both local and global. The interchangeable position constructed when referring to 'nations like India' and then putting '(and the United States)' within parenthesis, shows that India and the US have the same terror experiences and hence their responses could justifiably be the same (meaning military). The strategic use of the parenthesis functions as an equating device (equating the US with India) and garners special attention to the model nation: the US. The use of the comparative 'like' to equate Indian and US terror experiences also functions for US audiences in terms of simultaneously lauding the US citizens' nationalistic and patriotic support of their government in response to 9/11, and providing encouragement for future, uncritical support of the 'war on terror'.

The call to patriotism is problematic in this context because patriotism implies positive love for and pride in one's own country and its symbols, including a healthy questioning of national policies and procedures (Bar-tal & Staub 1997). But that is not what is being summoned here. Instead, what is being termed 'patriotism' is actually xenophobic 'nationalism' in disguise, where the love of one's country takes the form of unquestioning allegiance to jingoistic national government policies. The comparison of patriotism to a 'weapon' further adds fuel to the nationalistic agenda and fervour.

The juxtaposition of the binaries 'civilisation' and 'barbarism' deepens the chasm already in place between Us and Them and exacerbates the ideological incongruity of the two sides. In fact, the discourse restricts the possibilities to only two sides, whereas there are multiple sides and perspectives in the complex, geopolitical nature of terrorism. Finally, the discourse pitches the argument for unity against the backdrop of 'defence' of our way of life and our security. This approach implies that our unity against the 'terrorists' is a reaction to 'their' provocation, that our actions are justified because 'we' are defending ourselves. The discursive approach strategically removes our accountability and participation in the global, geopolitical crisis called terrorism. It is as if we played no part in the enactment of global policies that are now culminating in acts of terrorism.

Collectively then, these findings suggest that, within media discourse, terror attacks function as a locus for gathering together the in-group in order to satisfy specific local and global political goals identified by social elites and institutions as evidenced through overt promotion of uncritical 'patriotic' support for domestic government actions as well as the global US-led 'war on terror'.

*Playing the India–Pakistan religious difference card*

India's history is fraught with tensions emanating from religious differences between those following Hinduism and those following Islam. The creation of the Islamic country Pakistan in 1947 made these religious differences explicit and overt for the entire world to recognise. These tensions still exist in India today and have flared up time and again due to various agendas of social and political actors and groups in India as well as Pakistan. As it became evident in the days following the Mumbai attacks that those who conducted the attacks were Pakistani nationals, the terror attacks became a reminder of these longstanding tensions between the two religious groups as well as the two nations.

*HT* commentaries discursively employed the political and religious differences between the two countries to make ideological arguments in the debate on terrorism. Thus, after Pakistani President Asif Ali Zardari said that 'non-State actors operating from its soil perpetrated a horrendous carnage' in Mumbai, an *HT* op-ed dismissed the comment and the credibility of the president. 'Pakistan is *not going to get away* with the *usual smoke and mirrors game*' (*Hindustan Times* 2008d, emphasis added). The subtle intertextuality of the word 'usual' implicitly references and *establishes* past obfuscations and disingenuous attempts by the Pakistan government to allay suspicions of support for terrorist training on its soil. The threat that Pakistan will not 'get away with' attempting to disavow its role in the attacks, represents the Indian government as strong willed and capable of doing what is necessary to counter Pakistan's stance. This discourse positions India as truthful and decisive and opened space for *HT* commentaries to represent India's ongoing political problems with Pakistan as one of several issues contributing to the Mumbai terror attacks.

In contrast, the *NYT* discursively positioned the political differences between India and Pakistan, particularly as played out in Kashmir, as a much more salient and prominent contributor to the Mumbai attacks. This discourse highlights the interplay of global and local political strategies within the complex discursive arena of geographically specific mediated terror events. Two separate columns serve to illustrate this point:

> We fear that whoever was behind it, the carnage will unleash dangerous new furies between nuclear-armed India and Pakistan. And we fear it will divert even more of Pakistan's attention and troops away from fighting extremists on its western border with Afghanistan. (*New York Times* 2008a)

and

The idea that the road to stability in South Asia goes through Kashmir is as persuasive as the notion that the path to peace in the Middle East goes through Jerusalem. (Mishra 2008)

The *NYT* discourse focused on the tensions between India and Pakistan in the context of the Mumbai attacks specifically in terms of their global consequences (and implicitly in terms of the US led war on terror). The concern was that Pakistan would be drawn away from fighting the Taliban and al-Qaeda in its western borders with Afghanistan, where US troops were engaged and where, in addition to Iraq, the US was spearheading its anti-terrorism efforts. In the context of proffering advice on how India should respond to the attacks, the *NYT* strategically employed its discourse to support initiatives of the US Government. The *NYT* also zooms in on the Kashmir problem, making comparisons with complex land-occupation issues facing Israel and Palestine. Yet again, this focus serves to bring to the fore political strategies in alignment with US military policies in the region, policies that were put in place in order to wage the 'war on terror' post-9/11.

In contrast, it is noteworthy that none of the Indian editorials and op-eds mentioned the Kashmir issue, a deeply contested region along the border of India and Pakistan. The strategic omission of this issue potentially serves to obscure any Indian contributions to terrorist activities springing from the region and to divert public attention from this intractable political problem.

Pursuing its self-interested globalised discourse, *NYT* commentaries on the Mumbai attacks highlighted the religious backgrounds of the attackers to discursively connect Islamic fundamentalism with terrorism. Other issues that fuel terrorism – such as poverty, injustice, political and ideological differences and ambitions, social and cultural oppressions, etc – are absent from discourses in which Islam is tied intrinsically and singularly with terror.

Indian editorial commentaries, however, make only rare references to the religious background of the Mumbai attackers. The absence of this discursive focus, a dominant media focus in post-9/11 Western media discourse, may reflect a true ideological split between India and the US. Alternatively, this omission may be a strategic local inflection at once expressing sensitivity to the 150 million Muslim citizens of India and eliding religious sources of terror as a mechanism to fuse fragile national unity across religious divides in India (which prompted riots in Gujarat as recently as 2002). For the *NYT*, these nuances are too distant from the physical, nationalist and political centre of its readers to require attention in the post-9/11 discourses on terrorism that erase such 'subtleties'. Such realities apparently pose too inconvenient a truth, challenging military and political goals of the US in Afghanistan, Iraq and the region. Such distinctions between US and Indian media discourse also serve to maintain and reinforce the superior position of the US in terms of defining terror, whether at home or abroad.

### Giving peace a chance?

In another unexpected discursive turn, the *HT* commentaries were highly critical of the way in which the Indian government and politicians handled the Mumbai terror attacks. Time and again, frustration about the country's internal politics and corruption and mud-slinging amongst politicians came to the forefront of the discourses. Derogatory and sarcastic terms expressed and fuelled internal discontent with the government, diverging from the rallying that typically dominates post-crisis media discourse (Entman 2004). An *HT* editorial stated, 'The fact of the matter is that cynicism and laziness have been the hallmarks of our politicians' (*Hindustan Times* 2008e). The absence of nationalistic bravado, machismo or vengeance towards those threatening the security of the country and its people is striking. Indeed, this discourse shows the government of India and its political leaders as weak, incompetent, and pessimistic in nature.

There is disparity between the usual unifying nationalistic media discourses that rally citizens in support of domestic government policies and actions following crises, and the Indian commentaries that demonstrate the cultural and contextual use of the terrorism discourses in support of localised strategies. The frequency with which *HT* texts highlighted public frustration with the party in power and the more general status quo of politics in India opened up discursive fissures in the hegemonic discourse of elite societal institutions. The discursive distance between the media and the government represents what one scholar identified as infrequent yet rich 'seams' in which resources of resistance can be mined (Ross 2009). Such discourse becomes possible within a democracy of shifting power in part because the media must always equivocate their political alignment and provide a platform for dissent *within* that enables change without violence. Consequently, media remain always capable, if reluctant, of criticising rather than merely amplifying power.

In other examples of discursive divergence from the oft-beaten path of upholding the status quo in society, the *HT* editorials and op-eds took a path less travelled. The *HT* discourses presented negotiation, understanding, solidarity, commitment and peace as effective means of combating terrorism in India and the world:

> In such a situation the peace loving Indian patriotic citizens will have to combat terrorism with a commitment in order to create a terrorism free society rather than leaving it to the politicians alone or listening to the advice of the super power with [a] bad track record on terrorism. (*Hindustan Times* 2008f)

Surprisingly, some *NYT* commentaries showed similar discursive shading, though less frequently and prominently. The *NYT* too was critical of the US government's 'war on terror,' referring to it as 'America's so-called war on terror' and labelling it 'a catastrophe' (French 2008). Such criticism – although it appeared seven years, not weeks, after the 9/11 attacks – complemented and may potentially have encouraged a different Indian response to terror. This reading is supported by another commentary that said India had shown 'extraordinary restraint' and would need 'to continue to do so as the investigation moves forward' (*New York Times* 2008b). The *NYT* also critiqued the too-quick application of stigmatising labels, recognising that 'what you call someone matters. If he is a terrorist, he is an enemy of all civilised people, and his cause is less worthy of consideration' (Hoyt 2008).

These instances of discursive counterforce against the dominant current of terror discourse post 9/11 bring to the forefront media's role in opening the public sphere to alternative resolutions to terrorism. Such discourse calls on the people, rather than directly on governments, to be thoughtful and vigilant, not violent. It calls up understanding and empathy, not escalatory rhetoric that exaggerates and exacerbates differences. These media discourses present a refreshingly different perspective to the majority of discourses on terrorism. The fact that these discourses arose most prominently inside the country that suffered the terror attacks suggests that media are capable of a critical response that embraces human solutions to global problems.

## Discussion and conclusion

Our findings suggest that media in both India and the US contributed to global ideological discourses around terror that produced social identities, promoted nationalistic support for government actions, and invoked religious and political divisions between India and Pakistan as a cause for the Mumbai attacks. The similarities, more or less, ended there. The *HT* commentaries took a very different route when it came to suggesting solutions to the problem of terrorism. They were heavily critical of internal corruption and politics and were self-reflexive in their search for an appropriate response to terrorism. While the *NYT* too, displayed instances of discourses that went against the grain of the very terror discourse it had helped to construct post 9/11, such divergences from the leitmotif were too few and far between to appear to be anything more than the exception to the rule.

There are three important threads of discussion here that need elaboration. First, the Indian commentaries employ ideology that differentiates between Us and Them, Othering those who engage in terrorism. The differentiation works at the level of ostracising terror tactics and those who employ them. Apart from the discursive distancing of Us from people who employ terror to get their message across, however, the Indian texts also acknowledged economic, social, cultural and religious causes of terrorism. Recognition of these contributing factors mitigated judgments, opening the door to self-recognition within the Other and possible rapprochement as a means to reduce violence. In a way, the delineation of multiple causes of terror, in some of which the Indian nation might perceive itself to be complicit, served to bridge the distance between Us and Them, even affording Them an opportunity to see good within Us to which they might aspire. Even alongside recurrent Othering, discourses recognising social causes of terror enable the national media to be critical of their own nation and to provide a sphere for more productive exploration of complex issues. Such a discursive path must be opened further in order to encourage media to gradually abandon the well-worn trail of apocalyptic Othering.

Second, each country's media constructed unquestioning patriotic support of the national government as an ideal, driving the actions of Indian citizens to counter terror after the Mumbai attacks. The *NYT* discursive construction specified and prescribed particular qualities held to embody the patriotic. In fact, it represented patriotism as a weapon against the terrorists. The *HT* commentaries similarly upheld the desirability of patriotic fervour in Indian citizens, but a patriotism inflected with nonviolence that represented Indians as peace-loving people, and that could bring about social and political change through commitment and resolution – not through violence.

Third, the *NYT* commentaries focused on demonstrating to India and the rest of the world what a proper and swift response to terror should be. They unhesitatingly took it upon themselves to present strategies to/for India that were directed by the US political agenda in that region (as evidenced by the forceful inclusion of Pakistan and Islam in the coverage). *NYT* columns consistently and with little deviation supported US policies and constructed the unchallenged military, economic and political supremacy of the US. For India, however, the more self-critical stance, especially with regard to corruption and politics, reflected and refracted the numerous divisions of language and cultures across the vast nation.

The discourses observed in both India and the US reflected and maintained the unequal power distribution between the two nations and positioned the US as the dominant and controlling nation on issues of terrorism. However, both relied heavily upon antithetical constructions, implicit oppositions and explicit Othering to align themselves with each other against a common enemy: terrorism. While the *NYT* discourse displayed (with rare exception) all the familiar markings of media's monologic post-9/11 (anti)terrorist meta-discourse – complete with strategic ambiguities; unequivocal binaries; identification of terrorism with Islam; invocation of the global 'war on terror,' and calls for rapid, decisive military response – the *HT* discourse displayed cracks.

By calling up the specific and the local within the global discourse of terror, *HT* commentaries recognised complexities within and among the ideologies and practices of the terrorists and the Indian nation, and rejected a unitary identification of terror with Islam. Contextualising the Mumbai attacks within the global and the particular, the religious and the political, the structural and the systemic, *HT* commentaries shed light on some of the root causes, and potential long-term solutions, to terror. They softened the dehumanisation of the enemy Other and advocated thoughtful self-reflection and dialogue as an alternative to military attack. In this way, *HT* editorials and op-eds moved away from war journalism and toward peace journalism in ways not evident in the *NYT*. In so doing, the *HT* began to expose the hegemonic work of discourses that separate the dominant and the dominated, the powerful and the powerless. Lest we overstate this, however, it should be clear that alternatives to war journalism, even in the *HT*, were but fleeting shadows and narrow fissures in the dominant discourse that embraced manifest characteristics of war journalism. In the end then, both newspapers functioned far too often as the tools of global(ising) Western power elites who continue to wage war to obtain peace.

## References

Aly, Anne (2010). Shifting positions to the media discourse on terrorism: critical points in audience members' meaning-making experiences. *Media International Australia*, 134: 31–45.

Altman, Karen E & Thomas Nakayama (1991). Making a critical difference: a difficult dialogue. *Journal of Communication*, 41(4): 116–28.

Bar-Tal, Daniel & Ervin Staub (1997). *Patriotism in the lives of individuals and nations.* Chicago: Nelson-Hall.

Barthes, Roland (1977). *Image music text.* London: Fontana.

Barthes, Roland (1957). *Mythologies.* New York: Hill & Wang.

Bennett, W Lance (2003). *News: the politics of illusion.* 5th edn. New York: Longman.

Billeaudeaux, Andre, David Domke, John Hutcheson & Philip Garland (2003). Newspaper editorials follow lead of Bush administration. *Newspaper Research Journal,* 24(1): 166–84.

Bolívar, Adriana (1994). The structure of newspaper editorials. In Malcolm Coulthard (Ed). *Advances in written text analysis* (pp276–94). London: Routledge.

Burke, Kenneth (1945). *A grammar of motives.* Berkeley: University of California Press.

Carruthers, Susan L (2000). *The media at war: communication and conflict in the twentieth century.* New York: St Martin's Press.

Chakravartty, Paula (2002). Translating terror in India. *Television and New Media,* 3(2): 205–12.

Chouliaraki, Lilie (2004). Watching 11 September: the politics of pity. *Discourse and Society,* 15(2–3): 185–98.

Derrida, Jacques (1978). *Writing and difference.* Translated by Alan Bass. London: Routledge & Kegan Paul.

Entman, Robert (2004). *Projections of power: framing news, public opinion, and US foreign policy.* Chicago: The University of Chicago Press.

Fairclough, Norman (1998). Political discourse in the media: an analytical framework. In Allan Bell & Peter Garrett (Eds). *Approaches to media discourse* (pp142–62). Oxford: Blackwell.

Fairclough, Norman (1992). *Discourse and social change.* Cambridge, England: Polity Press.

French, Patrick (2008). They hate us: and India is us. *The New York Times*, December 8. [Online]. Available: www.nytimes.com/2008/12/08/opinion/08french.html [Accessed 27 July 2011].

Galtung, Johan (1998). Peace journalism: what, why, who, how, when, where. Paper presented in the workshop, 'What are journalists for?' TRANSCEND, Taplow Court, UK.

Graham, Phil, Thomas Keenan & Anne-Maree Dowd (2004). A call to arms at the end of history: a discourse historical-analysis of George W. Bush's declaration of war on terror. *Discourse & Society*, 15(2–3): 199–221.

Hackett, Robert (2007). Media terror. *Media Development*, 54(3): 3–6.

Hackett, Robert & Richard Gruneau (2000). *The missing news: filters and blind spots in Canada's press*. Ottawa: Canadian Centre for Policy Alternatives Garamond Press.

Hatfield, Katherine (2008). Falling towers, emerging iconography: a rhetorical analysis of twin tower images after 9/11. *Texas Speech Communication Journal*, 33(1): 62–73.

*Hindustan Times* (2008a). A nation that cannot afford to sleep. The *Hindustan Times*, November 28. [Online]. Available: www.hindustantimes.com/News-Feed/edits/A-nation-that-cannot-afford-to-sleep/Article1-354579.aspx [Accessed 27 July 2011].

*Hindustan Times* (2008b). Terror attacks. The *Hindustan Times*. November 30. [Online]. Available: www.assamtribune.com/scripts/details.asp?id=nov3008/edit3 [Accessed 25 August 2011].

*Hindustan Times* (2008c). Day after Wednesday. The *Hindustan Times*, December 9. [Online]. Available: www.highbeam.com/doc/1P3-1608871331.html [Accessed 25 August 2011].

*Hindustan Times* (2008d). Don't hide behind euphemisms. The *Hindustan Times*, 13 December. [Online]. Available: www.hindustantimes.com/News-Feed/editorials/Don-t-hide-behind-euphemisms/Article1-357637.aspx [Accessed 27 July 2011].

*Hindustan Times* (2008e). Politicians, shut up and listen. The *Hindustan Times*, November 30. [Online]. Available: www.hindustantimes.com/

News-Feed/edits/Politicians-shut-up-and-listen/Article1-355176.aspx [Accessed 27 July 2011].

*Hindustan Times* (2008f). The genesis of terrorism. The *Hindustan Times*, 26 December. [Online]. Available: www.highbeam.com/doc/1P3-1617927451.html [Accessed 25 August 2011].

Howard, Ross (2004). The media's role in war and peacebuilding. In Marina Caparini (Ed). *Media in security and governance* (pp147–58). Baden-Baden: Geneva Centre for the Democratic Control of Armed Forces.

Hoyt, Clark (2008). Separating the terror and the terrorists. *The New York Times*, December 14. [Online]. Available: www.nytimes.com/2008/12/14/opinion/14pubed.html [Accessed 27 July 2011].

Kattarwala, Nafisa (2010). The portrayal of Islam in the Indian mass media. Paper presented at the MeCCSA (Media, Communication and Cultural Studies Association) Conference, London, United Kingdom, January, 2010. [Online]. Available: www2.lse.ac.uk/media@lse/events/MeCCSA/pdf/papers/Kattarwala,%20H%20-%20The%20Portrayal%20of%20Islam%20In%20The%20Indian%20Mass%20Media.pdf [Accessed 9 May 2011].

Kristol, William (2008). Jihad's true face. *The New York Times*, December 1. [Online]. Available: www.nytimes.com/2008/12/01/opinion/01kristol.html [Accessed 9 May 2011].

Lazar, Annita & Michelle Lazar (2004). The discourse of the new world order: 'out-casting' the double face of threat. *Discourse and Society*, 15(2–3): 223–42.

Lee, Seow & Crispin Maslog (2005). War or peace journalism? Asian newspaper coverage of conflicts. *Journal of Communication*, 55(2): 311–29.

Leudar, Ivan, Victoria Marsland & Jiri Nekvapil (2004). On membership categorisation: 'us', 'them' and 'doing violence' in political discourse. *Discourse and Society*, 15(2–3): 243–66.

Lynch, Jake & Annabel McGoldrick (2005). *Peace journalism*. Stroud: Hawthorn Press.

Mishra, Pankaj (2008). Fresh blood from an old wound. *The New York Times*, December 2. [Online]. Available: www.nytimes.com/2008/12/02/opinion/02mishra.html [Accessed 9 May 2011].

National Readership Studies India (2006). National Readership Studies Council press release. [Online]. Available: www.slideshare.net/targetseo/national-readership-studies-india-nrs-2006 [Accessed 9 May 2010].

*New York Times* (2008a). The horror in Mumbai. *New York Times*, December 1. [Online]. Available: www.nytimes.com/2008/12/01/opinion/01mon1.html [Accessed 9 May 2010].

*New York Times* (2008b). The Pakistan connection. *New York Times*, December 6. [Online]. Available: www.nytimes.com/2008/12/06/opinion/06sat1.html?scp=1&sq=%22The%20Pakistan%20connection%22&st=cse [Accessed 9 May 2010].

Rajagopal, Arvind (2009). Violence, publicity, and sovereignty: lawlessness in Mumbai. *Social Identities*, 15(3): 411–16.

Ross, Susan Dente (2009). Limning terror: seams in the discourse of 'terrorism'. *Global Media Journal* 8(15). [Online]. Available: lass.calumet.purdue.edu/cca/gmj/fa09/gmj-fa09-dente-ross.htm [Accessed 27 July 2010].

Ross, Susan Dente & Philemon Bantimaroudis (2006). Frame shifts and catastrophic events: the attacks of September 11, 2001, and *New York Times*'s portrayals of Arafat and Sharon. *Mass Communication and Society*, 9(1): 85–101. [Online]. Available: www.tandfonline.com/doi/pdf/10.1207/s15327825mcs0901_5 [Accessed 27 July 2010].

Shekhar, Manisha (2009). Crisis management: a case study on Mumbai terrorist attack. *European Journal of Scientific Research*, 27(3): 358–71.

Simmons, Brian & David Lowry (1990). Terrorists in the news, as reflected in three news magazines, 1980–1988. *Journalism Quarterly*, 67(4): 692–96.

Siraj, Syed Abdul (2008). War or peace journalism in elite US newspapers: exploring news framing in Pakistan-India Conflict. Paper presented at the Annual Meeting of the International Communication Association, Montreal, Quebec, Canada, May. [Online]. Available: catalogo.casd.

difesa. it/geidefile/war_or_peace_journalism_in_elite_us_newspapers_
exploring_news_framing_in_pakistan-india_conflict.htm?archive=19155
9191973&file=war+or+peace+journalism+in+elite+us+newspapers+exp.
[Accessed 27 July 2010].

Steuter, Erin (1990). Understanding the media/terrorism relationship:
an analysis of ideology and the news in 'Time' magazine. *Political Communication*, 7(4): 257–78.

van Dijk, Teun (2006). Ideology and discourse analysis. *Journal of Political Ideologies*, 11: 115–40.

van Dijk, Teun (1995). Discourse analysis as ideology analysis. In
Christina Schäffner & Anita Wenden (Eds). *Language and peace* (pp17–33). Aldershot: Dartmouth Publishing.

Zaller, John (1994). Elite leadership of mass opinion: new evidence from
the Gulf War. In W. Lance Bennett & David Paletz (Eds). *Taken by storm: the media, public opinion, and US foreign policy in the Gulf War* (pp186–209). Chicago: University of Chicago Press.

Zaller, John (1992). *The nature and origins of mass opinion*. Cambridge:
Cambridge University Press.

# Chapter 8

# Peace journalism–critical discourse case study: media and the plan for Swedish and Norwegian defence cooperation

*Stig A Nohrstedt and Rune Ottosen*

In this chapter we discuss the relevance of Johan Galtung's peace journalism theory in dealing with the media coverage of historically oriented security policy issues such as Nordic defence cooperation. Previous research shows that national contexts have substantial framing impacts on mediated war discourses. After 9/11 and the global war on terror (GWOT), international politics have changed dramatically with new foreign and security policy alliances emerging. In the Scandinavian region, the previous division between NATO members (Denmark and Norway) and non-aligned countries (Finland and Sweden) is gradually reducing in importance and new patterns of cooperation are taking over. The Nordic countries are presently involved in formal defence cooperation through NORDCAPS (Nordic Coordinated Arrangement for Peace Support), NORDAC (Nordic Armaments Co-operation), and NORDSUP (Nordic Supportive Defence Structures). In November 2010, the Nordic defence ministers proposed a stronger alliance between the Nordic countries with a commitment for each to react if one of the others were subjected to threat or attack. At the same time the future presence of the Norwegian, Danish and Swedish forces in Afghanistan is under debate as most NATO members seem to be eager to set a date for withdrawing their International Security Assistance Force (ISAF) contingents by 2014. Interestingly, the issue of Afghanistan is absent from the public discourse on Nordic defence cooperation.

In this chapter we try to find out what this new situation means for security policy discourses in the media. By analysing the proposal for closer military cooperation between NATO-member Norway and non-aligned Sweden, jointly proposed by the two countries' commanders-in-chief in August 2007, we will critically discuss how useful Johan Galtung's peace journalism model is for analysis of such a debate. As a complementary approach, we propose critical discourse analysis (CDA) because of its more sophisticated method for contextualising.

## Earlier research

Our earlier studies of media coverage of the Gulf war (1990–91), the Kosovo war (1999), the Afghanistan war (2001) and the Iraq war (2003) have revealed the different framing of these conflicts in our respective countries' media (Nohrstedt & Ottosen 2001; Nohrstedt et al. 2002; Nohrstedt & Ottosen 2005). However, considering the close collaboration between Norway's and Sweden's troops in Afghanistan, and also with US and other NATO members' military forces during the GWOT, it seems important to analyse how these changes are discursively constructed for public information and deliberation. A particularly interesting and relevant case here is the ongoing political elitist debate within the Nordic Defence Forces about seeking a new role in the post-Cold War area. The main question addressed in this article is whether and how these strategic security-policy matters are constructed and manufactured for public opinion consumption.

### Methodological approach

The earlier research mentioned above concerning the Gulf War, Afghanistan, Kosovo and Iraq was all based on extensive empirical data with comparative studies of the media coverage in several countries including, of course, Sweden and Norway. Several methods were used including quantitative content analyses based on issues like genres, use of sources, and framing. Overall, these studies have used a combination of quantitative and qualitative data, the latter often dealt with using critical discourse analysis (CDA). The character of the study presented here differs from those mentioned above since the topic, Nordic defence cooperation, has not been a particularly 'hot' one in the news. This is actually our first finding – that is, that there is a lack of news journalism coverage of this important issue in mainstream media. Instead of concentrating our analysis on news reporting as we have in previous studies, our approach here is concerned with the ways in which editorials, debate and feature articles in mainstream media relate discursively to the original spin created by the two commanders-in-chief through which they brought the military collaboration plans to public attention. Furthermore, unlike our earlier studies involving cross-national comparisons, the aim in this article is a comparative analysis of different types of media in order to yield maximum variation in our data, irrespective of whether it comes from Norwegian or Swedish media.

Since the first quantitative result, the limited amount of substantial news material concerned with our proposed topic, is valid in both countries, the idea here is to look in more detail at what comments, if any, followed from the initial article on the debate in a situation where the space (that is, news coverage) for 'legitimate controversy' (Hallin 1986; see also about 'doxa' below) has been restricted to a minimum. The major purpose here is not so much to highlight the empirical results of our study on representations of the conditions of the public sphere in each two countries, but, rather, to lead an explorative inquiry into the value of the peace journalism model for media studies of conflict communication and opinion building.

Given these considerations, we selected both a mainstream Swedish newspaper as well as the online Norwegian newspaper *Nettavisen* for our analysis. The reason for choosing these particular news sources was that these were the ones that incorporated discussions of public opinion related to the chosen topic. The empirical findings from the content analyses of these cases are documented elsewhere and will not be presented in detail here (Nohrstedt & Ottosen 2010).

### A Nordic model?

Nordic countries are often held up as a role models for other countries, since the public image of Nordic countries is often linked to the positioning of humanitarian interests as paramount (Leira et al. 2007).

Issues such as the quest for equality, international solidarity, and the willingness to share some of their wealth with poor countries as development aid are all included in this public image. Norway has even tried to brand itself as a 'humanitarian great power' in its official foreign policy (Leira et al. 2007). Analysts, like the Norwegian scholar Terje Tvedt, have criticised this rhetoric and representation, claiming that Scandinavian countries should be judged by their actual policy rather than their projected image (Tvedt 2003). We support this criticism and question whether Norwegian and Swedish participation in the 'war on terror' as allies of the US has contributed negatively, rather than positively, to global affairs. To be more precise, we argue that this self-image might in itself become a risk factor for the two small countries. By ignoring the actual dangers of getting involved as an ally to the US in the GWOT, and by hiding this alliance behind humanitarian rhetoric, the two countries could easily be dragged into military adventures framed as peacebuilding and humanitarian intervention.

We also bring into our analysis Pierre Bourdieu's notion of 'doxa' or the doxic space (1998). Originally, the notion of doxa was employed by Greek rhetoricians as a tool for the formation of an argument by referring to common opinions. The doxa was often manipulated by sophists to persuade the people to follow the arguments of the leaders. In Bourdieu's use of doxa, he suggests that some issues are not introduced into public discourse because leaders simply try to avoid public discussions on certain topics. These issues are, so to speak, kept off of the agenda, leaving behind a false impression of consensus (von der Lippe 1991). We argue that doxa can be a useful concept for understanding why obviously relevant issues, such as the common risks posed to Sweden and Norway through participation in the GWOT, are left out of public debate when defence cooperation between Norway and Sweden is discussed in the media. The reasoning behind this is that opinion polls show strong opposition in both Sweden and Norway to having troops stationed in Afghanistan. Since there seems to be great unity among politicians in both Sweden and Norway that the two countries should support the US in the GWOT, they are apparently trying to avoid public debate on the issue by treating it as a topic 'beyond discussion'.

## The peace journalism discourse

Peace journalism has been proposed as an alternative to traditional war journalism by several scholars and journalists following its original formulation by Johan Galtung (2002). It has also been criticised (see the special issue of *Conflict and Communication Online* in 2007). We acknowledge Galtung's model for peace journalism as a useful tool for research and teaching (Ottosen 2010), but suggest (later on in this chapter) that for historical-related research, a peace journalism approach could be supplemented with critical discourse analysis (Nohrstedt & Ottosen 2010).

Jake Lynch has been a supporter of Galtung's peace journalism model and is an accomplished, published author in the field (Lynch & McGoldrick 2005; Lynch 2007, 2008; Galtung & Lynch 2010). In answer to the critics of peace journalism, Lynch claims that they underestimate leaders in the Western world when it comes to willingness and ability to manipulate the media. Especially in the phase of a conflict where there is a mobilisation to go to war based on rhetoric in favour of 'humanitarian intervention' (like in Yugoslavia in 1999 and prior to the war in Iraq in 2003), Lynch argues that propaganda must be contextualised by the media. It is vital, he argues, that the media is not seduced by propagandist rhetoric and does not adopt the vocabulary and arguments of spin-doctors in favour of war. Lynch stresses that the basic aim of peace journalists is to 'create opportunities for society at large to consider non-violent responses'.

Quoting Entman, Lynch argues that in order to give the public a fuller picture, journalists should make visible what the propaganda machinery leaves out – that is, peace alternatives and realistic information on the consequences of war (Lynch 2007, p2). We support Lynch's position and our own findings from several research projects fall very much in line with his arguments (Nohrstedt & Ottosen 2001, 2005). We put even more emphasis on the impact of psychological operations (PSYOPS) and their impact on media reporting. In retrospect many of the misleading stories defending the intervention in Iraq had their origin in disinformation that was a result of PSYOPS and propaganda (Eide & Ottosen 2008). One important PSYOPS operation was the US

Army pulling down the statue of Saddam Hussein and then portraying it as a spontaneous reaction from the people in Baghdad. The importance of propaganda before the war is underlined in new literature like Michael Isikoff and David Corn's book *Hubris,* where the authors argue that the Bush administration misled the public in their campaign for war to a level that has been underestimated by the media. Former US vice president Dick Cheney misused CIA resources by picking information that suited his argument for war, while simultaneously putting aside information that contradicted claims that Saddam Hussein had weapons of mass destruction (WMD).

For example, in a speech in front of veterans of foreign wars on 26 August 2002, Cheney presented a highly selective and tendentious account of data supplied by the CIA, to make a claim that was, in fact, unsupported by any evidence in the possession of the US intelligence community at the time: 'There is no doubt he is amassing WMD to use against our friends, against our allies, and against us' (Isikoff & Corn 2006, pp28–29). Isikoff and Corn reveal a forceful will in the Bush administration to go to war over whatever it chooses. When Karl Rove once told the then president about polls suggesting opposition in the public opinion against war, the president exploded: 'Don't tell me about fucking polls. I don't care what the polls say' (Isikoff & Corn 2006, p29). The extent of systematic lies repeated again and again had the desired impact, and public opinion changed to be more sympathetic to war as the solution to the 'Saddam Hussein problem'.

*Critique of peace journalism from a CDA perspective*

In the vibrant debate on peace journalism (PJ), CDA is underestimated as a supplement. CDA has emerged as one of the influential approaches within media studies in general and could play a vital role in research on war- and peace-journalism as well. We believe that the debate on journalism research can gain a lot if it draws more on this linguistically inspired analysis. There are a number of consequences if this idea is pursued in war- and peace-journalism.

If journalism is defined as a discourse, it is implied that the final journalistic products are perceived to carry and contain meanings on several levels. These levels cannot be collapsed into a single 'manifest content' level. As with other fields of communication, meaning is based on multi-level interrelations. This also means that in CDA, aspects of mediated conflict coverage that are rarely or not at all noticed in debates about journalism, such as the importance of the context, interdiscursive relations and the meaning of omissions, are addressed and integrated with the analysis. Considering that the concept of discourse is defined by its institutional dimension, the structural conditions and the organisational setting are at the centre of attention in the analysis. This is not unique to CDA but is treated in this approach as being fundamental to any reasonable conclusions. Hence when analysing media content, the layers of meanings related and alluding to other discourses beyond journalism itself are of particular importance. This interrelated set of discourses is, however, not randomly configured according to our application of CDA, but rather, is regarded as constituting a 'discursive order' – a term coined by Norman Fairclough (1995). We will exemplify the ways in which these theoretical points of departure are put to use in our analytical work, but first a few more comments must be made to state our position in the field of CDA research.

The label 'critical' is relevant as one common denominator in CDA research as it indicates the normative character of projects. It means that communication is explored with an intention to point out other possible realities than the one under investigation. This normative orientation also comes with a theoretical focus on relations of power, dominance and hegemony. These are all challenged as obstacles to the empowerment of non-elite peoples who are caught in the discursive nets spun by ideologues, public relations strategists, and politicians. As indicated above, one of the critical angles of CDA research is its insistence upon hidden assumptions and latent, but nevertheless relevant, cognitive or emotive discursive elements.

The CDA field is inhabited by three different 'schools': the socio-psychological Dutch variant with Teun van Dijk as the leading figure, the linguistic British school with Norman Fairclough as the most wellknown scholar, and the discourse-historical approach developed by the Austrian school with Ruth Wodak as its leader (Wodak 1996, 2001).

After Wodak's relocation to Lancaster, UK, the geographical dimension has become somewhat obsolete, and in addition, it should be mentioned that all these 'schools' are collaborating extensively and seem to mutually regard their differences as complementary assets.

In this article we rely mainly on the historically oriented variant as developed by Wodak and her colleagues (Wodak & Benke 2001). The main reason for this is their successful applications of inter-discursive analysis diachronically, and the insights they offer to understanding the operations of contextual conditions for the creation of meaning in different settings – for example, parliamentary debates, public ceremonies, media, exhibitions, and conversations overheard on the street corner. Here, due to practical limitations, we concentrate on journalism as a discourse related to defence policy in Scandinavian countries after the Second World War. Although this is a limited empirical basis for conclusions about the fruitfulness of applying CDA, we nevertheless hope to be able to make some critical, although constructive, comments to the debate about PJ. It makes sense because a war must be analysed as a historical process starting long before the first bullet is fired. To understand potential wars and conflicts in the years to come, we must examine the arguments in security policy debates today. As indicated above, we feel positive about the critique of mainstream war journalism coming from the peace journalism movement. But it seems to us that PJ could benefit from an integration of some of the theoretical ideas that CDA provides regarding understanding meaning-making as produced by discursive acts. If Norway and Sweden are to be involved in future wars, it might already be possible to find in the contemporary debate some reasons for this – not only in the arguments supporting a war-oriented policy, but also in the topics that are kept out of the debate. In this, we think CDA has advantages that are not captured by the peace journalism model.

In sum, we contend that the CDA approach can offer the following:

- way to manage the demands on contextual reflexivity that has been raised in the debate about peace journalism
- means of analysing propaganda discourses during peacetime, which are mainly neglected in the Galtung model, but which in

reality might be the most important stage for media effects on conflict escalation

- historical perspective – especially in the historical CDA approach as developed by Wodak and her associates – in which discursive uses of historical analogies and examples are emphasised.

In the examples we discuss below, two points in particular are important. First, that even a discourse about peace building and security plans may unintentionally be a step toward conflict escalation, and this possibility should not be left out of any critical analysis. Second, contextually speaking, we suggest that even a discourse qualified as 'peace journalism', to use Galtung's terminology, could, in the context of, for example, the GWOT, be more akin to 'war journalism' by virtue of its consequences. These are the challenges for the critical media research field studying mediated conflict reporting today.

### Empirical example 1: Norwegian media

In the autumn of 2007 the heads of Norwegian and Swedish defence, Sverre Diesen and Håkan Syrén, published a joint article in the Norwegian newspaper *Dagbladet* and the Swedish newspaper *Dagens Nyheter*, proposing closer cooperation between the two countries on military affairs and defence issues. Among the proposals were joint military exercises, military education, joint development of new military doctrines, and cooperation in buying military equipment such as warships and vehicles. In the background there was also the recent issue of Norway replacing its F-16 fighters with a new generation of fighters where the candidates were the Swedish plane JAS Gripen produced by SAAB, the European Eurofighter, and the US-produced Joint Strike Fighter (JSF) under construction by Lockheed Martin.

As mentioned in the methodological section of this chapter, by using case studies we now analyse how a few selected media in each country covered this initiative as a news event. We will also assess what the potential important issues were that were kept out of the news coverage. From Sweden, we use the example of the ways in which *Dagens Nyheter* and *Aftonbladet* reported about the Diesen–Syrén proposal.

*Dagens Nyheter* is the leading quality paper in Sweden and *Aftonbladet* is the largest tabloid in Sweden. From Norway, we draw our case study from a news story in the electronic newspaper *Nettavisen*, owned by the commercial TV station TV2. This is the only major newspaper in Norway that is a pure electronic publication. The other major electronic papers are web-versions connected to and owned by print newspapers. Our reason for choosing this internet outlet is that the readers are able to comment on articles in electronic debate forums, published after the articles themselves. By using this in our analysis, we are able to include some of the arguments in the public discourse following the article of interest.

The article in question was published in *Nettavisen* on 31 August 2007 and was titled 'Want a Norwegian–Swedish defence'. The article stated that a proposal on defence cooperation turned the traditional way of thinking about military affairs in the two countries upside down. Norway has traditionally been a NATO member while Sweden is an EU member. In the article, there was a link to the text published in *Dagbladet*. In this article, the question of sovereignty of the two countries was addressed immediately, but with a peculiar rhetorical twist, which did not invite discussion. This crucial issue was only touched upon and then 'dismissed': 'We must put all old sovereignty reflexes upside down (*på huvudet*)'. The issue of whether Sweden wanted to keep its non-alignment security policy could have raised an important debate, but was relegated to a historical past. Further, the two commanders underlined that the proposed collaboration was 'only' about purchase of submarines, tanks, and other military machinery. Also mentioned was the coordination of 'supply, education, training and doctrines'. The framing and tone was assuring and comforting. The new plans were presented as natural, uncontroversial and part of necessary development: 'The possibilities are great [up until the] year 2012 and will [expand] further in the future'. In other words, the cooperation would not restrict the freedom of actions – on the contrary, it would improve the relationship between the countries: 'A deeper Swedish–Norwegian collaboration provides opportunities to make our production of military forces more efficient. In this way we can strengthen our common influence within the entire European and Euro-Atlantic security cooperation'. This point is elaborated upon further:

> A stronger cooperation between Sweden and Norway is therefore a complement to the present collaboration structures in NATO and EU. It facilitates the national operative capacity for both of us at the same time as it prepares the ground for increased freedom of political action in the future.

In terms of macro-theme, the article describes how military cooperation makes it possible to finance necessary production and purchase of defence equipment. The selection of words and expressions implies cooperation is economically necessary and politically desirable. It is furthermore presented as entirely natural and uncontroversial: it is 'of course nothing new'; 'both sides ... will certainly keep their full national right to make decisions about the uses of the forces'; it has 'strong political support in both our countries'. However, a certain urgency of tone indicates that a choice of direction has to be decided: 'We now wish to get a clear and broad political mandate to proceed from idea to action. The time is short. In both our countries the defence forces face challenges the next coming years that make decisions about the direction urgent'.

In an interview with Sverre Diesen, attached to the article, he states that he foresees no significant practical problems with the proposal and regards it as a challenge to the politicians in the two countries. He further states that he has sent a written proposal to the Norwegian defence minister (at the time) Anne-Grete Strøm-Erichsen, claiming that it is now up to the politicians to decide how close the future defence cooperation between the two countries will be. He stresses that the proposal does not include the controversy of Norway's choice of a new generation of fighter planes.

*Nettavisen* asked Diesen in the interview whether he suspects there will be problems in NATO because of the proposal. Diesen responded that it is unproblematic for a NATO member like Norway and an EU member like Sweden to work closely together. He also mentioned that Sweden is already a member of NATO's partner organisation 'Partnership for Peace' (PfP). He further stressed that Sweden is already in a process of adapting to NATO standards in a number of areas. He did not anticipate that there would be practical problems because of the proposed cooperation, as each country would have full control over its own defence.

*Nettavisen* then asked Diesen to be more precise on the issue of 'common military doctrines'. Diesen answered:

> Norway has not decided [upon] a hierarchy of doctrines, but there are several documents offering guidelines on a national level. When we work together in an international context, in [the] UN, NATO, EU or in PfP, it is vital that one has a common doctrine which is decisive for the policy. Thus it's logical and practical that Sweden and Norway jointly contribute to [the] development of this doctrine.

Interestingly, he did not comment on the fact that Norway and Sweden both contribute to the NATO-led International Security Assistance Force (ISAF) in Afghanistan. Neither the journalists nor Diesen touched upon the historical fact that before Norway joined NATO, Sweden had suggested the establishment of a Nordic defence alliance as a possible alternative solution for Norway and Denmark. This suggestion played a major role in the public debate prior to Norway's decision to join NATO (Furre 1991). Many people on the left saw this as the preferred solution for Norway. Bjørgulv Braanen, the editor of the left-wing newspaper *Klassekampen*, also made a point of this in his commentary on 4 September, stating that it is a 'tragedy that the plans for a joint Nordic defence cooperation [were] smashed after [WWII] by US-loyal top-politicians who preferred membership in NATO'. *Klassekampen's* position is a dissenting voice in the Norwegian media landscape.

There is not enough space here to elaborate on the responses from the readers in *Nettavisen*. Let it suffice here to mention that 12 different contributions covered a number of issues. Several of the comments touched upon historical facts in the relationship between Sweden and Norway, contrary to the elite discourse (for more details, see Nohrstedt & Ottosen 2010). None of the contributions mentioned the fact that

Norway and Sweden are fighting together in Afghanistan, as US allies in the ISAF forces under NATO leadership, in the 'war on terror'. This fact, so vital for the future of GWOT, was not mentioned by *Nettavisen*, Diesen or any of the discussants.

## Empirical example 2: Swedish media

When the commanders-in-chief of Norway and Sweden publicly presented the plans for increased military collaboration, they used the format of a debate article in the leading quality newspaper *Dagens Nyheter* (*DN*) under the headline: 'New defence cooperation between Sweden and Norway' (*DN* 31 August 2007). As mentioned above, the article argues using general and vague language that old sovereignty ideas must be forgotten, and the text is intended to help the readers forget. Two themes are totally absent in the article – themes that would be entirely relevant to the historical-political substance of the matter. These are:

• the Swedish proposal after the Second World War of a Nordic Defence Alliance, which had substantial support among the general public in the Nordic countries as an alternative to NATO

• the fact that both countries are partners to US in the EU/NATO operations in Afghanistan as part of 'the global war on terror' (GWOT).

The semantic manoeuvres that the two commanders use, clearly intended to avoid the latter issue, is fascinating as an attempt not to raise concerns about possible conflict risks at the tangent of the far-reaching cooperation plans. Consequently throughout the article they use abstract and imprecise expressions when touching upon what kind of military joint venture that may come in the future: 'Euro-Atlantic security co-operation', 'the international community (UN/EU/NATO)', 'international peace operations', etc.

Since the proposed military cooperation is said to include 18 areas, only five of which are specified in the article, it is reasonable to expect that the collaboration will be extended to other NATO members. This, however, is not a theme of the article. On the contrary, it is quite re-markable how one-sided and emphatic it is when emphasising that freedom of action will grow out of the two-way cooperation.

In the subsequent media coverage of the proposed cooperation, silence, or consensus, are the predominant responses. The debate is mentioned in the news, but without reference to any crucial questions or critical comments by media personnel themselves or from the public. The leading tabloid *Aftonbladet* reports briefly about the main content of the proposal, with some quotations from the article – but no fur-ther comments or commentators are given a platform. The implication of closer cooperation with NATO as a military alliance is remarkably absent in this Social-Democratic newspaper. Curiously, while three Norwegian newspapers ran editorials, commenting on the proposal, none of them reported it in their news pages. Two of them were positive about the cooperation (*Trønderavisen* and *Bergens Tidende*), while *Nationen* was more neutral (all of them published on 1 September 2007).

However, the foreign editor of the *Dagens Nyheter* provided a com-ment. On the editorial pages, the newspaper has for a number of years proposed that Sweden should apply for NATO membership. The plans for Swedish–Norwegian military cooperation provided the foreign editor with an occasion to once more criticise the reluctance of the politicians to spell out in public what changes have actually taken place in the Swedish defence policy. The editorial's headline, 'Open door to NATO', indicates that the defence collaboration should naturally be fol-lowed up with a Swedish NATO membership application. Nevertheless, this is not something the editor expects to happen, primarily because left-wing politicians will continue their opposition given that 'there are only political losses to be made in a situation where the overwhelming majority of the Swedes are opponents to an application'. This 'remark-able' policy will continue, according to the editor:

> It is a policy where everything that is done points in the direction of an application being the natural consequence, at the same time as the official rhetoric pretends not to know what is actually going on.

He argues that it would be more honest to be forthrightly spoken, but does not express much hope of that, writing: 'what is happening is going to happen anyway'.

In an analytical comment on the proposal of defence cooperation in *Dagens Nyheter* on the same day (31 August 2007), Ewa Sternberg claimed that Swedish defence policy is changing in spite of public opinion: 'An alliance with Nordic neighbour-countries does not need to be perceived so negatively. Even if the co-operation with Oslo will bring us closer to Washington … In the future there may be a Finnish army, a Swedish airforce and a Norwegian navy in Scandinavia'.

In conclusion, the Swedish media discourse on the defence cooperation is constructed as a non-controversial and un-politicised issue, although one commentator did mention that it will tie Sweden closer to NATO. Otherwise, the rhetoric of the article signed by the two commanders seems to have been uncritically accepted, as though the proposed plans are simply the natural next steps on a road already chosen, and as if economic gains and operational improvements are the only objectives involved. The only critical point raised was when *DN* once again repeated its complaints that the Social-Democrats had not acknowledged in public that they had long since agreed to increased collaboration with NATO. That there could be any conflict-risks involved in becoming militarily engaged in the GWOT in Afghanistan or elsewhere was not mentioned in the Swedish discourse.

*The debate on a joint defence revisited*

In the summer of 2008, the heads of defence in Sweden and Norway picked up the debate again, this time including the head of defence in Finland. In a joint article, Sverre Diesen, Håkan Syrén and Juhani Kaskela suggested a joint Nordic defence system (*Aftenposten* 18 June 2008).

They referred to the article by Diesen and Syrén in August 2007 and stated that many of the suggestions had been discussed further. They mention a joint report presented to the ministers of defence in Norway, Sweden and Finland, where 140 suggestions for mutual defence cooperation had been identified. Out of these, they suggested that 40 could be implemented immediately. Among these are: 'maritime surveillance; surveillance of the airspace; mutual land forces; common areas for practice; mutual Nordic bases for sea, air, and land support; medical support; and military education.'

The main argument centres on the budget cuts experienced by the permanent forces in the three countries. The alternatives are mutual cooperation or capacity reductions. The reason for these cut backs are presented subtly. The doxa linked to Nordic participation in GWOT is as obscure here as it is in the article from August 2007. The issue is only indirectly dealt with in the beginning of the article: 'Most countries in the Euro-Atlantic area have gone through huge reorganisation to prepare their defence to deal with increasingly complex tasks nationally and internationally'.

When reading the whole report, the aim to coordinate joint efforts on GWOT is more clearly expressed. In point 42.2 in the document, the following rationale is stated clearly:

> This could mean ... shar[ing the] burden of a task in international operations by contributing assets from all three nations, simultaneously or in sequence, into one assignment. (Nordic Supportive Defence Structure 2008, pB:5)

Another way to put this, which is not pointed out in the media, is that the military capacity of all the Nordic countries has been reduced because resources have been drained as a result of participation as allies to the US in the GWOT in Afghanistan and Iraq. The question is whether the general public in the Nordic countries would have agreed to this trade-off and this use of military and economic resources if the choice had been presented to them in a frank and open manner. In the Swedish defence debate, the huge and often badly calculated costs for international military engagements have been hot potatoes for the government. Large parts of the Swedish defence industry have been bought up by US capital during recent decades, and the international collaboration in the GWOT seems to be the reason for continuing to spend large amounts of taxpayers' money on the defence sector. At the same time, it is the lever that will eventually dispose of the traditional non-alignment policy of both Finland and Sweden.

*The controversy over the Joint Strike Fighter*

On 20 November 2008, the Norwegian Parliament, after a short debate, made a decision to buy the US Lockheed Martin Joint Strike Fighter (JSF) as Norway's future fighter plane. The decision was arrived at after a long process in which the Swedish Saab Gripen plane was also a candidate. This debate was highly relevant to the other debate on closer Nordic defence cooperation. The Swedish government was involved in the marketing efforts to try to convince Norwegian politicians to choose the Swedish plane. Included in the proposed contract was a comprehensive plan for industrial, economical and military cooperation. A Norwegian decision to buy the Swedish plane would obviously have been an important step in strengthening Nordic cooperation. It would also have meant a more independent role for Norway within the US–Norwegian relationship and NATO. This issue was also controversial within the coalition government since the Sosialistisk Venstreparti (SV: the socialist left party) was in favour of the Swedish/Nordic solution while the Arbeiderpartiet (AP: the social democrats) supported the US JSF solution.

When the decision was made, it was met with disbelief from the Swedish Government and the Swedish media. The Swedish media and politicians had problems understanding the Norwegian decision since the Swedish Gripen plane, according to their estimates, would have been cheaper and one important step towards a stronger Nordic defence cooperation. In Norway the public debate and the media coverage was confusing since the government spokespersons insisted that the JSF solution was both cheaper and more suitable in terms of Norway's military commitments in international operations.

Once again the doxa of the mainstream media makes it almost impossible to confront the political and military elite on major issues, and the debate in Swedish and Norwegian media was reduced to a nationalistic quarrel between two neighbours (for further details, see Nohrstedt & Ottosen 2010). Both in Sweden and Norway, the unifying strategic interests indicate that both intend to continue as partners in arms on the battlefields in Afghanistan under US command, which, therefore, is not an issue in this debate.

## Conclusions

The peace journalism model as suggested by Johan Galtung is a useful tool as a checklist both for journalists and peace researchers. Since Galtung's approach is somewhat rigid, though, it has its obvious limitations and should thus be supplemented with other methods and theories. We suggest that Bourdieu's notion of doxa and the CDA approach could provide appropriate supplements. Although the question of audiences as active contributors to public discourse on war and peace has been addressed in some recent research, this chapter argues that a more sophisticated theoretical point of view would help bring the debate to a more reflexive level of understanding of the achievements and limits of the 'PJ program' (Kempf 2007, p4). The CDA approach to media studies incorporates levels of meanings and the relations between different actors in the discourse analysis as part of the context. The public debates in society have influences on media texts as do the discourses among politicians, PR firms and spin doctors, and vice versa. In particular, the CDA perspective helps to explore in what ways mediated discourses are interrelated with, for example, national and transnational security-policy discourses. In the empirical examples touched upon above, the silence around certain critical aspects of the plans for closer military cooperation between Finland, Norway and Sweden, and the hidden assumptions concerning the wider context of the US-led GWOT, are some such important – though discursively absent – inter-discursive relations.

Our point is that this silence about potential conflict risks and possible involvement in future wars is not accounted for in Galtung's model for war and peace journalism. On the contrary, by ignoring the potential conflict risks that may be contingent of deeper involvement in the GWOT, the journalistic examples above could in some respects be categorised as 'peace journalism', and in others as 'war journalism'. For example, although a common Nordic peaceful identity is appealed to, there is no opposition identity or enemy image mentioned. Further, there is an emphasis on preventing future wars – although by military means. On the other hand – and this would place the coverage in the war journalism category – the proposal of increased Nordic cooperation in the defence sector is making potential conflict risks 'opaque and secret', it is 'elite oriented', and it definitely does not 'uncover all cover-ups' (Galtung 2002). In addition we claim that the great variety of positions and points of view among the public, as demonstrated in our empirical examples, does not fit within either the war column or the peace column in Galtung's model. The elite positions in Galtung's war model are represented by the military and the politicians, but the ways in which they systematically avoid mentioning conflict risks, which may facilitate a process toward military conflict escalation, is not considered by the model. The reason for this is mainly because the Galtung model is limited in its reference to media coverage of open war. We on the other hand, would like to draw attention to the need to expand analysis to the previous stages in conflict escalation processes.

The discourse among ordinary people, though, might pick up historical links like the suggestion after the Second World War of a Nordic solution as an alternative to NATO for the Scandinavian countries. It might also mention possible scenarios other than those promoted by the elites. New digital media offers an opportunity for the public to put forward positions in opposition to the mainstream media (Nohrstedt & Ottosen 2010). In any case, we suggest that the multi-media landscape with its different discursive spaces should certainly have a place in the future debate on peace journalism.

Models such as Galtung's are probably not relevant in all conflict situations and stages. Used as a tool for assessing the journalistic contributions to conflict resolutions, they are not without problems because they are generalised and not properly contextualised. At the same time, it must be recognised that there is plenty of empirical evidence that much of the war reporting in mainstream media is constructed along the lines Galtung suggests. By using CDA as a supplement, we suggest that a more comprehensive analysis is possible. Such an analysis would examine both the systematic silencing of certain crucial aspects as well as promote the voices of ordinary people in public discourses on war and peace issues, with the objective of discovering the complex elements that comprise discursive constructions and structures that contribute to conflict escalation and wars.

We recommend the following as concluding points:

- Galtung's two polarised models have heuristic value for reflexive evaluation of journalistic practices – both internally within the trade and by interested people outside the profession; for example, media researchers and audiences. But they do not contain any recipe in any other ways.

- As a 'philosophy', peace journalism is far too broadly defined. It should preferably be replaced by some more appropriate term – for example, 'consequence-ethical reflexivity', which in our view better captures the kernel of the PJ 'program'.

- The PJ model might gain something from being combined with CDA or other context-oriented methods for analysis of and discussions about what discursive constructions best satisfy the requirements of a responsible and consequentially reflexive journalism.

- This should extend to the application field so that the role of journalism in the advent of conflict – the discursive handling of conflict risks – is exposed to critical examination.

### References

Bourdieu, Pierre (1998). *Acts of resistance: against the new myths of our time*. London: Polity Press.

Diesen, Sverre (2009). Hvorfor nordisk forsvarssamarbeide. *Aftenposten,* January 12, 2009. [Online]. Available: www.aftenposten.no/meninger/ kronikker/article2861077.ece [Accessed 25 August 2011].

Diesen, Sverre, Håkan Syrén and Juhani Kaskela (2008). Et nytt nordisk forsvar. *Aftenposten* 18 June 2008.

Fairclough, Norman (1995). *Media discourse*. London: Routledge.

Furre, Berge (1991). *Vårt hundreår: Norsk historie 1905–1990*. Oslo: Det Norske Samlaget.

Galtung, Johan (2002). Peace journalism: a challenge. In Stig Arne Nohrstedt, Rune Ottosen, Wilhelm Kempf, Heikki Luostarinen (Eds).

*Journalism and the new world order: studying war and the media* (pp259–72). Göteborg: Nordicom.

Galtung, Johan & Jake Lynch (2010). *Reporting conflict: new directions in peace journalism.* St. Lucia, Queensland: University of Queensland Press.

Hallin, Daniel (1986). *The uncensored war: the media and Vietnam.* New York: Oxford University Press.

Hume, Mick (1997). *Whose war is it anyway? The dangers of the journalism of attachment.* London: BM InformInc.

Isikoff, Michael & David Corn (2006). *Hubris: the inside story of spin, scandal and the selling of the Iraq war.* New York: Crown Publishers.

Kempf, Wilhelm (2007). Peace journalism: a tightrope between advocacy journalism and constructive conflict coverage. *Conflict and Communication Online,* 6(2). [Online]. Available: www.cco.regener-online.de/2007_2/pdf/kempf.pdf [Accessed 1 August 2011].

Leira, Halvard, Axel Borchgrevink, Nina Græger, Arne Melchior, Eli Stamnes & Indra Øverland (2007). *Norske selvbilder og Norsk utenrikspolitikk.* Oslo: Norsk Utenrikspolitisk Institutt (NUPI).

Lynch, Jake (2008). *Debates in peace journalism.* Sydney: Sydney University Press.

Lynch, Jake (2007). Peace journalism and its discontents. *Conflict & Communication Online,* 6(2). [Online]. Available: www.cco.regener-online.de/2007_2/pdf/lynch.pdf [Accessed 1 August 2011].

Lynch, Jake & Annabel McGoldrick (2005). *Peace journalism.* Stroud: Hawthorne Press.

Nohrstedt, Stig & Rune Ottosen (2010). Brothers in arms or peace? The media images of Swedish and Norwegian defence, and military co-operation. *Conflict and Communication Online* 9(2) [Online]. Available: www.cco.regener-online.de/2010_2/pdf/nohrstedt_ottosen.pdf [Accessed 1 August 2011].

Nohrstedt, Stig & Rune Ottosen (2005). *Global war: local news. media images of the Iraq war.* Gothenburg: Nordicom.

237

Nohrstedt, Stig & Rune Ottosen (2001). *Journalism and the new world order: Gulf War, national news discourse and globalisation.* Gothenburg: Nordicom.

Nohrstedt, Stig, Birgitta Höijer & Rune Ottosen (2002). *Kosovokonflikten, medierna och medlidandet.* Stockholm: Styrelsen för Psykologiskt Försvar Rapport.

Nordic Supportive Defence Structure (NORDSUP) (2008). *Progress report June 16, 2008.* Oslo: Norwegian Ministry of Defence.

Ottosen, Rune (2011). From psyops to miso? "Newspeak" in the information warfare in Afghanistan. Paper presented at the International Association of Media and Communications Researchers conference, Kadir Has University, Istanbul, 15 July.

Ottosen, Rune (2010). The war in Afghanistan and peace journalism in practice. *Media, War and Conflict,* 3(3): 1-18.

Syrén, Håkan & Sverre Diesen (2007). Nytt försvarssamarbete mellan Sverige och Norge. *Dagens Nyheter.* 31 August 2007.

Tvedt, Terje (2003). *Utviklingshjelp, utenrikspolitikk og makt: den Norske modellen.* Oslo: Gyldendal Norsk Forlag.

von der Lippe, Berit (1991). Kirurgisk krigføring eller kirurgisk mediedekning. In Jan Johnsen & Thomas Mathiesen (Eds). *Mediekrigen: søkelys på massemdienes dekning av golfkrigen* (pp145-67). Oslo: Cappelen Forlag.

Wodak, Ruth (2001). Critical discourse analysis in postmodern societies. *Special Issue of Folia Linguistica,* 35(1-2): 133-68. Berlin: de Gruyter.

Wodak, Ruth (1996). *Disorders of discourse.* London: Longman.

Wodak, Ruth & Gertraud Benke (2001). Neutrality versus NATO: the analysis of a TV-discussion on the contemporary function of Austria's neutrality. In Günter Bischof, Anton Pelinka & Ruth Wodak (Eds). *Neutrality in Austria, contemporary Austrian studies* (pp37-68), Volume 9. New Brunswick: Transaction Publishers.

# Chapter 9

# Conflict reporting and peace journalism: in search of a new model: lessons from the Nigerian Niger-Delta crisis

*Matt Mogekwu*

Conflict is a clash between hostile and opposing elements, ideas, or forces. It occurs at all levels of human interaction – in homes, institutions, and among groups. At some levels, these kinds of conflict are usually taken for granted and, most of the time, go unreported unless they have a bizarre nature to them. And when they are reported, it is usually in the local media as crime or as human interest stories. This chapter looks at conflict at an intra-national level in the context of peace journalism.

Such conflict occurs all around us today. Indeed, in many parts of the world, such conflicts have been transformed into a cultural norm. For so many years, conflict was the norm in such places as Northern Ireland, Lebanon, Sri Lanka, Sierra Leone, Liberia, Nicaragua and Colombia. In some of these countries, a generation would grow up knowing conflict as normalcy. For the most part, these were intra-national conflicts, although at times, the hands of foreign sponsors could be detected. But conflicts that are clearly international include what has occurred or is occurring in places like the Middle East, including the Iraqi and Afghan wars, and the Falklands/Malvinas war of 1982. These exemplify conflicts whose impacts were noticed and felt around the world.

Although the most recognisable conflict situation is war, all conflicts, to varying degrees, tend to threaten group, local, national and/or international peace. To deal with conflict, we must understand its nature and character, which implies an identification of the salient issues at play and the adoption of appropriate methods. There is thus, a need to focus on the causes of conflict, its nature and dynamics. Although it has been argued that the resolution of conflicts is only a 'minimalist condition' for the achievement of peace (Hansen 1987, p12) it is nonetheless a major effort in that direction. A more focused thought on conflict will elicit a couple of attempts at definitions that will offer a handle for understanding the phenomenon.

## Definition of conflict

Over half a century ago, Coser defined conflict as a struggle over values and claims to scarce status, power and resources in which the aims of the opponents are to neutralise, injure and eliminate the other (Coser 1956, p8). Almost 20 years later, Kriesberg (1973), in his treatise on the sociology of social conflicts, defined conflict as a relationship between two or more parties who believe they have incompatible goals. Later definitions have tended to build on these earlier attempts. Bonta defines conflict as 'the incompatible needs, differing demands, contradictory wishes, opposing beliefs or diverging interests which produce interpersonal antagonism and, at times, hostile encounters' (Bonta 1996, p405). He then goes on to define the resolution as 'the settlement or avoidance of disputes between individuals or groups of people through solutions that refrain from violence'.

The Heidelberg Institute for International Conflict Research (HIIK 2005, p2) defines conflict as:

> the clashing of interests (positional differences) on national values of some duration and magnitude between, at least, two parties (organized groups, states, groups of states, organizations) that are determined to pursue their interests and win their cases.

Some other definitions are more focused on violent disputes or armed conflicts. Singer and Small in their Correlates of War Project (CoW) define conflicts as violent disputes in which at least one of the combatant parties is a state, and there are at least 100 battle deaths. This definition focuses on the military (Singer & Small 1972, p8). Such a narrow construct of violence is also demonstrated in the definition by the Uppsala Conflict Data Program (UCDP) when it defines armed conflict as:

a contested incompatibility that concerns [a] government or territory, or both, where the use of armed force between two parties results in at least 25 battle related deaths. Of these two parties, at least one has to be the government of a state. (Wallensteen & Sollenberg 2005, p635)

The point to note in these various attempts at defining conflict is that, as the Jean Monnet Group (2006) notes, no limiting definition should be allowed, in order not to predetermine the analysis of conflicts; and that we should be aware of the need to not reduce conflicts' contextual characteristics, since this would not suit the complexity of the notion.

No matter how many definitions there are, there is a common thread containing elements of disagreement, either on points of principle, perception, policy, ideology, culture or expectation. But beyond this, a very important element in the discussion of conflict is that it occurs and progresses in stages. It is a cycle that can be broken or divided into a number of stages.

Anstey (1991) notes that the definition of conflict centres on two issues: relationships, and the fact that conflict is rooted in people's beliefs about goals as opposed to objective facts. Anstey then offers a two-part definition of conflict that is pertinent to this discourse. His definition essentially differentiates between 'latent' and 'manifest' conflict:

Conflict exists in a relationship when parties believe that aspirations cannot be achieved simultaneously, or perceive a divergence in their values, needs, and interests (latent conflict) and purposely employ their power in an effort to defeat, neutralize or eliminate each other to protect or further their interests in the interaction (manifest conflict). (Anstey 1991)

Eric Brahm (2003) draws a normal curve of progression of conflict which he breaks into seven stages/phases which include: the latent conflict stage, the conflict emergence stage, the conflict escalation stage, the stalemate stage, the de-escalation/negotiation stage, the dispute/settlement stage, and the post-conflict peacebuilding stage.

Douglas Noll (2000) identifies five phases of conflict escalation, each with its own characteristics and triggers. He argues that, as conflict escalates through various phases, parties tend to show behaviours indicating movement backward through stress. For Noll, the first phase is part of normal life in which people seek objective solutions in a cooperative manner. If at this phase, a solution is not found – especially because one of the parties sticks obstinately to his or her own point of view – the conflict escalates. In the second phase, the parties fluctuate between cooperation and competition and each party does everything possible to not show weakness. In the third phase, the parties each fear that the grounds for a common solution is lost. Interaction becomes hostile. As the conflict escalates into the fourth phase, each party is aware of the other's perspectives, but is no longer capable of considering the other's thoughts, feelings and situation. If not halted here, the conflict undergoes a dramatic increase in intensity. In the fifth and final phase, Noll notes that the conflict assumes mythical dimensions in which the parties sometimes have fantasies of omnipotence.

Johan Galtung, one of the founders of peace and conflict studies, developed a model of a conflict triangle in which he describes the architecture of conflict. According to Galtung (1996, p72), a conflict consists of behaviour (B), assumptions and attitudes (emotions) (A), and a contradiction (C). While the B-component is manifest (behaviour, by definition, is observable), both A and C are latent. Thus, conflict takes the form of a triangle and there are flows and interactions between the three corners of the triangle, which illustrate the dynamic nature of conflicts. To Galtung, conflict appears almost organic – in that it has its own lifecycle.

When we look at the various definitions and the stages and progression of conflict as enunciated by various scholars, we notice a gradual rise of conflict from a manageable level to a crescendo – where it essentially slips out of control. At this level, the best result that can be expected is that parties try to pick up the pieces, as it were, and go back to where the conflict began.

Noll's five stages, Brahm's seven stages, and Galtung's triangle, can be conveniently merged to produce two broad levels of conflict analysis, as suggested by Anstey: latent and manifest conflict. The latent level incorporates Noll's first two stages in which the parties seek objective solutions in a cooperative manner and later fluctuate between cooperation and competition; Kriesberg's first two stages of latent conflict and conflict emergence; and Galtung's attitude (A) and contradictions (C) elements of the conflict triangle. The manifest conflict level would include Galtung's behaviour (B) element and the later stages of the other models. The latent/manifest division is helpful in understanding how journalism can play a meaningful role in the pursuit of peace.

It is posited here that when conflict is confronted at the stage where its management is the least complex and unwieldy, where emotions have not peaked, and where attitudes and contradictions have not congealed into behaviours that are difficult to break, resolution is relatively easier to achieve. At Galtung's 'attitude' and 'contradiction' levels, ideas can still be suggested and considered and stand a better chance of preventing behaviours that translate into violence or manifest conflict.

It is important that such a distinction has been made between the two levels of conflict. More often than not, when we read about conflict, it is conflict of the manifest kind. Latent conflict is usually ignored because it is often not obvious enough to attract attention. It flies below the radar and is not recognised or appreciated for what it really is. On the other hand, manifest conflict is the stuff that makes for 'good' news and makes 'good' reporting. It does not call for much critical thinking. It is easier to describe and report than latent conflict, which calls for more profound understanding and analysis.

### Conflict reporting

In the first journalism course in any journalism curriculum, a journalism student learns the elements of newsworthiness. These include elements of conflict, oddity, proximity, magnitude, prominence, and human interest. Most of these elements can be identified in wars. Manifest conflict is the prime element of war. In wars, the high casualty figures make them very attractive to reporters. It is one element that elicits the 'wow!' reaction in news: for example, the bomb that was dropped has killed over 200 people! The combatants are usually prominent in their own merit, having acquired prominence prior to the war. In addition, different segments of the global audience can often identify with one or other of the fighting parties either because of cultural or religious affinities or by virtue of physical closeness, thus meeting the proximity element. Put together, these will create some human interest to which the reporter will cater. Thus, war, which is easily the highest level of manifest conflict, is very attractive to journalists. This is where the problem lies.

*Manifest conflict reporting*

Reporting about manifest conflict is less intellectually demanding than reporting on latent conflict, and journalists are more comfortable in doing so – just reporting the facts as presented (by spokespersons for different combatant groups) or as observed in the environment. Counting (dead) bodies is not much of an intellectual exercise. In fact, accuracy of casualty figures is not always of vital importance. Approximation is acceptable, especially as each group presents its own figures – usually more or less than the actual figures.

Some journalists who are involved in manifest conflict reporting may also see the positive incentives that derive from such reporting, such as the career recognition and, at times, prestige that may be accompaniments.

Because journalists are so intrigued with manifest conflict, this often results in them reporting on territoriality claims as in the Middle East, consequences of genocide as in Rwanda, fallouts of xenophobia as in South Africa and some European countries; actions of occupation forces as in Iraq and Afghanistan, insurgencies as in Sri Lanka, and civil wars as in Nigeria, Sierra Leone, Liberia and Ivory Coast. All of these situations provide easily reportable material for journalists. Such conflict reporting attracts attention. It is adrenalin-pumping for both the journalists and the audiences who have been conditioned to expect this kind of reporting to justify their patronage. Conflict reporting treats news as a commodity – something that has to sell. And as long as news is viewed as a commodity, especially by the mainstream media, manifest conflict reporting will be the most attractive variety. And as a principal revenue generating strategy for the media, it will be difficult to convince journalists to focus on events that have not reached the point of explosion. Such events would have to be spectacular!

When Saddam Hussein's Iraq was attacked, it was the spectacular 'victories' of the forces of the 'coalition of the willing' that were newsworthy and therefore were reported with enthusiasm. The toppling of the statue, the killing of different militia members on both sides, the killing of the two sons of Saddam and the display of their bullet-riddled bodies were enthusiastically reported for the satisfaction of media audiences and consumers. In the Israel–Lebanon war, the physical destruction of structures on both sides and the magnitude of casualties were what made front-page news, and top segment broadcasts. The Indian–Pakistani conflict thrived on the tension that the media helped generate with regard to the relative military/nuclear strength of both sides and the possibility of mutual destruction. The body count in Afghanistan done on a daily basis has been the core of the conflict reporting from that war.

As Lynch notes, 'objective news has three conventions in particular that also predispose it towards war journalism as [the] dominant form. They are: a bias in favour of event over process; a bias in favour of official sources; and a bias in favour of dualism' (Lynch 2008, p63). There is, of course, an economic dimension to consider. The economic interest of the media would dictate an emphasis on event over process. Process is obviously more time-consuming to report on than event. Also, getting information from official sources is less complex than seeking out possible view points from all stakeholders in the conflict, just as dualism is easier to deal with than pursuing different groups' perspectives and interests involved in the conflict. As Lynch concludes, 'the media are thus constrained to confine reports of conflict to violent events and … this can lead or leave violence to appear, by default, as the only colourable solution' (Lynch 2008, p63).

In most wars, the goal of journalists appears to be predicting the victor and the vanquished, the winner and the loser – if these roles are not discernible, it is assumed the conflict has been in vain. The no-winner, no-vanquished perspective is unattractive to the kind of conflict reporting in the media today. The conflict would have lost its appeal. It is important to emphasise that media alone do not have the capacity to resolve conflict – at whatever level. But the role and contribution of the media to the resolution of these conflicts can be invaluable.

## Latent conflict reporting

Almost as a rule, latent conflict hardly attracts attention. Yet it is at this level that conflict can best be managed by those whose interests are being considered and reported. For journalists and scholars who advocate peace journalism, the focus tends to be manifest conflict. I argue here that the application of peace journalism at the level of latent conflict reporting will more effectively help prevent the conflagration that manifest conflict usually exemplifies. Indeed, other scholars have noted the potential for such early intervention in interstate conflicts. Karl Deutsch proposed 'an early warning system' to register the amount of media attention given to a conflict area or an enemy country because 'continuing hostile attention in the mass media may tend to harden public opinion to such a degree as eventually to destroy the freedom of choice of the national government concerned' (Deutsch 1957, p202). His idea was 'to measure quantitatively the relative shares of attention allotted to particular interstate conflicts and issues in the general flow of news, the extent to which these are retained or forgotten by leaders, and the extent to which they have cumulative effects (Deutsch 1957, p204). Later, Cees Hamelink suggested an International Media Alert System (IMAS) to monitor media content in areas of conflict. 'This system would provide an "early warning" where and when media set the climate for crimes against humanity and begin to motivate people to kill others' (Hamelink 1997, p381).

Latent conflict is essentially a situation in which persons or groups or nations express differences in positions over values or ideas. It is at this level that protagonists are probably more likely to listen to one another and communicate more effectively. It is at this level also that mediation and negotiation have a greater chance of working. At the higher (manifest) level, violence would have been introduced and that constitutes one of the greatest obstacles to negotiation that could lead to peace. At the latent conflict level, it is even possible that one party does not know or acknowledge that a problem exists. This is similar to what occurs at the interpersonal level of human interaction (see Donahue & Kolt 1992). Therefore the need for face-saving is not as intense as it would be in manifest conflict where there would already be 'spectators'. This absence of the threat of 'losing face' in latent conflict makes it the preferred context for peace journalism.

## Peace journalism (today)

Since the introduction of peace journalism in the 1960s in Johan Galtung's article 'The structure of foreign news', in which he critiqued the prevailing style of journalism at the time (Galtung & Ruge 1965), other scholars have also focused on the phenomenon – many of them agreeing on some of its fundamental aspects. In a general sense, peace journalism is a form of journalism that frames stories in a way that encourages conflict analysis and a nonviolent response.

Lynch and McGoldrick (2005) have written that peace journalism concerns the choices of editors and reporters of what stories to report and about how to report them, that create opportunities for society at large to consider and value nonviolent responses to conflict. Lynch and McGoldrick's evaluative criteria provide us with some tips about what a peace journalist might try *not* to do, including a series of attitudes and behaviours that should be avoided, such as: portraying a conflict as consisting of only two parties contesting one goal; accepting stark distinctions between 'self' and 'other'; treating a conflict as if it is only going on in the place and at the time that violence is occurring; letting parties (to a conflict) define themselves by simply quoting their leaders' restatements of familiar demands or positions; concentrating always on what divides the parties; imprecise use of emotive words to describe what has happened to people; demonising adjectives and labels; and making an opinion or claim seem like an established fact.

Majid Tehranian has also identified similar issues regarding peace journalism. He describes peace journalism as:

247

> a kind of journalism and media ethics that attempts … to transform conflicts from their violent channels into constructive forms by conceptualising news, empowering the voiceless, and seeking common grounds that unify rather than divide human societies. (Tehranian 2002)

Similarly to Lynch and McGoldrick, Tehranian has also prescribed a '10 commandments' of peace journalism. He stressed that these 'commandments' are negotiable and suggestive rather than exhaustive. They include:

- Never reduce the parties in human conflict to two. Remember that when two elephants fight, the grass gets hurt. Pay attention to the poor grass.

- Identify the views and interests of all parties to human conflicts. There is no single truth. There are many truths.

- Do not be hostage to one source particularly those of governments that control the source of information.

- Develop a good sense of skepticism. Remember that reporting is representation. Bias is endemic to human conditions. You, your media organisation, and your sources are not exceptions.

- Give voice to the oppressed and peacemakers to represent and empower them.

- Seek peaceful solutions to conflict problems, but never fall prey to panaceas.

- Your representation of conflict problems can become part of the problem if it exacerbates dualism and hatreds.

- Your representation of conflict problems can become part of the solution if it employs the creative tensions in any human conflict to seek common ground and nonviolent solutions.

- Always exercise the professional media ethics of accuracy, veracity, fairness, and respect for human rights and dignity.

- Transcend your own ethnic, national, or ideological biases to see and represent the parties to human conflicts fairly and accurately.

Some of Tehranian's 'commandments' can be seen in Lynch and McGoldrick's prescriptions, and vice-versa. For instance, the advice to not portray a conflict as consisting of only two parties is common to both. This is an important point because, very often, mainstream media would often construct a conflict as between two major parties; for example, the US/Coalition forces against Iraq, or the Israelis against the Palestinians. Also, another point of similarity is the need to identify views and interests of all parties, realising that there are many truths, which need to be reported. And yet another is the avoidance of reporting and concentrating on violence, as this could become part of the problem. They also agree that journalists should go beyond reporting sources that control information, such as governments, instead giving everyone a voice.

However, Lynch and McGoldrick go beyond Tehranian's 'commandments' by advising against reporting that will do more to exacerbate than reduce the tension. This includes avoiding the use of emotive words such as 'genocide', 'massacre', and so on. They are powerful and may do more harm than good. Similarly, they advise against the use of demonising labels, such as 'terrorists', 'fundamentalists', and the like. The use of such adjectives, labels and emotive words go a long way in moulding negative (public) perceptions of the parties so described.

Taking a slightly different angle, Mayumi Futamura (2010) looks at peace journalism in relation to spirituality. He argues that society needs social dialogue in order to fundamentally change our values and norms. He believes that we as a human family need to adapt our focus on material wealth to incorporate inner experiences and spiritual wellbeing. He discusses journalism as a critical factor in this social equation:

> In order to create this kind of dialogue, I would like to look at the potential of journalism. Journalism already plays a key role in identifying important issues for people, but it can be used as a tool for creating value in people's lives only when the motivational forces behind it focus on the value of human life before financial gain. Journalism can make people apathetic, powerless or fearful, but at the same time, it can inspire people, make people reflect, and help people learn about others. (Futamura 2010, p1)

Good journalism as peace journalism?

Some scholars and practitioners will argue that journalism concerns itself with reporting the facts 'as they are'; recognising the need for objectivity and reporting as many sides of a story as possible; working within ethical parameters; and recognising the newsworthy elements of news. These are all useful. But when journalism is limited to these, it tends to become mechanical and less instrumental in bringing about peace in a conflict situation.

The kind of journalism that helps bring about peace is that which is discerning and can understand the mood and context in which an event occurs. It is journalism that understands the people involved in an event, their psychology and sociology, religion, and psyche, and the nuances surrounding the event as well as the consequences and ramifications of the conflict. This kind of journalism (as Futamura pointed out) inspires people, prompts them to reflect and helps them to learn about others.

If traditional journalism that mainstream journalists practise, with its emphasis on the rules mentioned above, is seen as 'good journalism', then the position of this chapter is that good journalism is not necessarily the same as peace journalism.

Peace journalism must be devoid of some of the parameters that tend to restrict mainstream journalism practice. It must free itself from the mainstream journalism straitjacket to be able to focus on bringing about change, preventing the escalation of crises, and doing its utmost to institute dialogue among people with conflicting ideas and values on any given issues at an intra- or international level. It should not be overly concerned with the showmanship and excitement of traditional journalism. It should not hide its goal, which is the prevention of violence. The promotion of peace should be its mission statement.

Obviously, this kind of journalism is a departure from traditional journalism and therefore requires a different mindset for journalists. It does not accommodate the brushfire approach to journalism that has been the modus operandi of mainstream/traditional journalism. This mindset is not expected of journalists who go through traditional journalism education and training. Peace journalists may still be trained in some fundamentals of journalism, such as good writing, accuracy, fairness and being guided by ethical standards. More importantly however, peace journalists must be well grounded in such areas as psychology, sociology, cultural studies, conflict management and resolution, indigenous knowledge systems of the local communities where they may be practising, and in similar disciplines that will help the journalist have a broad understanding of issues, persons involved and the contexts in which those issues are evolving. This will lead to a greater ability to discern and therefore a more effective intervention into issues that have the potential to explode into serious crises.

Traditional or 'good journalism' has not helped much to prevent manifest conflict. So a new approach should be tried. Peace journalism cannot be just *good* journalism. It is *determined* journalism. It is a serious endeavour and must be seen as such. It is patient and long-suffering and does not give up easily. Peace journalists must understand this and be comfortable with it.

The next important thing about the peace journalism advocated here is that, for the greatest impact, it has to operate at the level of latent conflict. That is the idea stage, where protagonists are most likely to listen to one another. Peace journalism that has been practised or advocated in literature so far concentrates more on manifest conflict – the stage at which war has already replaced negotiation, and the ability to work out a win–win solution becomes greatly diminished. In fact, when journalism focuses on manifest conflict, it tends towards war reporting or conflict reporting that is far removed from peace journalism.

Some of the suggestions and prescriptions mentioned in the literature noted earlier may have some relevance for the peace journalism advocated here. For instance, the suggestion not to reduce the parties in human conflict to two is very useful. There are many participants to any conflict and limiting them to two will prevent the journalist from looking at all the positions that have a bearing on the issues in question. We need to identify the views and interests of all parties. In this brand of journalism, we should be able to give voice to the oppressed and to peacemakers to represent and empower them. All of Tehranian's commandments would apply. From the prescriptions of Lynch and McGoldrick, the peace journalism advocated here should avoid concentrating always on what divides parties, and focus instead on efforts to reveal areas of common ground and goals that may be shared, or, at least, compatible. Similarly, peace journalism can heed the prescription of avoiding imprecise use of emotive words as being counterproductive to the goal of peace journalism.

## So, what is peace journalism?

In essence, peace journalism can be described as the kind of journalism that strives to *prevent* conflict from moving from a latent to a manifest level in order to avoid the violence that is often the main characteristic of manifest conflict. It also applies some fundamentals of traditional journalism. It is the stage at which the peace journalism I am describing here is applied that differentiates it from other forms of peace journalism described elsewhere by other scholars.

Peace journalism must be local and community-based and, as such, peace journalists cannot afford to be aloof. Journalists are involved because they are part of the community even if they are not part of the 'warring' parties. In intervening, journalists are also trying to protect their own interests. Maintaining a conducive environment for continuous and productive activities and interaction is in everyone's interest, including the media's. The rule of detachment (emphasised in mainstream journalism for the sake of 'objectivity') would not apply here because the media are corporate citizens of the locality. They must be determined to initiate and promote dialogue. But even as they pursue this goal of initiating dialogue and sustained conversation on the issues in question, they are simultaneously bringing the issues to the attention of national and ultimately international media.

When the issues become part of the national and international agenda, while still remaining below the level of manifest conflict, peace journalists are working to maximise peace prospects without getting involved in the kind of conflict reporting to which we are now accustomed. The local and community-centred nature of the peace journalism enunciated here is necessary because it is only in that state that the practitioners can feel drawn to the issues in contention. Distant media would neither be interested in local events nor feel the need to report on them until they have exploded, threatening national or international peace.

Peace journalism is persistent. It needs to carefully deconstruct all activities to make sense out of them and construct viable options out of the dilemma to 'sell' to the various parties. This endeavour can only be meaningfully pursued if the journalist is local to the environment.

Peace journalism should be interventionist in character. It aims to do at an earlier level what the fighting parties and mainstream media struggle to do after the conflict has become manifest and destruction has been perpetrated against groups. It works at winning the hearts and minds of people involved in a conflict. Hearts and minds would be more receptive to such overtures if serious harm has not yet been done. The intervention of peace journalism at the latent level would make this much easier.

Peace journalism should be considered a genre of its own – with rules, standards and ethics. Practitioners must appreciate the demands of this genre and be prepared to adapt. It should initiate its own curriculum for training and it should stand out as a journalism specialisation area.

The peace journalism advocated here could have been useful in many troublespots across the globe and in developing countries in particular, where initial grumbles and complaints have been allowed to fester into very serious violence. The Nigerian Niger-Delta situation is a good example of this, which will now be examined.

### The Nigerian Niger-Delta crisis

The Niger-Delta region of Nigeria occupies the portion of the country made up of the nine states of Abia, Akwa Ibom, Bayelsa, Cross River, Delta, Edo, Imo, Ondo and Rivers. The country has 36 states. This region provides the petroleum that generates over 60 percent of the country's GDP. But despite the fact that the region provides what has turned out to be the country's economic livelihood, the indigenous peoples of the region have continuously seen less than a trickle of the wealth.

According to Emeka Nkoro (2005), the conflict in the Niger-Delta region can be traced to the deep-seated neglect and marginalisation by the government and oil companies in supporting critical human development, infrastructure and provision of basic social amenities. The inhabitants in this region live in poverty in the midst of plenty. They have watched as oil was extracted from their land and the wealth derived used to develop other parts of the country far removed from their region. Most of these inhabitants are (small-scale) fishers and therefore dependent on the waters in the creeks for their livelihood. When the oil companies started exploring for oil, there was a lot of environmental degradation from spillages that the companies did little or nothing to rectify. The water was polluted, fishing was adversely affected and poverty deepened. Water-borne diseases, malnutrition and poor sanitation increased mortality among the ordinary people. Nkoro noted that one ethnic group in particular – the Ogoni – suffered from deprivation and poverty as their land was exploited and their source of livelihood seriously compromised:

> A practical case ... is that of the Ogoni community in the Niger-Delta of Rivers state whose case is being spearheaded by the Movement for the Survival of the Ogoni People (MOSOP) and the then human rights activist, Ken Saro-Wiwa. They pointed out like other communities in the Niger-Delta region that their lands have been devastated and degraded, their atmosphere has been polluted, water contaminated ... these as a result of the activities of the oil companies in the area. (Ngoro 2005, p1)

For years, the Ogoni people complained to authorities at all levels of government regarding the deprivation they were experiencing – lack of infrastructural amenities in their communities such as electricity, potable water and access to roads. But no one would listen. Then, slowly, the sense of deprivation led to frustration, which, in turn, led to anger. This was drawn out over many years. By November 1999, the Ogonis were incensed. As Nkoro notes:

> The Ogoni people issued a bill of rights which was sent to the federal government of Nigeria, demanding political freedom that will guarantee political control and use of Ogoni economic resources for

Ogoni development ... and the right to protect Ogoni environment
and ecology from further degradation. (Nkoro 2005)

At this point, the Ogonis had been forced to draw a line in the sand.
All they wanted was a change in their condition, but no one had listened
to them. The government, at all levels, did not enter into any kind of
dialogue with them. When they felt they had done all they could,
violence was introduced. The Ogoni situation became a serious conflict.
It attracted other minority groups who joined in the agitation for
resource control. This eventually led to what has now been referred to
as the Niger-Delta crisis that has claimed so many lives and heightened
the sense of insecurity in the country as a whole.

Obviously, the Niger-Delta story is more complex than has been
described here. But the idea of this narrative is to show how latent
conflict, when left unattended, can manifest itself in more serious,
violent forms.

At the earlier stages when the people started complaining about the
degradation of the environment, the authorities did not pay attention.
If they had, the killings, maiming, and kidnappings could have been
avoided. Apparently, their concerns were not wellarticulated or
sustained in ways that could attract the kind of attention they deserved.
Peace journalism could have done this – intervening at the level where
dialogue would still have been a viable option.

The Niger-Delta case is emblematic of crises in different parts of
the world that could have been avoided if necessary intervention had
occurred at the appropriate (latent) stage of the conflict.

Of course, it would be an overstatement to argue that the media
in itself could have been a sufficient counterpoise to the escalation of
the crises in the Niger-Delta or similar crisis areas around the world.
However, one could still argue that the media could be an effective
dialogue initiator. But most conflicts, especially at the latent stage, are
essentially local affairs. How would national and international media
intervene in a strictly local environment? This is a valid question that
helps underline the fact that preventive peace journalism must start
as a local endeavour. Externality is not necessarily a prerequisite for
peacebuilding if the local media intervene at the appropriate level.

The local media – print and broadcast – closest to the conflict should take up this responsibility of promoting dialogue among the parties. They could do this not only by repeating the 'event', but also by doing some analysis and confronting the relevant parties with facts that should be considered and discussed. Because the media are local, they understand the issues and all of the attendant nuances. Thus they are able to get involved and be persistent.

In fact, this notion of 'localised' journalism is nothing new. Community journalism that was promoted in the 1970s through the 1980s is locally oriented, yet professional in its coverage. It focuses on local neighbourhoods and, when it has to cover events outside, it focuses on the effects such events have on the local community (see, for example, Batten 1990; Broder 1994; Lauterer 2006). Similarly, civic journalism, which began to appear across the US in the 1990s, was seen by its proponents 'as central to the reconstruction of public life' (Friedland et al. 1994). Therefore, if local journalists in the Niger-Delta region had taken up the responsibility of helping to manage the crisis at the level where listening would have been a crucial factor in resolving the issues raised by the indigenous peoples of the region, the eventual violence might have been avoided.

In suggesting a way forward in the Niger-Delta conflict, again Nkoro noted that genuine conflict resolution efforts in Niger-Delta could be achieved by popular participation, equitable distribution of resources and free flow of information. This is very instructive. These suggestions would easily work at the latent conflict level, which should be the domain of the kind of peace journalism advocated here.

## Conclusion

There is resistance to the genre of journalism espoused here, especially from 'traditional' journalists. But it must be noted that this proposal does not call for the jettisoning of traditional, mainstream journalism. In fact, it calls for a different approach that should still work hand-in-hand with existing journalism practice. Journalism programs and institutions in countries should consider developing curricula that would take into consideration the need for producing practitioners of this genre of journalism. With continuous interaction and dialogue among various stakeholders such as government, civil society, journalism professionals, educators, various opinion leaders, and social and cultural organisations, the notion of peace journalism and capacity building endeavours for peace journalists will begin to crystallise.

Although the mass media do not necessarily start conflicts, they have been known to exacerbate them. The Rwandan conflict is a classic example. As Mogekwu (2000) noted:

> In 1992, Leon Mugesera, chairman of Habyarimanas (MRND) party in Gisenyi, known as the 'prophet of genocide', called for the Tutsis to be thrown into the Nyabarongo river so they could be 'sent to their Ethiopian fatherland'. *Radio Milles Collines* was used to make this call. Later, the dead Tutsis were indeed thrown into the river and swept into Lake Victoria. This extremist radio station continually broadcast violent xenophobic propaganda in a cruel and calculated plot to ethnically cleanse Rwanda.

Meanwhile, the extremist newspaper *Kangura* became famous when it published the '10 Bahuta commandments', ordering the Bahuta to break off all social contact with the Tutsis (Misser 1995). The message of hate continued unabated and is believed to have inflamed passions that led to the eventual massacre of over a million people in Rwanda. There are many other examples elsewhere. But just as the actions of the mass media play a serious role in affecting some kinds of behaviour, the media (and journalists) also aid and abet social and political conflict and disorder by their inaction. Peace journalism cannot afford inaction. Its practitioners should be the first on the scene of potential conflict, facilitating the right kind of action immediately. Journalists are getting used to being first responders when covering violent or mass tragedies. They arrive as early as other first responders such as police and fire trucks. They could also be first responders in conflicts that are still latent. But it would take the kind of peace journalism proposed here to do that.

Finally, it should be noted that, at this time, peace researchers have not yet produced a peace journalism welldefined enough that it could help to prevent conflict. Much of the discourse on peace journalism focuses on conflict resolution: that is, what journalists can contribute to the resolution of conflicts. These are conflicts that have gone through the various stages and phases of progression to the point where major damages have already been done. The question is: shouldn't peace journalism begin to turn its attention to the beginning stages of conflict where intervention will prevent escalation? The discourse production and search for peace journalism should continue until more satisfactory pictures emerge. No proposal should be seen as too outrageous or outlandish. History and experience have taught us that sometimes what looks crazy or improbable at one point becomes the norm at a later point. Citizen journalism would not have been given any credence two decades ago. Today, it is a reality. We must create spaces to accommodate new ideas. The peace journalism advocated here is one such new idea. In relation to mainstream journalism, this genre of journalism that I advocate here is not an 'either/or' but, instead, a 'both/and' proposition. There are ways of integrating both for the good of society. The discussion of whether peace journalism should continue to be mostly concerned with conflict resolution, or whether it should turn its hand to conflict prevention, is of great importance. I have argued that the latter makes more sense and calls for more attention than it has received thus far.

## References

Anstey, Mark (1991). *Negotiating conflict: insights and skills for negotiators and peace makers.* Kenwyn, South Africa: Juta & Co Ltd.

Batten, James (1990). Newspapers and communities: the vital link. In Jack Rosenberry & Burton St John III (Eds). *Public journalism 2.0: the promise and reality of a citizen-engaged press* (pp13–20).

Bonta, Bruce (1996). Conflict resolution among peace societies: the culture of peacefulness. *Journal of Peace Research*, 33(4): 403–20.

Brahm, Eric (2003). Conflict stages. In Guy Burgess & Heidi Burgess (Eds). *Beyond intractability.* [Online]. Available: mbb.beyondintractability. org/essay/conflict_stages/ [Accessed 2 August 2011].

Broder, David (1994). A new assignment for the press. Press Enterprise Lecture, No. 26. Riverside, California: The Press Enterprise.

Coser, Lewis (1956). *The functions of social conflict*. New York: Free Press.

Deutsch, Karl (1957). Mass communications and the loss of freedom in national decision-making: a possible research approach to interstate conflicts. *Journal of Conflict Resolution*, 1(2): 200–11.

Donahue, William & Robert Kolt (1992). *Managing interpersonal conflict*. London: Sage.

Friedland, Lewis, Jay Rosen & Lisa Austin (1994). *Civic journalism: a new approach to citizenship*. Civic Practices Network. [Online]. Available: www.cpn.org/topics/communication/civicjourn_new.html [Accessed 2 August 2011].

Futamura, Mayumi (2010). On establishing peace journalism. Peacewaves. [Online]. Available at www.peacewaves.net/peacejournalism.html [Accessed 2 August 2011].

Galtung, Johan (1996). *Peace by peaceful means: peace and conflict, development and civilization*. International Peace Research Institute. Oslo: Thousand Oaks.

Galtung, Johan & Mari Holmboe Ruge (1965). The structure of foreign news: the presentation of the Congo, Cuba and Cyprus crises in four Norwegian newspapers. *Journal of Peace Research*, 2(1): 64–90.

Hamelink, Cees (1997). Media, ethnic conflict and culpability. In Jan Servaes & Rico Lee (Eds). *Media and politics in transition: cultural identity in the age of globalization* (pp29–38). Leuven: Acco.

Hansen, Emmanuel (1987). *Africa: perspectives on peace and development*. London: Zed Books.

Heidelberg Institute for International Conflict Research (HIIK) (2005). Conflict barometer 2005: crisis, wars, coups d'état, negotiations, mediations, peace settlements. HIIK: Heidelberg. [Online]. Available: www.hiik.de/en/konfliktbarometer/pdf/ConflictBarometer_2005.pdf [Accessed 2 August 2011].

Jean Monnet Group (2006). Conflict: a literature review. University of Duisberg. [Online]. Available: www.europeanization.de/downloads/ conflict_review_fin.pdf [Accessed 2 August 2011].

Kriesberg, Louis (1973). *The sociology of social conflicts*. Englewood Cliffs, NJ: Prentice Hall.

Lauterer, Jock (2006): *Community journalism*. 3rd edn. Chapel Hill: University of North Carolina.

Lynch, Jake (2008). *Debates in peace journalism*. Sydney: Sydney University Press.

Lynch, Jake & Annabel McGoldrick (2005). *Peace journalism*. Stroud: Hawthorn Press.

Misser, Francois (1995). Rwanda: searching for the killers. WRITENET, *Rwanda: Update to End July 1995*, 1 August 1995. [Online]. Available: www.unhcr.org/refworld/docid/3ae6a6b64.html [Accessed 29 July 2011].

Mogekwu, Matt (2000). Media and the establishment of regional peace in Africa. In Ursula O Spring (Ed). *Peace studies from a global perspective: human needs in a cooperative world* (pp 296–325). Delhi: Maadhyam Book Services.

Nkoro, Emeka (2005). Conflict in the Niger-Delta: the way forward. [Online]. Available: www.Searchwarp.com/Swa20447.htm [Accessed 2 August 2011].

Noll, Douglas (2000). Conflict escalation: a five phase model. [Online]. Available: www.mediate.com/articles/noll2.cfm [Accessed 2 August 2011].

Singer, Joel & Melvin Small (1972). *The wages of war, 1816–1965: a statistical handbook*. New York: John Wiley & Sons Inc.

Tehranian, Majid (2002). Peace journalism: negotiating global media ethics. *Harvard International Journal of Press/Politics, 7*(2): 58–83.

Wallensteen, Peter & Margareta Sollenberg (2005). Armed conflict and its international dimensions, 1946–2004. *Journal of Peace Research, 42*(5): 623–35.

# Chapter 10

## Peace process or just peace deal? The media's failure to cover peace

*Virgil Hawkins*

In general, the news media in the West do not appear to be particularly interested in the outside world. Coverage has decreased considerably from the Cold War days when foreign news accounted for up to 45 percent of the time allocated for network television in the US (Moisy 1996, p9). This is of course paradoxical, given the growing connectedness of the world, and the fact that advancing information and communications technology increasingly allows the media to gather news from and transmit it to more of the world more quickly than it ever has before. It is also paradoxical given the proliferation of media corporations that appear to have gone global, and the rise of the internet, obviating the need for media audiences to be gathered in a single geographical space, easily reachable by physical forms of communication.

Within the limited media coverage of the world in the US, there are high levels of disproportion, largely along lines of geography, culture and socioeconomic status (Tai 2000). Perhaps most notably, the African continent finds itself considerably marginalised in Western media coverage (Golan 2008; Franks 2010). This can also be seen in the coverage of conflicts and peace processes (Hawkins 2002; Beaudoin & Thorson 2002, p57), resulting in stealth conflicts – those that go on largely without appearing on the media 'radar'. This marginalisation occurs despite the fact that conflicts in Africa have accounted for up to 88 percent of the world's conflict-related deaths since the end of the Cold War (Hawkins 2008, pp12–25).

Stealth conflicts are of particular concern considering the role of the media in the agenda-setting process that links actors in a position to respond to conflict. The media, particularly in the centres of power in the West, have the potential to influence public and policy responses to conflict, including expressions of concern, humanitarian aid, diplomatic pressure and, in some exceptional cases, military intervention. In this sense, the failure of the media to respond to conflict can also contribute to the lack of response to conflict by other actors. This is not to suggest that greater media coverage of a conflict will necessarily contribute to policies that will alleviate suffering and perhaps help move the conflict in the direction of a peaceful conclusion. Media coverage can often contribute to responses that have a negative impact on a conflict situation: through framing that does not reflect the reality on the ground, by oversimplification, and by taking sides. By the same token, much can be said for the potential of the media to influence public and policy responses in a positive way.

Does the disproportion in coverage levels seen in response to violent phases of conflict apply also to peace processes? This chapter examines the levels of media coverage that peace processes aimed at ending such stealth conflicts receive, relative to other more visible con-flicts. It is based largely on a quantitative comparison of coverage of the peace process in the Democratic Republic of Congo (DRC) with that in Israel–Palestine. It finds that there was proportionately less coverage of the peace process in the former case than there was in the latter, and that coverage was so limited and sporadic in the former that the media failed to refer to the series of events leading to the peace agreement as a 'process'. The chapter then goes on to discuss why this is so.

## Media coverage of peace processes

Peace is a process, not an event. It is not two signatures at the bottom of a document or a handshake among former enemies. This process neces-sarily goes far beyond any formal agreement, both in terms of time and in terms of how agreements are translated into change on the ground in the societies in question. And peace is not simply limited to the absence of violence ('negative peace'), but it can also be seen as a condition in which the root conflict, or causes of the violence, are eliminated ('positive peace') (Galtung 1985). Nor are peace processes the sole domain of elite players – the contribution of grassroots efforts should not be underestimated. For the purposes of this study, however, the use of the term 'peace process' will be limited to the time period starting at the point of substantive negotiations aimed at stopping violent confrontation, and ending at the conclusion of (or the failure to conclude) a peace agreement. Provisionally using this narrow definition permits a quantitative evaluation of media coverage of peace processes according to what could be considered to reflect the media's own definition of the term.

How do the media perform in covering 'peace processes' in this sense? While very little research has been conducted on this question, it is safe to say that the media perform quite poorly. In many cases, most of the little coverage that there is of conflict is focused on the violent phase, with very little on the peace process, or on the phases that precede and follow the violence (Jakobsen 2000). Indeed, the 'needs' of media corporations in going about the business of constructing news do not fit well with the needs of peace processes.

> A successful peace process requires patience, and the news media demand immediacy. Peace is most likely to develop within a calm environment and the media have an obsessive interest in threats and violence. Peace building is a complex process and the news media deal with simple events. (Wolfsfeld et al. 2008, p374)

Media coverage of conflicts tends to be based on 'violence journalism', in which conflict is a battle between two sides, not unlike the coverage of a sports event in which two teams contest victory (Lynch & Galtung 2010, pp1–8).

Such 'if it bleeds, it leads' newsroom mentalities can be widely observed in the end product, the levels of media coverage of conflict situations. Various studies have found news of the world being dominated by negativity – conflict, violence and crisis (Beaudoin & Thorson 2002, pp48–49; Williams 2004, pp44–45). Peace processes themselves often seem to attract little coverage, and coverage of a conflict tends to quickly evaporate when the peace agreement is concluded. But this is not always the case. A limited number of peace processes do manage to attract considerable coverage. A study of coverage of the world in the *Los Angeles Times*, for example, found that 60 percent of stories focusing on the Middle East referred to conflict resolution (Beaudoin & Thorson 2002, p57). This was not the case for Africa. Only 16 percent of stories focusing on Africa referred to conflict resolution, and Africa accounted for just four percent of all conflict resolution stories recorded.

As noted above, news of peace has an inherent disadvantage in attracting coverage – 'reporters search for "action" and when they find it their editors are more likely to place these stories in a prominent position' (Wolfsfeld 2004, p20). But while peace in itself may appear serene, inactive and thereby not newsworthy, peace processes are not necessarily uneventful or without drama. There is the tension of bitter foes coming to sit at the same table, the outbreaks of residual violence that threaten to ruin the process, the threats of walkouts, the breakthroughs along the way, the anticipation of a successful outcome, and (hopefully) the jubilation and celebration when an agreement is finally reached. This may be followed by the withdrawal of troops and perhaps historic elections. The secrecy of the negotiations could also contribute to the excitement of the proceedings. Not as dramatic as explosions and killings, admittedly, but there is certainly room for some form of 'action' or drama.

This kind of drama is most likely the basis for the coverage of peace processes that does make it to the newspapers and television stations. Beaudoin and Thorson's finding that there is, in fact, substantive coverage of conflict resolution – in some places rather than others – serves as a useful starting point for analysis. It raises the question of why some peace processes are able to attract considerable media coverage where others are not. With a view to addressing this question, this study is concerned with issue salience in the media agenda – the 'what is covered' (and, importantly, the 'what is *not* covered') rather than the 'how it is covered'. That is, it is about objects (first-level or traditional agenda-setting) rather than the attributes (second-level agenda-setting) (McCombs 2004, pp69–71). While the question of how a peace process is covered is certainly an important one, and more coverage does not necessarily contribute to a positive outcome (it can, as previously mentioned, often have a negative impact), quantity of coverage must also be taken into consideration. This is particularly the case given that coverage of peace processes is often negligible, meaning that even the potential for a positive impact is absent. Where coverage is absent, so too are incentives for elite involvement in mediation efforts, the application of pressure on the parties to the conflict, and other forms of support for the process. It is in this sense that this study focuses on the quantity of coverage.

By examining the levels of media coverage of the peace process that brought an official end to the conflict in the DRC – a stealth conflict consistently marginalised by the media in the outside world – and comparing it to the coverage of other more visible peace processes, this study hopes to contribute to our understanding of the media's perspectives on peace.

### The case of the Democratic Republic of Congo

The conflict in the DRC may be the deadliest of our times. It saw the direct involvement of armed forces from nine countries (and the indirect involvement of many others), and numerous non-state forces, both foreign and local. It was simultaneously a series of international, national and local conflicts and became known as Africa's First World War. In a series of mortality surveys conducted by the International Rescue Committee (IRC), the death toll was estimated at 1.7 million in 2000, 2.5 million in 2001, 3.3 million in 2003, 3.8 million in 2004, and 5.4 million in 2008 (IRC 2008). The results have recently been disputed by the Human Security Report Project as being far too high (HSRP 2010), but for the purposes of this study, it is important to note that during the period examined here (2001–2003) the 'known' (then undisputed) death toll stood at 2.5 million (IRC 2001), making it by far the deadliest conflict since the end of the Cold War.

In terms of a peace process, the Inter-Congolese Dialogue (ICD) from late 2001 to early 2003 (particularly 2002) is arguably the period most worthy of examination. While there had been a peace agreement before this (the Lusaka Agreement of 1999 set up the ICD but was

265

regarded as a failure), and while the conflict has continued at varying degrees of intensity at a local level (with foreign sponsorship) after the conclusion of the ICD, this phase of the peace process culminated in the withdrawal of all foreign forces, the establishment of a transitional government and the official end of the conflict.

This was not a peace deal agreed upon in secret that suddenly took the outside world by surprise, nor was it a series of impasses or frustrating blocking manoeuvres from uncommitted parties that bore no fruit. The talks were presided over by a former head of state (Ketumile Masire of Botswana), in Ethiopia and then in South Africa. There were setbacks, walkouts and some fighting on the ground (at one point rebels captured a town, prompting the government delegation to walk out, only returning when the rebels promised to withdraw), and yet there was progress and a series of major and conclusive agreements (Apuuli 2004). The results of these agreements – large-scale troop withdrawals by foreign forces (30 000 troops from Rwanda alone) and the establishment of a transitional government – were quite tangible and visible. In short, this was an event-filled conclusion to the world's deadliest conflict – there was plenty of 'news' to be reported. And yet very little of this process was being reported, and what was, was done so in a very piecemeal and disjointed manner.

Table 1: Timeline of the Inter-Congolese Dialogue (ICD) (2001–2003)

| Date | Event | Result |
|------|-------|--------|
| 15–23 Oct 01 | ICD opens in Addis Ababa | Talks break down |
| 26 Feb to 19 Apr 02 | ICD resumes with talks in Sun City | Agreement on power sharing framework reached |
| 25–30 Jul 02 | Rwanda–DRC peace talks | Bilateral peace agreement |
| 6 Sep 02 | Uganda–DRC peace talks | Bilateral peace agreement |
| 5 Oct 02 | Withdrawal of Rwandan troops ends | Complete withdrawal confirmed |

| Date | Event | Result |
|------|-------|--------|
| 30 Oct 02 | Withdrawal of Zimbabwean, Angolan, Namibian troops ends | Complete withdrawal confirmed |
| 25 Oct to 17 Dec 02 | Talks in Pretoria by all Congolese parties to conflict, political opposition, civil society | Comprehensive power sharing agreement reached, formal end of conflict |
| 2 Apr 03 | Pretoria agreement ratified in Sun City | Conclusion of the ICD |
| 4 Apr 03 | Promulgation of transitional constitution | |

In order to examine how extensively this peace process was covered by the media in the outside world, a study was conducted of media coverage by *The New York Times* (US), *The Times* (UK), *The Globe and Mail* (Canada), and *The Australian* (Australia). Leading media sources from the US and the UK were selected because of their ability to influence the global information flow and the level of interest/ response of other powerful global actors. Media sources from Canada and Australia were selected to examine the pervasiveness of trends in the global information flow. While both are Western countries, they can be seen as being distinct from the more powerful US and UK: Canada in terms of the government's approach to foreign affairs issues, and Australia in terms of its geographic distance from the centres of power. The particular newspapers selected are known as newspapers of record in their respective countries. While this particular study looks only at English language media, it can be noted here that previous studies on the levels of coverage of conflict that included non-English media sources found comparatively higher levels of coverage on the DRC in the French language media than English language media, and almost insignificant levels of coverage in the Japanese media (Hawkins 2002; 2008, pp109–11).

Using the LexisNexis database, a search was conducted for articles on the DRC during the period of the ICD. Articles were separated into those that focused primarily on the ongoing peace process and those that did not, including reporting centred around fighting and humanitarian suffering, as well as reporting unrelated to the conflict (such as volcanic eruptions and Belgium's apology for its role in the assassination of Patrice Lumumba). As many articles contained a mix of these topics, articles coded as those focusing primarily on the peace process were determined to be those in which the coverage of the peace process accounted for more than half the article. Coverage of the peace process here included that of the progress of the peace talks (successes and failures) and their aftermath (in this case most notably foreign troop withdrawals), initiatives, gestures and the interventions and application of pressure by outside parties.

None of the sources studied appeared to show much interest in the peace process. While *The New York Times*, for example, did at least cover each of the events in Table 1, it did so in very little depth. Perhaps most telling is the fact that 65 percent (31 of 48) of all articles focusing on the peace process were not full articles, but world briefings, none being more than 130 words in length. In fact the average length of an article on the peace process in this period was just 263 words. Of the events in the course of the ICD, the peace agreement between Rwanda and the DRC attracted the most coverage (five articles and one briefing), and the withdrawals were also covered. The Sun City peace talks that preceded this were mostly glossed over in world briefings, and, by the time talks were underway in Pretoria, what interest there was had mostly been lost. A world briefing mentioned that talks were resuming, but no updates were offered on the progress of the talks until two months later, when a single article informed readers that the Pretoria agreement had been signed. While this article did contain some information on the agreement and some background of the conflict, no analysis or follow-up articles were printed after this.

*The New York Times* had more to say about the peace process than the other sources studied. *The Times* printed a series of substantive articles on the Rwanda–DRC peace agreement, but little more. Only one substantive article was produced on the Sun City talks (231 words noting that the talks had collapsed) and none was forthcoming on the Pretoria talks or agreement or the ratification of the deal in Sun City in 2003 (world briefings are not included in the LexisNexis database for *The Times* and were not examined). The most detailed article dealing with the DRC in general was a 2874-word article by a reporter travelling with UK Secretary of State for International Development, Clare Short, on a four-day tour of the DRC, Burundi, Rwanda and Uganda. It is essentially a travel/adventure diary (not a news article) with hints of colonial nostalgia: they were 'buccaneers' who faced spies, rebels and food poisoning, and crossed the Congo River in a pirogue (Treneman 2002).

Canada's *The Globe and Mail* first acknowledged the existence of the peace talks in March 2002, with a 35-word brief noting that the DRC Government had pulled out of the peace talks in Sun City (it never mentioned there were talks going on to begin with). In the 18 months of the ICD, this newspaper published only four substantive articles on the entire peace process – one on the Rwanda–DRC peace deal, two (one article and one editorial) on the Pretoria agreement, and one editorial after the final Sun City agreement. With no apparent irony, the article on the Rwanda–DRC deal opens with the words 'It's a forgotten war' (Nolen 2002), and the final editorial, entitled 'The invisible war' invites readers to 'Spare a thought for the war that is not being brought live to living rooms across North America' (Anon 2003). In total, briefings that averaged 53 words accounted for 78 percent (14 of 18) of the articles published on the peace process.

*The Australian* newspaper took no half measures in its marginalisation of the DRC peace process. It needed only 672 words to cover the entire 18 months of the ICD: 41 words to note that talks would be starting in Addis Ababa, 37 words to report that Rwanda and the DRC would sign a deal, 568 words when that deal was signed, and 26 words after the ratification of the comprehensive agreement in April 2003. The newspaper missed the crucial talks and agreements at Sun City and Pretoria altogether. Oddly enough, in the same period it did report on other news in the DRC, such as the eruption of a volcano, students arrested for protesting high school fees, 17 people killed in a freak storm, illegal miners killed after being sealed into a mine, and alleged cannibalism. It had more to say in a single article about a Congo exhibition in Belgium than it did about the entire course of the peace process (Sutherland 2002). See Hawkins (2009) for a more detailed look at the coverage of the DRC conflict in *The Australian*.

## Some comparisons

It is useful to examine how the coverage of the peace process in the DRC compares to that of other peace processes. This section will begin by comparing the coverage in *The New York Times* of the peace process in the DRC in 2002 with coverage of the Israel–Palestine peace process in 2003. It should be noted from the outset that the lessons that can be learned from comparing two very different peace processes at different stages are limited and certainly need to be handled with care. There are, however, some similarities between the two peace processes in these periods, and, by focusing on a period of one year, a very basic comparison is possible.

In both cases, there were movements in the peace processes throughout the course of the year. Major agreements were debated for a number of months and were adopted. In both cases, agreements saw the withdrawal of foreign forces – Israeli forces from northern Gaza, and all foreign forces (except Uganda) from the DRC. The involvement in the process of the US at the presidential level in the Israel–Palestine case is clearly a major difference between the two, and this could be expected to serve as a major boost to coverage. On the other hand, whereas the Israel–Palestine case was a debate on a 'road map' towards an agreement (not by any means an agreement in itself), the DRC case saw the successful conclusion of a number of both international (bilateral) and national comprehensive agreements and the official end to the conflict. Furthermore, the DRC conflict was known to be the world's deadliest, with a death toll hundreds of times greater than that in Israel–Palestine. These points could conceivably have justified a boost in coverage of the DRC peace process.

A quantitative study of media coverage is clearly not needed to tell us that there was more coverage of the Israel–Palestinian peace process than there was of the DRC peace process. The question is how much more? Two previous studies that compared the overall coverage of these conflicts (the violence, humanitarian issues and the peace processes combined) in *The New York Times* (one covering the year 2000, Hawkins 2002; and one covering the year 2009 Hawkins unpublished) found that Israel–Palestine attracted 12–13 times more coverage than the DRC. This study, isolating the coverage of the peace processes (for 2002 in the case of the DRC and 2003 in the case of Israel–Palestine), found that there was 20 times more coverage for Israel–Palestine (more than 225 000 words) than there was for the DRC. That is, the peace process of the DRC conflict attracted comparatively less attention than did the violence and humanitarian aspects.

A similar comparison of the coverage of the DRC and Israel–Palestine peace processes in *The Australian* sent the disproportion to new heights, with coverage of the Israel–Palestine peace process being 115 times higher than coverage of the DRC peace process. In the case of *The Globe and Mail*, one day of coverage on the Israel–Palestine peace process (1 May 2003, when the 'road map' was unveiled) was more than enough to exceed the 18 months of coverage on the DRC peace process in that newspaper.

It is also worth pointing out that in *The New York Times* the average length of an article on the peace process in the case of Israel–Palestine was 864 words – almost three times longer than the average length of an article on the DRC peace process. This means that not only was there far more coverage of the Israel–Palestine peace process as a whole, but that each individual article dealt with the issue in far greater depth. The majority of articles on the peace process in the DRC simply noted, very briefly, that an event that had taken place (for example, talks breaking down, or a deal being signed), whereas articles on the peace process in Israel–Palestine included analysis, a variety of viewpoints, and depth. On a general methodological note, this also suggests that very different results may be obtained from quantitative studies of media coverage depending on whether numbers of articles are counted, or the numbers of words in the articles.

Comparisons with other less extreme examples (cases considered less relevant to powerful political interests) can also help boost our understanding of the coverage of peace processes. In this light, this study also looked at coverage in *The New York Times* of peace processes in Darfur, Kenya and Nepal. In the case of Darfur, the study followed the conclusion of peace talks in Nigeria in May 2006 that resulted in a peace agreement with one faction of the rebel Sudan Liberation Army (other groups did not sign). Substantive articles appeared in the paper on a daily basis for the first nine days of May, and in less than one month the quantity of reporting on the peace process for Darfur easily exceeded that for the 18 months of the DRC peace process.

An eruption of post-election violence left 1300 people dead and hundreds of thousands displaced in Kenya in late 2007 and early 2008. Former UN Secretary-General Kofi Annan attempted to mediate, and an agreement on power sharing was reached in March 2008. Coverage of the conflict itself was relatively heavy in *The New York Times*, as was the peace process that led to the power sharing agreement. The roughly two months of coverage of the peace process exceeded the 18 months of the DRC peace process.

Conflict in Nepal between government and Maoist rebel forces, while far less deadly than that in the DRC, was deadlier than that in Israel–Palestine or Kenya, with an estimated death toll of 13 000 people since 1996. The year 2006 saw the fall of the monarchy and a peace agreement with the rebels. The combined coverage of these two phases of the peace process in *The New York Times* (over a period of approximately eight months) was considerably greater than that for the course of the DRC peace process.

*Peace process or peace deal?*

One of the products of a peace process is a peace agreement, or deal. Peace deals do not happen overnight. They are almost invariably the result of long and painstaking negotiations, accompanied at times by impasses, setbacks, walkouts, prodding by third parties, and compromises. Such a 'process' may happen very quickly when one of the parties to the conflict vanquishes the other, as seen in Angola in 2002, Iraq in 2003, and Sri Lanka in 2009 (the 'agreement' of the vanquished is not really required), or when the conflict itself is very short, as seen in Kenya in 2008, for example. In the majority of cases, however, the process leading to a deal is a long and complex one.

Figure 1: Use of term 'peace process'. *The New York Times*, 2000–2009 (n=276).

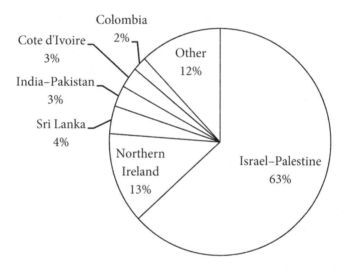

But do the media portray the series of events leading up to a peace agreement as a peace process? In most cases, they appear not to. This study conducted a LexisNexis search of the term 'peace process' in the headline or lead paragraphs of *The New York Times* articles for the period from 2000 to 2009, and recorded the conflict to which the term was referring. Figure 1 is a summary of the results. Over the course of the ten years examined, more often than not (63 percent of cases) the term 'peace process' was used in reference to a single conflict – that in Israel–Palestine. A considerable number of references was also found for Northern Ireland, but the use of the term was a rarity beyond these two cases. In some instances, the term was used not by the reporter writing the article, but by the political leader being interviewed (seen in the case of India–Pakistan and Somalia). In the case of the DRC, the term was used in just three articles with an average length of 107 words, and only one of these was during the course of the ICD. Interestingly, there also appears to be no 'peace process' for the two conflicts that are most heavily covered by the newspaper – those in Iraq and Afghanistan (there was only one reference for each), a reflection that the primary 'solution' in each case has been considered a military one.

The series of events that led to the Pretoria agreement in 2002, and its ratification in Sun City in 2003, was certainly a process. It had a clear beginning, a conclusion and a set of steps that got it from one to the other. It even had a name – the Inter-Congolese Dialogue. So why didn't the media call it a 'process'? In the case of Israel–Palestine, every twist and turn in the 'road' supposedly headed in the direction of peace has been reported – every proposal, every concession and gesture, every day of talks, every rejection and collapse. The dots along the timeline that has been presented by the media are so close together that there is somehow a connectedness, a sense of continuous action in a particular direction, however little apparent progress there had been. In the case of the DRC, however, the dots marked along the timeline were so few and far between (and so fleetingly and marginally recorded) that it was difficult for them to be connected in a coherent pattern, however process-like the series of events were. There were plenty of twists and turns along the road to the comprehensive peace agreement, but few of them were reported (or reported in any depth). As a result, the media reported the existence of a 'deal', 'accord' or 'agreement', but not a 'process'.

The notion of 'peace' itself tends to be heavily associated by the media with the conflict in Israel–Palestine, something that can also been seen in the use of artwork in the media. A search for the word 'dove' (a symbol of peace) in the online collection of political cartoons on the website Politicalcartoons.com, for the period 2000 to 2009, revealed that of those cartoons that included imagery of doves in reference to a specific conflict, 56 percent were on Israel–Palestine (a further eight percent were on the Israel–Lebanon conflict). There were no such cartoons appearing in reference to the DRC. The fact that the dove usually appeared in these cartoons about the Israel–Palestine conflict being eaten, blown up, decapitated, or otherwise maimed/threatened is ironically indicative of the fact that there has been little progress in achieving peace there. That the dove continues to be used primarily to refer to this particular conflict, regardless of this paradox, is indicative of how heavily the peace process there is being covered by the media.

*What factors determined the coverage?*

A number of studies have attempted to pin down the factors behind the newsworthiness of events. In 1965 Galtung and Ruge published a set of 12 factors that they found to be key determinants: frequency, threshold, unambiguity, meaningfulness, consonance, unexpectedness, continuity, composition, reference to elite nations, reference to elite people, reference to persons, and reference to something negative. Harcup and O'Neill (2001) reviewed these factors, made adjustments, and came up with the following ten, for the British press: the power elite, celebrity, entertainment, surprise, bad news, good news, magnitude, relevance, follow-up, and newspaper agenda. Golding and Elliott (1979) published a similar set of criteria, but, critically, added proximity to the mix. Shoemaker and Reese (1996) identified a 'hierarchy of influences', or five levels that influence news content: individual preferences and background, organisational routines, editorial policy and other organisational imperatives, extra-media influences, and ideology (at societal level). Allern, pointing to the need for a greater emphasis on commercial news criteria, added a number of criteria, perhaps most notably that 'the more resources – time, personnel and budget – it costs to cover, follow up or expose an event, etc., the less likely it will become a news story' (Allern 2002, p145).

In terms of factors specifically aimed at conflicts and peace processes, Hawkins (2008, pp189–202) proposed a list of factors behind the attention (not only of media, but also of policymakers, the public and academia) a conflict attracts: national/political interest, geographic proximity/access, ability to identify, ability to sympathise, simplicity, and sensationalism. Wolfsfeld (2004, pp15–23) identified immediacy, drama, simplicity, and ethnocentrism as factors that determine attention for events making up a peace process, although this focused on media based within the conflict zone, rather than outside it. So how well do these lists apply to the salience in the media agenda of the peace processes raised in this study? Of course, these lists are not manuals or checklists. Some criteria apply and others do not, and whether or not a particular situation will attract and sustain the media's attention depends not only on how many of these criteria it meets, but also on how strongly each of the criteria applies, not to mention from whose perspective they apply – in some cases one might be enough.

Comparing the cases of the DRC and Israel–Palestine, a number of factors are apparent. Although the elite nation (or power elite, national/ political interest) criteria may be somewhat ambiguous, Israel can be said to carry an elite nation status, largely because of the importance conferred on it by its elite nation allies. The rise in coverage that accompanied the US president's visit and proposal of the 'road map', and the rise accompanying the visits of other elites from the US, can be considered to serve as an example of the elite nations and elite people criteria. The meaningfulness/relevance/ability to identify factors can also apply in the Western world, not only because of the relatively high socioeconomic status of the participants, but also because the area of contestation is considered to be the Holy Land by Muslims, Jews and Christians alike. Continuity/follow-up are also relevant criteria – the conflict has always been the subject of heavy coverage and therefore it continues to be.

The DRC, on the other hand, had few of these criteria to recommend it as a news topic. None of the factors that applied to Israel–Palestine was relevant in this case. There was no direct or open involvement by elites (nation or person), and a conflict affecting poor black people apparently has limited relevance for those in the affluent white-dominated West. The limited elite interest in the conflict in the DRC undoubtedly served to deter media attention. As a conflict sparked by the invasion of US/ UK allies Rwanda and Uganda, and given the mining interests of powerful Western corporations, attention to the situation in the DRC was potentially embarrassing for elite interests in the West. From the elite perspective, those suffering in the DRC were not 'worthy victims' (Herman & Chomsky 1994, pp37–86). Furthermore, as the conflict was consistently marginalised from the outset, the trend continued throughout the peace process – a mark of continuity.

It is important to note that while the threshold/magnitude criteria may apply to domestic news or accidents, it is not relevant in the case of conflict and conflict resolution. The scale of a conflict (marked, for instance, by death toll) is, for all intents and purposes, unrelated to the level of media attention it attracts. As this study confirms, conflicts with relatively small death tolls often attract heavy coverage, while many of the world's deadliest conflicts are consistently absent from the media radar. The fact that the peace process for what was by far the world's deadliest conflict could only attract one-twentieth at most (less than one-hundredth at least) of the quantity of coverage of a peace process aimed at resolving a conflict with a death toll hundreds of times smaller makes the magnitude criteria altogether irrelevant.

The negative/bad news and good news criteria also didn't seem to have a considerable impact here. In the case of Israel–Palestine, there was little particularly good news (the successful conclusion of a deal, for example), and the failure of the process was gradual – there was no major negative incident that suddenly destroyed the entire peace process. To begin with, the starting point of the 'road map' was not met with a great deal of expectation. A political cartoon by Olle Johansson (reprinted here) summed up the mood of the times. A battered and very unenthused peace dove sitting on a shot-up signboard (to the Middle East) says sarcastically to the readers, 'Another peace plan … we're all thrilled'. Yet coverage of each intricate part of the peace process was reported in detail alongside the negativity of the violence. In the case of the DRC, the agreement was particularly good news. Although there was trouble brewing in Ituri, the bilateral peace deals were conclusive, as was the comprehensive peace agreement in Pretoria, which led to the establishment of a transitional government; and the large-scale troop withdrawals were very visible positive effects. This end to the world's deadliest conflict should have done something to offset the factors that prevented its coverage, but it did not.

None of the other peace processes studied (Darfur, Kenya, Nepal) came close to the levels of coverage of the Israel–Palestine peace process, but all attracted greater coverage than did the DRC peace process. None involved elite nations or elite people, but, importantly, in some cases there was elite interest in their resolution. In the case of Darfur, there was a degree of US policy interest, and the peace talks came at the peak of public interest in the US, coinciding with a series of highly coordinated nationwide rallies for Darfur. In the case of Kenya, an elite person (immediate past UN Secretary General Kofi Annan) stepped in as mediator.

© Olle Johansson 2003. Reproduced with permission

This is in line with studies finding that the media agenda largely follows the lead of the policy agenda – indexing (Bennett 1990) and (to a slightly lesser degree) cascading network activation (Entman 2004). Indexing holds that the media coverage reflects the strength of the voices in government. When there is consensus in government, the media will present that perspective; when there is debate within government, those perspectives will be offered; and the lack of policy voices will be matched by a lack of media coverage. In a somewhat more nuanced approach, the cascading network activation portrays agenda items originating primarily from the policy elites at the top of the 'cascade', but allows for items 'splashing' back up to the top from the lower tiers.

Other factors helped boost coverage. While the DRC and Israel–Palestine conflicts and peace processes were portrayed in very complex terms, the Darfur, Kenya and Nepal conflicts were reported in simplified one-on-one formats (the realities in each case were, of course, far from simple). Israel–Palestine is also essentially a one-on-one conflict, but the solution is reported in great detail and complexity. With so many actors at different levels with different motives and objectives, the DRC conflict has always been unsimplifiable. This has set it apart from other conflicts and can be considered a major factor in its marginalisation. In the case of Kenya, the element of unexpectedness/surprise also served as a major factor in the levels of interest. The conflict suddenly appeared in what was thought to be a relatively peaceful country. The media also attempted to connect readers to the conflict using the images already in their minds (meaningfulness/relevance). There were stories in *The New York Times* about the damage to the tourism industry and the dangers faced by marathon runners.

Commercial news criteria also need to be considered as major factors determining the levels of coverage; most notably, the proximity of news bureaus to the events. The long-term interest in the Israel–Palestine conflict has resulted in the stationing of numerous bureaus and reporters; most in Israeli-controlled West Jerusalem. As such, newsgathering is possible for however long a peace process goes on at little marginal expense. The same can be said of the Kenya process. Nairobi is one of the few places in Africa in which Western journalists are stationed. Jeffrey Gettleman, for example, reported for *The New York Times* on the conflict and peace process in Kenya from the newspaper's already established bureau there. There are no such bureaus in the vicinity of the DRC, making decisions to gather news from there expensive ones, with approved expeditions measured in days, not months. A short-term focus on the DRC peace process can be seen in *The Times* (UK), for example, with the bulk of the reporting during this period (the peace agreement with Rwanda) coinciding with a tour of the region by Africa-based journalist Michela Wrong.

Admittedly, the peace process for the DRC was conducted largely in relatively accessible South Africa (*The New York Times* has a bureau in Johannesburg), but covering both the peace process and the situation on the ground would have required two reporters. Such a split did not, however, prevent substantive coverage of the peace talks for Darfur taking place in Nigeria. Distance did little to stop coverage of the sensational volcanic eruption in eastern DRC. In each of the newspapers studied, less than one week of coverage of the eruption and its effects exceeded that of months of coverage of the peace process. In the case of *The Australian*, coverage of the eruption easily exceeded coverage of the entire 18-month peace process. A short stay to cover a sensational event (parachute journalism) makes good business sense, but a long stay to cover a peace process does not.

Finally, the influence of the elite news media on other news media, or intermedia agenda-setting (McCombs 2004, pp113–17), needs to be considered. With few foreign correspondents, smaller newspapers rely on other more powerful newspapers and agencies not only for their newsgathering capacity, but also for their judgements on newsworthiness. This pack journalism mentality results in a convergence of news agendas – many different newspapers end up reporting on the same peace process. Although information is certainly available from reputable sources (primarily news agencies) on events occurring in the DRC, a newspaper is unlikely to buy this news and publish it unless it is already considered by more powerful news sources as being newsworthy.

## Conclusion

It is no secret that the Western mainstream media marginalise conflict in Africa (or Africa in general, for that matter), giving much greater coverage to conflicts in Europe and the Middle East. This chapter has examined how these trends applied to peace processes, comparing the media coverage of the peace process in the DRC over the course of the Inter-Congolese Dialogue and the conclusion of a series of comprehensive peace agreements, with part of the peace process in Israel–Palestine (the announcement of the 'road map' in 2003) and, to a lesser degree, with peace processes in Darfur, Kenya and Nepal.

It found that, of the peace processes examined here, the DRC was by far the least covered. This was despite the fact that the conflict in the DRC was a multinational affair with a death toll hundreds of times greater than the others, and despite the scale of the achievements made possible by the successful conclusion of the peace agreements there – the withdrawal of tens of thousands of foreign troops and the establishment of an inclusive transitional government. Furthermore, the study found that, relative to the coverage of the violent phase of the conflict, the proportion of coverage of the peace process was considerably less for the DRC than it was for Israel–Palestine. In fact, the coverage of the peace process in the DRC was so little and so sporadic, that the media did not identify the organised set of events leading up to the peace agreement as a peace process. They were reported simply as peace deals or agreements.

The reasons for this marginalisation are complex, but include the lack of involvement and interest of elite nations and persons, the perceived failure of a predominantly white and affluent audience to identify, the sheer complexity, the fact that the conflict has been consistently marginalised in the past (continuity), commercial factors such as the lack of reporters permanently stationed in the vicinity, and the gravitational pull of powerful agenda-setters in the media.

Peace journalism focuses on the manner in which conflict, violence and peace are covered by the media. It is an approach that is not only critical in enhancing the public's understanding of conflict, but one that can also encourage and promote efforts towards peace. In this sense, it is certainly a worthy pursuit. At the same time, it is important not to lose sight of the fact that the majority of armed conflicts, and, critically, the peace processes aimed at ending them, are rarely covered by the media in any form. With a view to furthering understanding of these conflicts and enhancing the exploration of scenarios that will lead to a positive outcome, perhaps room can be made in the peace journalism movement for encouraging improvements in the quantity, as well as quality, of journalism related to armed conflict and its resolution.

*References*

Allern, Sigurd (2002). Journalistic and commercial news values: news organisations as patrons of an institution and market actors. *Nordicom Review*, 23(1–2): 137–52.

Anon (2003). The invisible war. *Globe and Mail*. Toronto. 4 April 2003. [Online]. Available: www.theglobeandmail.com/subscribe.jsp?art=385343 [Accessed 2 August 2011].

Apuuli, Kasaija (2004). The politics of conflict resolution in the Democratic Republic of Congo: the Inter-Congolese dialogue process. *African Journal on Conflict Resolution*, 4(1): 65–84.

Beaudoin, Christopher & Esther Thorson (2002). Spiral of violence? Conflict and conflict resolution in international news. In Eytan Gilboa (Ed). *Media and conflict: framing issues, making policy, shaping opinions* (pp45–64). Ardsley: Transnational Publishers.

Bennett, W. Lance (1990). Toward a theory of press-state relations in the United States. *Journal of Communication*, 40(2): 103–25.

Entman, Robert (2004). *Projections of power: framing news, public opinion, and US foreign policy*. Chicago: University of Chicago Press.

Franks, Suzanne (2010). The neglect of Africa and the power of aid. *International Communication Gazette*, 72(1): 71–84.

Galtung, Johan (1985). Twenty-five years of peace research: ten challenges and some responses. *Journal of Peace Research*, 22(2): 141–58.

Galtung, Johan & Mari Holmboe Ruge (1965). The structure of foreign news: the presentation of the Congo, Cuba and Cyprus crises in four Norwegian newspapers. *Journal of International Peace Research*, 1: 64–91.

Golan, Guy (2008). Where in the world is Africa? Predicting coverage of Africa by US television networks. *International Communication Gazette*, 70(1): 41–57.

Golding, Peter & Philip Elliott (1979). *Making the news*. London: Longman.

Harcup, Tony & Deirdre O'Neill (2001). What is news? Galtung and Ruge revisited. *Journalism Studies*, 2(2): 261–80.

Hawkins, Virgil (2009). National interest or business interest: coverage of conflict in the Democratic Republic of Congo in the *Australian* newspaper. *Media, War and Conflict*, 2(1): 67–84.

Hawkins, Virgil (2008). *Stealth conflicts: how the world's worst violence is ignored*. Aldershot: Ashgate.

Hawkins, Virgil (2002). The other side of the CNN factor: the media and conflict. *Journalism Studies* 3(2): 225–40.

Herman, Edward & Noam Chomsky (1994). *Manufacturing consent: the political economy of the mass media*. London: Vintage.

Human Security Report Project (HSRP) (2010). Human Security Report 2009/2010: the causes of peace and the shrinking costs of war. [Online]. Available: www.hsrgroup.org/human-security-reports/20092010/ overview.aspx [Accessed 2 August 2011].

International Rescue Committee (IRC) (2008). Mortality in the Democratic Republic of Congo: an ongoing crisis. [Online]. Available: www.rescue.org/special-reports/congo-forgotten-crisis [Accessed 2 August 2011].

International Rescue Committee (IRC) (2001). Mortality in eastern Democratic Republic of Congo: results from eleven mortality surveys. [Online]. Available: www.grandslacs.net/doc/3741.pdf [Accessed 2 August 2011].

Jakobsen, Peter (2000). Focus on the CNN effect misses the point: the real impact on conflict management is invisible and indirect. *Journal of Peace Research*, 37(2): 131–43.

Lynch, Jake & Johan Galtung (2010). *Reporting conflict: new directions in peace journalism*. St Lucia, Qld: University of Queensland Press.

McCombs, Maxwell (2004). *Setting the agenda: the mass media and public opinion*. Cambridge: Polity.

Moisy, Claude (1996). *The foreign news flow in the information age*. Cambridge: Harvard University.

Nolen, Stephanie (2002). Skepticism surrounds peace deal: Rwanda and Congo prepare to sign accord that could be historic, or another false hope. *Globe and Mail*. Toronto. 30 July: A9.

Shoemaker, Pamela & Stephen Reese (1996). *Mediating the message: theories of influence on mass media content*. London: Longman.

Sutherland, Tracy (2002). Congo exhibition to jolt nostalgic Belgians. *The Australian*, November 4: 16.

Tai, Zixue (2000). Media of the world and world of the media: a cross-national study of the rankings of the 'top 10 world events' from 1988 to 1998. *Gazette*, 62(5): 331–53.

Treneman, Ann (2002). Fixed in short time. *The Times*. 20 February: features.

Williams, Paul (2004). Britain and Africa after the cold war: beyond damage limitation? In Ian Taylor & Paul Williams (Eds). *Africa in international politics: external involvement on the continent* (pp41–60). Oxon: Routledge.

Wolfsfeld, Gadi (2004). *Media and the path to peace*. Cambridge: Cambridge University Press.

Wolfsfeld, Gadi, Eitan Alimi & Wasfi Kailani (2008). News media and peacebuilding in asymmetrical conflicts: the flow of news between Jordan and Israel. *Political Studies*, 56(2): 374–98.

# PART III

AGENCIES AND OPENINGS FOR CHANGE

# Chapter 11

# Can the centre hold? Prospects for mobilising media activism around public service broadcasting using peace journalism

*Jake Lynch*

> *Turning and turning in the widening gyre*
> *The falcon cannot hear the falconer;*
> *Things fall apart; the centre cannot hold;*
> *Mere anarchy is loosed upon the world,*
> *The blood-dimmed tide is loosed, and everywhere*
> *The ceremony of innocence is drowned;*
> *The best lack all conviction, while the worst*
> *Are full of passionate intensity.*
>
> William Butler Yeats, 'The second coming', 1920.

Peace journalism has developed as a fund of initiatives for editors and reporters, and latterly, evaluative criteria for content analysis by researchers. It has also been a source of impetus for change in media representations of conflict, from civil society. Hackett and Carroll (2006) consider the prospects for 'media activism' to 'democratise public communication'. In this chapter, I examine attempts to mobilise such activism around the coverage, by a public service broadcaster, of the Israel–Palestine conflict. This occurred in a context in which significant political agency was being applied at different levels and with conflicting effects on public policy towards the issue. In the process, I assess the 'credentials' of calls for peace journalism in public service broadcasting as a rallying point for building and sustaining effective alliances in social movements.

287

In early 2010, the Australian Broadcasting Corporation (ABC) agreed to purchase and transmit an independently produced documentary, *Hope in a slingshot*, by an emerging filmmaker, Inka Stafrace, which focuses on nonviolent resistance, by Palestinians, Israelis and internationals, to Israel's illegal military occupation of Palestinian territory. In this, and other respects, the film is a notable example of peace journalism.

Then, in a highly unusual twist, the distributor Ronin Films, received a letter from the ABC's Head of Television, Kim Dalton, informing them of his personal decision to intervene, rescinding the earlier offer to buy the film and announcing that the ABC would not now be screening it. *Hope in a slingshot* was, the letter declared, 'an opinion program' about a 'contentious' subject (Pike 2010). Under Clause 6.6.3 of its editorial policy the ABC would have to find another program that balanced the views expressed in the film and, as it had been unable to do so, *Hope in a slingshot* would have to be dropped from the schedule outright.

Two days after Dalton's intervention became public, Israeli commandoes raided and seized the MV *Mavi Marmara*, a vessel sailing through international waters carrying aid materials for Palestinians in the Gaza Strip, aimed at breaking a blockade on the territory imposed by the Israeli government.

In spite of Israel's vaunted 'withdrawal' from the Strip – dismantling settlements there, along with its army bases, in 2005 – it remains the de facto occupying power, since it retains control over Gazan air space, land borders and territorial waters (Amnesty et al. 2010, p9). The blockade was imposed as a further intensification of economic sanctions after the victory by Hamas in the Palestinian legislative elections of 2006, and continued through and beyond 'Operation Cast Lead', Israel's attack on Gaza in 2008–09.

The International Committee of the Red Cross reported that its effect was to prolong the suffering caused by the attack (ICRC 2009). Thousands of people whose homes Israel destroyed were still without shelter months later, the ICRC said, despite pledges of almost US$4.5 billion in aid, because Israel refused to allow cement and other building material into the Strip. The report also noted that hospitals were struggling to meet the needs of their patients due to Israel's disruption of medical supplies.

Gazans were 'trapped in despair', the report concluded, by these measures; measures which both the ICRC itself, and the UN High Commissioner for Human Rights, Navi Pillay, have pronounced illegal (Gray-Block 2010) as they are in contravention of Article 33 of the Fourth Geneva Convention of 1949, prohibiting collective punishments.

The *Mavi Marmara* set sail from Turkey at the head of a convoy of relief ships, carrying 10 000 tonnes of humanitarian aid including food, wheelchairs, books, toys, electricity generators, medicines, and building materials such as plaster and cement. News of Israel's attack on the vessel, in which nine activists were killed and several dozen injured, was greeted with fury around the world: a response channelled in street protests and demonstrations, including one in Sydney held at the traditional venue of the Town Hall steps and convened by a local civil society group, the Coalition for Justice and Peace in Palestine (CJPP).

Among the speakers was Sheik Taj el-Din al Hilaly from Lakemba Mosque in the city's southwest: a stronghold of Sydney's Lebanese Muslim community. Hilaly served for nearly 20 years as Mufti of Australia, a position to which he was appointed by the Australian Federation of Islamic Councils. During this time, he was criticised on numerous occasions, notably for public comments appearing to blame the incidence of rape on women's dress habits (AAP 2006). Hilaly was asked to step down from an official Muslim Community Reference Group after he called the Holocaust 'a ploy made by the Zionists' (in Kerbaj 2006).

Having retired from the role of Mufti in 2007, the slippage of Hilaly's once secure grasp on the allegiances of his followers appeared to be confirmed when, in March 2009, he was caught on CCTV cameras vandalising his own mosque; an incident he himself then reported to police, and attempted to blame on local youths. But there was little sign of this at the Town Hall demonstration, where his arrival at centre stage was greeted with loud approval. Hilaly spoke with passionate intensity. Holding up a large Turkish flag, he told the 4000-strong crowd that 'Turkey is coming' (in Munro 2010), before leading a rhythmic chant of 'Down, down Israel' (personal eyewitness experience).

## 'Flak' and 'legitimate controversy'

The unease this turn of events occasioned among some supporters of the protest is connected, in some important respects, with the ABC's decision not to screen *Hope in a slingshot*. The context for Kim Dalton's intervention can be conceptualised using the 'propaganda model' of media proposed by Edward Herman and Noam Chomsky. News should be seen, they say, as 'inculcating and defending the economic, social and political agenda of privileged groups that dominate the domestic society and the state' (Herman & Chomsky 2002, p298). One way in which this agenda is enforced is by hurling 'flak' in the direction of news organisations when they deviate from it. It works by 'conditioning the media to expect trouble' whenever they take on powerful interests (Herman & Chomsky 2002, p27).

Groups representing Australia's self-defined 'mainstream Jewish community' have been a source of flak in media, political and academic domains alike. Responding to a complaint, Australia's other public broadcaster, the minority-remit SBS, issued a directive to its journalists in 2009 not to use the term 'Palestinian land' since the territory in question was – according to a leaked internal memo – 'disputed' (Lynch 2009a). And modest changes to Australia's diplomatic stance – on questions such as referring the Goldstone Report on the Gaza attack for consideration by the UN Security Council – were followed by a deputation to then prime minister Kevin Rudd, at which threats were made to transfer the money and support of Jewish organisations to the opposition Liberal Party instead (Hartcher 2010).

Attempts were underway through this period to define and enforce, in the context of debate over Israel and Palestine, what Daniel Hallin called the 'zone of legitimate controversy [which] marks out and defends the limits of acceptable conflict [by] exposing, condemning, or excluding from the public agenda those who violate or challenge the political consensus' (Hallin 1989, p117). Notable among these attempts were interventions from a group of academics, led by Philip Mendes, a social work lecturer from Monash University in Melbourne, criticising what they called a 'fanatical form of pro-Palestinian orthodoxy' on Australian campuses (Mendes 2008). Mendes and his colleagues accused advocates of a cultural and academic boycott of Israel of 'essentialising' all Israeli Jews as being 'racist oppressors of the Palestinians' (Mendes 2008), and took to the columns of *The Australian* newspaper to accuse boycott advocates of belonging to the 'loony Left' (Mendes & Dyrenfurth 2009).

At stake, arguably, is whether the conflict can be represented in public debate, with recourse to frames derived from international law and human rights (as I have done here), without being 'pro-Palestinian' and anti-Israeli. Flak is a factor in academic circles too, with the present author having been obliged several times to defend interventions in public debate in the face of complaints from supporters in Australia, of the Israeli and Sri Lankan governments respectively. On the occasion of the *Mavi Marmara* rally, complaints centred on an email circular originally from the CJPP, forwarded to students and members of the Centre for Peace and Conflict Studies (CPACS) at the University of Sydney, publicising the event and urging them to 'bring Palestinian flags and banners'.

A subsequent meeting of CPACS' governing council heard objections that this amounted to a 'partisan' stance, 'supporting one side of the conflict over the other', in contravention of academic obligations to remain 'neutral'. Responses from council members emphasised that nothing in the centre's mission – formulated as 'Peace with Justice' – mandates neutrality over issues of human rights and international law, or in the face of 'massive inequality and injustice'. Palestinian flags could, in this context, be seen as 'an expression of solidarity with an oppressed people' rather than an indication of taking one side of a conflict against another.

It is in this spirit of solidarity that *Hope in a slingshot* is conceived and constructed. One reviewer called it 'an important document of Israel's brutal occupation of Palestine [in which] crimes committed with the full backing of the Western powers ... [lets audiences] view up-close the reality of life for millions of Palestinians' (Loewenstein 2010). It could therefore, be seen as rectifying an existing imbalance. Philo and Berry (2004) found that broadcast news in the UK persistently failed to offer any explanation of Israel's military occupation, how it came about, what international law says about it or its consequences for Palestinians.

Through hundreds of interviews and focus groups, they found lacunae, in understanding among the general public, to match these omissions. The British Broadcasting Corporation's (BBC) reporting changed significantly after the corporation's Board of Governors held their own inquiry into the issue, with Philo among the witnesses called, but no such exercise has taken place in Australia, where the coverage offered by television news generally displays the same pattern.

For all that, the ABC proved insistent that *Hope in a slingshot* not be shown, even when Ronin Films suggested two other documentaries as candidates for a 'balancing' slot in the same series. When members of the Senate in Canberra demanded an explanation of the corporation's stance, from Managing Director Mark Scott, he replied: 'I think finally the television division came to the view that it was not to the standard that they would want to acquire' (Senate Estimates 2010). No explanation was forthcoming of how this squared with the original decision to purchase the film.

## The shifting political context

Three months after the attack on the *Mavi Marmara*, the ABC did broadcast a bought-in film, in its *Foreign Correspondent* strand, from the BBC Panorama team, titled *Collision course*, in which reporter Jane Corbin pieced together an account of the incident, using what were described as newly acquired pictures of events on board. Weeks earlier, the BBC had itself broadcast this program, under the title *Death in the Med*, to a hail of complaints, mostly concerning the unchallenged reporting of unsupported Israeli military claims that live rounds were fired at their commandoes, and that passengers were carrying out a 'premeditated attack' when – as complainants pointed out – the premeditated attack was the one launched *by* the commandoes *on* the vessel, not the other way round (Lightbown 2010). Among those to take up the cudgels, with fresh complaints over the film after its showing on the ABC, were the groups involved in organising the Town Hall rally: Australians for Palestine and the Coalition for Justice and Peace in Palestine.

Corbin's account of the political context for the events depicted, given in the introductory section of her film, reproduced similar patterns of omission to those identified as dominant, in UK television news, by Philo and Berry: 'Hamas, which rules here, refuses to recognise Israel's right to exist', she averred. 'Militants have fired thousands of rockets at civilian targets in Israel in the past few years ... The Turkish Government and many Turkish charities support Hamas' (Corbin 2010).

Among the missing elements in Corbin's film and comments are as follows:

1.  Israel refuses to abide by the obligation to live within its legally recognised borders – with connivance by the US and allies – so there can be no certainty of what 'Israel' Hamas might be expected to 'accept'.

2.  There is abundant evidence of preparedness by Hamas leaders over recent years to call off their armed struggle if Israel would fully end its illegal military occupation of 1967 and live within its legally recognised borders (in Pilger 2007).

3.  There is a colossal disparity between the trickle of casualties resulting from Hamas rocket fire into Israel, and the death toll of 1300 – 400 of them children – in 'Operation Cast Lead', as well as the ongoing damage to life and property from Israeli air raids.

Should public service broadcasters be expected to behave differently? Not, certainly, according to the propaganda model, if the function of corporate media should be seen as inculcating and defending the political agenda of privileged groups that dominate the domestic society and the state. At the time of the events recalled here, however, that agenda was undergoing slight but significant modification.

Under the leadership of Kevin Rudd, Australia declared its aim to win a seat on the UN Security Council. Early in 2010, Ambassador Hesham Youssef, *chef de cabinet* to the Secretary General of the Arab League, visited Canberra to talk to politicians and officials, before making a series of other visits, including one to the Centre for Peace and Conflict Studies at the University of Sydney. He had informed everyone he met, he said at this meeting, that Australia could only look to Arab countries to support its UN bid, if it took steps to differentiate its position on Israel and Palestine from that of the US (personal communication).

This was shortly after the assassination in Dubai, of Mahmoud al-Mabhouh, a Hamas military commander, by suspected Mossad agents using fake travel documents from other countries, including several counterfeit Australian passports. The countries involved took one of two 'lines' in response. The 'softer' line was to call in the local Israeli ambassador for a 'dressing-down'; the 'harder' line was to order the expulsion of an Israeli diplomat. The Rudd government adopted the latter course – a development that prompted Jewish organisations to demand their meeting with Rudd, referenced earlier.

Just a couple of months later still, Rudd had gone, his ousting co-ordinated by a group of backbench powerbrokers in the ruling Labor Party, prominent among them being Mark Arbib, a Senator from New South Wales subsequently unmasked, by Wikileaks, as a longstanding US intelligence asset who had briefed his contacts at the American embassy on Rudd's travails and the leadership credentials of his deputy, Julia Gillard (Dorling 2010).

Gillard was the beneficiary of Rudd's fall, taking over unopposed, as Labor leader and Prime Minister in July 2010. Some 18 months earlier, at the time of the attack on Gaza, she had been standing in for Rudd. She characterised the onslaught as no more than Israel exercising its 'right to defend itself' against Hamas. Weeks later, she was welcomed to Tel Aviv at the head of a high-level political and business deputation, being greeted, according to reports, with fulsome thanks for having been 'alone in sticking by us'. In speeches and interviews Gillard gave during the trip, the word 'Gaza' did not once pass her lips. Hamas, she told questioners, would first have to 'renounce violence' if it wanted to qualify as a partner in any peace process sponsored by the 'quartet' of the UN, EU, US and Russia (no similar stipulation was made in respect of Israeli violence) (all in Lynch 2009b).

If a prime minister who was sending out signals of growing diplomatic distance from Israel, and thereby its sponsor in Washington – perhaps in pursuit of potential Arab support in Australia's bid for a UN Security Council seat – was ousted by a plot in which a secret US 'information source' was prominently involved, following explicit threats from pro-Israeli groups; and if the result was the installation of a more unambiguously pro-Israel head of government, then the Corbin explanation of the political context for the *Mavi Marmara* attack – along with the censorship of *Hope in a slingshot* and the directive to SBS journalists – could, indeed, be seen as inculcating and defending the agenda of powerful interests.

## Peace journalism and public service broadcasting

The propaganda model has been criticised, however, for attaching too little importance to plurality and variegation within media representations of key issues in public debate, and the scope for journalistic agency (Hackett 2006). A range of scholarship has emphasised these aspects: Hallin (1989) traced the migration of anti-war perspectives from the 'zone of deviance' to that of 'legitimate controversy'; Shoemaker and Reese (1996) set out a 'hierarchy of influences' on the work of the journalist; and Bourdieu (1999) saw journalism as a relatively autonomous 'field', albeit one that is in a 'structurally homologous' relationship with other fields within the same system.

Freedman calls the propaganda model 'a powerful reminder that the mainstream media are a crucial tool for legitimising the ideas of the most powerful social actors and for securing consent for their actions' (2009, p59), but prefers to focus on 'the exceptions, when the "default" position [of support for elite agendas] breaks down, precisely because, as someone who is committed to the transformation and democratisation of the existing media, they provide such important lessons' (Freedman 2009, p62).

Peace journalism is both a reform program for editors and reporters, and a fund of evaluative criteria for content analysis. It is value-explicit, aimed at 'creating opportunities for society at large to consider and value nonviolent responses' to conflict. It is, as Robert A Hackett declares in this volume, a 'challenger paradigm' to the hegemonic 'objectivity regime' of minority-world, Anglophone news, and one that should be seen as 'adjacent' to the media democratisation paradigm prompted by the movement, initiated through UNESCO, for a New World Information and Communication Order.

Peace journalism advocates have often looked to public service broadcasting as a promising field of media activism for transformation. 'Structural pluralism' in media, Tehranian suggests, 'may be considered a *sine qua non* of content pluralism' (2002, p79), to which Lynch and McGoldrick respond by calling for 'efforts to make the structural pluralism we already have work properly' (2005, p230), going on to reference several public service agreements governing the content of broadcast news in different countries.

A crucial provision of the agreement to which ABC journalists are supposed to adhere is enshrined in clause 6.6.3 of its 'Editorial policy', adduced in Kim Dalton's letter: 'The ABC is committed to impartiality and must demonstrate this in its opinion content through the presentation of a diversity of perspectives.' It echoes the previous chapter, which makes similar provisions for 'News and Current Affairs content', at clause 5.2.2:

> d) Be impartial. Editorial judgments are based on news values, not for example on political, commercial or sectional interests or personal views. Do not unduly favour one perspective over others.
>
> (e) Be balanced. Balance will be sought but may not always be achieved within a single program or publication; it will be achieved as soon as reasonably practicable and in an appropriate manner. It is not essential to give all sides equal time. As far as possible, present principal relevant views on matters of importance.

The overarching aim of both ABC news and opinion programming is to 'contribute to the diversity of content in the media' and position the ABC as 'a pace-setter in community discussion'. When these strictures were put to the test, however, in a complaint to the ABC about its coverage of the Australian government's Defence White Paper, in 2009, they were 'trumped' by a separate document, defining 'news values' as relied upon in the clause quoted above, drawn up by ABC news managers the previous year. These included:

- Prominence: status, power of the information source, or of the individuals or institutions involved in the event

- Personification: involvement of famous people even when what happens to them is commonplace.

The response to the complaint, by the ABC's Complaints Review Executive (CRE), made it clear that this definition of 'news values' was being used to exempt the corporation from reporting – in this case – the perspective that Australia should be reducing its defence expenditure, rather than increasing it (by an annual three percent above inflation) as provided for in the white paper. The CRE declared:

> In my view the nub of this issue is differing views on what is newsworthy and a matter of importance. From my reading of the correspondence from the listener he is arguing that the issue of whether Australia should spend as much on defence is the matter of importance, and that a wider range of views should be heard on that matter. ABC News argues that the specific release in May of the White Paper on Defending Australia in the Asia Pacific was the newsworthy topic ... The ABC has advised that an appropriate range of principal relevant views on those matters of importance has been presented in radio current affairs programs.

In practice, therefore, the source for a newsworthy development would have to be of a power or prominence equal to that of the government itself, to be entitled to expect their views on the subject to be reported. It is, in effect, a rare public affirmation of conventions deduced from outside by researchers: the habit of 'indexing' the bounds of legitimate controversy to the extent of elite discord (Bennett 1990), often defined by disagreements, in a representative democracy, between the governing party and the principal opposition. On this topic, disagreement is slight, at best: among the evidence adduced in the ABC's original response to the complaint, to show they had presented 'an appropriate range of principal relevant views', was an interview with Brendan Nelson, who had left office months earlier as defence minister in the previous Coalition-led government. The white paper 'basically restates commitments that had already been made by the previous government in the 2007 strategic update', he said (in Lynch 2009c).

So it is also, generally, with Australia's attitude towards the Israel–Palestine conflict. Rudd's brief (and slight) detour aside, Canberra has generally marched in lockstep with Washington, whichever of the two main parties has held office. Under Gillard, on 30 November 2010, Australia joined just six other countries – the US and Israel, and the handful of tiny states whose votes have essentially been bought, namely Marshall Islands, Micronesia, Nauru, Palau – in opposing a motion at the UN General Assembly which:

> reaffirmed the illegality of Israeli actions intended to change the status of Jerusalem … Reaffirming its commitment to the two-State solution of Israel and Palestine living side by side in peace and security within recognised borders, the Assembly also stressed the need for Israel to withdraw from Palestinian territory occupied since 1967, including East Jerusalem. (UNGA 2010)

An 'elite orientation' is a characteristic of 'war journalism', in the original table put forward by Johan Galtung (1998), since it predicates a bias towards 'official sources: a category topped by the leaders of national states' (McGoldrick 2006). For obvious reasons, political leaders seldom, if ever, *originate* moves to peace. Their position demands that they be seen to respond to an established public mood, or risk being isolated and undermined; famous leadership initiatives have usually followed a groundswell from beneath. The first moves towards peace therefore take place 'below the radar' of journalistic convention, so they are, in effect, being suppressed. Then, states are defined, in terms originally supplied by Max Weber, as political organisations that successfully claim a monopoly on the legitimate use of force in a given territory. Leaders of states therefore have access to a 'lever' that is denied to anyone else. So, if those leaders are also the most important sources for news, there is, ipso facto, bound to be a general, inbuilt bias towards force as a response to conflict.

This general proposition is borne out by the behaviour of the ABC over a range of issues where the effect has been the legitimisation of violence – the attacks on Gaza and the *Mavi Marmara*, and the threat of violence inscribed in the Defence White Paper – sanctioned by official sources, and the suppression of news about non-elite peace initiatives such as the campaign of nonviolent resistance to Israel's occupation of Palestinian territory, showcased in *Hope in a slingshot*. There is reason to regard this prevalence of war journalism as breaching the compact set out in the 'Editorial policy', the guidelines for journalists that are supposed to safeguard a wider conception of public interest. For instances where this interest may prove politically inconvenient, however, the definition of 'news values' is used to trump the apparent obligations under the policy for heterodox views and perspectives to be reported.

*Prospects for media activism*

This syndrome has become a focus of concern at the level of civil society, including from the ginger group, Friends of the ABC (FABC), which drew impetus from attempts to defend the corporation against editorial interference by the Coalition-led government of Prime Minister John Howard (1996–2007). When Ronin Films first drew attention to the intervention of Kim Dalton to reverse the ABC's initial decision to purchase *Hope in a slingshot*, FABC spokesperson Glenys Stradijot, quoted in *The Sydney Morning Herald*:

> said the decision took the commitment to bias avoidance to an absurd extreme. [Stradijot] said it was important for the ABC to stand up to the pressure on contentious issues such as the Middle East. 'If the ABC's bowing to that sort of pressure, that's not a good thing for an independent broadcaster'. (Sharp 2010)

Here, then, was an apparent opportunity to ally with an established civil society organisation to press the case for peace journalism, as a way to make the structural pluralism notionally provided for in the Australian mediascape work as it was apparently intended. The struggle being waged by Ronin Films, to get the original decision to buy and transmit the film reinstated – including an energetic program of public meetings featuring presentations by Inka Stafrace herself – was taking place in a political context in which a rare degree of agency was being exerted against the legitimisation of the use of force by the Israeli military – contrary to the usual response by Australian elites and against the wishes of 'mainstream Jewish' organisations and, perhaps, the US embassy in Canberra.

So it was that a decision was made to add visibility to this campaign, by staging a demonstration outside ABC headquarters in Sydney, as part of the biennial global conference of the International Peace Research Association (IPRA). Papers presented at the conference to the IPRA Peace Journalism Commission form the basis for the present volume, and commission members joined local activists in what was billed as 'the world's first ever demonstration for peace journalism' (Lynch 2010). The publicity leaflet for the event stated:

> *Hope in a slingshot* shows the realities of Israel's illegal military occupation of Palestinian territory … The ABC must acknowledge the biases inherent in news, especially about the Israel–Palestine conflict, and use other parts of its programming to rectify them.

It went on to state that if the corporation were to deliver successfully on its public service obligations:

> Audiences must have opportunities to see and hear the facts about Israel's occupation of Palestinian territory, its illegality and its consequences.

This appeal, however, proved impossible to join for Friends of the ABC, which turned down repeated invitations to add its name to the protest and confined itself, instead, to a less specific statement:

> There have been regular news and current affairs reports and a number of programs on the ABC (both television and radio) present-ing varied Israeli and Palestinian perspectives … Possibly the ABC's decision on *Hope in a slingshot* is influenced by fear of a backlash (real or perceived) from some in the community who tolerate no criticism of Israel. (Stradijot 2010)

The first of these statements overlooks the research evidence from Philo and Berry, in the very similar milieu of UK television journalism, that – if no deliberate remedial action is taken – a pattern of 'Israeli dominance' (Philo & Berry 2004, p259) supervenes, both in the choice of developments to report and in the way they are described, interpreted and framed. To cite 'varied Israeli and Palestinian perspectives' as having been presented is to ignore the power relations accounted for in the propaganda model and reflected, in coverage of this story, in the lopsidedness of the accounts and views that tend to reach the news. And the latter, of course, positions FABC on the same side of an important line as the bosses of SBS, who instructed their journalists, in effect, to remove the illegality of Israel's occupation from the domain of reportable fact, and to treat it as a criticism of Israel, to be 'balanced' like any other claim, instead.

If Friends of the ABC were to prove impossible to recruit to this form of media activism for peace journalism, what about the civil society groups that joined the protest over the *Mavi Marmara*? If they are to be engaged, clearly it would have to be on a different basis than the conflict-partisan position apparently inscribed in the chants of 'Down, down Israel'. Instead, peace journalism would have to enable its advocates to put forward a set of demands for public service broadcasting to restore to its coverage missing facts that are 'principal and relevant', in order to set the pace in community discussion. Is there, in calling for alternatives to a 'blood-dimmed tide loosed upon the world', an identifiable 'centre' in media representations; can it 'hold' or are its advocates doomed to 'lack all conviction'? The BBC's equivalent document, also called 'Editorial policies', states, as the aim of its journalism, to 'enable the national and international debate', but can one debate, or one community discussion, be identified and addressed; or are there many, each with its own terms of reference, which cannot be brought to mesh or match – an ever-widening gyre?

Hackett and Carroll consider the prospects for media activism as 'a nexus – a point of articulation between movements, transforming and lending coherence to the broad field of movement activism as a coun-ter-hegemonic formation' (2006, p199), but that assumes some degree of commensurability between the assumptions and aims of movement activism, on the one hand, and demands capable of being identified and articulated in media domains, on the other. In the context of peace journalism, public service broadcasting has been discussed as one such domain where strands can meet, and attain coherence; a proposition now presenting itself, in this tale of two documentaries and two demonstrations, in interrogative form.

In pursuit of a partial answer, at least, an experiment was conducted with two focus groups of Sydney Muslims, in which each group watched a set of television news stories about conflict, produced with familiar rhetorical structures and visual grammars of public service broadcasting. The two sets were 'versioned' to display framing characteristics categorised as war journalism and peace journalism respectively, following the methods outlined in Lynch and McGoldrick (2005) and Lynch (2008).

## Sydney's Muslims and the media

Before elaborating on this experiment, a brief digression is necessary, to set the context in which the Muslim peoples of Sydney have been treated and represented by the city's media. Manning (2004) found Muslims 'strongly associated with threat concepts' such as 'fundamentalist or terror or their derivatives', in a systematic content analysis study of the two main Sydney newspapers. Myconos and Watmough considered that 'the media, collectively, represents for many Muslims and people of Middle Eastern background an important site of racism' (2007, p7). They quote witness testimony from an investigation by Australia's Human Rights and Equal Opportunity Commission, that asked Muslims to recount experiences of racism encountered in daily life. 'I think the media is the main cause', one said, 'because kids are picking on Muslims at school and these kids get it from their parents and their parents get it from the media' (Myconos & Watmough 2007, p9). Lynch (2008) also found that two Australian newspapers were markedly more inclined to frame Islam or Muslims of Middle Eastern background as 'a problem' than their counterparts in the Philippines – another country with a significant Muslim minority, and ally of the US in the 'war on terror'.

Lynch's study included an interview with a senior journalist on *The Sydney Morning Herald*, which had commissioned, as a deliberate remedial measure, a series of articles called 'Faces of Islam', looking at 'how the Muslim community arrived in Australia, what kind of lifestyles and beliefs, [and] ethnic flavours are represented here' (in Lynch 2008, p173). This had come about as 'a response to a very negative representation of Muslims that has crept into the media here and also into the political debate in New South Wales', the journalist added (in Lynch 2008, p174).

There is, in other words, an active sense of contestation, in civil society in Sydney, over the representation of Muslims and Islam, both explicitly, and in the context of stories prominent on the news agenda in the period since '9/11' – the 'war on terror' itself; Afghanistan, Iraq, Iran, Israel and the Palestinians – all of which involve Muslim people as significant subjects, or, indeed, objects (in the sense of having things done to them). This testifies to the power of what Hackett and Carroll call 'hot pokers … [or] prods to activism', whereby 'social movements are catalysed and defined by what they perceive to be obstacles to valued goals' (2006, p143). A hegemonic political and media discourse in which Muslims and/or Islam have generally been problematised has brought with it – as a condition of its iteration – what Lewis calls 'slippage and dissociation' (2005, p11), inviting and prompting social movement activism to coalesce around the same set of issues, and its exponents to seek common cause with Sydney's Muslim community and its leadership, as at the Town Hall rally.

Hackett and Carroll find, among social movement activists, a 'widespread acceptance of the need for coalition building', along with a paradoxical 'divisiveness' that means 'most alliances are short term and focused on single issues' (2006, pp154–55). They suggest, among 'springboards for media activism', opportunities to form such alliances with 'non-media advocacy groups in civil society concerned with progressive social change', with the latter being defined by one of their subjects, as 'anybody concerned with human rights and social justice' (Hackett & Carroll 2006, p152). There is a strand of Muslim activist opinion in Sydney, perhaps represented by 'Sheikh Taj', which, on some issues at least, could not be said to identify with human rights and social justice concerns. But there are many others, across a broad cross-section of civil society, who have proved willing and capable allies in social movement activism for – in the CPACS formulation – 'Peace with Justice'.

Participants for the 'two versions' experiment were recruited by Kuranda Seyit, a prominent activist, media producer and social entrepreneur, who was appointed shortly before the 9/11 attacks as press officer for the Australian Federation of Islamic Councils (which had previously appointed 'Sheik Taj'), and later set up FAIR, the Forum on Australia's Islamic Relations. In the latter guise, he organised a set of media awards, to recognise socially responsible reporting by a range of local media, including newspapers and television programs as well as 'talkback' radio. As a consummate media activist, Seyit selected the participants for this study to represent a range of views and perspectives on the commensurability, or otherwise, of goals valued in Muslim social movement activism, with distinctions observable in public service broadcasting.

These distinctions were built into the two versions of a 20-minute news bulletin showcasing a recent episode on each of six familiar stories:

1. the anniversary of the 9/11 attacks
2. the funeral of an Australian soldier killed in Afghanistan
3. the latest political row over provisions for asylum seekers in Australia
4. the 'peace talks', brokered by US Secretary of State Hillary Clinton, between Israeli Prime Minister Binyamin Netanyahu and Palestinian President Mahmoud Abbas
5. Iran's 'nuclear ambitions' as 'revealed' by the opening of its nuclear power station at Bushehr
6. Iraqi security, in light of the latest attack by suicide bombers on an army recruitment station in Baghdad.

Pictures for the bulletins were drawn from material broadcast on SBS Television's evening bulletin, *World news Australia*, with some extra original elements gathered locally. The items were voiced by SBS journalists, so each reporter recorded the voice-over track for the same story in each bulletin, with adjustments to script and content to reflect distinctions in the peace journalism model. The experiment formed one part of the data collection for a larger study, ongoing at the time of writing, aimed at formulating a Global Standard for Reporting Conflict (see Lynch & McGoldrick 2010), in which aspects of peace journalism are particularised and compared across media and across countries under five headings, following Shinar. In this study, the peace journalism model could be recognised for:

* exploring backgrounds and contexts of conflict formation, and presenting causes and options on every side so as to portray conflict in realistic terms, transparent to the audience
* voicing views of all rival parties
* highlighting creative ideas for conflict resolution, development, peacemaking and peacekeeping
* exposing lies, cover-up attempts and culprits on all sides, and revealing excesses committed by, and suffering inflicted on, people of all parties
* paying attention to peace stories and postwar developments. (Shinar 2007, p200)

In the context of the stories chosen, these criteria tended to be fulfilled, as often as not, by putting into practice Johan Galtung's summarising observation that 'peace journalism makes audible and visible the subjugated aspects of reality' (in Lynch & McGoldrick 2005, p224). In a media milieu in which the 'Faces of Islam' series was conceived by the *Herald* as a belated corrective, the inclusion in news reports about these conflicts, of Muslim perspectives, would automatically 'qualify' as peace journalism at least under Shinar's second heading.

To take, for example, the treatment of the fourth story in the bulletin, on the Israel–Palestine peace talks, the peace journalism version included an interview recorded separately for the exercise with Bishara Costandi, a Palestinian refugee now resident in Sydney and an activist with the CJPP. In the clip chosen for the package, he described the consequences for Palestinians of Israel's military occupation of their territory by inviting Australians to consider it in terms recognisable to themselves. Imagine setting out, he said, to go from 'Marrickville to Glebe' (two wellknown adjacent Sydney suburbs) only to face '14 checkpoints' along the way.

It also featured a sequence of maps showing 'the amazing disappearing Palestine', to illustrate the ongoing encroachment by Israel since the formation of the Jewish state in 1948, and it spelt out some background issues, commonly glossed over, euphemised or omitted altogether. A section of the script said:

> The settlements are considered illegal under international law, and the majority of world opinion wants to see Israel pull back to its recognised borders, leaving these streets and houses under Palestinian control.

The package thereby strengthened the peace journalism 'credentials' of this story under Shinar's first and third headings, while filling in some familiar gaps in public understanding identified in the UK study by Philo and Berry.

So how did an audience of Sydney Muslims in the eight-strong group who watched the peace journalism version – featuring this treatment of the Israel–Palestine conflict, along with similar variants on the other conflicts on the list – respond? What, if anything, did their responses reveal about the potential for commensurability between this remedial approach to public service broadcasting and their own perceptions of 'hot poker' issues that act as prods to social movement activism?

As it turned out, a significant pattern was established from the outset. When the bulletin was switched off at the end, and the group asked for overall responses, the very first comments came from M, a student of law and journalism who worked parttime as a lifeguard, and J, a part-time university lecturer:

> M: It was very fair, very balanced.

> J: A bit more balanced than a lot of SBS. I've complained to SBS several times; you get the usual bland reply, [but] I guess that [the bulletin they had just watched] was reasonably balanced.

This positive reaction, and willingness to perceive significant distinctions, based on expanding the range of principal relevant viewpoints, was immediately opposed, however, by B, a middle-aged man who described himself as unemployed and a some-time charity worker. He said:

> Can I be honest? I don't want to beat about the bush: I think M, studying journalism, is always going to be diplomatic. To me, I think it was biased and prejudiced and one-sided ... the media here, let's say, I call it a brain-washing because a lot of people don't like to read, so their only source of normal access to knowledge is through the media and the media is one-sided.

Pressed further on why he thought the bulletin 'balanced', M said:

> I guess, the selection of interviews from different perspectives. There wasn't a clear, blatant agenda. You could initially at the start have thought it was a sympathetic slant for the Palestinians but then the Israeli perspective was given, the same thing with most of the other stories, so there was a variety of interviews and it gives at least the viewer a sense of, 'I could do further research into this, I'm not going to take up one perspective, I heard all different perspectives about the subject matter'.

This comment chimes with the update I have proposed elsewhere, and built into content analysis methods for the Global Standard study, of Galtung's original distinction between 'war journalism' as 'propaganda-oriented' and peace journalism as 'truth-oriented'. Concepts of meaning-making have been 'decentred', this argument goes, since the original structuralist text that gave rise to the model, *The structure of foreign news*, published in 1965, notably by Stuart Hall with the insight that an event 'has no fixed meaning, no meaning in the obvious sense, *until* it has been represented' (1997, p7).

Hall, in the Media Education Foundation lecture from which these words are taken, continues:

The process of representation has entered into the event itself. In a way, it doesn't exist meaningfully until it has been represented, and to put that in a more hifalutin way is to say that representation doesn't occur after the event; representation is constitutive of the event. It enters into the constitution of the object that we are talking about. It is part of the object itself; it is constitutive of it. It is one of its conditions of existence, and therefore representation is not outside the event, not after the event, but within the event itself. (Hall 1997, pp7–8)

This challenges the notion of fidelity to a stable, pre-existing reality, which is implicit in the formulation 'truth-oriented', leading to a re-conceptualisation of this distinction in which peace journalism can be recognised as that which:

offer[s] and draw[s] attention to vantage points from which to inspect propaganda from the outside. Articles scored on this indicator [in an exercise in content analysis gauging the extent of peace journalism] if they contained material likely to open war propaganda to what Hall (1980) calls 'negotiated' or 'oppositional' readings. (Lynch 2008, p143)

The multiplicity of perspectives, prompting and equipping audiences with cues and clues they can use to develop their own views, referred to by M, above, contains a distinct echo of this point.

Later, S, a senior executive in a civil society organisation, commented:

If the news was to be written by Muslim journalists you'd have a different perspective, but the reality is that we don't have our own news station, we don't have our own TV and so on.

As the discussion developed, S went further by referring to the:

Huge amount of mistrust and pessimism, scepticism and lack of confidence within the Australian Muslim community [regarding media representations] … There's [a] lack of confidence that the Muslim point of view is ever going to get across or what they're going to read is ever going to be fair to the Muslim community. And, to be honest, I think this is fed by some of our leaders also, who have had that point of view, so they reinforce it [at] any chance that comes up ... [to] confirm their point of view, rather than seeing that isolated good comment [for example] that we should be out of Afghanistan, we should be providing aid, we should be rebuilding and so on [referring to interviews recorded for item number 2 on the list above]. So it's a self-perpetuating state of mind that is basic right the way through the Muslim community.

To the suggestion that the familiar patterns had been 'dislodged' by some of the material in the peace journalism bulletin, she replied: 'but it's not different enough for the community here: you'd have to hit us in the face with a wet fish, I think'. An intriguing suggestion emerged, from some of the other participants, of an incipient generation gap in responses and expectations. A, a part-time office worker for the Australian Federal Police, offered the following assessment of the comments by S and B:

Because they're older, they've had more experience and lived in this country longer. We're [including M, of the participants quoted here, as well as herself] so young, we haven't developed our ideas, like they're not as consolidated. So when they watch news they may be desensitised to some of the crap, they're like 'Ugh, same old stuff', but when I watch the news and I think it's something fresh I go 'Oh my god that was refreshing' ... As young people, when we see something new we don't go 'Argh, they're brainwashing me', we go 'Oh look'. It's that glimpse of hope that there's a slight change.

In response to this prompt, M responded positively to the story about the Israel–Palestine peace talks in particular:

I think it was very effective because, like H [another participant, who described herself as a housewife] said, it gave the story a reality, it contextualised it. When you speak of Palestine in the Middle East, most general Australians get turned off, it doesn't concern us, we're not over there, we don't feel their pain, we don't understand what they're doing. When he used the example – it was a brilliant example, Glebe and Marrickville – general Australians, the vast masses, can relate to that because they are familiar with that. So it gave it context, which is what more journalism needs to do.

## Conclusion

Peace journalism has been criticised for inscribing in calls for media reform 'an overly individualistic and voluntaristic perspective' (Hanitzsch 2007), downplaying the importance of media structures in governing the content of news representations of conflict. Perhaps the best-known critique of this kind is the propaganda model, but this, in turn, is criticised for going, as it were, too far in the other direction, underplaying the scope for journalistic agency and attaching too little importance to plurality and variegation, and moments when they may be extended.

Public service broadcasting has been identified as a media domain in which a mandate to represent a diversity of views and perspectives, and assemble accounts of the facts with due attention to backgrounds and contexts, 'should' afford more opportunities for peace journalism. Peace journalism has, in some contexts, proved an animating concept in social movement activism and professional development, as well as scholarly research. To consider the prospects for media activism, to foster journalistic agency within public service broadcasting to get more peace journalism, by evoking and activating its mandate provisions, therefore presents itself as an obvious application of the concept.

Successful media activism depends on alliances with progressive forces, formed and calibrated according to the needs of particular issues. In Australia in 2010, activists were supplied with a 'hot poker' by the Israeli military's attack on the *Mavi Marmara* aid vessel, which brought peace campaigners into alliance with the leadership of Sydney's Muslim community. Significant political changes were underway in the background, with the Australian government deviating – slightly and temporarily, but significantly – from its customary uncritical pro-Israel stance. And the ABC, the country's principal public service broadcaster, was coming under pressure over its decision to rescind plans to broadcast a documentary highlighting nonviolent resistance to Israel's illegal military occupation of Palestinian territory.

This presented a hot poker to media activism too, raising demands in the domain of public service broadcasting, but the most prominent civil society organisation providing independent views on the ABC and its output declined to join in. As with the protests over the *Mavi Marmara* attack itself, Sydney's Muslim community may supply potential partners for alliances to press for change. This potential depends on willingness, by Muslim activists, to identify peace journalism demands vis-à-vis public service broadcasting, as effective ways to surmount obstacles to what they would regard as valued goals.

The commensurability between these two potential allies – peace journalism advocates and Muslim activists – depends on being able to delineate the boundaries of a 'centre', and call for their expansion to include the subjugated aspects of reality, while distinguishing that from a partisan stance in the conflicts themselves. Could peace journalism in public service broadcasting serve as an effective rallying call for such an alliance, or would the Muslim activists see any change that might result as 'too little', preferring to create and consume news 'written by Muslim journalists' instead? Comments in the focus group discussion suggest that the answer is 'yes' in some cases, and 'no' in others: perhaps depending on the generational background of the individual concerned.

Peace journalism, as a value-explicit approach to media practice and analysis, confers a responsibility on its adherents to seek opportunities for practical application. That directs their attention to media activism, and public service broadcasting remains an appealing domain in which to attempt to bring it to bear. Alliance-building for this form of media activism is possible but, in Sydney in 2010, it was underdeveloped, and therefore did not, arguably, make the most of the conjunction of events underway at the time – an experience that holds important lessons for future attempts – both in Australia and elsewhere.

* The research by Jake Lynch and Annabel McGoldrick on a Global Standard for Reporting Conflict is supported under the Australian Research Council's Linkage Projects funding scheme (No. LP0991223) with partnership by the International Federation of Journalists, and Act for Peace.

## References

Amnesty, et al. (2010). Dashed hopes: continuation of the Gaza blockade. Report by Amnesty International and a group of 24 other aid agencies and human rights organisations. [Online]. Available: www.amnesty.org.uk/ uploads/documents/doc_21083.pdf [Accessed 2 August 2011].

Australian Associated Press (2006). Ethnic leaders condemn Muslim cleric. *The Age.* 26 October. [Online]. Available: www. theage.com.au/news/national/ethnic-leaders-condemn-muslim-cleric/2006/10/26/1161749223822.html [Accessed 2 August 2011].

Bennett, W Lance (1990). Towards a theory of press-state relations. *Journal of Communication,* 40(2): 103–25.

Bourdieu, Pierre (1999). *On television.* Translated by Priscilla Parkhurst Ferguson. New York: New Press.

Corbin, Jane (2010). Collision course. *ABC Foreign correspondent.* 8 September. Transcript cited [Online]. Available: www.abc.net.au/foreign/ content/2010/s3005778.htm [Accessed 2 August 2011].

Dorling, Philip (2010). Yank in the ranks. *Sydney Morning Herald.* 9 December. [Online]. Available: www.smh.com.au/technology/technology-news/yank-in-the-ranks-20101208-18pwi.html [Accessed 2 August 2011].

Freedman, Des (2009). Smooth operator? The propaganda model and moments of crisis. *Westminster Papers in Communication and Culture,* 6(2): 59–72.

Gray-Block, Aaron (2010). Gaza blockade illegal, must be lifted: UN's Pillay. *Reuter News Report.* [Online]. Available: www.reuters.com/article/ idUSLDE65404020100605 [Accessed 2 August 2011].

Hackett, Robert (2006). Is peace journalism possible? Three frameworks for assessing structure and agency in news media. *Conflict and Communication Online,* 5(2). [Online]. Available: www.cco.regener-online.de/2006_2/pdf/hackett.pdf [Accessed 2 August 2011].

Hackett, Robert & William Carroll (2006). *Remaking media: the struggle to democratise public communication.* London: Routledge.

Hall, Stuart (1997). Representation and the media. *Media Education Foundation Transcript*. [Online]. Available: www.mediaed.org/handouts/pdfs/HALL-REPMEDIA.pdf [Accessed 2 August 2011].

Hall, Stuart (1980). Encoding/decoding. In Stuart Hall, Dorothy Hobson, Andrew Lowe & Paul Willis (Eds). *Culture, media, language: working papers in cultural studies, 1972–79* (pp128–38). London: Hutchinson.

Hallin, Daniel (1989). *The uncensored war: the media and Vietnam.* Berkeley: University of California Press.

Hanitzsch, Thomas (2007). Situating peace journalism in journalism studies: a critical appraisal. *Conflict and Communication Online*, 6(2). [Online]. Available: www.cco.regener-online.de/2007_2/pdf/hanitzsch.pdf [Accessed 2 August 2011].

Hartcher, Peter (2010). What am I, chopped liver? How Rudd dived into schmooze mode. *Sydney Morning Herald*. 21 June. [Online]. Available: www.smh.com.au/opinion/politics/what-am-i-chopped-liver-how-rudd-dived-into-schmooze-mode-20100621-ys5g.html [Accessed 2 August 2011].

Herman, Edward & Noam Chomsky (2002). *Manufacturing consent: the political economy of the mass media*. 2nd edn. New York: Pantheon Books.

International Committee of the Red Cross (2009). Gaza: 1.5m people trapped in despair. *ICRC*. [Online]. Available: www.icrc.org/eng/resources/documents/report/palestine-report-260609.htm[Accessed 2 August 2011].

Kerbaj, Richard (2006). 'I'm misunderstood' excuse is wearing thin. *The Australian*. 27 October. [Online]. Available: www.theaustralian.com.au/news/nation/im-misunderstood-excuse-is-wearing-thin/story-e6frg6nf-1111112425591[Accessed 2 August 2011].

Lewis, Jeff (2005). *Language wars: the role of media and culture in global terror and political violence.* London: Pluto Press.

Lightbown, Richard (2010). Analysis of BBC Panorama 'Death on the Med' exposes blatant pro-Israel bias. *Redress*. [Online]. Available: www.redress.cc/global/tclementevans20100828 [Accessed 2 August 2011].

Loewenstein, Antony (2010). 'Reviews: *Hope in a slingshot*,' *Hopeinaslingshot.com.* [Online]. Available: hopeinaslingshot.com/reviews/ [Accessed 2 August 2011].

Lynch, Jake (2010). The world's first ever demonstration for peace journalism? *TRANSCEND Media Service.* 5 July. [Online]. Available: www.transcend.org/tms/2010/06/the-world%E2%80%99s-first-demonstration-for-peace-journalism/ [Accessed 2 August 2011].

Lynch, Jake (2009a). Do you ever feel like the walls are closing in? *New Matilda.* 15 September. [Online]. Available: newmatilda.com/2009/09/15/ ever-feel-walls-are-closing [Accessed 2 August 2011].

Lynch, Jake (2009b). Politicide or politic: Gillard and the Gaza muzzle. *Sydney Morning Herald.* 10 July. [Online]. Available: www.smh.com.au/ opinion/politicide-or-politic-gillard-and-the-gaza-muzzle-20090709-deju. html?page=-1 [Accessed 2 August 2011].

Lynch, Jake (2009c). Australia's ABC attempts to justify rise above inflation of military spending. *Pressenza.* 20 August. [Online]. Available: www.pressenza.com/npermalink/australiaxs-abc-attempts-to-justify-rise-above-inflation-of-military-spending [Accessed 2 August 2011].

Lynch, Jake (2008). *Debates in peace journalism.* Sydney: Sydney University Press.

Lynch, Jake & Annabel McGoldrick (2010). A global standard for reporting conflict and peace. In Richard Lance Keeble, John Tulloch & Florian Zollmann (Eds). *Peace journalism, war and conflict resolution* (pp87–104). London: Peter Lang Inc.

Lynch, Jake & Annabel McGoldrick (2005). *Peace journalism.* Stroud: Hawthorn Press.

Manning, Peter (2004). *Dog-whistle politics and journalism.* Sydney: Australian Centre for Independent Journalism.

McGoldrick, Annabel (2006). War journalism and objectivity. *Conflict and Communication Online,* 5(2). [Online]. Available: www.cco.regener-online.de/2006_2/pdf/mcgoldrick.pdf [Accessed 2 August 2011].

Mendes, Philip (2008). John Pilger on Israel/Palestine: a critical analysis of his views and sources. *Australian Journal of Jewish Studies*, 22: 97–112.

Mendes, Philip & Nick Dyrenfurth (2009). Racism risk in calls for Israeli boycott. *The Australian*. 19 September. [Online]. Available: www.theaustralian.com.au/news/opinion/racism-risk-in-calls-for-israeli-boycott/story-e6frg6zo-1225776845035 [Accessed 2 August 2011].

Munro, Kelsey (2010). Sydney marchers in global wave of protest against killings and blockade,' *Sydney Morning Herald*. 2 June. [Online]. Available: www.smh.com.au/national/sydney-marchers-in-global-wave-of-protest-against-killings-and-blockade-20100601-wvgl.html [Accessed 2 August 2011].

Myconos, George & Simon Watmough (2007). *Perceptions of Islamic and Middle Eastern people in Australian media: scope for improvement*. Melbourne: Centre for Dialogue, La Trobe University.

Philo, Greg & Mike Berry (2004). *Bad news from Israel*. London: Pluto Press.

Pike, Andrew (2010). *Ronin Films news release*. 7 January. [Online]. Available: www.roninfilms.com.au/read/3502.html [Accessed 2 August 2011].

Pilger, John (2007). Children of the dust. *New Statesman*. 28 May. [Online]. Available: www.newstatesman.com/middle-east/2007/05/pilger-israel-children [Accessed 2 August 2011].

Senate Estimates (2010). Transcript. Senate Environment and Communications Legislation Committee: Estimates. [Online]. Available: www.aph.gov.au/hansard/senate/commttee/S13340.pdf [Accessed 2 August 2011].

Sharp, Ari (2010). ABC in firing line over balancing act. *Sydney Morning Herald*. 29 May. [Online]. Available: www.smh.com.au/national/abc-in-firing-line-over-balancing-act-20100528-wldr.html [Accessed 2 August 2011].

Shinar, Dov (2007). Peace journalism: the state of the art. In Dov Shinar & Wilhelm Kempf (Eds). *Peace journalism: the state of the art* (pp199–210). Berlin: Regener.

Shoemaker, Pamela & Stephen Reese (1996). *Mediating the message.* White Plains, NY: Longman.

Stradijot, Glenys (2010). ABC self-censors: what you don't see on the ABC. *News and Views*, FABC newsletter, Winter. [Online]. Available: friendsoftheabc.org/newsletters/Update2010_6.pdf/view [Accessed 2 August 2011].

Tehranian, Majid (2002). Peace journalism: negotiating global media ethics. *Harvard International Journal of Press/Politics,* 7(2): 58–83.

UNGA (2010). General Assembly concludes two-day debate, adopting six resolutions on question of Palestine, situation in Middle East. *UNGA.* [Online]. Available: unispal.un.org/UNISPAL.nsf/47D4E277B48D9D368 5256DDC00612265/508B96508E1AF713852577EC0050EE99 [Accessed 2 August 2011].

# Chapter 12

## Globalisation of compassion: women's narratives as models for peace journalism

*Elissa J Tivona*

Unprecedented advances in global interconnectivity have accelerated the pace of globalisation. In a few short decades, globalisation has come to characterise changes across wide ranging disciplines. Consider increased consolidation of economic markets and global business interests, heightened awareness of climate crises and the planet's finite carrying capacity, instantaneous interaction across the internet, and expanded consciousness of worldwide human rights abuses and extreme discrepancies in resource distribution.

In 2001, Mark Juergensmeyer, author of *Terror in the mind of God: the global rise of religious violence*, added another unexpected dimension to globalisation with his investigation of major world religions. In his book, he describes this phenomenon from an insider's perspective, analysing the rhetoric of male religious fanatics who have captured public attention and mobilised men by the thousands (Juergensmeyer 2001). These leaders and their followers brazenly assert a willingness to sacrifice people in the service of God, the angry and vengeful father. However, what do wives, sisters, mothers and daughters of these religious warriors do when they awaken each morning, and how might their actions reveal very different dreams and aspirations?

Women's alternative acts comprise data for my research, derived from stories of 1000 women collectively nominated for the Nobel Peace Prize in 2005 in a landmark Swiss initiative to draw attention to a very different and remarkable kind of globalisation: *the globalisation of compassion*. The results of my research strongly indicate that the warriors' impulse to usher in the ultimate rule of a particular God through violence and force has a strong gender correlate. According to a rhetorical analysis of peace and reconciliation narratives – as recorded in *1000 peacewomen across the globe* (Association 2005), the collected stories of the 1000 Nobel nominees of every religious persuasion and background – women are engaged in activities quite different from their male counterparts. This idea is corroborated by eminent peace researcher Elise Boulding, who writes in *The cultures of peace: the hidden side of history*, that 'The holy war culture is a male warrior culture headed by a patriarchal warrior-god. It demands the subjection of women and other aliens to men, the proto-patriarchs, and to God (or the gods)' (Boulding 2000, p17). An understanding of women's global performance represents an altogether new prospect for humanity; in particular, the globalisation of compassion, which has emerged as the critical focus of my research.

The result of rhetorical analysis of peace and conflict narratives in combination with systematic analysis of how different rhetorical acts are portrayed (or not portrayed) in world media reinforces a growing sense that humanity is deeply imperilled by continued refusal to distinguish the actions of women as global citizens, as peace activists, and as spiritual visionaries, from those of men. Although it may appear that the fundamental drama of holy war between good and evil is embedded in all human beings, the obsession with supremacy is – my research suggests – predominantly male. I argue that these furies are especially unique to a hegemonic understanding of religious history, revealing a profound ignorance of multifaceted feminist expressions of spirituality. Furthermore, it is my thesis that significant progress in the world in establishing reconciliation and positive peace (Galtung 1996) across cultures depends on deepening our collective understanding of these underlying feminist principles, strengthening our ability to interpret them and, above all, incorporating them into daily public discourse, notably through the media.

Most recently, author and social critic Jeremy Rifkin embraced this view in *The empathic civilisations: the race to global consciousness in a world in crisis* (2009). Rifkin notes:

What is required now is nothing less than a leap to global empathic consciousness and in less than a generation if we are to resurrect the global economy and revitalise the biosphere. The question becomes this: what is the mechanism that allows empathic sensitivity to mature and consciousness to expand through history. (Rifkin 2010)

Leading peace researchers Galtung and Lynch (2010) offer peace journalism as a promising tool for expediting this foundational shift, and the findings of my own research provide compelling evidence for this conviction. Like many of my colleagues, I originally undertook research to better understand ways to reshape a world that is currently being mediated almost exclusively through the lens of war and conflict narratives. By contrast, the women I feature in my research speak eloquently through very different kinds of actions, and the principles underlying their actions embody many of the conceptual currents running throughout peace journalism. I contend that a powerful strategy to globalise compassion – to move empathic sensitivity from a theoretical ideal to a practical reality – is to regularly highlight these acts, performed daily across every continent, as featured news.

At the conclusion of my research, I put forward a set of hypothetical categories for reframing news stories, with the intention of infusing compassionate behaviour into mainstream public discourse. Ultimately, shifting perceptions of the newsworthy from 'if it bleeds, it leads' to 'if it heals, it reveals' requires a reformulation of the performances that are highlighted on a day-to-day basis: performances modelled by women activists across the globe. I think of each category as a strand of discussion that can be consciously incorporated in the media to weave a tapestry of peace. As it turns out, this formulation is a vivid and useful extension of the peace journalism model, especially the following doctrines: to give voice to the views of all rival parties at every level; to offer creative ideas for conflict resolution, development, peacemaking and peacekeeping; and to pay attention to peace stories and postwar developments (Lynch & McGoldrick 2005). Bringing women's peacebuilding creativity into the foreground of public awareness, by means of the public media, constitutes a momentous step forward in the advancement of global justice and lasting peace.

## Different notions of globalisation

Unarguably the organised and systematic perpetuation of warfare is, and has been throughout history, largely the domain of men, even though it is common to hear war characterised as a byproduct of 'human nature'. Typically women, the exclusive child bearers and most frequent life-sutainers of young children across drastically different cutures, conduct the affairs of homemaking and care giving, to whatever extent possible, out of the direct line of fire. However, throughout the late 20th and now the early 21st centuries, technological advances have extended the reach of deadly violence far outside artificially constructed battle lines, cosquently endangering the security of all sentient life (Heyzer 2004). One could plausibly argue that ubiquitous weapons of mass destruction have in and of themselves globalised warfare, taking it far beyond the limited notion of exclusive engagement between combatants. In such a lethal environment, collateral damage, or more accurately injury and death of civilians (largely women and children), is unavoidable.

However, more and more women in the world, inordinately impacted by toxic violence perpetrated by militaries, militias and/or terrorists across every continent, are consolidating distinct and potent activities as antidotes and finding creative strategies to stretch a net of compassion over the most vulnerable and powerless in every society. This movement can be understood as the globalisation of compassion. This paradigm of globalisation is characterised by what Johan Galtung refers to as positive peace (as contrasted to negative peace, which is defined simply as the cessation or absence of active violence regardless of how tentative the ceasefire). In a positive peace model however, solutions represent the introduction of harmony, analogous to the positive health model, which is characterised by wellness rather than simply the absence of symptoms. In Galtung's global analysis, notions of direct personal violence (such as inter-gender or gang-related), inter-state violence, and all forms of indirect violence including structural, cultural and nature-related violence are inseparable. To establish true positive peace, harmony must be reasserted and sustained across multiple dimensions. My research underscores the multitude and diversity of models for positive peace currently operating on the ground, represented by the collection of the 1000 peacewomen's narratives. In each model, one or more women stand at the centre of innovation, and in so far as the models achieve harmonious results and inspire replication, compassion (and positive peace) are indeed becoming globalised.

Looking back several decades, feminist theorists Nancy Hartsock and Irene Diamond foreshadowed the vital need for this form of global consciousness, predating Rifkin by three decades. As early as 1981, they offered a cautionary note to pay 'close attention to women's activity rather than men's and the consequent thoroughgoing focus on whole human beings', which 'necessitates the development of more encompassing categories of analysis of political life' (Diamond & Hartsock 1981, p719).

With the goal in mind of creating a systematic set of globally relevant positive peace categories, I constructed a research study to explore women's intentional peacebuilding activities. Results of the study confirmed my hypothesis that the vast majority of women's rhetorical acts remain imperceptible to the general media, in stark contrast to repetitious and dominant narratives of divisiveness, often erupting in bloodshed and currently labelled as headlines or as featured news stories. The conclusion that public discourse is saturated by the rhetorical acts of men comes as no great surprise. However, by shifting focus away from dominant foreground noise, and then systematically analysing the nature and impact of global peacebuilding activity (too often lost in the background), this investigation seeks to shed light on a more balanced and salient understanding of human performance on the world stage and provide hope for more durable cultures of peace in the future.

*Background of the '1000 peacewomen initiative'*

It is prudent to keep in mind that according to the Women's Refugee Commission (WRC), four out of five of the world's nearly 45 million people who were forced to seek safety in a country not their own or who were internally displaced within their own borders are women, children and young people. Women and adolescent girls are especially vulnerable to exploitation, rape and abuse (WRC 2010). This estimate of women and children comprising nearly 80 percent of total refugee and internally displaced populations worldwide is consistent with ongoing research by the United Nations High Commissioner for Refugees (UNHCR 2009). The plight of these individuals has reached epic proportions, begging a wide range of questions including: What resources do these women and children require; how are these most effectively provided; who provides them; and how can such vast numbers of people be reintegrated into either the former or renewed cultures from which they fled?

In 2003, these and other critical questions became a motivating catalyst for Swiss parliamentarian and Council of Europe member Ruth Gaby Vermot-Mangold. In her capacity with the European Union, Vermot-Mangold visited refugee camps and war-torn regions across Europe: in Azerbaijan and Armenia; in Bosnia and Kosovo; and in Serbia, Georgia, and Chechnya. During these journeys, she became acutely aware of wreckage left in the wake of war. Yet everywhere she travelled, she met and visited with hundreds of women who laboured tirelessly under dire circumstances: struggling to restore stability and security to the lives of families, friends, and communities; to sustain nonviolence; to reconcile with former enemies; and to build viable alternatives to overcome intractable conflict. These creative and courageous efforts to rehabilitate the shattered lives of survivors and to implement strategies for moving forward went virtually unnoticed; these projects and programs left scarcely a trace in the world outside their narrow sphere of influence and action.

Dismayed by this state of affairs in which women were being so completely obscured within the background of public discourse, Vermot-Mangold (2005) determined to reduce global ignorance. She assembled an international team of 20 women, who in turn helped organise nine evaluation panels based on geographic regions. Together, they set an ambitious agenda to identify, publicise and network the deeds and stories of 1000 women labouring in and for peace. The association drafted criteria for nomination and sent out the first candidate call over the internet in 2003, satisfied with the presumption that nominators could and would capably define women's peace work on an inductive basis. As nominations began to flow in, they discovered that the scope of women's peace work runs the gamut of what we now recognise and define under the rubric of peacebuilding, inclusive of all the necessary and simultaneous activities vividly described by Elizabeth Ferris, Senior Fellow at the Brookings Institution – and co-director of the Brookings–Bern Project on Internal Displacement, in her keynote address to the 2009 International Conference on Peace and Reconciliation. Ferris stated:

> Former UN Secretary-General Boutros Boutros-Ghali originally presented peacebuilding as 'action to identify and support structures which will tend to strengthen and solidify peace in order to avoid relapse into conflict'. Since then, the concept of peacebuilding has expanded to include addressing the root causes of conflict, early warning and response efforts, violence prevention, advocacy, civilian and military peacekeeping, military intervention, humanitarian assistance, ceasefire agreements, and the establishment of peace zones. (Ferris 2009)

In less than two years, more than 2000 women performing work across many of these dimensions and others were submitted for nomination. Every nominee had to be submitted by at least two individuals and their references carefully vetted by association members and evaluation panels. Interestingly, a key criterion for nomination was that each candidate's work had to exemplify the work of many. In other words, the association believed that if the same call went out on any given day, there would be a high likelihood for a completely different set of women engaged in peace innovations across the world to be nominated and selected.

The prevalence of peacebuilding efforts at the grassroots was recently highlighted in a July 2010 interview between Krista Tippett, host of National Public Radio's (NPR) *Speaking of faith*, and John Paul Lederach, a veteran of crisis mediation for over three decades in over 25 countries and five continents. In the interview, Lederach recounts stories about grassroots peace initiatives in specific localities on very different continents. He notes:

> Because I work at both a grassroots level and a very high political level; in some ways, to be very honest, the sophistication by which

they're doing it at a local level is leap years ahead of how politics is typically done, which is an all-or-nothing kind of format in which every decision is gauged primarily on whether if we haven't won, we have at least assured the other cannot carry victory away. (2010)

Throughout the interview, Lederach shares his direct experiences with women and men, from local communities and without benefit of news coverage or fanfare, who are recrafting their understanding of the 'other'. This is accomplished by forging highly improbable relationships with others, who have typically been their enemies over years of conflict and violence.

In a similar fashion, the narratives of 1000 peacewomen (and scores of other women who remain unrecorded and undocumented) echo this theme. These women consistently employ compassion, creativity and cross-cultural sensitivity in order to transform conflicts in profound ways that government officials and government-appointed negotiators, while enjoying the spotlight of constant media attention, have failed to realise, despite years of effort.

## Summary of research methodology and analytical methods

Moved by this monumental undertaking and curious to assess the impact of the 1000 peacewomen stories on public discourse, I undertook a qualitative document analysis (QDA) in accordance with the emerging method described by David Altheide et al. (2008). In so doing, I made use of two comparable sets of data. The first dataset consisted of nine peacewomen narratives, identified by a systematic sampling process to ensure diversity. From *1000 peacewomen across the globe* (Association 2005), the text compilation of the stories of all 1000 women included in the project, I selected one narrative at random from each of the nine geographic regions represented. The 1000 narratives in this volume constituted an unprecedented source for content analysis and provided both the inspiration and the starting point for the research. Each entry in the book was a record of the nominee's initiative, as drafted by a native-speaking journalist who typically conducted a face-to-face or telephone interview. I analysed each narrative with an eye to clarifying and bringing forward the 'core rhetorical act' (the term I used for the characteristic performance of each peacewoman) represented by the woman's specific labour in her particular context on behalf of building peace.

Following this random selection, I paired each of the sampled stories with a headline news story, also collected systematically through a LexisNexis search of wire service news stories feeding popular media outlets. The specific news or *foreground* story was selected from all those occurring in the peacewoman's country of origin on the day of (or the day after) press conferences held in 50 worldwide locations, announcing the nomination of 1000 women from 153 countries as collective recipients of the Nobel Peace Prize for 2005. The resulting pairs (a background *1000 peacewomen across the globe* narrative coupled with a foreground news story) were called local focus dyads (LFDs) and created the basis for the QDA.

Using all the LFDs, I structured a meta-analysis to address several overarching and puzzling questions. By contrasting core rhetorical acts featured in media from the same region as the nine women (and occurring on the same day the nomination was made public), my goal was to gain insights into the following:

- What characterises rhetorical acts of empowered women?
- What characterises rhetorical acts featured by news media?
- By juxtaposing these two types of rhetoric, how is the discourse on peace and war distorted and how are activities of women rendered invisible?
- What new possibilities for peace emerge when we rack focus[1] and reverse background and foreground representations?

The investigation sought to draw attention to lessons learned from a synthesis of peacewomen enterprises, viewed through the lens of

---

1   To 'rack focus' is a term used by television news camera crews, literally meaning to change the focus of a single shot, for effect, while the camera is running. The effect sought is usually to connect an item in the foreground, conceptually, with one in the background of the shot – hence the viewer's attention is directed first to the one, then to the other.

subject matter that is amplified on the world stage versus subject matter that is omitted. One day I hope similar scrutiny will be given to the 991 other stories in the *1000 peacewomen across the globe* compilation in a search for even greater insight.

Table 1 provides a composite of the rhetorical acts of the nine selected peacewomen, individually referred to as the 'rhetor'. To identify the defining rhetorical act represented in each story, as well as in each news article paired with it, I developed and followed a rigorous process of iterative coding, adapted from Strauss and Corbin's methodology of grounded theory (1990, 1994), moving from each woman's specific work within her local context to a broader statement summarising the core rhetorical act represented by that work. Then, I repeated the systematic coding process for the companion news stories in each LFD.

Table 1 Peacewomen's core rhetorical acts

| 'Background' rhetor | Core rhetorical act |
| --- | --- |
| Durga Devi<br>Region – South Asia<br>Country – India | RHETOR aspires to social productivity through women's empowerment projects |
| Amelia Rokotuivana<br>Region – Oceania<br>Country – Fiji | RHETOR unites constituents for public benefit: an end to French nuclear testing and colonisation |
| Nina Kolybashkina<br>Region – Europe<br>Country – Ukraine | RHETOR demonstrates peacebuilding and reconciliation strategies using skills as an interpreter |
| Alma Montenegro de Fletcher<br>Region – Latin America and Caribbean<br>Country – Panama | RHETOR seeks justice for all through available but limited legal channels |
| Landon Pearson<br>Region – North America<br>Country – Canada | RHETOR demonstrates lifelong dedication to advocating for human rights on behalf of children |

| 'Background' rhetor | Core rhetorical act |
|---|---|
| Zanaa Jurmed<br><br>Region – Eastern Asia<br><br>Country – Mongolia | RHETOR employs multiple strategies to achieve democratic civil society in Mongolia. Multidimensional nature of her work, most recently 're-focused' on the 'social sphere' to more directly develop human capacity |
| Genoveva Ximenes Alves<br><br>Region – Southeast Asia<br><br>Country – East Timor | RHETOR transforms local school into school for peace and serves in multiple leadership capacities in program she helped create |
| Jeanne M Gacoreke<br><br>Region – Africa<br><br>Country – Burundi | RHETOR gives direct assistance to women and children traumatised by sexual abuse and related war crimes, works to raise awareness to break through taboo of silence concerning atrocities. |
| Palwasha Hassan<br><br>Region – Asia and Middle East<br><br>Country – Afghanistan | RHETOR directs resources to empower destitute Afghan women and protect their human rights |

Finally, the axial codes for the study (open codes grouped categorically) were rooted in Karlyn Kohrs Campbell's 'Elements of descriptive analysis for rhetorical acts' (1982). According to Campbell, truth does not exist independently of people's social interaction. She notes:

> Whereas the [empirical] scientist would say, 'the most important thing is the discovery and testing of truth', the rhetorician (one who studies rhetoric and takes a rhetorical perspective) would say, 'truth cannot walk on its own legs. It must be carried by people to other people. It must be made effective through language, through argument and appeal'. (Campbell 1982, p3)

Thus I predicated the findings of the study on the assumption that news reporting is a fundamental means for carrying truth to the general public and functions as a significant mechanism to frame public perception. The overriding question is, if this vehicle delivered alternate news, might there be other more salient perceptions dominating public discourse?

## Globalisation of compassion

The QDA confirmed one mechanism for globalising cultures of war like those characterised by Mark Juergensmeyer and others: that is, the media's persistent foregrounding of stories of conflict featuring hierarchical rank, with a preference for official sources, and ubiquitous neglect of global peacebuilding achievements and collaborative problem-solving. The media's failure to boldly feature peace-related accomplishments – models of reconciliation, cooperation, rehabilitation and compassion that might be repeated and adapted to other contexts – depletes the human knowledge base, thwarting our capacity to reverse cultures of violence and replace them with durable and peaceable cultures. Even more damaging is the realisation that as long as we persist in the belief that essential human nature is violent and self-serving, the more we continue to report stories about ourselves to reinforce these beliefs, and the more social constructs become extensions of these beliefs about ourselves.

Several of the stories drawn from the compilation *1000 peacewomen across the globe*, viewed in the context of LFDs, highlight the collective ignorance created to a large extent by the ever narrowing thematic repertoire of the popular media. Conversely, the study suggests a set of alternate thematic threads (detailed in sections to follow), crafted from the fabric of these women's stories, and woven together into a novel narrative tapestry. The process of racking focus, from war journalism to peace journalism, shifting the stories of women's compassionate peacebuilding activities from a dimly lit background into a brightly illuminated foreground, is the process referred to in this study as the globalisation of compassion.

For example, in one LFD, the story of Mongolian 'professor, turned political activist', Zanaa Jurmed (Association 2005, p951), is paired with a foreground news story dealing with the infusion of large amounts of cash into the Mongolian private sector by the World Bank. The foundational premise of this viewpoint is that growing the private sector is essential to economic capacity-building throughout the country. Unfortunately, the recent global recession has demonstrated how fast this logic can unravel, and, in the wake of that unravelling, revealed the frightening scarcity of social safety nets.

Zanaa Jurmed's story demonstrates an alternate line of reasoning. After years directly involved in the political process of building a modern democratic civil society in Mongolia, Jurmed perceived a critical need to refocus energy more directly on the social sphere. In this arena, she initiated and founded a number of women and human rights NGOs nationwide, including the National Watch Network Center of the Convention on the Elimination of All Forms of Discrimination Against Women (CEDAW) (Association 2005, p951). From this perspective, development and protection of human capital take precedence over development and protection of money and the interests of those who control and manipulate monetary resources. Such rhetorical acts, referencing social concern for those nearer to the middle or bottom of the socioeconomic continuum, along with compassion and care for vulnerable populations, rarely dominate the headlines. In the terms outlined in the peace journalism model, her story is 'people-oriented' whereas the World Bank story is 'elite-oriented'.

In addition to Jurmed's work, multiple initiatives in this study illustrate the same point, including: women's empowerment projects among the destitute in India and in Afghanistan, peacebuilding and reconciliation strategies in the Ukraine; Canadian human rights initiatives for global children, justice for all in Panama, peace education programs in East Timor, and assistance to sexually abused victims of war in Burundi. Each program is important for the social benefit it brings to people. Nevertheless, as repeatedly illustrated in each LFD, economic stories featuring people-to-material transactions overshadow these socially significant narratives where people-to-people transactions prevail. When the victims of conflict and violence appear in the news, they are usually, according to Galtung and Lynch, 'able-bodied white males' from 'our' side; whereas peace journalism is 'a journalism of attachment to all actual and potential victims' (in Galtung & Lynch 2010, p17).

News services consistently fixate on the values underpinning a competitive free market economy to the exclusion of other values. War journalism is 'propaganda-oriented'. Propaganda here refers to attempts to 'shape perceptions, manipulate cognitions and direct behaviour' (Jowett & O'Donnell 1999, p6). And in this regard the news media are complicit in undermining a public consciousness of ideals that millions of women have exemplified for millennium: compassion, generosity, and service to others. Jurmed, like hundreds of thousands of women who function with limited resources under extreme conditions, managed to help heal and transform lives through dedication to direct service rather than through the generation of greater wealth at the top of the social spectrum. Practically speaking, from the perspective of the women who initiate, advocate for, and work in these social programs, progress is measured by the benefits achieved from the bottom up rather than, in terms of economic prospects, from the top down. Rhetorical acts of this nature appear to have intrinsic value regardless of whether money changes hands. In these cases, progress becomes the embodiment of people-to-people interventions celebrating the worth and dignity of many, not simply people-to-capital interventions measured in economic terms with the highest rewards for the most successful elites.

Some economists argue that social programs have value only to the extent that they rehabilitate people to engage productively in the market. Proponents of this perspective discuss services offered (for example, in the context of peace education, women's empowerment, and trauma recovery programs), strictly in terms of their success or failure at restoring recipients' willingness to re-engage in the pursuit of affluence. What is sorely missing from this point of view is the notion of 'sufficiency' that is embedded in women's rhetorical acts throughout this study. In a world where a chief executive officer of a major corporation earns more than enough to feed an entire population in some countries for a year, the peacewomen in my study repeatedly engage in acts that demonstrate real world strategies to rebalance such a distorted notion of progress. If the rhetoric of female-based compassion were to be on par with (or even supersede) the rhetoric of male-based economic expansion, we might be able to better view ourselves as a global human family and act as though each human being, and all of our resources, mattered.

The peacewomen I investigated provide role models in terms of their practical implementation of compassionate acts and efforts. These locally enacted but globally instructive projects represent a 'webocracy' – a web of achievable, sustainable, and secure livelihoods for countless people across every continent.

The work of Nina Kolybahskina of the Ukraine exemplifies another seminal shift, in this case around the idea of how *human security* is characterised by the media. Her core rhetorical act is bridging diversity: initiating acts of coming together for the collective good of all. This activity distinguished many of the rhetorical acts of her colleagues, yet collectively such stories rarely find their way into public discourse. Instead, the media repeatedly associates human security with force, presumably under the assumption that sufficient force correlates with order. In this limited paradigm, imposing order is portrayed as far and away more critical to citizen security than all other strategies for deep healing, causes to which so many peacewomen are dedicated. I argue that order *and* healing must go together. The media, however, overwhelmingly opts to feature force and coercion over the use of other tactics.

As a young woman, Nina Kolybahskina trained as an interpreter; as she matured, she discovered that her role as an interpreter gave her special insight into the rhetoric of multiple sides in conflict situations. Through the act of translation, she became more and more adept at gleaning the common needs underlying points of conflict. Her narrative notes:

> That job taught her that translation requires not merely shifting between languages, but also finding common points between the systems of thinking of diverse groups. Later, in managing social projects, she realised that providing basic social services was essentially a work of translating the needs of community members into the language of project proposals and policy recommendations. (Association 2005, p101)

The rhetorical act of *interpreting* takes on much broader significance in this narrative. Beyond casting the words of one language into another language, Kolybahskina learned to use words as pathways into the heart of issues and as clues to how people frame and express their own needs. As she grew more skilled in this regard, her work evolved: she was no longer strictly engaged in resolving disputes, where some points are won and others lost, but rather in finding ways to meet the needs of whole populations, regardless of the side of a conflict they represented. Her role became bonding people around their collective destinies rather than dividing them according to their competing interests. However, few global citizens know of Nina Kolybahskina's work with the Network of Intercultural Exchange and Inter-Ethnic Tolerance in the Ukraine. Practically all forms of media remain silent with regard to rhetorical acts of this nature. Rather, media place continual and repetitious emphasis on clashes of oppositional interests. In a world saturated with stories of self-interested forces fighting for supremacy over *the other* to secure their own exclusive wellbeing, peaceful conflict resolution is rendered an aberration and largely unachievable.

## Security, progress and agency

These two stories are representative of the findings of my study, which concludes with an analysis of three overarching thematic currents: human security, progress, and sustained agency. When the background acts of peacewomen and the foreground acts of news stories are clustered in these categories and then considered side by side, distinctly different patterns of meaning for each category emerge. It is important to note, in the context of this research, that the thematic labels are useful devices to illustrate divergent inductive descriptions. However, they should in no way be confused with definitions previously established by international bodies (for example, the United Nations High Commissioner for Refugees [UNHCR] or the United Nations Development Programme [UNDP]). For example, in 1994, the UNDP comprehensively scrutinised human security from many angles. The term 'human security', as applied in the context of the United Nations, implies a set of very specific meanings (UNDP 1994). In the context of this research, the term is used as a label for two opposite perspectives – one featured regularly in the news media and the other altogether absent from the news media. The following tables provide a summary of the thematic framework and display the conceptual conclusions that I drew on each side of the Dyads for all three categories. The left side shows meanings and considerations that emerged from an analysis of background narratives, while the right side shows meanings and considerations that emerged from an analysis of foreground news stories. Depending on whether one takes a background or foreground perspective, the understanding of each theme differs dramatically.

*Theme 1 – progress*

Based on analysis of the core rhetorical acts in the peacewomen's narratives, progress is considered in terms of social and relational achievements. From the point of view of news, progress relies exclusively on expansion of material wealth. There are three differentiating factors along the dimension of progress.

| Progress | |
|---|---|
| **Peacewomen – background narratives** | **News stories – foreground narratives** |
| Progress considered in light of social, relational achievements. | Progress relies exclusively on expansion of material wealth. |
| • Acts of social compassion, concern and care for vulnerable populations (internally displaced persons, refugees, etc) | • Acts of economic expansion and material wealth |
| Progress is defined in terms of measures instituted for the public good/social welfare, not simply economic advancement (eg education, trauma recovery, women's empowerment programs). | Progress measured exclusively in economic terms. All human development reduced to economic terms versus awareness and cultivation of alternate values. |

| Progress | |
|---|---|
| **Peacewomen – background narratives** | **News stories – foreground narratives** |
| • People-to-people transactions | • People-to-material transactions |
| Social initiatives 'count' as progress, worthy of positive regard and public interest. | As evidenced by repetition of the Dow Jones and other stock market metrics. |
| • Bottom-up strategies accounting for sufficiency | • Top-down strategies accounting for supremacy |
| Wellbeing for many/most whenever possible, rather than for designated few. | Emphasis on individuals or corporations acting as individuals relied upon to provide the means for others to advance. |

*Theme 2 - human security*

Based on an analysis of peacewomen's narratives, human security and wellbeing are achieved through acts of unity and collectivity, whereas, in the media, human security is depicted as being achieved through powerplays between 'champions' and a demonised 'other'.

| Human security | |
|---|---|
| **Peacewomen – background narratives** | **News stories – foreground narratives** |
| Human security and wellbeing achieved through acts of unity, collectivity. | Human security achieved through power-plays between 'champions' and 'demons'. |
| • Collectivity: summoning healing strategies, reconciling with the other, weaving social safety nets, and building on the synergy of recovery. | • Duality: stressing divisive, oppositional, combative acts. Assignments of victors and vanquished. Reports of victories and defeats (eg Who is hurt, harmed or defeated? Who escapes harm, triumphs, ranks?) Distinguishing opposing sides, obstacles and barriers. |
| • Generational awareness and sustenance: stewardship and long-term sustainability where there are multiple winners. | |

| Human security | |
|---|---|
| **Peacewomen – background narratives** | **News stories – foreground narratives** |
| | • Emphasis on hierarchical rank: winners and losers, scores and hierarchies. Heavy reliance on numbers and statistics. For example, sport and sporting spectacles. Naming individual stars or leaders in starring roles. |

## Theme 3 – sustained agency

In terms of sustained agency, women's peacework is consistently occupied with building capacity, strengthening the ongoing pursuit of tangible results to address complex problems. In the media, sustained agency seems to disappear from view altogether. Instead, the emphasis is on images of victimhood and helplessness, where people are perpetually portrayed as being at the mercy of random, incoherent circumstances.

| Sustained agency | |
|---|---|
| **Peacewomen – background narratives** | **News stories – foreground narratives** |
| Sustained agency implies the capacity for ongoing pursuit of tangible results to address complex problems. | Sustained agency disappears altogether; instead media emphasis shifts perception to images and descriptions of victims of circumstance trapped in states of helplessness. |
| • Acts of healing and reconciliation, including reports on collective wellbeing and on participatory and collaborative initiatives. Creation of proactive social safety nets. | • Reports of transitory or repetitive outbreaks of crime, violence, and atrocity. |
| • Macro: long-term approaches to problems and problem-solving. | • Micro: short-term approach to problems and problem-solving. |

| Sustained agency | |
| --- | --- |
| Peacewomen – background narratives | News stories – foreground narratives |
| • Multidimensional: holistic approaches and social programs to address multiple faces of social problems. | • Uni-dimensional: fragmented and reactive programs and responses to social problems addressing a single facet at any given time. |

*Reinserting peace into public discourse*

These categories contrast headline news (which currently frame human understanding of reality by featuring gendered information in the foreground) with peace narratives that unfold in the background, just outside our field of view. Consequently, the public remains unaware of peace performances, especially as enacted by global women on the world stage on a daily basis.

Yet these themes are simply starting points. The observations and conclusions that follow indicate a critical and immediate need for more in-depth research into such gendered journalism and a comprehensive examination of alternative news reporting strategies. Humanity requires more accurate and representative views of the full bandwidth of human performance, which allow us to reclaim a belief that peace and reconciliation are possible and to demonstrate the many ways in which these results are achievable on a global basis.

Since I began by questioning the trajectory of world history as viewed through the lens of 'warrior theologies', replete with violent clashes between ultimate good and ultimate evil, I want to return to the idea that there may in fact be other viewpoints that can help us shift this trajectory. I argue that, at present, the international news media reflect the dominant storylines as determined *only* by warriors in one form or another – economic, political and religious. In this sense:

• Public discourse depends exclusively on economic indicators to measure human progress, ignoring most, if not all, other indicators.

- Mediated public discourse describes human security in terms of highly competitive and hierarchical powerplays between polarised forces (for example, religiously framed views of good and evil), which often rely on perpetuation or escalation of violence to affirm victory.

- Public discourse serves up fragmented incidents of victimisation (whether inflicted by human or natural causes) along with incoherent, short-term, and/or uni-dimensional propositions intended to fix or rescue the victims.

These findings are consistent with the foundational work of pioneering feminists where patriarchal systems are described as primarily valuing rational intellectual expression over emotional compassion; competitive power relationships and hierarchical rank over relational, collaborative structures; and labour performed in the public sphere over labour and productivity performed at home (in the private sphere) involving nurturing multiple generations (Harding 2003; Eisler 1995; Barlow 2000). What this study contributes to this august body of scholarship is explicit evidence that public media mirrors and intensifies prevailing values. It also finds that public audiences tolerate and often perpetuate this system at our own peril.

Globalisation of compassion requires a dramatic and immediate shift of focus, with a firm commitment to foregrounding stories of women's peacebuilding activities. This approach requires fieldworkers to proactively engage international media to modify how news media is generated in our world, drawing on the global peace journalism movement of educators and activists. Among the thousands of gifted writers and producers of message streams are individuals of goodwill, who empathise in attempts to 'ungender' journalism so that it more closely resembles peace journalism. This study is a wake-up call to professionals to cease framing news as the exclusive dominion of warriors but rather, to highlight the empathic and compassionate province of the peaceable and, by so doing, to effect an essential paradigm shift away from 'if it bleeds, it leads' and toward 'if it heals, it reveals'.

Pragmatically, an incident in my local community illustrates the possibilities for precisely this type of change. For several consecutive years an Abrahamic Interfaith group has sponsored a community service project called Bloodbonds, a campaign that asks members of the Muslim, Christian and Jewish faith communities to affirm the strength of their common heritage by donating blood rather than shedding blood. During these campaigns, ToAHS (Tent of Abraham, Hagar and Sarah) has successfully filled the local hospital bloodmobile to capacity, in an unmistakable act of collective service. This past year I had the occasion to publicly address the managing editor of the local newspaper and propose a challenge. I asked the paper to proactively contribute to public awareness of collaboration and service represented by Bloodbonds as opposed to 'business as usual' with news features of sectarian and religious violence. The outcome was promising; the local paper conceded and featured stories both before and following the event, highlighting the collaborative effort among the three Abrahamic faith communities.

Worldwide, journalists are pivotal partners in influencing decision-makers and reshaping opinions. Their commitment to healing and revealing stories means creatively re-crafting the steady deluge of information we listen to and see day after day. A synthesis of the findings of my study suggests at least six alternate and viable news strands comprising a tapestry of peace, which could contribute to ungendering the news environment. These categories provide frames for public discourse more in line with a true and rebalanced understanding of reality. These include:

- mending wounds and alleviating suffering
- weaving social safety nets
- crafting cultures of conflict resolution; *repurposing* cultures of violence
- creating innovative patterns and designs
- knitting together local and global
- affixing badges of honour to peace construction.

I invite academics and activists, and producers and consumers of media, to collaborate in drawing attention to one or more of these strands. I argue that the timing for a new journalistic framework could not be better. Established news agencies and global networks are hungry to reinvent themselves, especially given intense pressure created by the internet's ease of alternative information delivery. I encourage colleagues to look beyond underlying principles of *persuasive* rhetoric – devoted to establishing truth by ever escalating adversarial viewpoints. The outcome of this practice is a fixed perception of intractable conflict (Tannen 1998). I suggest re-imagined stories, constructed around Foss and Griffin's notions of 'invitational rhetoric' (Foss & Griffin 1995). At the heart of this argument is a push for the strong amplification of healing and revealing news: stories of peace and reconciliation between former warriors and perceived enemies. Such a practice would serve well to divert energy away from elites and extremists alike, many who easily hijack the media to serve underlying agendas and many who have vested interest in sustaining conflict and inflammatory realities. The survival of our species would be far better served by shifting the focus to the rest of us who harbour intense longing and vested interest in long-term security and achievable peace.

There are strong indications that this shift is well underway, specifically attributable to the seeming unlimited reach of the internet. As mentioned before, a strong advocate of this point of view is Jeremy Rifkin, who discusses this shift in his latest book, *The empathic civilisation: the race to global consciousness in a world in crisis* (2009). In a January 2010 *Huffington Post* article, he heralds recent scientific discoveries that contradict previous assumptions that humans are naturally aggressive and self-serving:

> Biologists and cognitive neuroscientists are discovering mirror-neurons – the so-called empathy neurons – that allow human beings and other species to feel and experience another's situation as if it were one's own. We are, it appears, the most social of animals and seek intimate participation and companionship with our fellows.

> Social scientists, in turn, are beginning to re-examine human history from an empathic lens and, in the process, discovering previously hidden strands of the human narrative which suggests that human evolution is measured not only by the expansion of power over nature, but also by the intensification and extension of empathy to more diverse others across broader temporal and spatial domains. (Rifkin 2010)

It appears that Rifkin's book provides a new interpretation of the history of civilisation, as seen through this lens of human empathy (or what I refer to as compassion). Many feminists may read his book and his blog with a sigh of weary cynicism, exasperated with the scientific sector's enormous ignorance of the body of research and proofs put forward by feminist scholars and activists for decades. The central notion of empathic human nature is not a new discovery for women, but has been woven throughout women's culture, women's rhetoric and women's spirituality, and has been substantially documented by researchers from first-wave feminists through to the present day (Boulding 2000). Nevertheless, despite the long delay created by the untenable gender bias in research and academia, Rifkin does offer an interesting historical analysis of how empathy is extended by quantum developments in information distribution channels. He attempts to explain the mechanism 'that allows empathic sensitivity to mature and consciousness to expand through history':

> Communication revolutions not only manage new, more complex energy regimes, but also change human consciousness in the process. Forager/hunter societies relied on oral communications and their consciousness was mythologically constructed. The great hydraulic agricultural civilisations were, for the most part, organised around script communication and steeped in theological consciousness. The first industrial revolution of the 19th century was managed by print communication and ushered in ideological consciousness. Electronic communication became the command and control mechanism for arranging the second industrial revolution in the 20th century and spawned psychological consciousness ... By extending the central nervous system of each individual and the society as a whole,

communication revolutions provide an ever more inclusive playing
field for empathy to mature and consciousness to expand. (Rifkin 2010)

This astute analysis is an efficient characterisation of developments
that rocked *mankind* throughout the grand sweep of history,
accounting for the full gamut: clusters of hunter-gatherers, religious
holy warriors and modern imperial regimes concentrating wealth
and resources for their own benefit. However, it still lacks a cogent
analysis of *womankind's* activities during all this time. The history of
civilisation, as described by Rifkin and countless other social analysts, is
a recounting of the actions and reactions of warrior men. Unfortunately
their stories dismiss thousands of vanquished indigenous civilisations
that might have evolved quite differently; civilisations where qualities
predominantly ascribed to women, whether presumed to be intrinsic or
socially constructed, of nurturance, compassion and empathy, were well
developed and highly regarded (Eisler 1995).

My conclusion is that the scientific elite, with the collusion of every
form of recorded media, has systematically rendered the identifiable
agency of women and their particular capacity for compassion
completely invisible. For example, according to Rifkin, empathy was
only recently 'discovered' by accident while observing the brainwaves of
monkeys (Rifkin 2009). One can only wonder whether mirror neurons
and the empathic nature of humanity might have been 'discovered' and
acknowledged sooner if women had been considered worthy of research.
Similarly, what other critically important scientific advancements are
missing as a result of this oversight?

In the rush to 'resurrect the global economy and revitalise the
biosphere' (Rifkin 2010), we can no longer afford persistent neglect
of women's agency; we are called upon to locate the consistent guides
who have preserved and extended the boundaries of compassion
through collective and revealing acts of healing: healing sisters and
brothers; attending to allies and former enemies; reaching out in local
communities and across borders; and, indeed, restoring mother earth
herself. These women include the 1000 peacewomen across the globe
studied here, and women across every continent and border.

## References

Altheide, David, Michael Coyle, Katie DeVriese & Christopher Schneider (2008). Emergent qualitative document analysis. In Sharlene Harding & Patricia Leavy (Eds). *Handbook of emergent methods* (pp127–51). New York: The Guilford Press.

Association 1000 Women for the Nobel Peace Prize 2005 (Association) (2005). *1000 peacewomen across the globe*. Zurich: Scalo Publishers.

Barlow, Tani (2000). International feminism of the future. *Signs: Journal of Women in Culture and Society*, 25(4): 1099-105 (Special issue, Feminisms at a Millennium).

Boulding, Elise (2000). *Cultures of peace: the hidden side of history*. Syracuse: Syracuse University Press.

Campbell, Karlyn Kohrs (1982). Elements of rhetorical action. [Online]. Available: www.voxygen.net/cpa/articles/campbellelements.htm [Accessed 27 September 2011].

Campbell, Karlyn Kohrs & Susan Schultz Huxman (2008). *The rhetorical act: thinking, speaking and writing critically*. Belmont: Wadsworth Publishing.

Diamond, Irene & Nancy Hartsock (1981). Beyond interests in politics: a comment on Virginia Sapiro's 'When are interests interesting? The problem of political representation of women'. *The American Political Science Review*, 75(3): 717–21.

Eisler, Riane (1995). *The chalice and the blade: our history, our future*. New York: Harper Collins.

Ferris, Elizabeth (2009). Peace, reconciliation, and displacement. Paper presented to the UCLA Conference on Peace and Reconciliation: Embracing the Displaced, July 2009. [Online]. Available: www.brookings.edu/speeches/2009/0707_internal_displacement_ferris.aspx [Accessed 2 August 2011].

Foss, Sonja & Cindy Griffin (1995). Beyond persuasion: a proposal for an invitational rhetoric. *Communication Monographs*, 62(1): 2–18.

Galtung, Johan (1996). *Peace by peaceful means: peace and conflict development and civilisation.* London: Sage.

Galtung, Johan & Jake Lynch (2010). *Reporting conflict: new directions in peace journalism.* St Lucia, Qld: University of Queensland Press.

Harding, Sandra (2003). *The feminist standpoint theory reader: intellectual and political controversies.* New York: Routledge Taylor and Francis Group.

Heyzer, Noeleen (2004). Preface: Women, peace and security. *UNIFEM Supporting Implementation of UN Security Council Resolutions 1325.* New York: UNIFEM. [Online]. Available: www.peacewomen.org/assets/image/Resources/wps_womenpeace_security_analysis_sc1325.2004.pdf [Accessed 2 August 2011].

Jowett, Garth & Victoria O'Donnell (1999). *Propaganda and persuasion.* 3rd edn. London: Sage.

Juergensmeyer, Mark (2001).*Terror in the mind of god: the global rise of religious violence.* Berkeley: University of California Press.

Lederach, John Paul (2010). The art of peace. Interview with Krista Tippett on speaking of faith. [Online]. Available: being.publicradio.org/programs/2010/art-of-peace/ [Accessed 3 August 2011].

Lynch, Jake & Annabel McGoldrick (2005). *Peace journalism.* Stroud: Hawthorn Press.

Rifkin, Jeremy (2010). The empathic civilisation: rethinking human nature in the biosphere era. *The Huffington Post.* [Online]. Available: www.huffingtonpost.com/jeremy-rifkin/the-empathic-civilization_b_416589.html [Accessed 3 August 2011].

Rifkin, Jeremy (2009). *The empathic civilisation: the race to global consciousness in a world in crisis.* New York: Tarcher Penguin.

Strauss, Anselm & Juliet Corbin (1994). Grounded theory methodology: an overview. In Norman Denzin & Yvonna Lincoln (Eds). *Handbook of qualitative research* (pp217–85). Thousand Oaks: Sage.

Strauss, Anselm & Juliet Corbin (1990). *Basics of qualitative research: grounded theory procedures and techniques.* Newbury Park, CA: Sage Publications.

Tannen, Deborah (1998). *The argument culture*. New York: Random House.

United Nations Development Program (1994). *Human development report 1994: new dimensions of human security*. United Nations Development Program. [Online]. Available: hdr.undp.org/en/reports/global/hdr1994/chapters/ [Accessed 3 August 2011].

United Nations High Commissioner for Refugees (2009). *About us: history of UNHCR*. [Online]. Available: www.unhcr.org/pages/49c3646cbc.html [Accessed 3 August 2011].

Women's Refugee Commission (2010). Displaced women and girls at risk: identifying risk factors and taking steps to prevent abuse. [Online]. Available: www.womensrefugeecommission.org/reports/cat_view/68-reports/72-refugee-protection [Accessed 3 August 2011].

Vermot-Mangold, Ruth-Gaby (2005). Editorial: the idea. In *1000 peacewomen across the globe*. Zurich: Scalo Publishers.

# Chapter 13

# Examining the 'dark past' and 'hopeful future' in representations of race and Canada's Truth and Reconciliation Commission

*Peter A Chow-White and Rob McMahon*

The Canadian state is presently engaged in a court-mandated process of 'reconciliation' with its aboriginal populations. This process includes the efforts of the Truth and Reconciliation Commission, which will document the history of abuses that took place in government-funded, church-run schools during the 19th and 20th centuries. It is also being publicly defined and framed through media: newspapers, television newscasts, internet blogs and other forms of public communication. For many Canadians, whose daily experiences are far removed from this process, these mediated forms of communication are key sources of information about and engagement with 'reconciliation'.

In this chapter, we consider a case study of a mediated representation of the reconciliation process, using a model we developed from adapting peace journalism (PJ). PJ draws from broader work on media and conflict that recognises the potential of media to exacerbate direct and structural violence (Becker 1981; Cottle 2006; Lynch & McGoldrick 2005b; Wolfsfeld 2004; Young 2008). PJ theory incorporates principles of conflict analysis to promote news production practices that aim towards conflict transformation (Lynch & McGoldrick 2005a; Shinar 2003). Proponents argue that PJ can help expand the discursive field of conflict and render more visible its logic and effects – for example, through an analysis of attitudes, behaviour and contradiction, or the 'ABC conflict triangle' (Galtung 2000). This helps open policy options and issues to public discussion (Spencer 2005). PJ researchers like Lee and

Maslog (2006) conduct quantitative empirical studies to investigate the interplay between media representations and violence in news content, including its role in taking an interventionist 'preventative advocacy' stance, for example, in editorials and columns urging reconciliation (p314; see also Galtung 1998). Finally, practice-oriented PJ scholars and activists advance tools and guidelines that working journalists can use to increase their awareness of conflict resolution techniques in coverage of war and violence (Galtung 2000; Lynch & McGoldrick, 2005b).

We argue that a PJ model for analysing 'cold' conflict (see McMahon & Chow-White, 2011) can help researchers examine news discourse about the reconciliation process. Our model develops PJ in two ways. Theoretically, it incorporates insights from critical race theory to consider 'cold' conflicts, such as those between racialised groups in postcolonial societies. One shortcoming noted by PJ scholars, including Matt Mogekwu in this volume, is the field's focus on 'hot' conflicts or direct violence (see also El-Nawawy & Powers 2010). Our model offers PJ researchers an analytical tool to examine prolonged and extended, or 'cold', conflicts, such as struggles over representations of race and racism (Entman & Rojecki 2000; Hall 1981; van Dijk 2009).

Methodologically, our model draws on and operationalises both agenda-setting theory (McCombs 1994; McCombs & Shaw 1977) and framing theory (Entman 2007; Weaver 2007). The selection of news stories, the salience of issues, and the sources that journalists draw from are all points of negotiation in the production of discourses. Journalists employ discursive frames to interpret and structure meanings about events or people, and make choices about what parties are included and excluded and how they are portrayed in media content (West 1990). For critical race theorists, each of these choices and the aggregate story that is told (or left untold) are key moments in the racialisation of the public sphere (Omi & Winant 1994).

Examples of 'cold' conflicts, and attempts by governments, non-governmental organisations and others to redress them, are ongoing around the world. For example, work is being done in South Africa to rebuild society after the formal deconstruction of the apartheid system. We chose to analyse news coverage of the formal reconciliation process in Canada to look for examples of journalism that captures attempts at reconciliation alongside the ongoing effects of structural racism against First Nations communities and individuals. Our approach recognises that the concept of 'reconciliation' is highly contested, and can be seen as an ongoing individual and collective process (Truth and Reconciliation Commission of Canada nd). In her comparative discussion of truth commissions in South Africa and Germany, Andrews (2003) notes the difficulty of establishing reconciliation in formerly divided societies:

> The power of truth commissions lies not so much in discovering truth – in the form of new facts – as in acknowledging it. Moreover, once the facts of the past have been established ... the challenge of deciphering meaning behind such facts still remains. (Andrews 2003, p49)

Defining this process as the formation of 'collective memory', Andrews points out that the resulting 'national narratives' document stories of the past, which are then situated within the context of the present. Truth commissions allow members of society to 'witness the dynamics of the making of collective memory, with all of the tensions and ambiguities this entails' (Andrews 2003, p62). If certain stories are left out of this process, voices can become subsumed or erased in the construction of collective memory. For example, in their study of Australian Aborigines, Banerjee and Osuri describe the process of 'institutional forgetting' (2000). They argue that, in the Australian context, representations of the past have historically been embedded within a narrative of power shaped by broader political and economic inequalities: 'the content of the past, present and future is preserved within the dominant identity that is thus able to present a history that "washed away" Aboriginal rights to land' (Banerjee & Osuri 2000, p274).

In Canada, historic relations between the state and aboriginal people are similarly problematic. The formal process of reconciliation can be read as the latest chapter in a centuries-long struggle for aboriginal rights and self-determination vis-à-vis the state. The federal government's 2008 apology for residential schools and support for the Truth and Reconciliation Commission process is an encouraging development. However we argue that this development should still be critically scrutinised. In this chapter we do this by exploring some early mediated representations of Canada's reconciliation process through an empirical analysis of a broadsheet newspaper series about the 'state of affairs' of First Nations peoples in British Columbia. This empirical site is conceived as a self-reflexive attempt by working journalists to highlight concrete examples of 'reconciliation', but a deeper look demonstrates more complex and contradictory processes at play (Galtung 1998).

## PJ Theory and 'cold' conflict

PJ research has largely focused on examples of 'hot' conflict, such as media coverage of wars or other forms of direct violence. PJ researchers uncover those news production practices and narrative structures that promote a 'culture of peace', as well as those that harden dichotomies between discursively constructed 'enemies' in a mediated field of conflict (see for example Dente Ross et al. 2009; Galtung 2000; Lynch & McGoldrick 2005b). However, some PJ scholars suggest the field needs to pay clearer attention to the roles that structural factors, such as religious, national, transnational and ethnic identities, play in conflicts (El-Nawawy & Powers 2010). Where 'hot' conflicts erupt between parties in violent displays of direct force, 'cold' conflicts take place in more subtle (though still damaging) arenas of culture and media representation (Cottle 2006; Shinar 2003). In expanding its consideration of these cold conflicts, PJ theory can support research into representations of long-term cultural conflicts, including those between racialised communities in multicultural societies (LeBaron & Pillay 2006). The work of sociologists (Omi & Winant 1994), political philosophers (Fraser 2003), and critical scholars of race and media (Downing & Husband 2005; Jiwani 2006) highlights the potential of discursively constructed boundaries between racialised communities to result in material inequalities and systemic domination; that is, in structural violence (Galtung 1969; see Galtung 2000 for definitions of direct, structural and cultural forms of violence). For example, Green (1995) and Lawrence (2004) argue that legal and discursive frameworks justify the systemic domination of aboriginal groups by the Canadian state. From this perspective, media representations can perpetuate an ahistorical, hierarchical, racialised social structure that can become codified in discursive forms, including 'common sense', public opinion, government policy and institutional practice.

Critical scholars have demonstrated how journalism practices can inadvertently reproduce these broader power inequalities in the overt language of 'old' or 'legacy' racism (Hall 1981; Said 1978), and in the more coded discourse of 'new' racism (Downing & Husband 2005; van Dijk 2009). Hall described how researchers can challenge 'old' racism through examining the 'relations of representation' and the 'politics of representation' (Hall 1981). The 'relations of representation' refers to levels of inclusion and exclusion of racialised voices in media discourse (Hall 1981; Henry & Tator 2002; West 1990).

The politics of representation explores qualitative elements of 'old' racism, focusing on the language used in news discourse and the quality and accuracy of media representations of race. Critical scholars identified a number of consistent stereotypes, such as the recurring tropes of the 'slave-figure', 'native' and 'clown/entertainer' (Hall 1981; Said 1978). In Canada, researchers have described the historical prevalence and contemporary persistence of negative representations of aboriginal Canadians in the mass media (Lambertus 2004; Roth 2005; Winter 1992). For example, Harding writes that during the 1990s 'aboriginal issues were framed, much as they were 130 years earlier, in ways that protect dominant interests and signify aboriginal people as a threat to such interests' (Harding 2006, p224). While these efforts are important and necessary to the ongoing project of exposing and critiquing media representations, there are problematic assumptions buried in the use of the term 'old' to describe such forms of racism. We propose the alternate term 'legacy racism' to foreground the observation that examples and effects of so-called 'old' racism continue to be reproduced in contemporary discourse and social relations. 'Legacy' racism seeks to recognise the ongoing impacts of past processes on present realities and future possibilities (Hall 1997; Hill-Collins 2004).

In the early 21st century, scholars of 'new' racism like Bonilla-Silva (2001) and Hill-Collins (2004) developed a body of theory that identified more subtle expressions of racism. Legacy racism, with its overt biological markers of identity, is relatively easy to identify, and is quantitatively decreasing given widespread public condemnation. Scholars of 'new' racism draw attention towards emergent forms of racism expressed in the more fluid, coded terrain of culture (Barker 1989; Bonilla-Silva 2001; Chow-White 2009; Jiwani 2006). While overtly racist discourses are absent in most news discourse, repetitive structural patterns of 'new' racism remain; for example, in the framing of 'neutral' topics like immigration or housing, or in the deployment of terms like 'welfare mothers' or 'terrorists' (van Dijk, 2009). Critical race scholars argue that to counter these new forms of racism, analysis must consider 'common sense'. Bonilla-Silva (2001) argues this can be done through examining several processes, including: increasingly covert discourses and practices, the avoidance of racial terminology, the invisibility of structural mechanisms that reproduce inequalities and the re-articulation of old practices in new forms. Hill-Collins describes specifically how new racism is articulated in media discourse:

> The new racism relies more heavily on the manipulation of ideas within mass media. These new techniques present hegemonic ideologies that claim that racism is over. They work to obscure the racism that does exist, and they undercut antiracist protest. (Hill-Collins 2004, pp54–55)

For critical race scholars, new racism is revealed by research that exposes 'naturalised' and fluid hierarchies, frameworks, and images. Our PJ model for 'cold' conflicts (McMahon & Chow-White, 2011) draws on these insights to offer a tool for researchers to expose both forms of racism.

To develop our PJ model, we operationalised elements of agenda-setting and framing theory. Many PJ researchers employ a methodology based in agenda-setting that focuses on overt expressions of language and representation (see, for example, Lee & Maslog 2006). According to agenda-setting theory, by highlighting certain issues, the news media confers on them a level of social relevance and importance, and issues are more likely to be debated, attacked or justified if they are validated in the media (Coleman et al. 2009; McCombs & Shaw 1977). While McCombs and other agenda-setting scholars argue that the media tells us what to think about, some push that argument further (Nesbitt-Larking 2001). Where agenda-setting theory measures the presence and salience of issues, a framing approach focuses on the qualitative meanings attached to issues, and the values embedded in media representations (Entman et al. 2009; Jiwani 2006; Pan & Kosicki 2003; Weaver 2007). This approach moves beyond a consideration of overt content analysis to also examine the implicit frameworks media producers employ to interpret and structure the placement of issues, events, and actors in discourse.

PJ researchers suggest that 'theoretically, peace journalism is supported by framing theory' (Lee et al. 2006, pp501-02). Framing theory is also supported by critical race scholars who found agenda-setting a useful and necessary tool, but insufficient on its own to accurately capture the more subtle or implicit representations of 'new' racism (Hall 1996). As a parallel to these methodological developments, our model incorporates the insights of both agenda-setting and framing to comprehensively expose 'cold' conflicts.

*A PJ model for 'cold' conflict*

This section briefly describes our PJ model for 'cold' conflict (McMahon & Chow-White, 2011). Our model works to uncover examples of value-based language, highlight the perspectives of various stakeholders to the conflicts examined, and explore the discursive field of power relations these statements operate within. The model emerged from our engagement with a strategically chosen empirical example of 'reconciliation' news coverage, which helped ground and enrich our theoretical argument. It includes four frames developed from PJ theory alongside techniques that reveal processes of 'legacy' and 'new' racism.

To identify processes of legacy racism, our model employs two analytical techniques. First, it examines the presence and/or absence of voices in the news discourse, particularly voices from marginalised and/or racialised communities. Second, it looks for evidence of previously identified, historically persistent negative stereotypes.

Table 1: Model for analysis of 'cold' conflicts

| Legacy racism |
| --- |
| Presence/absence of voice |
| Evidence of historically persistent stereotypes |
| **New racism** |
| Framing of parties in negotiation and conflict |
| Re-articulation of old stereotypes in new forms |
| Decontextualisation of key issues |
| **Peace journalism: four frames** |
| Cooperation and reconciliation in conflict transformation |
| Reporting 'invisible' effects of structural racism |
| Complicates stereotypes (directly and indirectly) |
| Community leadership and self-determination |

Our model explores the more subtle discourses of new racism through three analytical techniques. First, it examines the framing of parties in conflict and negotiation. This is done to explore whether these frames obscure and naturalise asymmetrical power relations by failing to acknowledge their existence (Galtung 2000). As Jiwani reminds us, in discursively formed allegiances or conflicts 'the freedom to choose which side is "right" is accorded only to those who have the power to define and decide the limits of the debate' (Jiwani 2006, p44). Second, our model seeks to capture the re-articulation of old racist frames and stereotypes in new forms, including in more subtle discourses of 'common sense'. Third, our model points out the decontexualisation of certain issues, such as the omission of appropriate legal and historical contexts.

Finally, our model employs four analytical frames that highlight examples of PJ. These frames draw on existing PJ theory and incorporate insights from critical race theory, and emerge from our strategically chosen empirical site. The first frame identifies instances of cooperation, reconciliation and hope that simultaneously acknowledge past and present injustices. PJ scholars note the important role that mediated representations play in (re)constructing the effects of conflict transformation (Peleg 2006; Shinar 2003). They analyse conflicts as ongoing processes, as opposed to discrete events with a fixed start and end. In this way PJ works to 'broaden the field within which contestation, argument and disagreement can take place' (Spencer 2005, pp180–81; see also LeBaron & Pillay 2006; Lynch & McGoldrick 2005a).

The second frame identifies examples of the long-term impacts of violence, both direct and indirect, on racialised communities. PJ scholars argue that comprehensive coverage of conflict must move beyond the direct effects of violence to also consider its structural impacts (Becker 1981; Galtung 2000; Spencer 2005). When these indirect impacts are made more visible and concrete, they become discrete objects that can be examined and critiqued (Lynch & McGoldrick 2005a; see also Zandberg 2010). This approach can be enriched by critical race theory, which seeks to expose the long-term, structural effects of racism (Bonilla-Silva 2001; Hall 1997; Hill Collins 2004).

The third frame highlights examples of attempts by journalists to confront and counteract stereotypes that are connected to ideologies embedded in distinct chains of meaning activated and reproduced in recurring images. Hall's (1981) analysis of the politics of representation describes how stereotypes can be directly challenged through the presentation of individuals in non-stereotypical positions (see also Attille & Blackwood 1986; Dennis 2009; Entman & Rojecki 2000; Henry & Tator 2002). Media producers can confront and break the chains of associations activated each time a problematic racialised stereotype is invoked (Jiwani 2006). Stereotypes can also be challenged through the recognition of hybridity, which counteracts a static, homogenising approach to identity and suggests a more fluid and complex conception of identity (Cottle 2000; Hall 1981). Our model demonstrates examples of such hybrid images.

The last frame in our model identifies racialised groups and individuals as rational, goal-oriented political actors rather than passive, emotional 'victims', and identifies the historical continuity of leadership in a variety of institutional fields. Following the arguments of postcolonial scholars, this frame highlights multifaceted representations that demonstrate the agency of all involved parties in enacting change

353

and struggling for justice and self-determination, as opposed to portraying one side as 'oppressors' and the other as dominated 'victims' (Fanon 1963; Said 1978). One of the racial projects of postcolonial scholars has been to recoup subaltern voices in historical texts, tell counter stories, and frame colonial subjects as agentic actors (Shome & Hegde 2002; Spivak 1999). PJ researchers similarly seek to expose instances of parties in conflict that are portrayed along a 'zero-sum' axis, where one side is represented as 'oppressor' and the other as 'victim' in an asymmetrical binary logic (Galtung 2000; Lynch & McGoldrick 2005a; Spencer 2005). This frame seeks to highlight the agency of all involved parties in enacting change and struggling for justice.

## Case study: reporting on reconciliation in Canada

We now turn to an application of our PJ model to an empirical site of analysis. We previously used this site to develop our model (McMahon & Chow-White, 2011); here we examine it in more detail as a case study. The eight *Vancouver Sun* stories ran as a series titled 'Dark past, hopeful future' over an eight-day period from 13 to21 June 2008 (see Table 2). The series is an attempt by the newspaper to document a perceived shift in race relations following the Canadian government's 2008 apology for its treatment of First Nations children in residential schools, and the early stages of the $60 million Indian Residential Schools Truth and Reconciliation Commission (TRC). The TRC is mandated to document the history of abuses that took place in these government-funded, church-run schools (Milloy 1999). Our analysis avoids specific comment on these events and issues, instead assuming a general desire to move forward processes of reconciliation by all involved parties.

This case study offers a set of media discourses that aim to capture optimistic attempts at reconciliation alongside the aftermath and ongoing effects of the systemic abuse of generations of First Nations individuals and communities. We see it as a self-conscious form of journalism that highlights post-conflict or reconstruction activities, while also recognising the after-effects of violence. It is a publicly symbolic attempt at relationship-building between First Nations and non-aboriginal communities in British Columbia. But at the same time, we find examples of the continuity and re-articulation of legacy and new racism. The following analysis treats this series as a complex set of discourses resulting from implicit media production practices, rather than critiquing the actions of individual reporters.

Table 2 Stories from *The Vancouver Sun* series 'Dark past, hopeful future'

| Headline | Date published | ID |
|---|---|---|
| Aboriginal educators find hope amid dismal student results | 13 June 2008 | Steffenhagen |
| Many paths to healing | 14 June 2008 | Todd |
| First Nations have key role in Games | 16 June 2008 | Lee1 |
| First Nations resort turns the corner | 17 June 2008 | Constantineau |
| First Nations celebrate new cultural centre | 18 June 2008 | Lee2 |
| First Nations take early steps towards better health | 19 June 2008 | Fowlie1 |
| New treaty negotiations spark cautious optimism | 20 June 2008 | Fowlie2 |
| Currents of history | 21 June 2008 | Sinoski |

*Note:* The series URL: www2.canada.com/vancouversun/features/apology/series.html

## Legacy racism and new racism in media representations of reconciliation

*Legacy racism: the persistence of colonial stereotypes*

A quantitative examination of the case study reveals that all of the stories in *The Vancouver Sun* series include First Nations voices. This indicates that, in terms of the relations of representation, racialised communities are making progress. Most of the stories include the voices of both elite sources and everyday people, moving beyond a two-party source dichotomy to demonstrate differentiation within the First Nations community. That said, not all voices are represented, and so the relations of representation continue to be restricted in stories where the voices of everyday or oppositional First Nations people are limited or excluded. For example, the voices of organised groups opposed to the 2010 Olympics, such as Mostly Water (Mostly Water 2009), are not included, despite several mentions of the event.

The series also contains several examples of persistent colonial-era stereotypes demonstrating that challenges in the politics of representation continue. Harding (2006) discovered that negative stereotypes of aboriginal peoples in the Canadian news media are remarkably stable over time. We find continued evidence of his findings. For example, one story leads by marshalling the frame of the 'violent and irresponsible native'. Starting a story this way offsets simultaneous attempts in the story to build a narrative of community struggle and individual redemption, as is evident in this quote:

> Life at the Penticton Indian Band took a dramatic turn about four years ago after Dustin Joseph Paul killed three friends in an unprovoked drug-and-alcohol-fuelled shooting rampage. Paul, who snorted cocaine and drank heavily at a popular party spot on the reserve before the killings, said at trial he began shooting because a voice in his head told him that doing so, and then slitting his own throat, would lead to a better life. (Fowlie1)

While this example in part reflects conventional storytelling practices such as personalisation and dramatisation, framing the story this way is problematic given the attendant (and in this case, unacknowledged) historical and cultural stereotypes it invokes. Scholars argue the process of public witnessing is an important part of 'reconciliation' (Llewellyn 2002). However, this story (re)opens personal histories of pain and suffering to public witnessing, and invokes a chain of associations including images of alcohol and drug abuse, criminal deviancy, and 'savage' behaviour that recall stereotypes like the 'drunken Indian' or 'savage' (Harding 2006; Hall 1981). As Jiwani notes: 'in projecting onto the colonised traits that were considered excessive (sexuality, immorality, emotionality, fecundity, and so on) the colonisers were able to construct an image of themselves as intelligent, rational, superior, moral, and controlled' (Jiwani 2006, p33). Since the story is framed this way, the article's later discussion of community-driven First Nations health policies and practices is pushed to the background.

*New racism: problematising the 'culture of negotiation'*

We also found examples of more subtle discourses of new racism in the series. We explore these examples by looking at the positioning of parties in representations of conflict, the re-articulation of old racist frames in new forms, and the omission of key historical, legal and cultural contexts.

Some of the newspaper articles framed parties in conflict and negotiation in ways that obscure and naturalise asymmetrical power relations by failing to acknowledge their existence. This process was apparent in the (re)production of discursively formed allegiances or conflicts. In British Columbia, First Nations and non-aboriginal parties have made public statements expressing a desire towards negotiation rather than litigation to manage conflict (see, for example, Transformative Change Accord 2005). However, the series undermines this goal by repeatedly contrasting 'reasonable' state negotiators with 'emotional' First Nations leaders. In a story about the 2010 Winter Olympic Games, Squamish nation hereditary chief Joe Mathias is initially described as a 'defender of native rights who preferred to negotiate rather than litigate' (Lee1). The rest of the story constructs and employs a binary division between 'negotiators' (benevolent government and corporate groups and the First Nations communities that cooperate with them), and 'litigators' (First Nations communities that express reluctance and suspicion of their initiatives). Echoing the tendency of news frames to gain salience through repetition (Entman et al. 2009), this frame is elaborated on in another story about treaty negotiations. The then minister of Aboriginal Relations and Reconciliation for the province of British Columbia, Mike de Jong, points out the successes of the treaty negotiation process as based in reasoned negotiation and compromise, while, in contrast, oppositional First Nations parties are described as expressing 'immense frustration', 'anger', skepticism, and, at best, 'cautious optimism' (Fowlie2). Minister de Jong is described as:

> Hopeful that over the next year there will be further progress with reconciliation deals, such as the one recently approved by the Musqueam Indian Band. De Jong said that deal is an example of an approach 'designed to build a culture of settlements through *negotiation rather than litigation*'. (Fowlie2, emphasis added)

This quote concludes a story filled with optimistic, negotiation-oriented statements from government representatives, and pessimistic, emotional and reluctant statements from oppositional First Nations leaders. The 'litigators' are portrayed using generalised, negative language, as is apparent in this quote:

> The common table itself was born out of immense frustration by a group of first nations ... 'We cannot accept the current one size fits all approach with inadequate policy/mandates being imposed by your governments' negotiators,' wrote a group of then about 50 first nations that called themselves the Unity Protocol. 'The level of anger and frustration is reaching levels of which you have been repeatedly warned'. (Fowlie2)

Viewed across the series, this frames 'good' First Nations communities in relation to 'bad' ones and the dominant society. Parties in negotiation become valorised as either 'positive' or 'negative' depending on their synchronicity with the dominant corporate/government frame, echoing the findings of previous research on labour/management framing in news coverage (Hackett 1991). This situates the right of aboriginal people to employ legal measures to ensure fair consultation and accommodation in a framework of deviancy.

New racism is also present in the series through the re-articulation of old racist frames in new forms. *The Vancouver Sun* series demonstrates a shift in language from the historical frame of the 'white man's burden' to its re-articulation as a benevolent, government- and corporate-driven 'culture of negotiation'. As noted earlier, some aboriginal political groups support the principle of a 'culture of negotiation'. However, when employed in a way that undermines the agency of these groups and increases the relative discursive position of government/corporate decision-makers and their allies, the descriptor becomes another example in the long struggle over the language of aboriginal rights – and of state attempts to define and structure access to those rights through discursive and legal strategies (Green 1995). Viewed in this way, the 'culture of negotiation' can naturalise pre-existing power structures and render oppositional perspectives non-threatening, homogenised and contained.

The 'culture of negotiation' frame is positioned throughout the series as a result of government largesse, rather than First Nations self-determination. Words like 'giving', 'allowed', and 'building' imply agency and benevolence on the part of government/corporate parties, and are positioned against the passive acquiescence or litigious resistance of some First Nations groups. For example, in a discussion of the legacy of residential school policies, portrayals of government benevolence appear in language that reflects active attempts at reconciliation: 'the apology *gave first nations a chance* to press their point' (Steffenhagen, emphasis added). This quote undermines First Nations agency in this process: rather than the culmination of First Nations-led demands for justice and hard fought legal battles, the apology is framed as 'giving' these communities a chance to present an argument for self-determination. Even stories that work to document First Nations communities' shift towards greater independence portray their actions as stemming from state benevolence, not community-driven agency. This is seen in quotes like '*giving first nations a hand* in developing programs to fit their needs' (Fowlie1, emphasis added).

Finally, new racism is supported in the decontexualisation of certain issues; specifically the omission of appropriate legal and historical contexts. As noted, policy documents released by First Nations political organisations make clear the position of many groups to achieve solutions over land claims and other disputes through negotiation rather than litigation. For example, a statement by former Assembly of First Nations National Chief Phil Fontaine states that 'good faith negotiation is preferable to litigation, but clearly this is not the final word from the courts or First Nations on these fundamental matters' (Assembly of First Nations 2005). This statement demonstrates that the Assembly of First Nations was willing to negotiate in good faith. At the same time, it reserved the right to seek alternative remedies through the courts if negotiations – over such issues as land claims – did not prove fruitful, noting that negotiation is 'not the final word from the courts or First Nations'.

However, aside from the exception of one story about treaty negotiations that elaborates on the appropriate legal context, the series suppresses discussion of important cases such as Delgamuukw (Culhane 1998) and cornerstone reports such as the Royal Commission on Aboriginal Peoples (1996). This oversight represses the long history of First Nations-led political and legal struggle that has preceded the 'culture of negotiation'. Instead of explaining the legally mandated requirements for business and government to seek aboriginal cooperation for economic developments, the articles describe relationships between organisations such as the Vancouver Organizing Committee (VANOC) in charge of planning the 2010 Winter Olympics and aboriginal communities as driven by the goodwill of corporate and government organisations. For example, a business deal is described as an attempt by VANOC '*to include first nations* in economic, social and cultural opportunities' (Lee1, emphasis added). But this statement neglects the relevant context of the court-mandated requirement of the organisation to seek permission to conduct business on First Nations claimed territories. Further decontextualisation is highlighted in the language used to describe First Nations communities' frustration with the treaty process. Rather than explaining specific, concrete problems and challenges, a story on treaty negotiations employs vague terms, such as 'six key issues' and 'significant roadblocks'. At one point, the treaty process is described as having 'dragged on for years with only a few notable successes' (Fowlie2), but without any context as to why.

# Writing reconciliation? Elements of peace journalism in media discourse

Despite these notable examples that reproduce and re-articulate legacy and new forms of racism, *The Vancouver Sun* series also demonstrates a clear attempt to focus on the ongoing transformational effects of recncilion-oriented activities. This section elaborates on some of these frames.

## Cooperation and reconciliation in conflict transformation frame

This frame expresses change as bringing about long-term conflict transformation (including material transformations and attempts to address structural violence). It is contrasted against framing 'reconciliation' as an event with a fixed start and end, hardening dichotomies between parties, and operating only on a symbolic level. Several stories in the series emphasise community-driven cooperation and hope (accompanied by an acknowledgement of past injustices). For example, some articles highlight concrete examples of cooperation through formal mechanisms like public apologies and financial reparations delivered from non-aboriginal institutions such as the United Church and the federal government. Others describe community-driven economic development projects. For example, one story describes how a First Nations community transformed a former residential school into a thriving business. In acknowledging the site's past alongside its optimistic future, and highlighting community-driven partnerships with non-aboriginal communities, the story offers a symbolic and physical example of reconstruction:

> St Eugene school educated about 5,000 first nations children between 1912 and 1970 and sat derelict for 30 years before a combination of government funds, band money and private capital transformed the property into a quality resort. '*The decision to transform the site of so much pain and suffering into a new tourism business was not easy*'. ... [St Mary's band Chief Sophie] Pierre and resort officials invoke the words of late band elder Mary Paul when explaining the decision to create the resort. '*Since it was within the St Eugene Mission School*

361

*that the culture of the Kootenay Indian was taken away, it should be within the building that it is returned,* Paul said. (Constantineau, emphasis added)

Another story frames the economic partnership between the four First Nations host communities, government and corporate parties in the lead-up to the 2010 Winter Olympics as a 'history-making opportunity'. This partnership is presented as the result of entrepreneurship, First Nations agency, and local initiative:

> The Vancouver relationship [between First Nation and non-First Nation groups] is so strong that the four host First Nations are consulted on nearly everything, and VANOC actively seeks to include first nations in economic, social and cultural opportunities. (Lee1)

Importantly, this story includes relevant legal context, such as a description of the Delgamuukw case, that 'implicitly gave strength to first nations' claims that their aboriginal title hadn't been extinguished' (Lee1). By noting this fact in the lead paragraph, the story sets up a frame that the business negotiations leading to the Olympic partnership result from the history of ongoing legal and political struggles on the part of First Nations communities to achieve self-determination.

### Reporting 'invisible' effects of structural racism frame

*The Vancouver Sun* series also offers examples of media discourses that highlight the long-term repercussions of the structural violence of colonial public policies. For example, the series describes the ongoing negative effects of the government's residential schools policy while also acknowledging the successes of indigenous forms of health and spirituality. This relational approach to representing structural racism across time is apparent in this quote:

> The school dropout rate is still high among aboriginal students ... and first nations students are still being taken into care by government agencies. *Much of this stems from the pain and loss they suffered by being forced into residential schools...*'The residential schools were like a shock, an explosion on the people, and we still feel the

reverberations' [said Shawn Atleo, then regional chief of the Assembly of First Nations]. (Sinowski, emphasis added)

Journalists tend to write about the experiences of individuals, to 'humanise' otherwise abstract issues. At the same time, it is important to situate individuals in the appropriate social, cultural, political and economic structures that impact their lives. The example highlighted above demonstrates an example of this technique.

An article about the 2010 Winter Olympics notes that Chief Leonard Andrew of the Lil'wat has a 'deep skepticism, born of long experience, about grandiose ideas' (Lee1). The story includes appropriate context for this skepticism, explaining it as the result of long-term policies like the residential school system, racism against aboriginal communities, and social problems within his community. Chief Andrew is given an opportunity to express his legitimate concerns and hopes within a discursive framework that situates his statements in a broader context.

*Complicates stereotypes frame*

*The Vancouver Sun* series offers examples of direct and indirect attempts to counter longstanding stereotypes. Several articles discuss the efforts of First Nations leaders working in professional fields like law, politics and education – moving beyond the historical stereotype of uncertain, emotion-driven First Nation leadership (Harding 2006). One story highlights leaders like Frank Calder (the first full status aboriginal person to attend Chilliwack high school and the University of British Columbia, and a former elected Member of the Legislative Assembly) and Gordon Antoine (who founded the Nicola Valley Institute of Technology). These individuals received recognition through achievements such as the Order of British Columbia and Order of Canada, demonstrating that they are viewed as leaders not only by their own communities, but also by the non-aboriginal community (Sinoski).

The series also includes representations of aboriginal cultural forms that are expressed in the language of contemporary business. While references to 'artistic branding' bring up arguments about the commodification of material culture and community-'owned' intellectual property (see Brown 2003) that are beyond the scope of this chapter, they nonetheless demonstrate a shift in the portrayal of aboriginal art as an 'exotic remnant of the past'. For example, a story about a new cultural centre challenges the stereotype of aboriginal culture as the relic of a lost culture:

> The new $30-million Squamish Lil'wat Cultural Centre, [is] a living museum that pays homage to the art, history and culture of the first nations. '*We are not a museum culture, we are a living culture,*' said Joy Joseph McCullough, the education director for the Squamish. (Lee2, emphasis added)

*The Vancouver Sun* series also illustrates indirect methods of countering stereotypes through several examples of cultural hybridity. One article discusses the history of religious syncretism in First Nations communities, through which some former residential school students combined aboriginal and non-aboriginal religious traditions in a new form of spiritual practice. This highlights the fluid and diverse nature of religious practices in British Columbia:

> Like many aboriginals, [David] Belleau was trying to heal through a complex mix of aboriginal rituals, Western psychotherapy, Alcoholics Anonymous, traditional art and dance and, surprisingly to some, Christianity ... Many aboriginals are accepting church apologies and offering forgiveness, *while exploring a blend of spiritual and psychological practices, both aboriginal and Western.* (Todd, emphasis added)

### Community leadership and self-determination frame

Finally, some of the stories in *The Vancouver Sun* series portray First Nations leaders as pushing forward ongoing constructive change in their communities, and in broader society, in fields such as law, politics and education. These developments are accompanied with an acknowledgement of past struggles and successes achieved by First Nations leaders. As opposed to the frame of government/corporate benevolence (as discussed in our 'new' racism analysis), this frame highlights the long struggle of First Nations peoples to achieve social justice in a variety of institutional fields. They are presented as rational, goal-oriented political actors rather than passive, emotional, 'victims' of colonial power. For example, the series includes statements by Grand Chief Stewart Philip from the Union of British Columbia Indian Chiefs that are critical of the government's current approach to the treaty process in British Columbia. This demonstrates an active political argument for increased self-determination in treaty negotiations:

> I stated at the outset that I have no faith in the common table given the fact that the policy underlying the treaty process hasn't changed ... What we need is a dramatic fundamental structural change in legislation and policy and practice because the status quo is just an impediment to us reaching those goals. (Grand Chief Stewart Philip, cited in Fowlie2)

This frame also highlights the historical continuity of leadership in First Nations communities. In fact, one story focuses on multi-generational leadership driven by the agency of individuals and communities, as apparent in this quote:

> They were born into a world bent on assimilation, but first nations elders like Frank Arthur Calder and Grand Chief George Manuel refused to buckle under colonial control. Instead, following a trail blazed by their ancestors, the two men pulled themselves from the residential school mire to doggedly pursue a centuries-long fight for the rights of their people. (Sinowski)

This frame of First Nations self-determination and leadership is further echoed in discussions of community-led health policies and projects. Where warranted, existing problems are explained in the context of government (not First Nations) neglect, and articles note efforts to recoup culture and build relationships led by First Nations community members. For example, one story presents reconstruction in the field of education through an acknowledgement of the historical movement from state control to First Nations self-determination. This shift is framed in terms of hope, pride, and reconciliation through concrete mechanisms like an agreement that gives First Nations more control of educational administration:

A result of a landmark deal signed in 2006, which recognizes the right of first nations to control their own schools and gives them a stronger role in educating aboriginal students in public schools ... *'It's recognition, finally, that first nations people can do it, and they need to do it for our own children,'* said [First Nations educator Kathi] Dickie. (Steffenhagen, emphasis added)

The series also includes statements that validate different knowledge systems, as demonstrated in descriptions of First Nations professionals who 'don't have academic degrees but do have firm community roots' (Fowlie1). This comment serves to counteract tendencies to diminish First Nations knowledge by contrasting it to Western 'rational' belief systems (Dei et al. 2000).

## Conclusion

Peace journalism theory and research has largely focused on analysing 'hot' conflicts and direct violence. In this chapter, we use our PJ model to demonstrate one way researchers might investigate the more subtle discursive terrain of 'cold' conflicts (McMahon & Chow-White, 2011). We proposed the concept of 'legacy' racism as an alternative to 'old' racism, to recognise the continuing impact of past racist policies and practices on groups and individuals. Finally, we critically analysed a case study of news coverage about 'reconciliation' activities between First Nations and non-aboriginal communities in Canada.

*The Vancouver Sun* series exhibits some characteristics that reflect the normative suggestions put forward by proponents of peace journalism and critical race theory; however, many of these brief articulations are far overshadowed by ongoing evidence of both legacy and new racism towards First Nations people. Our model demonstrates these contradictions most clearly in its discussion of the recurring frame of the 'culture of negotiation'. This frame may be a *prima facie* example of PJ, since it appears to highlight a process of negotiation and conflict transformation between equal parties. However, our model reveals that the frame in fact undermines First Nations agency and constructs an asymmetrical binary between 'benevolent' corporate/state parties and 'frustrated, emotional' First Nations groups. Explained this way, the 'culture of negotiation' becomes an expression of new racism. This demonstrates that putatively self-reflexive, 'reconciliation'-oriented news representations can at times perpetuate systemic domination of racialised communities.

Critical race theorists have long contended that structural racism is not solely based in media discourses. Similarly, PJ researchers and critics question whether mediated approaches to peacebuilding are effective in securing material change and transforming conflict. Our case study underscores these points. Ongoing evidence of both legacy and new racism in 'reconciliation' media suggests that such coverage does not always challenge structural racism, and in fact may reproduce it in new forms.

However, we also found news discourse can simultaneously contain seeds of progressive reform. Our model exposed nascent tendencies towards PJ, enabling us to highlight examples of discourses that challenge stereotypes, expose the structural effects of violence, demonstrate the fluid and contingent nature of group-based identities and offer appropriate contextual explanations. By helping researchers highlight such examples of PJ, while also exposing ongoing processes of legacy and new racism, we hope our analytical model is useful for projects of peacebuilding and reconciliation.

## References

Andrews, Molly (2003). Grand national narratives and the project of truth commissions: a comparative analysis. *Media, Culture and Society,* 25(1): 45–65.

Attille, Martina and Maureen Blackwood (1986). Black women and representation. In Charlotte Brunsdon (Ed). *Films for women* (pp202–28). New York: Garland.

Banerjee, Subhabrata Bobby & Goldie Osuri (2000). Silences of the media: whiting out Aboriginality in making news and making history. *Media, Culture and Society,* 22(3): 263–84.

Barker, Martin (1989). *Racism.* London: Routledge.

Becker, Jörg (1981). Communication and peace: the empirical and theoretical relation between two categories in social sciences. *The Journal of Peace Research,* 19(3): 227–40.

Bonilla-Silva, Eduardo (2001). What is racism? The racialized social system framework. In Eduardo Bonilla-Silva (Ed). *White supremacy and racism in the post-civil rights era* (pp21–58). Boulder: Lynne Rienner Publishers.

Brown, Michael (2003). *Who owns native culture?* Cambridge: Harvard University Press.

Chow-White, Peter (2009). Data, code, and discourses of difference in genomics. *Communication Theory,* 19(3): 219–46.

Coleman, Renita, Maxwell McCombs, Donald Shaw & David Weaver (2009). Agenda-setting. In Karin Wahl-Jorgensen & Thomas Hanitzsch (Eds). *The handbook of journalism studies* (pp147–60). New York: Routledge.

Cottle, Simon (2000). Introduction. Media research and ethnic minorities: mapping the field. In Simon Cottle (Ed). *Ethnic minorities and the media: changing cultural boundaries* (pp1–31). Philadelphia: Open University Press.

Cottle, Simon (2006). *Mediatized conflict.* Berkshire: Open University Press.

Culhane, Dara (1997). *The pleasure of the crown: anthropology, law and First Nations.* Burnaby: Talonbooks.

Dei GJS, Hall BL and Rosenberg DG (Eds) (2000). *Indigenous knowledges in global contexts: multiple readings of our world.* Toronto: University of Toronto Press.

Dennis, Jeffrey (2009). Gazing at the black teen: con artists, cyborgs and sycophants. *Media, Culture and Society,* 31(2): 179–95.

Downing, John & Charles Husband (2005). *Representing 'race': racisms, ethnicities and media.* London: SAGE Publications.

El-Nawawy, Mohammed & Shawn Powers (2010). Al-Jazeera English: a conciliatory medium in a conflict-driven environment? *Global Media and Communication*, 6(1): 61–84.

Entman, Robert (2007). Framing bias: media in the distribution of power. *Journal of Communication*, 57(1): 163–73.

Entman, Robert & Andrew Rojecki (2000). *The black image in the white mind: media and race in America*. Chicago: The University of Chicago Press.

Entman, Robert, Jörg Matthes & Lynn Pellicano (2009). Nature, sources, and effects of news framing. In Karin Wahl-Jorgensen & Thomas Hanitzsch (Eds). *The handbook of journalism studies* (pp175–90). New York: Routledge.

Fanon, Franz (1963). *The wretched of the earth*. New York: Grove Press.

Galtung, Johan (2000). *Conflict transformation by peaceful means: a participants' and trainers' manual*. Geneva: UNDP.

Galtung, Johan (1998). High road, low road: charting the course for peace journalism. *Track Two: Constructive Approaches to Community and Political Conflict*, 7(4): 7–10.

Galtung, Johan (1969). Violence, peace, and peace research. *Journal of Peace Research*, 6(3): 167–91.

Green, Joyce (1995). Towards a détente with history: confronting Canada's colonial legacy. *International Journal of Canadian Studies*, 11: 85–105.

Hackett, Robert (1991). *News and dissent: the press and the politics of peace in Canada*. Norwood, New Jersey: Ablex.

Hall, Stuart (1997). Old and new identities, old and new ethnicities. In Anthony King (Ed). *Culture, globalization and the world system: contemporary conditions for the representation of identity* (pp19–39). Minneapolis: University of Minnesota Press.

Hall, Stuart (1981). The whites of their eyes: racist ideologies and the media. In George Bridges & Rosalind Brunt (Eds). *Silver linings* (pp89–93). London: Lawrence and Wishart.

Harding, Robert (2006). Historical representations of Aboriginal people in the Canadian news media. *Discourse and Society,* 17(2): 205–35.

Henry, Francis & Carol Tator (2002). *Discourses of domination: racial bias in the Canadian English-language press.* Toronto: University of Toronto Press.

Hill Collins, Patricia (2004). The past is ever present: recognizing the new racism. In Patricia Hill Collins (Ed). *Black sexual politics: African Americans, gender, and the new racism* (pp53–86). New York: Routledge.

Jiwani, Yasmin (2006). *Discourses of denial: mediations of race, gender, and violence.* Vancouver: UBC Press.

Lambertus, Sandra (2004). *Wartime images, peacetime wounds: the media and the Gustafsen Lake standoff.* Toronto: University of Toronto Press.

Lawrence, Bonita (2004). *'Real' Indians and others: mixed-blood urban native peoples and indigenous nationhood.* Vancouver: UBC Press.

LeBaron, Michelle & Venashri Pillay (2006). *Conflict across cultures: a unique experience of bridging differences.* Boston: Intercultural Press.

Lee, Seow Ting, Crispin Maslog & Hum Shik Kim (2006). Asian conflicts and the Iraq War: a comparative framing analysis. *The International Communication Gazette,* 68(5-6): 499–518.

Lee, Seow Ting & Crispin Maslog (2006). War or peace journalism? Asian newspaper coverage of conflicts. *Journal of Communication,* 55(2): 311–29.

Llewellyn, Jennifer (2002). Dealing with the legacy of native residential school abuse in Canada: litigation, ADR and restorative justice. *University of Toronto Law Journal,* 52(3): 253–300.

Lynch, Jake & Annabel McGoldrick (2005a). Peace journalism: a global dialog for democracy and democratic media. In Robert Hackett & Yuezhi Zhao (Eds). *Democratizing global media: one world, many struggles* (pp269–88). Lanham: Rowman and Littlefield.

Lynch, Jake & Annabel McGoldrick (2005b). *Peace journalism.* Stroud: Hawthorn Press.

McCombs, Maxwell (1994). News influence on our pictures of the world. In Jennings Bryant & Dolf Zillmann (Eds.) *Media effects: advances in theory and research* (pp1–16). Hillsdale, Howe: Lawrence Erlbaum Associates.

McCombs, Maxwell & Donald Shaw (1977). *The emergence of American political issues: the agenda-setting function of the press.* St. Paul: West Publishing Co.

McMahon, Rob & Peter Chow-White (2011). News media encoding of racial reconciliation: developing a peace journalism model for the analysis of 'cold conflict'. *Media, Culture & Society*, 33(7): 989–1008.

Milloy, John (1999). *A national crime': the Canadian government and the residential school system, 1879 to 1986.* Winnipeg: University of Manitoba Press.

Mostly Water (2009). Olympic spotlight. *Mostly water.* [Online]. Available: mostlywater.org/topics/olympics. [Accessed 23 June 2009].

Nesbitt-Larking, Paul (2001). From experience to editorial: gatekeeping, agenda-setting, priming and framing. In Paul Nesbitt-Larking (Ed). *Politics, society and the media* (pp315–48). Petersbourgh: Broadview Press.

Omi, Michael & Howard Winant (1994). Racial formation. In Michael Omi & Howard Winant (Eds). *Racial formation in the United States: from the 1960s to the 1990s* (pp53–76). London: Routledge.

Pan, Zhongdang & Gerald Kosicki (2003). Framing as a strategic action in public deliberation. In Stephen Reese, Oscar Gandy & August Grant (Eds). *Framing in the new media landscape* (pp35–66). Mahwah, NJ: Erlbaum.

Peleg, Samuel (2006). Peace journalism through the lenses of conflict theory: analysis and practice. *Conflict and Communication Online*, 5(2). [Online]. Available: www.cco.regener-online.de/2006_2/pdf/peleg.pdf [Accessed 3 August 2011].

Ross, Susan Dente, Diane Louise Carter & Ryan Thomas (2009). Reporting the U.S./Mexico border in times of peace. *Media Development*, 56(1): 35–39.

Roth, Lorna (2005). *Something new in the air: the story of first peoples television broadcasting in Canada*. Ithaca: McGill-Queen's University Press.

Royal Commission on Aboriginal Peoples (1996). *Report of the Royal Commission on Aboriginal peoples*. Ottawa: CCG Publications.

Said, Edward (1979). *Orientalism*. New York: Vintage Books.

Shinar, Dov (2003). The peace process in cultural conflict: the role of the media. *Conflict and Communication Online*, 2(1). [Online]. Available: www.cco.regener-online.de/2003_1/pdf_2003_1/shinar.pdf [Accessed 3 August 2011].

Shome, Raka & Radha Hegde (2002). Postcolonial approaches to communication: charting the terrain, engaging the intersections. *Communication Theory*, 12(3): 249–70.

Spencer, Graham (2005). *The media and peace: from Vietnam to the war on terror*. New York: Palgrave Macmillian.

Spivak, Gayatri (1999). Can the subaltern speak? In Charles Lemert (Ed). *Social theory: the multicultural and classic readings* (pp548–52). 2nd edn. Boulder: Westview Press.

Transformative Change Accord (2005). *Transformative change accord*. [Online]. Available: www.gov.bc.ca/arr/social/down/transformative_change_accord.pdf [Accessed 3 August 2011].

Truth and Reconciliation Commission of Canada (nd). About us. *Truth and Reconciliation Commission of Canada*. [Online]. Available: www.trc.ca/websites/trcinstitution/index.php?p=10 [Accessed 3 August 2011].

van Dijk, Teun (2009). News, discourse, and ideology. In Karin Wahl-Jorgensen & Hanitzsch, Thomas (Eds). *The handbook of journalism studies* (pp191–204). New York: Routledge.

Weaver, David (2007). Thoughts on agenda setting, framing, and priming. *Journal of Communication*, 57(1): 142–47.

West, Cornel (1990). The new cultural politics of difference. In Russell Ferguson, Martha Gever, Trinh Minh-Ha & Cornel West (Eds). *Out there:*

*marginalization and contemporary cultures* (pp19–38). Cambridge: MIT Press.

Winter, James (1992). *Common cents: media portrayal of the Gulf War and other events*. Montreal: Black Rose Books.

Wolfsfeld, Gadi (2004). *Media and the path to peace*. Cambridge: Cambridge University Press.

Young, Sally (2008). The broadcast political interview and strategies used by politicians: how the Australian prime minister promoted the Iraq War. *Media, Culture and Society,* 30(5): 623–40.

Zandberg, Eyal (2010). The right to tell the (right) story: journalism, authority and memory. *Media, Culture and Society,* 32(1): 5–24.

# Notes on contributors

**Stuart Allan** is professor of journalism in the Media School at Bournemouth University, UK. He has published widely on the news reporting of war, conflict and crisis. Related books include *Journalism after September 11* (second edition 2011, co-edited with Barbie Zelizer), *Reporting war: journalism in wartime* (2004, co-edited with Zelizer), *Online news: journalism and the internet* (2006), *Digital war reporting* (2009, co-written with Donald Matheson) and *Citizen journalism: global perspectives* (2009, co-edited with Einar Thorsen). He is a book series editor, and serves on the editorial boards of several peer-reviewed journals.

**Birgit Brock-Utne** is affiliated to the University of Oslo as a professor in education and development. She is currently a visiting professor of peace studies at the University of Otago, New Zealand. She has a PhD in peace studies and previously worked as a researcher at PRIO (the Peace Research Institute of Oslo). From 1987 until 1992 she was a professor at the University of Dar es Salaam, Tanzania. She has been a visiting professor in Japan (University of Hiroshima, Fall 2002) and in the US (Antioch University, Spring 1992; Indiana University, Spring 2005; Wartburg College, Spring 2010). She has written, co-authored and co-edited many books and scholarly articles within the field of peace studies, education and development, and languages in Africa.

**Peter Chow-White** is assistant professor in the School of Communication at Simon Fraser University in Vancouver, Canada. He is co-author with Lisa Nakamura of the edited book *Race after the internet* from Routledge. His work has appeared in *Communication Theory*, the *International Journal of Communication*, *Media, Culture & Society*, *PLoS Medicine*, and *Science, Technology & Human Values*. He is currently working on two research projects. In the first project, he is collaborating with scientists who are developing a molecular diagnostic technology for cancer to research the management of personal genetic information in healthcare settings. In his second project, he is writing a book from his research on social media and data mining.

**Robert A Hackett** is professor of communication at Simon Fraser University, Vancouver, BC, Canada, co-director of NewsWatch Canada; and co-founder of OpenMedia.ca and other media democratisation initiatives. He has written extensively on journalism, political communication, and media representation. His recent works include *Remaking media: the struggle to democratize public communication* (2006, co-written with William Carroll), and *Democratizing global media: one world, many struggles* (2005, co-edited with Yuezhi Zhao). Hackett serves on the editorial boards of *Journalism Studies* and four other journals in the field.

**Virgil Hawkins** is an associate professor at the Osaka School of International Public Policy (OSIPP), Osaka University, Japan. He previously worked on NGO programs in the field of health and poverty reduction in Asia and Africa. His primary research interest is in unravelling the tendency of key actors in the world, including policymakers, the media, the public and academia, to collectively marginalise the world's deadliest armed conflicts, most notably those in Africa. He is the author of *Stealth conflicts: how the world's worst violence is ignored* (2008) and writes a blog of the same title.

**Richard Lance Keeble** has been professor of journalism at the University of Lincoln since 2003. Before that he was the executive editor of *The Teacher*, the weekly newspaper of the National Union of Teachers and he lectured at City University, London for 19 years. He has written and edited 18 publications including *Secret state, silent press: new militarism, the gulf and the modern image of warfare* (1997), *The newspapers handbook* (2005), *Ethics for journalists* (2008), *The journalistic imagination: literary journalists from Defoe to Capote and Carter* (2007, co-edited with Sharon Wheeler), *Communicating war: memory, media and military* (2007, co-written with Sarah Maltby) and *Peace journalism, war and conflict resolution* (2010, co-edited with John Tulloch & Florian Zollmann). He is also the joint editor of *Ethical Space: The International Journal of Communication Ethics.*

**Lioba Suchenwirth** is writing her PhD at Lincoln University's School of Journalism, focusing on peace journalism projects in post-conflict societies. She holds an MPhil in peace and conflict studies from the University of Oslo and has been working as a freelance journalist from Central America and Mexico since 2005.

**Jake Lynch** is associate professor and director of the Centre for Peace and Conflict Studies, University of Sydney, former senior professional journalist and TV presenter, chief investigator for the Australian Research Council Global Standard in Conflict Reporting project; an executive member of the Sydney Peace Foundation and secretary general of the International Peace Research Association, having organised and hosted its Sydney conference in July 2010. Publications include several books and many book chapters and refereed articles on peace and peace journalism. In 2008, Jake was guest editor of a special edition of the Routledge scholarly journal, *Global Change, Peace and Security*, with contributions based on presentations to a major conference he organised at the University of Sydney. He is also the author of several think-tank reports and many articles in public media including *The Sydney Morning Herald*, *The Australian* and *The Canberra Times*. He is the on-screen host of *News Goo*, a streamed television program produced by the New Matilda current affairs website. In 2009–2010 he wrote a weekly column, combining commentary on world affairs with media analysis and literacy issues, for the TRANSCEND Media Service website. He is a regular contributor to radio and television. Jake has senior production credits on three documentary films, including the multi-award winning *Soldiers of peace*, narrated by the Hollywood actor Michael Douglas.

**Annabel McGoldrick** is a clinical psychotherapist, PhD candidate and part-time lecturer at the University of Sydney. She is also an experienced professional journalist, most recently as a reporter for *World News Australia*, on SBS Television. Before that, Annabel covered conflicts in Indonesia, Thailand and Burma, and former Yugoslavia. Her publications include *Peace journalism* (2005, co-written with Jake Lynch), as well as chapters in several books and several academic journal articles. She edited and presented two educational video documentaries, *News from the Holy Land* (2004) and *Peace journalism in the Philippines* (2007). She has led professional training workshops for journalists and peace workers in many countries, including the US, UK, Indonesia, the Philippines, Nepal, Armenia and Norway.

**Rob McMahon** is a doctoral candidate in the School of Communication at Simon Fraser University in Canada. He researches and writes on indigenous media policy and practice, and his work has appeared in *Media, Culture & Society*, the *Canadian Journal of Communication and Media Development*. He was a visiting scholar at the Centre for Global Communications Studies at the University of Pennsylvania, and has worked as a journalist in Canada.

**Matt Mogekwu** is associate professor of journalism in the Roy Park School of Communications at Ithaca College in the state of New York. He was chair of the Journalism Department from 2008 to 2010. Mogekwu earned his BA in journalism from the University of Wisconsin – Whitewater, an MA in communications from Michigan State University, and a PhD in journalism/mass communication from Indiana University, Bloomington – all in the US. His research has focused on media and peace building, international communication, press freedom and sustainable development in Africa and capacity building for media practitioners in developing countries and has published widely in journals and books. Mogekwu has been faculty member and administrator in universities in South Africa, Nigeria, Sierra Leone, Swaziland and the US. He is a member of many international media/journalism associations.

**Stig Arne Nohrstedt** is the author of numerous books, articles and conference papers on war journalism, journalism ethics, and crisis and conflict communication. As full professor at Örebro University, Sweden, he is head of the media and communication program at the undergraduate and postgraduate levels, including a newly started international MA in global journalism. He is associate professor at the National Defense College in Sweden and peer reviewer at the Swedish National Bank's Research Council.

**Rune Ottosen** is professor of journalism at Oslo and Akershus University College, Norway. He previously worked as a journalist in various Norwegian media, as Information Director and Research Fellow at the International Peace Research Institute, Oslo (PRIO), and as a research fellow at the Norwegian Journalist Federation. Since 1996 he has taught at Oslo College and part-time at the Sami College in Kautokeino, Norway. He and Professor Stig Arne Nohrstedt have written and edited several books and articles on war and media. These include a comparative international study of the Gulf Conflict coverage in several countries, *Journalism and the new world order: studying war and the media* (2002, co-edited with Heikki Luostarinen), *Journalism and the new world order: Gulf War, national news discourses and globalization* (2001, co-edited with Stig Arne Nohrstedt), *US and the others: global media images on 'The war on terror'* (2004, co-written with Stig Arne Nohrstedt), and *Global war – local views: media images of the Iraq War* (2005, co-written with Stig Arne Nohrstedt).

**Susan Dente Ross** is professor of English and former research associate dean at Washington State University and director of Paxim, a peace communication research group. A former longtime reporter, editor, and newspaper owner, she writes creative nonfiction offering voice to the powerless. A Fulbright Scholar, faculty fellow, media consultant, and peace journalism trainer in Canada, Cyprus, Ecuador, Greece, Israel, Jordan, Palestine, and Turkey, her recent publications include *Peace journalism in times of war* (2009, co-edited with Majid Tehranian) and *Images that injure: pictorial stereotypes in the media* (2003, co-edited with Paul Lester), as well as chapters in *Mediation: journalism, war and conflict resolution* (2009, edited by Keeble et al.), *Race/gender/media: considering diversity across audiences, content, and producers* (2009, edited by Lind), and *Discovering new pathways to peace* (2009, edited by Shiba & Kawamura).

**Sudeshna Roy** is assistant professor of communication at Stephen F Austin State University, Texas, US. She is a critical media studies scholar with special focus on representation of multinational organisations and media's role in conflict and peace processes. She is also an intercultural communication scholar working with race, ethnicity, gender and identity. Her article has been published in Purdue University Press online journal *Comparative Literature and Culture*. Her most recent co-authored chapter appears in the book *Mass media: coverage, objectivity and changes* (2010, edited by Kovács).

**Ibrahim Seaga Shaw** is senior lecturer in media and politics in the Department of Media, Northumbria University in Newcastle Upon Tyne. His research and teaching interests encompass democracy and media agenda-setting, peace journalism and global justice, media representations of conflict and humanitarian intervention. He has published articles in *International Communication Gazette* (2009), *African Journalism Review* (2007), *Globalisation, Societies and Education* (2007), *Ethical Space* (2009), and in the *Journal of Global Ethics* (2010). He is also author of *Human rights journalism* (Palgrave forthcoming December 2011). He obtained his PhD from the Sorbonne in 2006 and has been a member of the Bristol Legacy Commission since 2008.

**Elissa J Tivona** (PhD) is adjunct professor, international education, Colorado State University, Department of International Education. She was instrumental in the creation of the interdisciplinary peace and reconciliation studies program, recently upgraded to a minor at CSU and authored the curriculum for the keystone class, Education for Global Peace. She is the recipient of the Peace Ambassador Award in recognition of work with the Israel Palestine Center for Research and Information in Jerusalem and advocacy work on behalf of J-Street Colorado) and interfaith Living Room Dialogues. Elissa is widely acknowledged for convening the International Perspectives on Peacemaking Conference in Boulder, Colorado and is widely published in academic as well as popular media.

# Index

Made in United States
North Haven, CT
25 January 2022